OFFICER CANDIDATE TESTS: COMPLETE PREPARATION FOR THE ASVAB, AFOQT, AND ASTB

LearningExpress®

NEW YORK

Library of Congress Cataloging-in-Publication Data
Officer candidate tests: complete preparation for the ASVAB, AFOQT, and ASTB.—1st ed.
    p. cm.
  ISBN-13: 978-1-57685-771-7 (pbk. : alk. paper)
  ISBN-10: 1-57685-771-9 (pbk. : alk. paper)   1. United States—Armed Forces—Examinations.
2. United States—Armed Forces—Officers.
  U408.5.P363 2011
  355.0076—dc22

           2010034695

Printed in the United States of America

9 8 7 6 5 4 3 2 1

First Edition

ISBN-13: 978-1-57685-771-7
ISBN-10: 1-57685-771-9

For more information or to place an order, contact LearningExpress at:
  2 Rector Street
  26th Floor
  New York, NY 10006

Or visit us at:
  www.learnatest.com

Editor: Marco A. Annunziata
Production Editor: Michael B. Detweiler
Editorial Assistant: Alex Duym

CONTENTS ▶

CONTENTS

CONTENTS

CONTRIBUTORS ▶

The following individuals contributed to the content of this book.

Julia Hayden (TSgt. USAF, Ret.) served for twenty years in various military broadcasting, public affairs, and combat video documentation assignments. She is a long-time military blogger, and contributes regularly to a number of general interest websites. She lives in San Antonio, Texas, where she is a partner in a boutique publishing firm, Watercress Press, and writes historical novels under the pen name Celia Hayes.

CDR Bill Paisley is a former F-14 Tomcat radar intercept officer with 25 years of active and reserve service. He holds two undergraduate degrees in education and an MA in National Security. He lives in northern Virginia and works as a modeling and simulation professional for the U.S. Navy.

Mike Segretto has been an assessment writer for ten years while also creating a wide assortment of informational and entertainment material for various online sites and print publications. He holds a degree in film and English from Hofstra University.

Special thanks to Scott A. Thornbloom, Heath Alvarez, the U.S. Army, and U.S. Navy for providing us with many of the beautiful images used in this book.

CHAPTER 1

WHY SHOULD I BECOME AN OFFICER?

CHAPTER SUMMARY

Congratulations on taking the first step toward a career as a military officer! As you prepare for your test, know that you have come to the right place for up-to-date information on the entire process. This chapter describes the benefits and advantages of choosing a career as an officer in the U.S. Air Force, the U.S. Army, the U.S. Navy, or the U.S. Marine Corps.

To serve one's country in a military capacity is almost the oldest of all duties required of citizens in a free and democratic society, as the ancient Greeks and the early Romans would attest. However, with the end of the selective service draft in 1973, military service in the United States transitioned to an all-volunteer basis, both for officer and enlisted specialties in all services. Although only a relatively small portion of the population of the United States currently serves on active or reserve duty, the influence of veterans in the larger community, the satisfaction of having served, and the benefits of service are very real.

The need for a select, skilled, and highly professional military remains. A study of history, ancient and modern, encourages the belief that a standing and effective military is essential to national survival. "Peace is the dream of the wise," observed the explorer Sir Richard Burton. "War is the history of man." With the advanced machinery and technology used to fight, supply, transport, and to guard against attack, modern war has increased demands on those who serve. A modern military requires a higher level of commitment and more rigorous training than may be imparted through putting on a uniform and undergoing a few weeks or months of close-order drill and weapons training. Many modern military career fields are so challenging or complex that they demand extended training and a degree of dedication from the individual that only comes from having freely chosen to pursue mastery. Military service is not for everyone, nor should it be—but the benefits of having served are incalculable.

Meeting the Challenge

"Duty, Honor, Country" has long been the motto of the U.S. Military Academy at West Point, but it is felt no less by other members of the services, officer and enlisted alike. The sense of pride and connection to the history of this country are intangible but powerful motivators to becoming an officer in the U.S military. There is also the camaraderie, the satisfaction of being part of a close-knit and purposeful community charged with protecting the freedoms and interests of our nation, at home and abroad.

Another intangible aspect of becoming an officer is the prospect of challenge on several levels: challenging yourself; achieving something perhaps you thought you might not be able to do—the challenge of mastery over yourself. There is also the challenge of greater responsibility at an earlier age than is customary in most civilian occupations. No matter in which branch of service, as a commissioned officer you would be directly responsible as a leader and manager for upholding the standards required to achieve the mission of your unit. U.S. military members are stationed in more than 130 foreign countries, throughout the United States and its territories, at diplomatic missions, and aboard ships at sea. Wherever they are, they are performing a range of missions from direct combat and combat support to technical and medical support, humanitarian missions, and training at every level and in every conceivable specialty, from classroom to the field. The military will offer an unprecedented range of possibilities to those who are qualified and motivated, whether they serve for a short period of time or for a career of 20 years or longer.

A Career with a Future

While the specific terminology used for the ten commissioned officer ranks vary across the uniformed services, the insignia used to designate them are fairly similar, and the system of numbering officer ranks from 1 to 10 makes it easier to compare across the uniformed services. Base pay is calculated based upon rank and is uniform across all services.

O-1 is the lowest regular commissioned officer rank, which is second lieutenant or ensign. After at least 18 months of active service, a second lieutenant is eligible for promotion to first lieutenant (lieutenant junior grade in the Navy or Coast Guard). An O-2 is eligible for promotion to O-3, captain (or Navy/Coast Guard lieutenant) after four years' time in service. Until this point, fully qualified officers have been promoted to the next rank almost automatically, although superior performers may be promoted as soon as they have served a sufficient time in their current rank. At ten years' time in service, the next rank is O-4 (major or lieutenant commander). Approximately 80% of those best qualified will be promoted to that rank; the remainder, if not eventually promoted, will have to separate from the service. At 16 years of time in service, the next promotion to O-5 is even more competitive; only 70% of the best qualified will advance to that rank. At 22 years of service, only 50% of those qualified will be promoted to O-6 (colonel or commander). Less than 1% of career officers will make it to the next plateau, which is flag, or general officer rank (O-7 through O-10). Officers promoted to O-5 are obligated to serve at least 28 years; O-6s must serve 30. Regardless, the mandatory retirement age for general officers is 62, although this may be postponed to 64.

Warrant officers bridge the gap between enlisted and officer ranks. Warrant officers in the grade of W-1 are nominated and approved in that grade by the secretary of the particular service, and are most usually drawn from the enlisted ranks to serve in very specialized, highly technical positions. Those serving in the grade of W-2 to W-5 are also commissioned officers. They presently serve in all uniformed services except the Air Force. Each service utilizes warrant officer programs in a different manner, but generally warrant officers are utilized primarily as highly skilled technical experts.

COMPARABLE GRADES ACROSS THE BRANCHES					
PAY GRADE	ARMY	NAVY	MARINE CORPS	AIR FORCE	COAST GUARD
O-10	General	Admiral	General	General	Admiral
O-9	Lieutenant General	Vice Admiral	Lieutenant General	Lieutenant General	Vice Admiral
O-8	Major General	Rear Admiral (UH)	Major General	Major General	Rear Admiral (UH)
O-7	Brigadier General	Rear Admiral (LH)	Brigadier General	Brigadier General	Rear Admiral (LH)
O-6	Colonel	Captain	Colonel	Colonel	Captain
O-5	Lieutenant Colonel	Commander	Lieutenant Colonel	Lieutenant Colonel	Commander
O-4	Major	Lieutenant Commander	Major	Major	Lieutenant Commander
O-3	Captain	Lieutenant	Captain	Captain	Lieutenant
O-2	First Lieutenant	Lieutenant (Junior Grade)	First Lieutenant	First Lieutenant	Lieutenant (Junior Grade)
O-1	Second Lieutenant	Ensign	Second Lieutenant	Second Lieutenant	Ensign
W-5	Chief Warrant Officer	Chief Warrant Officer	Chief Warrant Officer 5		Chief Warrant Officer
W-4	Chief Warrant Officer	Chief Warrant Officer	Chief Warrant Officer 4		Chief Warrant Officer
W-3	Chief Warrant Officer	Chief Warrant Officer	Chief Warrant Officer 3		Chief Warrant Officer
W-2	Chief Warrant Officer	Chief Warrant Officer	Chief Warrant Officer 2		Chief Warrant Officer
W-1	Warrant Officer		Warrant Officer		
E-9 Special	Sergeant Major of the Army	Master Chief Petty Officer of the Navy	Sergeant Major of the Marine Corps	Chief Master Sergeant of the Air Force	Master Chief Petty Officer of the Coast Guard

COMPARABLE GRADES ACROSS THE BRANCHES (continued)					
PAY GRADE	ARMY	NAVY	MARINE CORPS	AIR FORCE	COAST GUARD
E-9	Command Sergeant Major or Sergeant Major	Master Chief Petty Officer	Sergeant Major or Master Gunnery Sergeant	Chief Master Sergeant	Master Chief Petty Officer
E-8	First Sergeant or Master Sergeant	Senior Chief Petty Officer	First Sergeant or Master Sergeant	Senior Master Sergeant	Senior Chief Petty Officer
E-7	Platoon Sergeant or Sergeant First Class	Chief Petty Officer	Gunnery Sergeant	Master Sergeant	Chief Petty Officer
E-6	Staff Sergeant	Petty Officer, First Class	Staff Sergeant	Technical Sergeant	Petty Officer, First Class
E-5	Sergeant	Petty Officer, Second Class	Sergeant	Staff Sergeant	Petty Officer, Second Class
E-4	Corporal or Specialist	Petty Officer, Third Class	Corporal	Senior Airman	Petty Officer, Third Class
E-3	Private First Class	Seaman	Lance Corporal	Airman, First Class	Seaman
E-2	Private	Seaman Apprentice	Private First Class	Airman	Seaman Apprentice
E-1	Private	Seaman Recruit	Private	Airman, Basic	Seaman Recruit

A Good Paycheck

Despite the challenges of serving on active duty—such as long hours, frequent moves, and assignments to distant and sometimes uncomfortable places—there are also substantial tangible benefits to a military career, especially for commissioned officers. Base pay, benefits, and allowances are relatively generous. Additional allowances are made for service in special duties, or areas, for specialized skills. Many such allowances increase with rank and service time.

Officer pay grades and allowances are published for the whole world to see on the Defense Finance and Accounting Service (DFAS) website, found at www.dfas.mil/militarypay.html. In addition to the basic military pay charts that we have provided for you on the following pages, on the DFAS website you will also be able to the see the additional incentives and allowances for health professional officers, submarine duty, aviation careers, hazardous duty, and more. Before you even begin the process of becoming an officer, these pay charts can help you get an idea of the amount of money you can make. See the table on the following pages for the monthly dollar amounts of officers' basic pay, based on years of service, for 2011. If you are a commissioned officer, you will most likely be starting out at pay grade O-1. You will probably move up to pay grade O-2 within your first two years of service and to pay grade O-3 a few years later. As you climb the pay grade ladder, promotions become increasingly competitive. One reason for the competition is that Congress limits the number of officers in the very highest pay grades. Warrant officers start out at the W-1 pay grade and move up to W-5.

2011 MILITARY MONTHLY BASE PAY RATES
COMMISSIONED OFFICERS
YEARS OF SERVICE

Pay Grade	Under 2	Over 2	Over 3	Over 4	Over 6	Over 8	Over 10	Over 12	Over 14	Over 16	Over 18	Over 20	Over 22	Over 24	Over 26
O-10 See Note 1												15401	15476	15797	16358
O-9												13470	13664	13944	14433
O-8	9531	9843	10050	10108	10366	10798	10898	11308	11426	11779	12291	12762	13078	13078	13078
O-7	7919	8287	8457	8592	8838	9079	9360	9639	9919	10798	11541	11541	11541	11541	11599
O-6	5870	6448	6872	6872	6898	7193	7233	7233	7643	8370	8797	9223	9466	9711	10188
O-5	4893	5512	5893	5966	6204	6346	6659	6889	7185	7639	7856	8070	8313	8313	8313
O-4	4222	4887	5213	5286	5588	5913	6316	6632	6850	6976	7049	7049	7049	7049	7049
O-3	3712	4208	4542	4952	5189	5449	5617	5895	6038	6038	6039	6039	6039	6039	6039
O-2	3207	3653	4207	4349	4438	4438	4438	4438	4438	4438	4438	4438	4438	4438	4438
O-1	2783	2898	3503	3503	3503	3503	3503	3503	3503	3503	3503	3503	3503	3503	3503

COMMISSIONED OFFICERS WITH MORE THAN FOUR YEARS OF ACTIVE SERVICE AS AN ENLISTED MEMBER OR WARRANT OFFICER
YEARS OF SERVICE

Pay Grade	Under 2	Over 2	Over 3	Over 4	Over 6	Over 8	Over 10	Over 12	Over 14	Over 16	Over 18	Over 20	Over 22	Over 24	Over 26
O-3E See Note 2				4951	5189	5449	5618	5895	6128	6263	6445	6445	6445	6445	6445
O-2E				4349	4438	4580	4819	5003	5140	5140	5140	5140	5140	5140	5140
O-1E				3501	3740	3878	4020	4159	4349	4349	4349	4349	4349	4349	4349

WARRANT OFFICERS
YEARS OF SERVICE

Pay Grade	Under 2	Over 2	Over 3	Over 4	Over 6	Over 8	Over 10	Over 12	Over 14	Over 16	Over 18	Over 20	Over 22	Over 24	Over 26
W-5												6821	7167	7424	7710
W-4	3836	4125	4245	4361	4562	4761	4961	5264	5530	5782	5988	6189	6486	6728	7006
W-3	3502	3648	3799	3847	4005	4313	4635	4786	4961	5142	5466	5684	5816	5956	6145
W-2	3081	3257	3411	3522	3619	4059	4214	4366	4552	4698	4830	4988	5091	5174	5174
W-1	2719	2943	3093	3189	3445	3746	3881	4070	4257	4403	4538	4701	4701	4701	4701

Pay Grade	Under 2	Over 2	Over 3	Over 4	Over 6	Over 8	Over 10	Over 12	Over 14	Over 16	Over 18	Over 20	Over 22	Over 24	Over 26
ENLISTED															
YEARS OF SERVICE															
E-9							4635	4740	4872	5029	5185	5436	5649	5874	6215
E-8						3794	3962	4066	4191	4325	4568	4692	4902	5018	5305
E-7	2638	2879	2989	3135	3249	3444	3554	3751	3914	4025	4568	4692	4902	5018	5305
E-6	2281	2510	2621	2728	2840	3094	3193	3382	3441	3484	3533	3533	3533	3533	3533
E-5	2091	2230	2338	2448	2620	2800	2947	2965	2965	2965	2965	2965	2965	2965	2965
E-4	1915	2014	2123	2231	2327	2327	2327	2327	2327	2327	2327	2327	2327	2327	2327
E-2	1645	1645	1645	1645	1645	1645	1645	1645	1645	1645	1645	1645	1645	1645	1645
E-1 >4	1467	1467	1467	1467	1467	1467	1467	1467	1467	1467	1467	1467	1467	1467	1467
E-1 <4 with less than four months	1357														

Note 1. Basic pay for an O-7 to O-10 is limited by Level II of the Executive Schedule. Basic pay for O-6 and below is limited by Level V of the Executive Schedule.

Note 2. Applicable to O-1 to O-3 with at least four years and one day of active duty or more than 1460 points as a warrant and/or enlisted member. See DoDFMR for more detailed explanation on who is eligible for this special basic pay rate.

Housing and Food Allowances

One of the opportunities afforded military personnel is the ability to live free of charge in military housing on their assigned base. Just think of it: no rent or mortgage payment to pay every month! However, since military housing is limited, not all officers get this benefit. If you cannot get housing at the base, you can live off base and get a monthly housing allowance to offset your rent or mortgage payments. A new law that recently went into effect increases the basic housing allowance for most military personnel. The exact amount of the allowance depends on housing prices in the geographic area in which you are stationed.

In addition to generous housing allowances, the military also offers a monthly food allowance called a subsistence allowance. You can get about $225 each month to help pay for your food. While you cannot buy a lot of caviar on that budget, it is taxfree money and a good benefit.

Other Benefits

Life as a military officer has several other benefits, too. Officers get free health and dental care, low-cost life insurance, generous vacation time of 30 days per year, a 20-year retirement plan, tuition assistance that often covers from 75% to 90% of education costs, legal assistance that includes several free legal services for personal matters, shopping privileges at base commissaries and exchanges, recreation programs, and membership in prestigious officers' clubs. Plus, the post-9/11 GI Bill provides expanded benefits for qualified military personnel.

Education and Tuition Assistance

In addition to the service academies, the military branches maintain more than 300 schools, which together offer over 10,000 courses. Qualified military members are eligible for tuition assistance programs, to include the post–9/11 GI Bill. Those intending to make the military a career may take advantage of a number of in-house professional education/development courses offered by the Army War College, the School for Command Preparation, the U.S. Navy Command Leadership School, and the Air Force Commander's Professional Development School, among others.

Secure Retirement

After 20 years total of active federal military service, both officer and enlisted ranks may retire, with a pension amounting to half of their base pay at the highest rank held. This may not seem like a very long period of time in which to become eligible for a lifetime pension, but be assured that when long duty hours, deployments, round-the-clock availability, constant permanent changes of station—and, for some career fields, considerable physical risk—are considered, 20 years in the active military are comparable to 30 or more years in any other profession. Many military members do choose to retire at that point, and transition into a meaningful second career in private industry, or in civil service. Some combine a second career with part-time service in the various military reserves, depending on the inclination of the individual and the needs of the reserve unit.

Post-Service Career Opportunities

Of inestimable benefit to veterans in establishing a post-service career is the perception that the military is acknowledged to be a ruthless meritocracy, functioning in a world where success and failure are immediately visible. In other words, success advances, failure does not. This truth develops a fairly realistic mind-set among veterans, along with an ability for setting goals and meeting them in an efficient manner, and in coping and adapting to adversity. Some 93.5% of jobs within the military have a direct counterpart in the civilian world, and that includes management and leadership functions. Those skills practiced within the military translate very readily to civilian life—and in most cases, an officer is more likely to have performed in the role of manager and leader.

Now that you have a better idea of what choosing a career as an officer in the military entails, the following chapter will discuss the different paths to getting you started.

2 ▶ BECOMING A COMMISSIONED OFFICER

CHAPTER SUMMARY

Within each service, there are separate and distinct paths to the same end: a commission as a serving officer. Each route, whether it is through a service academy, a collegiate Reserve Officer Training Course (ROTC), officer candidate school, a direct commission, or a commission from the ranks, is outlined in detail in this chapter.

There are number of paths to becoming a commissioned officer in the branches of the U.S. Military. Each possesses a distinct set of advantages and requirements; some are more open to the general applicant, others are more restricted. Some require extensive preparation while still a teenager; some may be taken by individuals in their 20s. All have the same eventual goal: commission as an officer in the service of this country.

The Service Academies

The service academies are the oldest and most prestigious within the military, and until the twentieth century, were the principal method of schooling officers to serve as leaders in the uniformed services of the United States. Today, however, these academies provide only about 13% of the new military officers commissioned per year. West Point, Annapolis, the Air Force Academy, and the Coast Guard Academy function as four-year coeducational colleges, with tuition, room, and board paid by the military services. Undergraduates are members of the military, and considered to be *officers in training*. Upon graduation, they are commissioned as second lieutenants or ensigns (O-1), the lowest officer rank, and have an obligation to serve a specified number of years in their chosen branch of service. Competition for a service academy is fierce; prospective undergraduates must

- be at least 17, but not yet 23 years of age, as of July 1 of the year of admission
- be a citizen of the United States; if naturalized, the naturalization must be completed prior to entry
- have a good moral character
- pass a physical aptitude exam
- pass a medical exam

Candidates for admission to West Point, Annapolis, and the Air Force Academy must also receive a nomination from an approved source, such as a member of Congress. Admission to the Coast Guard Academy is by merit.

There are other means of obtaining a nomination; for example, children of Medal of Honor recipients may be appointed, should they meet admission requirements. Appointments are also open for the children of career military personnel, and for the children of military members who were killed in action, or rendered completely disabled due to injuries received in action, or are currently prisoners of war or missing in action.

Let us take a look at each of the academies in more detail.

The United States Military Academy at West Point

West Point, or more properly, the U.S. Military Academy at West Point, is located in the Hudson River Valley, approximately 50 miles north of New York City. It is the oldest of the service academies, established in

1802. During the Revolution, the fortified garrison at West Point protected the Upper Hudson River, and prevented the British from sailing upriver and dividing the rebellious Colonies. Today the campus is a national landmark and popular tourist destination, being thickly planted, with scenic outlooks over the Hudson River, historic sites, monuments, and buildings. Originally founded to provide qualified engineers, for 20 years it was the only such school in the nation. During the early nineteenth century, Academy graduates designed most of the nation's bridges, harbors, and roads.

A View of West Point from the Hudson River

Today, West Point offers a balanced curriculum of arts and sciences, allowing an undergraduate, known as a cadet, to choose among 40 majors; it still emphasizes engineering. The student body usually runs to about 4,300, graduating a class of about 1,000 each year. Classes are kept small, most often less than 18, with a faculty-to-student ratio of 1:8.

Competition for admission to West Point, like all of the uniformed service academies, is rigorous. Once selected for a place in the corps of cadets, the challenge of meeting the academic and physical standards does not relent. A cadet is a member of the U.S. Army, receiving a full scholarship as well as an annual salary. Room, board, medical, and dental care are provided. Graduates are awarded a bachelor of science degree and a commission in the U.S. Army, and are obligated to serve five years on active duty and three years in an inactive reserve status (subject to recall to active duty, if the need arises during that period). More information about West Point is available at the Academy's official website, http://admissions.usma.edu.

The United States Naval Academy

Annapolis, or the U.S. Naval Academy, is located in Annapolis, Maryland. The campus is relatively small, about 330 acres located on a site where the Severn River enters Chesapeake Bay, 33 miles east of Washington, DC, and 26 miles southeast of Baltimore, Maryland. Like West Point, the entire campus is a national landmark. It was first housed in a Revolutionary War–era fort, Ft. Severn, which had been part of the military defenses of Annapolis. It was founded in 1845, at the direction of the then-Secretary of the Navy, George Bancroft, with the purpose of providing a solid education and apprenticeship training for sailors.

Annapolis is accredited as a technological institution, and awards a bachelor of science degree to graduates. Presently, Annapolis offers a core curriculum plus 21 major fields of study to all midshipmen, or plebes. Each class of about 1,200 young men and women are commissioned as either ensigns (O-1) in the U.S. Navy or second lieutenants in the U.S. Marine Corps, and are obligated to serve at least five years on active duty. Graduates selected to serve as pilots or naval flight officers (navigators or weapons officers) incur longer active service obligations because of the additional training required.

The Navy provides tuition, room and board, and medical/dental care for cadet midshipmen, as well as regular pay, although various student-associated fees are deducted from it. Similar to West Point, cadets at Annapolis are considered to be members of the military, with commissary and exchange privileges, space-available travel aboard military aircraft, and commercial transportation and lodging discounts. More about the U.S. Naval Academy can be found on the official website http://www.usna.edu/homepage.php.

The United States Air Force Academy

The U.S. Air Force Academy is located on an 18,000-acre mountainside campus near Colorado Springs, Colorado. It is the newest of the service academies, founded in 1954 by Congressional legislation in the wake of the National Security Act of 1947 that established the Air Force as a separate military service. The first graduating class swore in at Lowry Air Force Base and lived and trained in WWII–era temporary buildings before moving to the permanent campus in 1958. The campus was designed by the firm of Skidmore, Owings, and Merrill, and presents a unified, ultramodern appearance anchored by the distinctive Cadet Chapel. Over a four-year course of instruction, the student body of about 4,400 undergraduate cadets is prepared to serve as career officers in the U.S. Air Force.

Currently, the Academy offers 31 academic majors, with a core curriculum including courses in science, engineering, and the humanities. Sixty percent of graduating cadets complete majors in science and engineering fields. The average class size is less than 20, and the instructor-to-student ratio is 1:8. Graduating cadets earn a bachelor of science degree, are commissioned as second lieutenants (O-1) in the Air Force, and must serve at least five years of active service and three in the inactive reserve.

The Cadet Chapel at the United States Air Force Academy

The Air Force Academy is regarded as one of the most rigorously selective colleges in the nation and thus competition for an appointment is fierce. Cadets are considered to be members of the military and paid a small stipend. They also have access to military facilities such as commissaries, base exchanges, clubs, and recreational facilities. The Air Force provides tuition, room and board, and medical and dental care for cadets. More information can be found at the U.S. Air Force Academy's official website, http://www.usafa.af .mil/information/baseinfo/

The United States Coast Guard Academy

The U.S. Coast Guard Academy is the smallest of the service academies in terms of campus size 'and student body. It occupies just over 100 acres of waterfront land in New London, Connecticut. In peacetime, the U.S. Coast Guard is under the authority of the Department of Homeland Security; in a time of war it would be placed under the authority of the Department of Defense. Like the other military academies, its mission is to provide skilled and welltrained officers for the parent service.

The Coast Guard has its origins in the Revenue Cutter Service established in 1790 to enforce customs and navigation law. It was founded in 1876 as the *School of Instruction for the Revenue Cutter Service* at New Bedford, although for a number of years the Academy was the sailing clipper *Chase*, a roving school with no permanent berth. Eventually, the Revenue Cutter Service and the Lifesaving Service merged to form the modern Coast Guard, and the school moved to permanent shore quarters at Fort Trumbull, a Revolutionary War Army post near New London. When the school outgrew that facility, land for a new campus on the west bank of the Thames River was purchased and additional land was donated by the town. Ground was broken in 1931 for the present academy. An unusual element of the Coast Guard Academy's facility is the *USCGC Eagle*. The *Eagle* is a full-rigged sailing barque, and serves as a sail-training ship. It is the United States' only active-duty tall ship; it and the *USS Constitution* are the only commissioned sailing ships in inventory. The *Eagle's* home port is at the Academy, but it serves as a training ship during the summer.

USCGC Eagle

The Coast Guard Academy has a total student/ cadet body of about 900. Each year, approximately 2,500 students apply for an appointment; 250 will eventually be granted an appointment. Unlike the other service academies, admission is based only on merit; a congressional nomination is not necessary. The Coast Guard Academy awards graduates a bachelor of science degree but offers only eight majors: civil, mechanical, or electrical engineering; naval architecture/marine engineering; operations research/computer analysis; marine/environmental science; government, and management. Upon graduation, cadets are commissioned as ensigns (O-1), and generally serve as deck watch officers. They are obligated to serve at least five years of active-duty service. Nearly 80% of Coast Guard Academy graduates continue on to postgraduate schools, and 85% choose to serve beyond the initial five-year commitment. Current information is available at the U.S. Coast Guard Academy's website, http://www .uscga.edu.

The Uniformed Services University of Health Sciences

Another and relatively unknown pathway toward a commission as a serving officer is through the Uniformed Services University of Health Sciences, specifically the F. Edward Hebert School of Medicine. Unlike the uniformed services academies, the medical school is a postgraduate establishment, for the purpose of serving in the civil or military medical services.

The F. Edward Hebert School of Medicine is in Bethesda, Maryland, adjacent to the Naval Medical Center and the National Institutes of Health. The medical school is part of a federally run health science university. It bears a similarity to the other service academies in that students are formally members of the uniformed services, and offers a year-round four-year educational program in exchange for a seven-year active-duty service commitment. The course of studies is almost 700 hours longer than is found at similar schools of medicine in the United States. The additional hours focus on subjects related to the requirements of military physicians, such as epidemiology, tropical medicine, field exercises, and leadership. Of nearly 4,000 alumni of the medical school, more than 75% are currently serving in the uniformed branches or in the U.S. Public Health service.

Students enter as commissioned officers with the rank of second lieutenant or ensign (O-1), in the Army, Navy, Air Force, or U.S. Public Health service. Civilians and currently serving military personnel are eligible for admission. Prospective students must

- be citizens of the United States
- be at least 18 years old at the time of matriculation, but no older than 30 as of June 30 in the year of admission (civilians and enlisted personnel); applicants over the age 30 may apply on a case-by-case basis; student applicants who have been on active duty as commissioned officers may exceed the age limit by a period equal to the time served on active duty, if the student will be no older than 35 on June 30 in the year of admission
- meet the general requirements for holding a commission in the uniformed services

Applicants must apply through the American Medical College Application Service (AMCAS), using the designation code 821 (or current designation number) assigned to the School of Medicine by AMCAS. Applications must be properly routed through AMCAS, as it is currently not possible to apply directly to the School of Medicine for the M.D. program. More and current information about the F. Edward Hebert School of Medicine can found on the school's official website, http://www.usuhs.mil/med school/fehsom.html.

The Reserve Officer Training Corps Programs

At present, the Reserve Officer Training Corps (ROTC) is the most common means of being commissioned as an officer in the Armed Forces, accounting for more than 44% of new officers. More than a thousand universities and colleges offer an ROTC program for four of the five uniformed military services: Army, Navy, Air Force, and Marines. The Coast Guard does not have a formal ROTC program, but does offer a military officer training program to college students, discussed later in this chapter.

Depending upon the service and the program offered, student applicants may qualify for scholarships covering tuition and fees, plus a monthly stipend. ROTC students must take additional classes focusing on military skills both general and specific to their chosen service, as well as participating in regular drills, and in extended military training camps for several weeks each summer. Upon successful completion of an ROTC program, graduates are commissioned as second lieutenants or ensigns (O-1), and may either serve as officers on active duty or as members of a reserve or National Guard unit. Now, let us take a look at each branch's ROTC programs.

The Army Reserve Officer Training Corps

The Army ROTC programs normally require an elective class and a lab per semester. Students who have opted for less than the full four-year program may participate in an accelerated summer course, and incur only a three-year service obligation as long as they have not also obtained a scholarship. While ROTC courses may require much out-of-classroom fieldwork, they are geared to fit into a normal academic schedule. ROTC cadets are not limited to a specific academic major, but may select almost any course of study offered by their school.

ROTC scholarships are available; however, cadets who win such scholarships are still obligated for a four-year active duty service. Selected cadets may also serve part time in the Army Reserve or in the Army National Guard. Graduates are commissioned as second lieutenants.

Prospective ROTC cadets must be U.S. citizens between the ages of 17 and 26, must have a high school diploma or equivalent, and a high school GPA of at least 2.50. They must score a minimum of 920 on the SAT (math/verbal) or 19 on the ACT (exclusive of the required writing test scores). Cadets must also meet physical standards and agree to accept a commission and the active service commitment in either the active duty or reserve component. Further information about Army ROTC programs can be found at the Army's official website, http://www.go army.com/rotc.

The Navy/Marine Reserve Officer Training Corps

Naval ROTC cadets are called midshipmen, and fall into two general categories—scholarship midshipmen or college program midshipmen. The Navy's Scholarship Program is highly selective and offers scholarships at over 160 colleges and universities across the country. Normally, prospective midshipmen apply during their senior year of high school or during their college freshman year. The Navy pays tuition and fees as well as an allowance for books and a small stipend for living expenses during the school year. Some colleges that participate in the Naval ROTC Scholarship program also offer additional scholarships to cover room and board, or at least a portion of it. Scholarship applicants must also meet fitness requirements and pass an entrance medical exam.

College Program Midshipmen are those who have been accepted into a Naval ROTC program without a scholarship. Requirements for entry into the program and for participation in ROTC activities are identical in either case, as well as the commissioning and active-service obligations. Should a College Program Midshipman perform exceptionally well academically and in the ROTC program, he or she may also be offered a scholarship. College Program students choosing to major in a technical field such as engineering, sciences, or math—which translate to skill sets valued by the Navy—have an edge with regard to the shorter-term scholarships.

ROTC student midshipmen are also divided into three tracks:

- Navy Option (those who will serve in the Navy proper)
- Marine Option (those who will serve in the Marines)
- Navy Nurse Option (those who will eventually serve as nurses in the Navy medical command)

Midshipmen participate in various specialty summer cruises. During their first summer cruise, cadets will travel either to San Diego, California, or to Norfolk, Virginia, for career orientation training. They will familiarize themselves with activities in the fleet—surface ships, submarines, aviation, or the Marines—and will receive hands-on training in various skills, before eventually choosing their own career specialty. Naval officer skill fields include

- surface warfare
- naval aviator (pilot)
- flight officer (navigator or weapons officer)
- submarine officer
- explosive ordnance disposal
- special warfare

During subsequent summer cruises, midshipmen will focus on their chosen field. Nurse Option Midshipmen will also have summer cruises tailored for their career. During their summers, Marine Option Midshipmen will attend a session at the USMC's Mountain Warfare Training Center at Pickel Meadows in California's Sierra Nevada Mountains, and a six-week course at the Marine Officer Candidate School at Marine Corps Base Quantico, Virginia.

Students intending to participate in Navy ROTC must

- be citizens of the United States
- be no less than 17 years of age by September 1 of the year of beginning college, and no older than 23 on June 30 of that year
- *not* have reached their 27th birthday by June 30 of the year in which graduation/commissioning is expected
- have earned a high school diploma or equivalent by August 1 of the year planned to enter the NROTC program
- meet physical qualifications
- have no moral reservations or personal convictions preventing the bearing of arms

- *not* have 30 or more semester hours or 45 or more quarter-hours of college credit at the time of application

Academic qualifications include a minimum SAT score of 530 in reading and 520 in math. Minimum ACT scores must be 21 in math, 22 in English. Applicants in the top 10% of their graduating class will be considered.

For more complete and current information, be sure to refer to the websites http://www.navy.com/navy and http://officer.marines.com.

The Air Force Reserve Officer Training Corps

The Air Force ROTC (AFROTC) and ROTC scholarship programs have historically been the largest and most long-established source of commissioned officers in the Air Force. AFROTC units are located on nearly 150 college and university campuses, with at least 900 other institutions participating in a cross-town agreement, permitting their students to participate in AFROTC classes and activities at a nearby college or university with an active ROTC program.

The academic or classroom portion of the Air Force's ROTC program is called **Aerospace Studies**; cadets must attend these classes each semester. The first- and second-year cadets take the General Military Course, a weekly one-hour academic course intended to familiarize cadets with the basic concepts of military service. Third- and fourth-year cadets move on to the Professional Officer Course, a weekly, three-hour academic course designed to prepare them for active duty.

All cadets must also participate in Leadership Laboratory, a weekly half-hour class that develops leadership and teamwork skills and promotes *esprit de corps* and general military tradition. In Leadership Laboratory, upper division cadets assist the ROTC leadership cadre with preparing the first- and second-year cadets for Field Training. Field training is a month-long boot camp–style course at the Air Force Officer Training School at Maxwell Air Force Base,

Alabama. The Field Training program is intended to evaluate cadets for ability and to determine potential for the upper-division Professional Officer Course. Cadets are rated on their preparation for Field Training; on physical fitness, leadership skills, professional qualities, communication skills, judgment, and decision-making; and on general military knowledge and bearing. Those cadets who have not participated in junior-division ROTC activities will attend a week of mandatory academic classes at Maxwell, before Field Training begins, and must pass a written final before continuing. Those cadets who have not completed the Air Force Officer Qualifying Test (AFOQT) as part of the application for an Air Force ROTC scholarship must do so before attending Field Training.

The AFROTC offers three- and four-year scholarships to high school seniors and two- or three-year scholarships to those already enrolled as cadets. In order to be eligible for any scholarship, all candidates must complete the Air Force Officer Qualifying Test, or AFOQT. Scores on the AFOQT are rated as percentiles from 1 to 99, so each candidate will be rated against all other candidates applying through a particular program: AFROTC, OTC, enlisted commissioning programs, Guards, or Reserves. Each accession source for officer candidates has established its own cut-off score. There is no set standard score available; however, an ongoing survey of Air Force pilot selectees conducted by the military pilot–oriented website www.wantscheck.com currently gives the following average scores for AFOQT: pilot, 85; navigator-technical, 78; verbal, 66; quantitative, 69; and academic, 70.

During their junior year, most cadets will apply for their active-duty career field. Besides aeronautical or rated (flying) career fields such as pilot, navigator/combat systems officer, and air battle manager positions, they may also apply for nonrated positions in missile operations and management, intelligence, maintenance, meteorology, civil engineering, security forces, and administration and personnel.

Prospective Air Force ROTC cadets must be enrolled in an accredited university or college that hosts an ROTC detachment, or has an agreement with a nearby institution that does. Cadets must be of good moral character and in good physical condition. Those who have been diagnosed with asthma or have been prescribed certain drugs for treatment of ADD/ADHD at any time in their life may be prevented from serving in the military, but this prohibition may be waived, depending on various factors. A cadet on a scholarship must be a U.S. citizen and at least 17 years old. Cadets must be of legal age in the state in which they will be attending, or at least 17 years of age with parent or guardian consent. Cadets must pass a military certified physical exam, meet Air Force weight and height standards, and maintain the required standards of weight, as well as standards of appearance, decorum, discipline, and military and academic performance. Those intending to serve as rated (flying) officers must be commissioned before reaching the age of 29. Those intending to serve in technical, nontechnical, and nonrated positions, must be commissioned by age 30, although this may be waived up to the age of 35. Cadets who are single with dependents, or married to a military member with dependents, must also have a dependent care plan in place. More information can be found at the official AFROTC website, http://afrotc.com/admissions.

The Coast Guard College Student Pre-Commissioning Initiative

The Coast Guard does not have a formal ROTC program, but does offer the College Student Pre-Commissioning Initiative (CSPI) for college sophomores and juniors attending certain colleges. Students who meet the qualifications are sworn into the Coast Guard and must successfully complete the enlisted Coast Guard basic training course upon admission to this program. They would then receive active duty pay at the rate of an E-3, and a scholarship that pays for tuition, fees, and textbooks during their junior and senior year of college, as well as medical insurance benefits. During their junior year, they must also attend the Officer Indoctrination School at the Coast Guard Academy, or receive equivalent on-the-job training at various operational units, and complete all academic requirements for their degree. Upon graduation, and before being commissioned as an ensign (O-1), candidates must attend the 17-week Coast Guard Officer Candidate School. Graduates of this program have an active duty commitment of at least three years. Students who, for one reason or another, are not able to meet these requirements are still obligated to serve their original Coast Guard enlistment as an enlisted service member.

To be considered for the CSPI, a candidate must be a U.S. citizen and meet all physical requirements and standards for a commission in the Coast Guard. He or she must be enrolled as a sophomore or junior in a four-year degree program at an approved institution with a 25% minority student enrollment, and have at least 60 credits completed toward a degree. An applicant must be able to get a bachelor's degree within 24 months after entering this program, and maintain a GPA of 2.50 or better. He or she must also have scored *at least*

- 1100 combined on the SAT, *or*
- 23 composite on the ACT, *or*
- a 4 AQR/4PFAR on the ASTB, *or*
- a General Technical (GT) score of 109 on the ASVAB

More about the CSPI can found on the USCG website, http://www.gocoastguard.com/find-your-career/officer-opportunities/programs/college-student-pre-commissioning-initiative.

Officer Candidate Schools and Officer Training Schools

If you are a college graduate who is interested in serving as a commissioned officer, but did not participate in an ROTC program (and still meet certain age restrictions), all military services and the Coast Guard operate Officer Candidate Schools (OCS) or Officer Training Schools (OTS). These schools offer courses that are much more accelerated than the four academies or the college-based Reserve Officer Training Corps. Most services also have an accelerated course for certain credentialed professionals such as doctors, chaplains, or lawyers, who require only basic familiarity with military customs, courtesies, and traditions.

The services require officer candidates who are participating in an ROTC program also to participate in some version of their officer candidate course, either during the summer vacation or upon college graduation. After ROTC, the various services' officer training schools are the second most common means of acquiring a commission; at the present time, approximately 21% of the services' officers earn a commission in this manner.

In addition, some fields and specialties require extensive additional training, such as flight school. Generally, an individual volunteering for lengthy specialized training will incur a longer period of obligated active duty service.

The Army Officer Candidate School

The Army Officer Candidate School (OCS) is located at Fort Benning, Georgia. It offers a 12-week course, which allows it to be somewhat more immediately responsive than the U.S. Military Academy or Army ROTC programs in meeting Army needs for junior officers. Officer candidates are drawn either from active-duty enlisted applicants or directly from civilian life. The admission process is highly selective, including a careful review by a board of serving officers, and accepts approximately 60% of applicants.

An applicant must be a U.S. citizen, possess a minimum four-year college degree, and earn a minimum General Technical (GT) score of 110 on the ASVAB. He or she must meet the minimum height and weight standards, and pass a complete military physical. Applicants must be at least 19, and no older than 29, although candidates up to the age of 34 may request a waiver.

Civilian candidates must be able to obtain a security clearance and must meet the normal requirements for enlistment, which generally means no convictions by either civil or military courts. Prior enlisted candidates must have no more than ten years active federal military service at the time of commissioning. Following commissioning, an active-duty service commitment of three years is required. Learn more about the Army Officer Candidate School here: http://www.goarmy.com/ocs/index.jsp

The Navy Officer Candidate School

The Navy Officer Candidate School is currently located at Naval Station Newport, Rhode Island; it is one of five specialized officer training schools located there. Conducted by senior enlisted Navy and Marine Corps instructors, the basic officer course is a challenging 12-week program, combining academic coursework and military-style physical fitness training and teamwork exercises, with an emphasis on the core values of the Navy.

To qualify for admission, an applicant must be a U.S. citizen and have received a four-year bachelor of science or bachelor of arts degree from an accredited institution. Applicants must be in good physical condition, and pass a full medical examination; they must also be at least 19 years of age, and no older than 35, depending on the career field or program selected.

Graduates will have an active-duty commitment of at least four years. Engineering officers must serve a minimum of five years; pilots and flight officers are obligated for eight to ten years, depending on the type of aircraft. Medical Service Corps officers, dentists, and nurses will have to serve only three years, at a minimum. Generally, the Navy officer career path alternates between shore and sea assignments, and sea tours usually average less than 50% of the time actually at spent at sea. For more details, be sure to visit http://www.cnic.navy.mil/newport/index.htm.

The Marine Corps Officer Candidate School

The Marine Corps Officer Candidate School is located at Marine Corps Base Quantico in Virginia. Candidates are assigned to either a six- or ten-week course, or to two six-week courses over separate summers, depending upon whether they have been drawn from an ROTC training program, have graduated from such a program, or have applied from the ranks of enlisted Marines. A core principle of the Marine Corps is that every Marine is a combat rifleman, so a Marine officer will be trained as a combat officer, regardless of his or her occupational specialty.

Navy OCS Commissioning

Marine Corps OCS Commissioning

Academic subjects include the history of the Marine Corps, principles of leadership, the Uniform Code of Military Justice, and general topics such as land navigation and military and weapons drill. In addition to academics, there is a strong emphasis on infantry tactics and small-unit leadership carried out in field exercises, at the platoon, squad, and fire-team levels.

Candidates for the Marine Corps Officer Candidates School must be in or have graduated from an accredited four-year college or university with an SAT score of 1000 or higher, an ACT score of 22 or higher, or an ASVAB General Technical (GT) score of 74 or higher. Those who wish to serve as aviation officers must also have a qualifying score on the ASTB. In addition, they must be at a high level of fitness, for the training is physically demanding. It is expected, for example, that officer candidates in the second session of their summer ROTC training will run and hike an average of 250 miles during the six-week training course. Visit the official USMC Officer Training school website, http://www.ocs.usmc.mil.

The Air Force Officer Training School

The Air Force Officer Training School is a 13½-week course held at Maxwell Air Force Base, near Mont-gomery, Alabama. The tradition of training at Maxwell goes back to 1910, when the Wright brothers briefly opened one of the world's first flying schools on that spot, which would later become a military air base. Besides conducting Basic Officer Training, Maxwell also hosts the Air University as well as offering continuing professional training for military officers at higher ranks. The Basic Officer Training course is intended to provide commissioned officers for both the active duty Air Force and the reserve element, drawing in college graduates directly from the civilian world as well as those with prior military experience.

Air Force Officer Training School classes begin at staggered and overlapping intervals, so that an advanced class will serve as the leadership and administrative cadre for a beginning class. The initial six weeks of training are intended to orient the candidate to Air Force standards, with an emphasis on physical training, drill and ceremonies, and military customs. Other areas of training will include academic courses in military history, and leadership, field exercises, small arms training, and team building. During the last six weeks, the focus of the course is on leadership and management within the Air Force structure, as the upper-class cadets mentor and lead a new, incoming junior class. To graduate, officer cadets must exceed established standards for physical and academic fitness and demonstrate a high degree of military bearing and leadership. Applicants for Air Force Officer training school must be graduates of an accredited college or university with a degree in either technical or nontechnical fields. Technical fields such as engineering are in higher demand than nontechnical degrees, thus competition among applicants with a nontechnical degree is fierce.

As in all other services, an officer applicant must be a U.S. citizen and be at least 18 years of age but not have reached the age of 35 by the time of commissioning. Those applying for a pilot or navigator position must have been commissioned and enter flight-specific training by the age of 30. Applicants must be in good health and good physical condition, and meet Air Force weight standards. Applicants must also have completed the AFOQT. Results on each of the sixteen subtests in the AFOQT are combined into five composite scores: Pilot, Navigator, Academic Aptitude, Verbal, and Quantitative, each of which are a percentile score and a predictor of success in various career specialties, to include aviation. Graduates are commissioned as second lieutenants, with an active duty service obligation of 4 years, although navigators/battle managers incur a 6-year active duty obligation, and pilots a 10-year obligation, beginning from the time they are awarded an aeronautical rating. For further information, see http://www.air force.com/opportunities/officer/training.

The Coast Guard Officer Candidate School

The Coast Guard Officer Candidate School is a 17-week long course held at the U.S. Coast Guard Academy at New London, Connecticut, described earlier in this chapter. As in officer training schools for other services, the emphasis here is divided between leadership training and acquainting student/cadets with the peculiar ethos of the Coast Guard—historically oriented toward regulating commerce, service and safety at sea, rather than a strictly military and defensive role. An applicant must have a baccalaureate degree from an accredited college or university and have maintained a cumulative GPA of 2.5, be a U.S. citizen, and able to pass a full medical screening. Applicants for a reserve commission must be between the ages of 21 and 30. Applicants currently on active duty who wish to apply for a temporary commission must be between the ages of 21 and 34. Applicants must also score, *at a minimum,*

- a combined verbal and math score of 1100 on the SAT 1, *or*
- 23 composite on the ACT, *or*
- a 109 General Technical (GT) score on the ASVAB

Graduates will receive a commission at the rank of ensign (O-1) and have a three-year active-duty requirement. More information is available at http://www.uscga.edu.

Direct Commission

The military services offer direct commissions and abbreviated officer training courses to applicants with in-demand professional qualifications, which accounts for approximately 11% of the commissioned officer corps. Chaplains, lawyers, and medical staff—specifically doctors, nurses, and pharmacists—are the usual professions to be regularly offered a direct commission, although there are certain technicians and professions, usually in the engineering fields, who may also be offered such. In the case of direct commission officers, the officer training course is comparatively brief, and intended to familiarize them with the customs, traditions, and administrative practices peculiar to their branch of service.

The Army

The U.S. Army offers direct commissions to those qualified to serve in the Army Medical Department, in the Judge Advocate General's Corps, and in the Army Chaplain Corps. Needs and requirements for these professionals vary widely, and the various familiarization courses are designed to integrate formerly civilian personnel with the Army. The most current information on the Army's direct commission programs may be found at http://www.goarmy.com/careers/direct.jsp.

The Navy

The U.S. Navy's Direct Commission Officer's Indoctrination course is held at Naval Station Newport, Rhode Island, one of five officer training courses held there. While there are certain specialized technical skills needed by the Navy and the Navy Reserve, such needs arise on an irregular basis. Generally, routine opportunities for a direct commission as a naval officer are in the fields of medicine, the ministry, and the law, with occasional needs with regard to civil engineering and supply/logistics functions. The required course is two weeks long, and fairly intensive, providing basic knowledge of Navy traditions and basic military customs and courtesies, along with management and leadership skills relevant to a serving officer. More information on the Navy's Direct Commission Officer's Indoctrination Program may be found at www.ocs.navy.mil/dcoic.asp.

More information on applying for a direct commission in the legal field may be found at http://www.jag.navy.mil.

The Marines

The U.S. Marine Corps does not offer a direct commission officer program.

The Air Force

The Air Force Commissioned Officer Training is a five-week basic course held at Maxwell-Gunter AFB, Alabama, for those professionals who have been offered a direct commission to serve in the Air Force medical, legal, and chaplaincy fields. Owing to their specialized experience and high level of education, such officers may also enter service at the rank of first lieutenant (O-2) or captain (O-3), rather than at the lowest officer rank of second lieutenant (O-1). Like similar Army and Navy courses, Commissioned Officer Training is intended to familiarize such professionals with military traditions and practices and acquaint them with the principles of military leadership and management.

The Coast Guard

The Coast Guard's Direct Commission Officer School is located at the Coast Guard Academy in New London, Connecticut. The course is generally five weeks in length, and is intended to school those with professional degrees who are coming directly into the Coast Guard officer ranks from the civilian world to meet critical needs, as well as those who come from Coast Guard enlisted ranks, or who have held commissions in other services. The course will familiarize such newly commissioned officers with the Coast Guard mission and history, with customs and courtesies, and with basic leadership skills and managerial practices. Those with prior military experience may be assigned to a three- or four-week course, only.

Direct Commission from Enlisted Ranks

Approximately 11% of the newly commissioned officers come by means of a direct commission from enlisted ranks. All the uniformed services encourage enlisted personnel, through different programs, to enroll in continuing education and to work toward a degree.

Programs for commissioning military members include the Army's Green to Gold program, which involves a scholarship to attend college and participate in a local ROTC program. The Navy offers the Seaman to Admiral Program for young NCOs, as well as the Medical Enlisted Commissioning Program, which focuses primarily on enlisted members who wish to pursue a degree in nursing. The Marine Corps has a variety of different programs to earn a commission for those who have a degree, wish to seek a degree, or exhibit outstanding leadership skills.

The Air Force offers the AECP (Airman Education and Commissioning Program), which, like the Army's Green to Gold, allows young enlisted members to attend collage while participating in a local ROTC program. The Air Force also has the Nurse Enlisted Commissioning Program, intended for those enlisted members interested in pursuing a nursing degree. Finally, the Coast Guard has the Pre-Commissioning Program for Enlisted Personnel. All of these programs are available only to those currently serving as enlisted members of the military.

Officers who have graduated from a commissioning program may go directly to their first duty station or go on to additional training. Some of the training courses are relatively brief; others are not. Air Force undergraduate pilot training, for example, is a year-long process. Basic flight training is conducted at Columbus Air Force Base in Mississippi, Laughlin Air Force Base in Texas, or Vance Air Force Base in Oklahoma, with specialized courses at other bases. Naval flight training for Navy and Marine officers is centralized at Pensacola Naval Air Station, Florida. Serving as a nuclear submarine and surface ship officer also involves extended and challenging training courses. Such duties are extremely attractive to consider, being personally and professionally rewarding. However, competition for such assignments is extremely competitive, the courses themselves are challenging, and completing such training will substantially increase the length of the service obligation.

Regardless of the road traveled toward a commission, the prospective officer candidate will encounter some manner of aptitude or qualification assessment along the way, and scoring well on that test will be a major steppingstone. The test you will take depends on the military service in which you are most interested. The different tests used by the uniformed services to screen officer candidates—ASVAB, AFAST, AFOQT, or ASTB (Alternate Flight Aptitude Selection Test) are discussed in the following chapter.

CHAPTER

3 ▶ THE OFFICER CANDIDATE TESTS

CHAPTER SUMMARY

Each military service screens officer candidates in part by using a battery of tests to determine fitness for service, and in what capacity, according to the needs and standards required by the service. These test batteries are discussed in detail in this chapter.

The United States Military uses three main batteries of exams in the process of selecting officer candidates: the Armed Services Vocational Battery (ASVAB), the Air Force Officer Qualification Test (AFOQT), and the Aviation Selection Test Battery (ASTB). The Air Force uses the AFOQT and the Navy uses the ASTB to screen both aviation and nonaviation officer candidates. The ASTB is also used by the Marine Corps and the Coast Guard to screen aviation candidates; nonaviation officer candidates for those branches, however, must take the ASVAB. The Army also utilizes the ASVAB to screen officer candidates, but prospective Army helicopter pilots must take the Army's Alternate Flight Aptitude Selection Test (AFAST). The ASVAB, AFOQT, and ASTB are discussed and reviewed at length in this chapter and throughout this book; the AFAST, because it is used solely to screen Army pilots, is not. For comprehensive AFAST review and practice, be sure to buy LearningExpress's *Military Flight Aptitude Tests*.

The Armed Services Vocational Aptitude Battery (ASVAB)

The Armed Services Vocational Aptitude Battery (ASVAB) is a multiple-aptitude test battery used by all the uniformed services to test prospective enlistees for general aptitude and fitness for the military, and to match their skills and education to an appropriate military occupational specialty (MOS). This is done by combining the scaled, or standard, scores of individual subtests to produce an additional set of composite scores, called *Line Scores*.

The General Technical Line Score

The Army, the Marine Corps, and the Coast Guard also use ASVAB Line Scores to screen officer candidates, specifically with the General Technical (or more simply, the GT) Line Score. The GT score is found by combining the standard scores on the Arithmetic Reasoning subtest of the ASVAB and the total of the standard scores on the Word Knowledge and Paragraph Comprehension subtests.

Army officer candidates must earn a minimum GT score of 110; Marine Corps officer candidates must score a minimum of 115, if not utilizing the SAT or ACT as a qualifying test score. Prospective Coast Guard officers must score a minimum of 109 on the ASVAB GT. The Coast Guard also offers officer candidates the option of using an SAT or ACT score as a qualifier. They must have a combined score of 1100 on the verbal/math SAT, or an ACT score of 23.

The Arithmetic Reasoning Subtest

The Arithmetic Reasoning subtest consists of word problems describing everyday life situations, designed to measure reasoning skills and understanding of

- operations with whole numbers
- operations with fractions and decimals or money
- ratio and proportion
- interest and percentage
- measurement of perimeters, areas, volumes, and time and temperature

The Word Knowledge Subtest

The Word Knowledge subtest consists of questions that ask you to choose the correct definitions of verbs, nouns, adjectives, and adverbs. These questions come in two forms:

- definitions presented alone, with no context
- words in the context of a short sentence

The Paragraph Comprehension Subtest

The Paragraph Comprehension subtest consists of 15 questions, based on several short passages on a variety of topics. No prior knowledge of the subject is required; all the information you will need to answer the questions will be found in the passage. The questions test two different skills:

- literal comprehension—that is, your ability to identify stated facts, identify reworded facts, and determine a sequence of events
- implicit, inferential, or critical comprehension—that is, your ability to draw conclusions; identify the main idea of a paragraph; determine the author's purpose, mood, or tone; and identify style and technique

Other Subtests

The following is a detailed description of each of the remaining subtests on the ASVAB. Most ASVAB subtests require knowledge of the subject as covered in high school courses or other related reading. The two sections that do not depend on knowledge of the subjects in advance are the Paragraph Comprehension and Assembling Objects sections. As we just discussed, in the Paragraph Comprehension questions you will be able to find the answers using the information given in the paragraph provided. The Assembling Objects section tests your natural spatial aptitude skills.

The General Science Subtest

The General Science subtest consists of questions that are designed to measure your ability to recognize, apply, and analyze basic scientific principles in the areas of

- life science: botany, zoology, anatomy and physiology, and ecology
- physical science: force and motion, energy, fluids and gases, atomic structure, and chemistry
- earth and space science: astronomy, geology, meteorology, and oceanography

The Math Knowledge Subtest

The Math Knowledge subtest contains questions designed to measure your understanding and ability to recognize and apply mathematical concepts, principles, and procedures. The questions cover

- number theory: factors, multiples, reciprocals, number properties, primes, and integers
- numeration: fractions, decimals, percentages, conversions, order of operations, exponents, rounding, roots, radicals, and signed numbers
- algebraic operations and equations: solving or determining equations, factoring, simplifying algebraic expressions, and converting sentences to equations
- geometry and measurement: coordinates, slope, Pythagorean theorem, angle measurement, properties of polygons and circles, perimeter, area, volume, and unit conversion
- probability: analyzing and determining probability

The Electronics Information Subtest

The Electronics Information subtest consists of questions that are designed to measure basic knowledge of principles of electrical and electronics systems:

- electrical tools, symbols, devices, and materials
- electrical circuits
- electricity and electronic systems
- electrical current, voltage, conductivity, resistance, and grounding

The Auto and Shop Information Subtest

The Auto and Shop Information subtest includes questions on automotive repair and building construction. General shop practices are also included. The CAT-ASVAB (see following section) splits these two subtests into separate subtests, but combines results into one score. The questions cover the following topics:

- automotive components
- automotive systems
- automotive tools
- automotive troubleshooting and repair
- shop tools
- building materials
- building and construction procedures

The Mechanical Comprehension Subtest

The Mechanical Comprehension subtest consists of problems—many of them illustrated—covering general mechanics, physical principles, and principles of simple machines such as gears, pulleys, levers, force, and fluid dynamics. Problems involving basic properties of materials are also included. The questions may test knowledge, application, and analysis of

- basic compound machines: gears, cams, pistons, cranks, linkages, belts, and chains
- simple machines: levers, planes, pulleys, screws, wedges, wheels, and axles
- mechanical motion: friction, velocity, direction, acceleration, and centrifugal force
- fluid dynamics: hydraulic forces and compression
- properties of materials: weight, strength, expansion and contraction, absorption, and center of gravity
- structural support

The Assembling Objects Subtest

The Assembling Objects subtest consists of illustrated questions that test your ability to determine how an object should look when its parts are put together. These questions measure

- general mechanics and physical principles
- aptitude for discerning spatial relations
- problem-solving abilities

The Armed Services Vocational Battery: Paper-and-Pencil versus Computer-Adaptive

Candidates for military enlistment and officer programs take the *production* version of the ASVAB. (The student version of the exam offered to high school juniors and seniors is often referred to as the *institutional* version.) Depending on where an enlistee takes the ASVAB, he or she will take either the computer-adaptive version of the ASVAB, called the CAT-ASVAB, or the paper-and-pencil version. Candidates taking the ASVAB at a Military Entrance Processing Station (MEPS) will take the computer version, while those taking the ASVAB at a reserve center or Mobile Examination Team (MET) site will take the paper-and-pencil version.

The paper-and-pencil version of the production ASVAB consists of nine subtests. The majority of test takers, approximately 70%, take the CAT-ASVAB. The CAT-ASVAB is a computer-adaptive test, which means that the test adapts to your ability level. The computer will give you the first question, and, if you answer correctly, it gives you another question on the same subject—but one that is a bit harder than the first. The questions get harder as you progress, and after you answer a certain number of questions correctly, the computer skips to the next subtest.

Following are breakdowns of both test formats, with the relevant subtests for the GT Line Score highlighted in boldface.

NUMBER OF ITEMS AND TESTING TIME FOR THE PAPER-AND-PENCIL ASVAB		
SUBTEST	NUMBER OF QUESTIONS	TIME (MINUTES)
General Science (GS)	25	11
Arithmetic Reasoning (AR)	30	36
Word Knowledge (WK)	35	11
Paragraph Comprehension (PC)	15	13
Math Knowledge (MK)	25	24
Electronics Information (EI)	20	9
Auto and Shop Information (AS)	25	11
Mechanical Comprehension (MC)	25	19
Assembling Objects (AO)	25	15
Totals	225 Items	149 Minutes

NUMBER OF ITEMS AND TESTING TIME FOR THE CAT-ASVAB		
SUBTEST	NUMBER OF QUESTIONS	TIME (MINUTES)
General Science (GS)	16	8
Arithmetic Reasoning (AR)	16	39
Word Knowledge (WK)	16	8
Paragraph Comprehension (PC)	11	22
Math Knowledge (MK)	16	20
Electronics Information (EI)	16	8
Auto Information (AI)	11	7
Shop Information (SI)	11	6
Mechanical Comprehension (MC)	16	20
Assembling Objects (AO)	16	16
Totals:	145 Items	154 Minutes

The CAT-ASVAB also differs from the paper-and-pencil version in the following ways:

- Each subtest must be completed within a certain timeframe; most individuals complete the subtest within that time.
- Once you have completed a subtest, you do not have to wait for everyone else to finish; you may move on to the next subtest.
- As you complete each subtest, the computer displays the number of items and amount of time remaining for that subtest in the lower right-hand corner.
- Once an answer has been submitted, you cannot review it or change it.
- Test scores are available as soon as the test session is complete.

THE NEW iCAT-ASVAB

At the time of the printing of this book, the military was in the preliminary stages of rolling out an internet-based version of the CAT-ASVAB, known as the iCAT-ASVAB. This new version offers all the benefits of computerized adaptive testing and allows for the expansion of the CAT-ASVAB to significantly more testing locations, especially to National Guard and Service computer-based learning centers.

The Air Force Officer Qualifying Test

The Air Force Officer Qualifying Test, or AFOQT, is a paper-and-pencil test that somewhat resembles the SAT and the ACT. In order to become an officer and to be accepted into training in the career field of pilot or navigator, you must maximize your scores in each of its 12 sections. If you are an AFROTC cadet, you must also pass in order to attend field training between your sophomore and junior years of college. The combined scores on the AFOQT are rated as percentiles from 1 to 99, so the higher the score, the better the chance of acceptance. Candidates for the pilot/navigator career field are ranked against all other candidates applying through a particular program and testing during that testing cycle. Each accession source for officer candidates (AFROTC, OTC, enlisted commissioning programs, Guards, or Reserves) has established its own cut-off score for each cycle. Consult with the command administering your test for current specifics on required scores.

Cadets are allowed to take the AFOQT only twice during their college years. If you have already completed at least a bachelor's degree, you will take the AFOQT as part of your application process for acceptance into the 12-week officer commissioning program, Officer Training School (OTS). For additional information about the OTS option, contact your local Air Force recruiter or talk to an officer at a nearby university's Air Force ROTC program.

If you fail the test the first time, you may take it again after a six-month waiting period. This gives you an opportunity to review and study those areas in which you may be weak or less confident. Anyone who fails the test on the second try is removed from the ROTC program.

The Air Force Officer Qualifying Subtests (AFOQT)

The AFOQT is made up of 12 subtests. The following chart shows subtests and the time allotted for each.

NUMBER OF ITEMS AND TESTING TIME FOR THE AFOQT		
SUBTEST	NUMBER OF QUESTIONS	TIME (MINUTES)
Verbal Analogies	25	8
Arithmetic Reasoning	25	29
Word Knowledge	25	5
Math Knowledge	25	22
Instrument Comprehension	20	6
Block Counting	20	3
Table Reading	40	7
Aviation Information	20	8
Rotated Blocks	15	13
General Science	20	10
Hidden Figures	15	8
Self-Description Inventory	220	40
Totals:	470 items	177 minutes

The Verbal Analogies Subtest

The Verbal Analogies subtest measures your ability to reason and to see relationships between words. You are to choose the answer that best completes the analogy developed at the beginning of each question. Candidates have 8 minutes to complete the 25 questions in this subtest.

The Arithmetic Reasoning Subtest

The Arithmetic Reasoning subtest measures your mathematical reasoning and problem-solving ability. Candidates have 29 minutes to complete the 25 questions in this subtest.

The Word Knowledge Subtest

The Word Knowledge subtest measures your vocabulary comprehension. For each question, you must choose the answer that most closely means the same as a given word. Candidates have 5 minutes to complete the 25 questions in this subtest.

The Math Knowledge Subtest

The Math Knowledge subtest measures your ability to use learned mathematical relationships. Candidates have 22 minutes to complete the 25 questions in this subtest.

The Instrument Comprehension Subtest

The Instrument Comprehension subtest measures your ability to determine the position of an aircraft in flight by reading instruments showing its compass heading, its amount of climb or dive, and its degree of bank to right or left. In each test item, the left-hand dial is labeled *Artificial Horizon*. The small aircraft silhouette remains stationary on the face of this dial, while the positions of the heavy black line and the black pointer vary with the changes in the position of the aircraft in which the instrument is located. Candidates have 6 minutes to complete the 20 questions in this subtest.

The Block Counting Subtest

The Block Counting subtest measures your ability to see into a three-dimensional stack of blocks to determine how many pieces are touched by the numbered blocks. It is also a test of your abilities to observe and to deduce what you cannot specifically see. Candidates have 3 minutes to complete the 20 questions in this subtest.

The Table Reading Subtest

The Table Reading subtest measures your ability to read tables quickly and accurately. Candidates have 7 minutes to complete the 40 questions in this subtest.

The Aviation Information Subtest

The Aviation Information subtest measures your knowledge of aviation. Candidates have 8 minutes to complete the 20 questions in this subtest.

The Rotated Blocks Subtest

The Rotated Blocks subtest measures your ability to visualize and manipulate objects in space. For each question in this test, you will be shown a picture of a block. You must find a second block that is identical to the first. Candidates have 13 minutes to complete the 15 questions in this subtest.

The General Science Subtest

The General Science (GS) subtest measures your knowledge in the area of science. Candidates have 10 minutes to complete the 20 questions in this subtest.

The Hidden Figures Subtest

The Hidden Figures subtest measures your ability to discern a simple figure in a complex drawing. Candidates have 8 minutes to complete the 15 questions in this subtest.

The Self-Description Inventory Subtest

The Self-Description Inventory subtest measures your personal traits and attitudes. It consists of a list of statements that you must read carefully and decide how well each one describes you. Candidates have 40 minutes to respond to the 220 statements in this inventory.

The Air Force Officer Qualifying Test Composite Scores

The scores from each of the preceding 12 subtests are combined to create five composite scores, which are then used to help determine your aptitude for the various officer career fields within the Air Force. The five composite scores cover the areas of pilot, navigator-technical, academic aptitude, verbal, and quantitative. All cadets take the complete test, whether they are seeking to become a pilot or to enter any of the Air Force's other career specialties. The five composite blocks are described as follows.

The Pilot Composite

The Pilot composite measures the knowledge and abilities necessary to complete pilot training successfully, such as quantitative ability, knowledge of aviation and mechanical systems, ability to determine aircraft altitude and attitude by instruments, understanding of aeronautical concepts, ability to read scales and interpret tables, and some spatial comprehension. The subtests that comprise this composite score are

- Arithmetic Reasoning
- Math Knowledge
- Instrument Comprehension
- Table Reading
- Aviation Information

The Navigator-Technical Composite

The Navigator-Technical composite measures the knowledge and abilities necessary to complete navigator training successfully. It shares many of the subtests included in the pilot composite, but those subtests measure the determination of aircraft altitude. The Navigator-Technical composite does not measure knowledge of aeronautical concepts. Instead, it measures verbal aptitude, some spatial or visual abilities, and knowledge of general science. The subtests that comprise this composite score are

- Verbal Analogies
- Arithmetic Reasoning
- Math Knowledge
- Block Counting
- Table Reading
- General Science

The Academic Aptitude Composite

The Academic Aptitude composite score measures verbal and quantitative knowledge and abilities. The academic composite score combines all of the subtests used to score both the verbal and quantitative composites:

- Verbal Analogies
- Arithmetic Reasoning
- Word Knowledge
- Math Knowledge

The Verbal Composite

The Verbal composite measures verbal abilities and knowledge. It is comprised of the two subtests that measure the ability to recognize relationships among words and the ability to understand synonyms:

- Verbal Analogies
- Word Knowledge

The Quantitative Composite

The Quantitative composite measures a number of quantitative abilities and knowledge. It includes the two subtests that measure the ability to understand and reason with arithmetic relationships; to interpret data from graphs and charts; and to apply mathematical terms, formulae, and relationships:

- Arithmetic Reasoning
- Mathematical Knowledge

Chapters 5 and 9 contain material and practice exercises to assist you in refining your skills with regard to the various portions of the AFOQT.

The Aviation Selection Test Battery

The Aviation Selection Test Battery (ASTB) was developed for use in the selection of candidates for Navy, Marine Corps, and Coast Guard pilot and flight officer programs. Like the AFOQT, a segment of the battery is also utilized to judge the general fitness and aptitude for selection of nonflying officers for the Navy's Officer Candidate School and the Coast Guard's nonaviation officer commissioning program.

The ASTB is administered at most Navy and Marine Corps recruiting centers. Depending on your testing location, you may have the option to take a web-based version of the ASTB called APEX.NET. Unlike the ASVAB, the paper-and-pencil and web-based versions of the ASTB are identical in terms of content and specifications. An advantage of taking the APEX.NET version, however, is the immediate availability of your scores. You should consult your recruiter about your different test options.

The Aviation Selection Test Battery Subtests

The full ASTB consists of six subtests: the Math Skills Test (MST), Reading Skills Test (MCT), Mechanical Comprehension Test (MCT), Spatial Apperception Test (SAT), Aviation and Nautical Information Test (ANIT), and Aviation Supplemental Test (AST). Although most examinees take the entire test battery, those test takers not interested in military aviation have the option of taking only the Officer Aptitude Rating (OAR) portion of the test, which consists of the Math Skills Test, Reading Comprehension Test, and Mechanical Comprehension Test. Nonaviation officer candidates are encouraged to talk to their recruiters about whether they or not they are required to take the full ASTB. The breakdowns of each of the ASTB's subtests can be found in the following table, with the OAR portion of the battery highlighted in boldface.

NUMBER OF ITEMS AND TESTING TIME FOR THE ASTB		
SUBTEST	NUMBER OF QUESTIONS	TIME (MINUTES)
Math Skills Test (MST)	30	25
Reading Skills Test (RST)	27	25
Mechanical Comprehension Test (MCT)	30	15
Spatial Apperception Test (SAT)	25	10
Aviation and Nautical Information Test (ANIT)	30	15
Aviation Supplemental Test (AST)	34	25
Totals:	176 items	115 minutes

The Math Knowledge Subtest

The Math Knowledge subtest measures a candidate's ability to apply mathematical processes in solving equations, and the understanding of basic concepts in arithmetic, algebra, data analysis, and some geometry, and includes solving for variables, fractions, roots, exponents, and the calculation of angles, areas, and perimeters of geometric shapes. The test items include both equations and word problems. Some require solving for variables, others are time-and-distance problems, and some require the estimation of simple probabilities. Practice for this subtest can be found in Chapters 6 and 10.

The Paragraph Comprehension Subtest

The Paragraph Comprehension subtest measures a candidate's ability to extract information from a written paragraph, analyze written information, and form logical conclusions based on the information provided. Skills required for this subtest are relatively straightforward, but it is important to remember that the correct answer to each item must be derived solely from the information incorporated in the given test paragraph. Practice for this subtest can be found in Chapters 6 and 10.

The Mechanical Comprehension Subtest

The Mechanical Comprehension subtest measures a candidate's ability to see and understand the nature of physical relationships and to solve practical problems related to mechanical principles; topics contained in this subtest would normally be included in an introductory high school physics course. Questions measure candidates' knowledge of principles related to gases and liquids, and their understanding of how these properties affect pressure, volume, and velocity. The subtest also includes questions relating to the components and performance of engines, principles of electricity, gears, weight distribution, and the operation of simple machines such as pulleys and fulcrums. Practice for the MCT can be found in Chapters 6 and 10.

The Spatial Apperception Subtest

The Spatial Apperception subtest measures and evaluates the candidate's ability to visualize spatial relationships from various orientations. Each item consists of a view from inside the cockpit, which the examinee must match to one of five external views. These items capture the ability to visualize the orientation of objects in three-dimensional space. Practice for the SAT can be found in Chapters 6 and 10.

The Aviation and Nautical Information Subtest

The Aviation and Nautical Information subtest measures and assesses familiarity with aviation history, nautical terminology and procedures, and aviation-related concepts such as aircraft components, aerodynamic principles, and flight rules and regulations. This subtest may be the most easily improved by review, being largely a test of knowledge rather than of aptitude. Practice for this subtest can be found in Chapters 6 and 10.

The Aviation Supplemental Subtest

The Aviation Supplemental subtest measures the candidate's ability to apply concepts from a variety of subjects in order to solve test items. This will typically contain a variety of items that are similar in format and content to the items in the preceding subtests.

The Aviation Selection Test Battery Ratings

Candidates who take only the OAR portion of the ASTB will receive only an OAR rating; candidates who take the complete ASTB will receive four separate ratings (including the OAR) that are obtained from different combinations of subtest scores. The six subtests in the complete ASTB battery are combined into four result sets used to make determinations in assigning potential officers. The first, the Academic Qualifications Rating (AQR) is a combination of all results, but the strongest component is weighted toward the Math Knowledge subtest. The Pilot Flight Aptitude Rating (PFAR) is also a combination of all results, but weighted heavily toward the Aviation & Nautical Information and Spatial Apperception subtests. The Flight Officer Flight Aptitude Rating (FOFAR) is a combination of all test results, but weighted heavily toward the Math Knowledge subtest. Finally, the OAR is most heavily weighted by scores on the Math Knowledge, Paragraph Comprehension, and Mechanical Comprehension subtests. The first three ratings—the AQR, the PFAR, and the

FOFAR—predict a candidate's future performance in aviation. The OAR is used to predict academic performance in Navy Officer Candidate School (OCS) and Coast Guard Officer Candidate School. Here are the categories and possible scores:

- Academic Qualification Rating (AQR) 1–9
- Pilot Flight Aptitude Rating (PFAR) 1–9
- Flight Officer Flight Aptitude Rating (FOFAR) 1–9
- Officer Aptitude Rating (OAR) 20–80

The Academic Qualification Rating

The Academic Qualification Rating (AQR) is used to predict a candidate's academic performance in Aviation Preflight Indoctrination (API) and primary phase ground school. Performance on the MST weighs most heavily here, but an AQR rating is affected by a test taker's performance on all other subtests. The Coast Guard uses this rating and the PFAR to determine eligibility for its flight training programs.

The Pilot Flight Aptitude Rating

The Pilot Flight Aptitude Rating (PFAR) is used to predict a Student Naval Aviator's (future Aviators) performance in primary flight training. Performance on the ANIT and the SAT weigh the most heavily in the formulation of the rating, but a PFAR rating is affected by a test taker's performance on all other subtests. The Coast Guard uses this rating and the AQR to determine eligibility for its flight training programs.

The Flight Officer Flight Aptitude Rating

The Flight Officer Flight Aptitude Rating (FOFAR) is used to predict a Student Naval Flight Officer's (future Weapon Systems Officers, Electronic Warfare Officers, Tactical Coordinators, Bombardiers, and Navigators) performance in primary flight training. Like the AQR, performance on the MST weighs most heavily here, but the FOFAR rating is affected by a test taker's performance on all other subtests as well.

Officer Aptitude Rating (OAR)

As mentioned, an examinee who takes only the OAR portion of the ASTB will receive only one score—the Officer Aptitude Rating (OAR). The OAR score is used to predict academic performance in Navy Officer Candidate School (OCS).

THE LEARNINGEXPRESS TEST PREPARATION SYSTEM

CHAPTER SUMMARY

Taking an officer candidate exam can be tough. It demands a lot of preparation if you want to achieve a top score. The LearningExpress Test Preparation System, developed exclusively for LearningExpress by leading test experts, gives you the discipline, attitude, and advantage you need to be a winner.

First, the bad news: Taking an officer candidate test is no picnic, and neither is getting ready for it. Your future career as a military officer depends on getting a high score on many parts of the test, and there are all sorts of pitfalls that can keep you from doing your best on this all-important exam. Here are some of the obstacles that can stand in the way of your success:

- Being unfamiliar with the format of the exam
- Being paralyzed by test anxiety
- Leaving your preparation to the last minute
- Not preparing at all!
- Not knowing vital test-taking skills, such as how to pace yourself through the exam, how to use the process of elimination, and when to guess
- Not being in tip-top mental and physical shape
- Working through the test on an empty stomach or shivering through the exam because the room is cold

What is the common denominator in all these test-taking pitfalls? One word: *control*. Who's in control, you or the exam?

Now the good news: The LearningExpress Test Preparation System puts you in control. In just nine easy-to-follow steps, you will learn everything you need to know to make sure that you are in charge of your preparation and your performance on the exam. Other test takers may let the test get the better of them, other test takers may be unprepared or out of shape, but not you. You will have taken all the steps you need to take to get a high score on any officer candidate exam.

Here's how the LearningExpress Test Preparation System works. Nine easy steps lead you through everything you need to know and do to get ready to master your exam. Each of the following steps involves some reading and activities that will help build confidence. It is important that you do the activities along with the reading, or else you will not be getting the full benefit of the system. Each step tells you approximately how much time that step will take you to complete.

Step 1.	Get information	30 minutes
Step 2.	Conquer test anxiety	20 minutes
Step 3.	Make a plan	50 minutes
Step 4.	Learn to manage your time	10 minutes
Step 5.	Learn to use the process of elimination	20 minutes
Step 6.	Know when to guess	20 minutes
Step 7.	Reach your peak performance zone	10 minutes
Step 8.	Get your act together	10 minutes
Step 9.	Do it!	10 minutes
Total		**3 hours**

We estimate that working through the entire system will take you approximately three hours, although it is perfectly okay if you work faster or slower than the time estimates assume. If you can take a whole afternoon or evening, you can work through the whole LearningExpress Test Preparation System in one sitting. Otherwise, you can break it up and do just one or two steps a day for the next several days. It is up to you—remember, you are in control.

Step 1: Get Information

Time to complete: 30 minutes
Activities: Read Chapter 3, "The Officer Candidate Tests," and Chapter 8, "Sample Officer Candidate Test Questions."

Knowledge is power. The first step in the LearningExpress Test Preparation System is finding out everything you can about the officer candidate exam you will be taking. Once you have your information, the next steps in the LearningExpress Test Preparation System will show you what to do about it.

Straight Talk about Your Officer Candidate Test

It is important for you to realize that your score on an officer candidate test does not determine what kind of person you are. There are all kinds of things a written exam like this cannot test: whether you can give and follow orders, whether you can become part of a unit that works together cohesively, whether you will show courage under fire, and so on. Those kinds of things are hard to evaluate and are not tested on this kind of exam.

What Is on Most Officer Candidate Tests

The skills that officers have to know are varied. Following are the most commonly tested subjects.

- Arithmetic Reasoning
- Assembling Objects
- Auto and Shop Information
- Aviation Information
- Block Counting

- Electronics Information
- General Science
- Hidden Figures
- Instrument Comprehension
- Math Knowledge
- Mechanical Comprehension
- Nautical Information
- Paragraph Comprehension
- Reading Skills
- Rotated Blocks
- Spatial Apperception
- Table Reading
- Verbal Analogies
- Word Knowledge

If you have not already done so, stop here and read Chapters 3 and 8 of this book for a complete overview of the officer candidate tests. Keep in mind that each branch of the military has its own qualifying tests. Then, move on to the next step and get rid of that test anxiety!

Step 2: Conquer Test Anxiety

Time to complete: 20 minutes
Activity: Take the Test Stress Test.

Having complete information about the exam is the first step in getting control of the exam. Next, you have to overcome one of the biggest obstacles to test success: test anxiety. Test anxiety not only impairs your performance on the exam itself, but can even keep you from preparing! In Step 2, you will learn stress management techniques that will help you succeed on your exam. Learn these strategies now, and practice them as you work through the exams in this book, so they will be second nature to you by exam day.

Combating Test Anxiety

The first thing you need to know is that a little test anxiety is a good thing. Everyone gets nervous before a big exam—and if that nervousness motivates you to prepare thoroughly, so much the better. It is said that Sir Laurence Olivier, one of the foremost British actors of the twentieth century, threw up before every performance. His stage fright did not impair his performance; in fact, it probably gave him a little extra edge—just the kind of edge you need to do well, whether on a stage or in an exam room.

The Test Stress Quiz is on page 39. Stop here and answer the questions on that page to find out whether your level of test anxiety is something you should worry about.

Stress Management before the Test

If you feel your level of anxiety getting the best of you in the weeks before the test, here is what you need to do to bring the level down again.

- **Get prepared.** There is nothing like knowing what to expect. Being prepared will put you in control of test anxiety. That is why you are reading this book. Use it faithfully, and remind yourself that you are better prepared than most of the people taking the test.
- **Practice self-confidence.** A positive attitude is a great way to combat test anxiety. This is no time to be humble or shy. Stand in front of the mirror and say to your reflection, "I'm prepared. I'm full of self-confidence. I'm going to ace this test. I know I can do it." Say it into a recording device and play it back once a day. If you hear it often enough, you will believe it.
- **Fight negative messages.** Every time someone starts telling you how hard the exam is or how it is almost impossible to get a high score, start telling them your self-confidence messages. If you are telling yourself that you do not do well on exams or that you just cannot do this, do not

listen. Just listen to your self-confidence messages instead.

- **Visualize.** Imagine yourself reporting for your first flight. Think of yourself developing flight plans, preflighting an airplane, or delivering cargo. Visualizing success can help make it happen—and it reminds you why you are preparing for the exam so diligently.
- **Exercise.** Physical activity helps calm your body down and focus your mind. Besides, being in good physical shape can actually help you do well on the exam. Go for a run, lift weights, go swimming—and do it regularly.

Stress Management on Test Day

There are several ways you can bring down your level of test anxiety on test day. To find a comfort level, practice the following techniques in the weeks before the test, and use the ones that work best for you.

- **Deep breathing.** Take a deep breath while you count to five. Hold it on the count of one, and then let it out on the count of five. Repeat several times.
- **Move your body.** Try rolling your head in a circle. Rotate your shoulders. Shake your hands from the wrist. Many people find these movements very relaxing.
- **Visualize again.** Think of the place where you are most relaxed: lying on the beach in the sun, walking through the park, or whatever. Now close your eyes and imagine you are actually there. If you practice in advance, you will find

that you only need a few seconds of this exercise to experience a significant increase in your sense of well-being.

When anxiety threatens to overwhelm you right there during the exam, you can still do things to manage the stress level.

- **Repeat your self-confidence messages.** You should have them memorized by now. Say them quietly to yourself, and believe them!
- **Visualize one more time.** This time, visualize yourself moving smoothly and quickly through the test, answering every question right and finishing just before time is up. Like most visualization techniques, this one works best if you have practiced it ahead of time.
- **Find an easy question.** Skim over the test until you find an easy question, and answer it. Getting even one circle filled in gets you into the test-taking groove.
- **Take a mental break.** Everyone loses concentration once in a while during a long test. It is normal, so you should not worry about it. Instead, accept what has happened. Say to yourself, "Hey, I lost it there for a minute. My brain is taking a break." Put down your pencil, close your eyes, and do some deep breathing for a few seconds. Then you are ready to go back to work.

Try these techniques ahead of time, and see if they work for you!

You only need to worry about test anxiety if it is extreme enough to impair your performance. The following questionnaire will provide a diagnosis of your level of test anxiety. In the blank before each statement, write the number that most accurately describes your experience.

0 = Never   1 = Once or twice   2 = Sometimes   3 = Often

_____ I have gotten so nervous before an exam that I simply put down the books and did not study for it.

_____ I have experienced disabling physical symptoms such as vomiting and severe headaches because I was nervous about an exam.

_____ I have simply not showed up for an exam because I was afraid to take it.

_____ I have experienced dizziness and disorientation while taking an exam.

_____ I have had trouble filling in the little circles because my hands were shaking too hard.

_____ I have failed an exam because I was too nervous to complete it.

_____ **Total: Add up the numbers in the blanks above.**

Your Test Stress Score

Here are the steps you should take, depending on your score:

- **Below 3:** Your level of test anxiety is nothing to worry about; it is probably just enough to give you the motivation to excel.
- **Between 3 and 6:** Your test anxiety may be enough to impair your performance, and you should practice the stress management techniques listed in this section to try to bring your test anxiety down to manageable levels.
- **Above 6:** Your level of test anxiety is a serious concern. In addition to practicing the stress management techniques listed in this section, you may want to seek additional, personal help. Call your local high school or community college and ask for the academic counselor. Tell the counselor that you have a level of test anxiety that sometimes keeps you from being able to take an exam. The counselor may be willing to help you or may suggest someone else you should talk to.

Step 3: Make a Plan

Time to complete: 50 minutes
Activity: Construct a study plan.

Maybe the most important thing you can do to get control of yourself and your exam is to make a study plan. Too many people fail to prepare simply because they fail to plan. Spending hours on the day before the exam poring over sample test questions not only raises your level of test anxiety, but also is simply no substitute for careful preparation and practice.

Do not fall into the cram trap. Take control of your preparation time by mapping out a study schedule. The four sample schedules on the following pages are based on the amount of time you have before your officer candidate test. If you are the kind of person who needs deadlines and assignments to motivate you for a project, here they are. If you are the kind of person who does not like to follow other people's plans, you can use the suggested schedules here to construct your own.

Even more important than making a plan is making a commitment. You cannot review everything you know about becoming an officer in one night. You have to set aside some time every day for study and practice. Try for at least 20 minutes a day.

Even 10 minutes a day, with half an hour or more on weekends, can make a big difference in your score—and in your chances of making the grade you want!

Schedule A: The 30-Day Plan

If you have at least a month before you take your officer candidate test, you have plenty of time to prepare—as long as you do not waste it! If you have less than a month, turn to Schedule B.

Time	Preparation
Days 1–4	Skim over the written materials from your specific training program, particularly noting 1) areas you expect to be emphasized on the test and 2) areas you do not remember well. On Day 4, concentrate on those areas.
Day 5	Take the appropriate diagnostic test.
Day 6	Score the diagnostic test, using the answer key at the end. Read the list of subsections on the sample test given in Chapter 8. Identify two areas that you will concentrate on before you take the practice exam.
Days 7–10	Study the two areas you identified as your weak points. Do not worry about the other areas.
Day 11	Take the appropriate practice test.
Day 12	Score your practice test, using the answer key at the end. Identify one area to concentrate on before you continue.
Days 13–18	Study the one area you identified for review. In addition, review both the diagnostic and the practice test you have taken. Give special attention to the answer explanations and the length of time it took you to complete the exams.
Day 19	Take the online practice test.
Days 20–21	Study the one area you identified for review.
Days 22–25	Take an overview of all your training materials, consolidating your strengths and improving on your weaknesses.
Days 26–27	Review all the areas that gave you the most trouble in the diagnostic, practice, and online practice exams.
Day 28	Take the diagnostic test one final time. Note how much you have improved!
Day 29	Review one or two weak areas.
Day before	Relax. Do something unrelated to the test and go to bed at a reasonable hour.

Schedule B: The 10-Day Plan

If you have two weeks or less before you take the exam, you may have your work cut out for you. Use this 10-day schedule to help you make the most of your time.

Time	Preparation
Day 1	Take the appropriate diagnostic test and score it, using the answer key at the end. Skim through the list of subject areas on the exam in Chapter 8 to find out which areas need the most work—based on your exam score.
Day 2	Review one area that gave you trouble on the diagnostic test.
Day 3	Review another area that gave you trouble on the diagnostic test.
Day 4	Take the appropriate practice exam and score it, using the answer key at the end.
Day 5	If your score on the practice test does not show improvement from the diagnostic test on the two areas you studied, review them. If you did improve in those areas, choose a different trouble spot to study today.
Day 6	Take the online practice test.

Day 7	Choose your weakest area from your online practice exam to review.
Day 8	Review any areas that you have not yet reviewed.
Day 9	Take the diagnostic test again and score it.
Day 10	Use your last study day to brush up on any areas that are still giving you trouble.
Day before the exam	Relax. Do something unrelated to the test and go to bed at a reasonable hour.

Step 4: Learn to Manage Your Time

Time to complete: 10 minutes to read; many hours of practice!
Activities: Practice these strategies as you take the sample tests in this book.

Steps 4, 5, and 6 of the LearningExpress Test Preparation System put you in charge of your exam by showing you test-taking strategies that work. Practice these strategies as you take the sample tests in this book, and then you will be ready to use them on test day.

First, you will take control of your time on the exam. Officer candidate exams each have a time limit, which may give you more than enough time to complete all the questions—or may not. It is a terrible feeling to hear the examiner say "five minutes left" when you are only three-quarters of the way through the test. Here are some tips to keep that from happening to you.

- **Follow directions.** If the directions are given orally, listen closely. If they are written on the exam booklet, read them carefully. Ask questions before the exam begins if there is anything you do not understand. If you are allowed to write in your exam booklet, write down the beginning time and the ending time of the exam.
- **Pace yourself.** Glance at your watch every few minutes, and compare the time to how far you have gotten in the test. When one-quarter of the

time has elapsed, you should be a quarter of the way through the section, and so on. If you are falling behind, pick up the pace a bit.

- **Keep moving.** Do not waste time on one question. If you do not know the answer, skip the question and move on. Circle the number of the question in your test booklet in case you have time to come back to it later.
- **Keep track of your place on the answer sheet.** If you skip a question, make sure you skip on the answer sheet, too. Check yourself every five to 10 questions to make sure the question number and the answer sheet number are still the same.
- **Do not rush.** Although you should keep moving, rushing will not help. Try to keep calm and work methodically and quickly.

Step 5: Learn to Use the Process of Elimination

Time to complete: 20 minutes
Activity: Complete the worksheet on Using the Process of Elimination.

After time management, your next most important tool for taking control of your exam is using the process of elimination wisely. It is standard test-taking wisdom that you should always read all the answer choices before choosing your answer. This helps you find the right answer by eliminating wrong answer choices. And, sure enough, that standard wisdom applies to your exam, too.

Let us say you are facing a general science question that goes like this:

13. "Biology uses a *binomial* system of classification." In this sentence, the word *binomial* most nearly means
    a. understanding the law.
    b. having two names.
    c. scientifically sound.
    d. having a double meaning.

If you happen to know what *binomial* means, of course, you do not need to use the process of elimination, but let us assume that, like many people, you do not. So you look at the answer choices. "Understanding the law" does not sound very likely for something having to do with biology. So you eliminate choice **a**—and now you have only three answer choices to deal with. Mark an X next to choice **a** so you do not read it again.

On to the other answer choices. If you know that the prefix *bi-* means "two," as in *bicycle*, you will flag choice **b** as a possible answer. Make a check mark beside it, meaning "good answer, I might use this one."

Choice **c**, "scientifically sound," is a possibility. At least it is about science, not law. It could work here, although, when you think about it, having a "scientifically sound" classification system in a scientific field is kind of redundant. You remember the *bi-* thing in *binomial* and probably continue to prefer choice **b**. But you are not sure, so you put a question mark next to choice **c**, meaning "well, maybe."

Now, choice **d**, "having a double meaning." You are still keeping in mind that *bi-* means "two," so this one looks possible at first. But then you look again at the sentence the word belongs in, and you think, "Why would biology want a system of classification that has two meanings? That wouldn't work very well!" If you are really taken with the idea that *bi-* means "two," you might put a question mark here. But if you are feeling a little more confident, you will put an X. You have already got a better answer picked out.

Now your question looks like this:

13. "Biology uses a *binomial* system of classification." In this sentence, the word *binomial* most nearly means
   X **a.** understanding the law.
   ✓ **b.** having two names.
   ? **c.** scientifically sound.
   ? **d.** having a double meaning.

You have got just one check mark, for "good answer." If you are pressed for time, you should simply mark choice **b** on your answer sheet. If you have got the time to be extra careful, you could compare your check-mark answer to your question-mark answers to make sure that it is better. (The binomial system in biology is the one that gives a two-part genus and species name like *Homo sapiens*.)

It is good to have a system for marking good, bad, and maybe answers. We are recommending this one:

X = bad
✓ = good
? = maybe

If you do not like these marks, devise your own system. Just make sure you do it long before test day—while you are working through the practice tests in this book—so you will not have to worry about it during the actual exam.

Even when you think you are absolutely clueless about a question, you can often use the process of elimination to get rid of one answer choice. If so, you are better prepared to make an educated guess, as you will see in Step 6. More often, the process of elimination allows you to get down to only two possibly right answers. Then you are in a strong position to guess. And sometimes, even though you do not know the right answer, you find it simply by getting rid of the wrong ones, as you did in the previous example.

Try using your powers of elimination on the questions in the worksheet Using the Process of Elimination now. The answer explanations given there show one possible way you might use the process to arrive at the right answer.

The process of elimination is your tool for the next step, which is knowing when to guess.

Use the process of elimination to answer the following questions.

1. Ilsa is as old as Meghan will be in five years. The difference between Ed's age and Meghan's age is twice the difference between Ilsa's age and Meghan's age. Ed is 29. How old is Ilsa?

   a. 4

   b. 10

   c. 19

   d. 24

2. "All drivers of commercial vehicles must carry a valid commercial driver's license whenever operating a commercial vehicle." According to this sentence, which of the following people need NOT carry a commercial driver's license?

   a. a truck driver idling his engine while waiting to be directed to a loading dock

   b. a bus operator backing her bus out of the way of another bus in the bus lot

   c. a taxi driver driving his personal car to the grocery store

   d. a limousine driver taking the limousine to her home after dropping off her last passenger of the evening

3. Smoking tobacco has been linked to

   a. increased risk of stroke and heart attack.

   b. all forms of respiratory disease.

   c. increasing mortality rates over the past ten years.

   d. juvenile delinquency.

4. Which of the following words is spelled correctly?

   a. incorrigible

   b. outragous

   c. domestickated

   d. understandible

Answers

Here are the answers, as well as some suggestions as to how you might have used the process of elimination to find them.

1. d. You should have eliminated choice **a** immediately. Ilsa cannot be 4 years old if Meghan is going to be Ilsa's age in five years. The best way to eliminate other answer choices is to try plugging them into the information given in the problem. For instance, for choice **b**, if Ilsa is 10, then Meghan must be 5. The difference in their ages is 5 years. The difference between Ed's age, 29, and Meghan's age, 5, is 24. Is 24 two times 5? No. Then choice **b** is wrong. You could eliminate choice **c** in the same way and be left with choice **d**.

2. c. Note the word *not* in the question, and go through the answers one by one. Is the truck driver in choice **a** "operating a commercial vehicle"? Yes, idling counts as "operating," so he needs to have a commercial driver's license. Likewise, the bus operator in choice **b** is operating a commercial vehicle; the question does not say the operator has to be on the street. The limo driver in choice **d** is operating a commercial vehicle, even if it does not have a passenger in it. However, the cabbie in choice **c** is *not* operating a commercial vehicle, but his own private car.

3. a. You could eliminate choice **b** simply because of the presence of the word *all*. Such absolutes hardly ever appear in correct answer choices. Choice **c** looks attractive until you think a little about what you know—are there not fewer people smoking these days, rather than more? So how could smoking be responsible for a higher mortality rate? (If you did not know that *mortality rate* means the rate at which people die, you might keep this choice as a possibility, but you would still be able to eliminate two answers and have only two to choose from.) Choice **d** is plain silly, so you could eliminate that one, too. Now you are left with the correct choice, **a**.

4. a. How you used the process of elimination here depends on which words you recognized as being spelled incorrectly. If you knew that the correct spellings were *outrageous, domesticated*, and *understandable,* then you were home free. You probably knew that at least one of those words was spelled wrong.

Step 6: Know When to Guess

Time to complete: 20 minutes
Activity: Complete the worksheet on Your Guessing Ability.

Armed with the process of elimination, you are ready to take control of one of the big questions in test taking: Should I guess? The first and main answer is yes. Some exams have what is called a guessing penalty, in which a fraction of your wrong answers is subtracted from your right answers—but officer candidate exams do not tend to work like that. The number of questions you answer correctly yields your raw score. So you have nothing to lose and everything to gain by guessing.

The more complicated answer to the question Should I guess? depends on you, your personality, and your guessing intutition. There are two things you need to know about yourself before you go into the exam:

- Are you a risk taker?
- Are you a good guesser?

You will have to decide about your risk-taking quotient on your own. To find out if you are a good guesser, complete the worksheet on Your Guessing Ability that follows. Frankly, even if you are a play-it-safe person with terrible intuition, you are still safe in guessing every time. The best thing would be if you could overcome your anxieties and go ahead and mark an answer. But you may want to have a sense of how good your intuition is before you go into the exam.

YOUR GUESSING ABILITY

The following are ten really hard questions. You are not supposed to know the answers. Rather, this is an assessment of your ability to guess when you don't have a clue. Read each question carefully, just as if you did expect to answer it. If you have any knowledge at all about the subject of the question, use that knowledge to help you eliminate wrong answer choices.

ANSWER GRID

1. ⓐ ⓑ ⓒ ⓓ
2. ⓐ ⓑ ⓒ ⓓ
3. ⓐ ⓑ ⓒ ⓓ
4. ⓐ ⓑ ⓒ ⓓ

5. ⓐ ⓑ ⓒ ⓓ
6. ⓐ ⓑ ⓒ ⓓ
7. ⓐ ⓑ ⓒ ⓓ
8. ⓐ ⓑ ⓒ ⓓ

9. ⓐ ⓑ ⓒ ⓓ
10. ⓐ ⓑ ⓒ ⓓ

1. September 7 is Independence Day in
   a. India.
   b. Costa Rica.
   c. Brazil.
   d. Australia.

2. Which of the following is the formula for determining the momentum of an object?
   a. $p = mv$
   b. $F = ma$
   c. $P = IV$
   d. $E = mc^2$

3. Because of the expansion of the universe, the stars and other celestial bodies are all moving away from each other. This phenomenon is known as
   a. Newton's first law.
   b. the big bang.
   c. gravitational collapse.
   d. Hubble flow.

4. American author Gertrude Stein was born in
   a. 1713.
   b. 1830.
   c. 1874.
   d. 1901.

5. Which of the following is NOT one of the Five Classics attributed to Confucius?
   a. *I Ching*
   b. *Book of Holiness*
   c. *Spring and Autumn Annals*
   d. *Book of History*

6. The religious and philosophical doctrine that holds that the universe is constantly in a struggle between good and evil is known as
   a. Pelagianism.
   b. Manichaeanism.
   c. neo-Hegelianism.
   d. Epicureanism.

7. The third Chief Justice of the U.S. Supreme Court was
   a. John Blair.
   b. William Cushing.
   c. James Wilson.
   d. John Jay.

8. Which of the following is the poisonous portion of a daffodil?

   a. the bulb
   b. the leaves
   c. the stem
   d. the flowers

9. The winner of the Masters golf tournament in 1953 was

   a. Sam Snead.
   b. Cary Middlecoff.
   c. Arnold Palmer.
   d. Ben Hogan.

10. The state with the highest per capita personal income in 1980 was

   a. Alaska.
   b. Connecticut.
   c. New York.
   d. Texas.

Answers

Check your answers against the correct answers below.

1. **c.**
2. **a.**
3. **d.**
4. **c.**
5. **b.**
6. **b.**
7. **b.**
8. **a.**
9. **d.**
10. **a.**

How Did You Do?

You may have simply gotten lucky and actually known the answer to one or two questions. In addition, your guessing was more successful if you were able to use the process of elimination on any of the questions. Maybe you didn't know who the third Chief Justice was (question 7), but you knew that John Jay was the first. In that case, you would have eliminated choice **d** and therefore improved your odds of guessing correctly from one in four to one in three.

According to probability, you should get $2\frac{1}{2}$ answers correct, so getting either two or three right would be average. If you got four or more right, you may be a really terrific guesser. If you got one or none right, you may need to work on your guessing skills.

Keep in mind, though, that this is only a small sample. You should continue to keep track of your guessing ability as you work through the sample questions in this book. Circle the numbers of questions you guess on as you make your guess; or, if you don't have time while you take the practice exams, go back afterward and try to remember which questions you guessed at. Remember, on an exam with four answer choices, your chances of getting a right answer is one in four. So keep a separate "guessing" score for each exam. How many questions did you guess on? How many did you get right? If the number you got right is at least one-fourth of the number of questions you guessed on, you are at least an average guesser, maybe better—and you should always go ahead and guess on a real exam. If the number you got right is significantly lower than one-fourth of the number you guessed on, you would, frankly, be safe in guessing anyway, but maybe you would feel more comfortable if you guessed only selectively, when you can eliminate a wrong answer or at least have a good feeling about one of the answer choices.

Step 7: Reach Your Peak Performance Zone

Time to complete: 10 minutes to read; weeks to complete!

Activity: Complete the Physical Preparation Checklist.

To get ready for a challenge like a big exam, you have to take control of your physical as well as your mental state. Exercise, proper diet, and rest will ensure that your body works with, rather than against, your mind on test day, as well as during your preparation.

Exercise

If you do not already have a regular exercise program going, the time during which you are preparing for an exam is actually an excellent time to start one. You will have to be pretty fit to pass your physical ability test anyway. And if you are already keeping fit—or trying to get that way—do not let the pressure of preparing for an exam fool you into quitting now. Exercise helps reduce stress by pumping wonderful good-feeling hormones called endorphins into your system. It also increases the oxygen supply throughout your body and your brain, so you will be at peak performance on test day.

A half hour of vigorous activity—enough to raise a sweat—every day should be your aim. If you are really pressed for time, every other day is okay. Choose an activity you like and get out there and do it. Jogging with a friend always makes the time go faster, as does listening to music.

But do not overdo it. You do not want to exhaust yourself. Moderation is the key.

Diet

First of all, cut out the junk. Go easy on caffeine and nicotine, and eliminate alcohol and any other drugs from your system at least two weeks before the exam. Promise to treat yourself the night after the exam, if need be.

What your body needs for peak performance is simply a balanced diet. Eat plenty of fruits and vegetables, along with protein and carbohydrates. Foods that are high in lecithin (an amino acid), such as fish and beans, are especially good brain foods.

Rest

You probably know how much sleep you need every night to be at your best, even if you do not always get it. Make sure you do get that much sleep, though, for at least a week before the exam. Moderation is important here, too. Extra sleep will just make you groggy.

If you are not a morning person and your exam will be given in the morning, you should reset your internal clock so that your body does not think you are taking an exam at 3 A.M. You have to start this process well before the exam. The way it works is to get up half an hour earlier each morning, and then go to bed half an hour earlier that night. Do not try it the other way around; you will just toss and turn if you go to bed early without getting up early. The next morning, get up another half an hour earlier, and so on. How long you will have to do this depends on how late you are used to getting up. Use the following Physical Preparation Checklist to make sure you are in tip-top form.

PHYSICAL PREPARATION CHECKLIST

For the week before the test, write down what physical exercise you engaged in and for how long and what you ate for each meal. Remember, you are trying for at least half an hour of exercise every other day (preferably every day) and a balanced diet that is light on junk food.

Exam minus 7 days

Exercise: _____ for _____ minutes
Breakfast: _____
Lunch: _____
Dinner: _____
Snacks: _____

Exam minus 6 days

Exercise: _____ for _____ minutes
Breakfast: _____
Lunch: _____
Dinner: _____
Snacks: _____

Exam minus 5 days

Exercise: _____ for _____ minutes
Breakfast: _____
Lunch: _____
Dinner: _____
Snacks: _____

Exam minus 4 days

Exercise: _____ for _____ minutes
Breakfast: _____
Lunch: _____
Dinner: _____
Snacks: _____

Exam minus 3 days

Exercise: _____ for _____ minutes
Breakfast: _____
Lunch: _____
Dinner: _____
Snacks: _____

Exam minus 2 days

Exercise: _____ for _____ minutes
Breakfast: _____
Lunch: _____
Dinner: _____
Snacks: _____

Exam minus 1 day

Exercise: _____ for _____ minutes
Breakfast: _____
Lunch: _____
Dinner: _____
Snacks: _____

Step 8: Get Your Act Together

Time to complete: 10 minutes to read; time to complete will vary.
Activity: Complete the Final Preparations worksheet.

Once you feel in control of your mind and body, you are in charge of test anxiety, test preparation, and test-taking strategies. Now it is time to make charts and gather the materials you will need to take to the exam.

Gather Your Materials

The night before the exam, lay out the clothes you will wear and the materials you have to bring with you to the exam. Plan on dressing in layers, because you will not have any control over the temperature of the exam room. Have a sweater or jacket you can take off if it is warm. Use the checklist on the following worksheet, Final Preparations, to help you pull together what you will need.

Do Not Skip Breakfast

Even if you do not usually eat breakfast, do so on exam morning. A cup of coffee does not count. Do not eat doughnuts or other sweet foods, either. A sugar high will leave you with a sugar low in the middle of the exam. A mix of protein and carbohydrates is best: cereal with milk and just a little sugar or eggs with toast will do your body a world of good.

Step 9: Do It!

Time to complete: 10 minutes, plus test-taking time
Activity: Ace the Officer Candidate Test!

Fast forward to exam day. You are ready. You made a study plan and followed through. You practiced your test-taking strategies while working through this book. You are in control of your physical, mental, and emotional state. You know when and where to show up and what to bring with you. In other words, you are better prepared than most of the other people taking the officer candidate test with you. You are psyched!

Just one more thing. When you are done with the exam, you will have earned a reward. Plan a celebration. Call your friends and plan a party, or have a nice dinner for two—whatever your heart desires. Give yourself something to look forward to.

And then do it. Go into the exam full of confidence, armed with test-taking strategies you have practiced until they are second nature. You are in control of yourself, your environment, and your performance on exam day. You are ready to succeed. So do it. Go in there and ace the exam! And, then, look forward to your future career as an officer in the U.S. military.

FINAL PREPARATIONS

Getting to the Exam Site

Location of exam site: _____

Date: _____

Departure time: _____

Do I know how to get to the exam site?   Yes _____   No _____   (If no, make a trial run.)

Time it will take to get to exam site _____

Things to Lay Out the Night Before

Clothes I will wear   _____

Sweater/jacket   _____

Watch   _____

Photo ID   _____

Four #2 pencils   _____

Other Things to Bring/Remember

_____   _____

_____   _____

_____   _____

_____   _____

CHAPTER

5 ▶ DIAGNOSTIC TEST FOR THE AIR FORCE OFFICER QUALIFYING TEST

CHAPTER SUMMARY

This is the first of two sample Air Force Officer Qualifying Tests (AFOQT) in this book. This diagnostic is based on the actual format and content of the official AFOQT. Use it to see how you would do if you took the exam today and to determine your strengths and weaknesses as you plan your study schedule. Information on official AFOQT scoring can be found in Chapter 3.

Subtest 1: Verbal Analogies

1.	ⓐ	ⓑ	ⓒ	ⓓ
2.	ⓐ	ⓑ	ⓒ	ⓓ
3.	ⓐ	ⓑ	ⓒ	ⓓ
4.	ⓐ	ⓑ	ⓒ	ⓓ
5.	ⓐ	ⓑ	ⓒ	ⓓ
6.	ⓐ	ⓑ	ⓒ	ⓓ
7.	ⓐ	ⓑ	ⓒ	ⓓ
8.	ⓐ	ⓑ	ⓒ	ⓓ
9.	ⓐ	ⓑ	ⓒ	ⓓ

10.	ⓐ	ⓑ	ⓒ	ⓓ
11.	ⓐ	ⓑ	ⓒ	ⓓ
12.	ⓐ	ⓑ	ⓒ	ⓓ
13.	ⓐ	ⓑ	ⓒ	ⓓ
14.	ⓐ	ⓑ	ⓒ	ⓓ
15.	ⓐ	ⓑ	ⓒ	ⓓ
16.	ⓐ	ⓑ	ⓒ	ⓓ
17.	ⓐ	ⓑ	ⓒ	ⓓ

18.	ⓐ	ⓑ	ⓒ	ⓓ
19.	ⓐ	ⓑ	ⓒ	ⓓ
20.	ⓐ	ⓑ	ⓒ	ⓓ
21.	ⓐ	ⓑ	ⓒ	ⓓ
22.	ⓐ	ⓑ	ⓒ	ⓓ
23.	ⓐ	ⓑ	ⓒ	ⓓ
24.	ⓐ	ⓑ	ⓒ	ⓓ
25.	ⓐ	ⓑ	ⓒ	ⓓ

Subtest 2: Arithmetic Reasoning

1.	ⓐ	ⓑ	ⓒ	ⓓ
2.	ⓐ	ⓑ	ⓒ	ⓓ
3.	ⓐ	ⓑ	ⓒ	ⓓ
4.	ⓐ	ⓑ	ⓒ	ⓓ
5.	ⓐ	ⓑ	ⓒ	ⓓ
6.	ⓐ	ⓑ	ⓒ	ⓓ
7.	ⓐ	ⓑ	ⓒ	ⓓ
8.	ⓐ	ⓑ	ⓒ	ⓓ
9.	ⓐ	ⓑ	ⓒ	ⓓ

10.	ⓐ	ⓑ	ⓒ	ⓓ
11.	ⓐ	ⓑ	ⓒ	ⓓ
12.	ⓐ	ⓑ	ⓒ	ⓓ
13.	ⓐ	ⓑ	ⓒ	ⓓ
14.	ⓐ	ⓑ	ⓒ	ⓓ
15.	ⓐ	ⓑ	ⓒ	ⓓ
16.	ⓐ	ⓑ	ⓒ	ⓓ
17.	ⓐ	ⓑ	ⓒ	ⓓ

18.	ⓐ	ⓑ	ⓒ	ⓓ
19.	ⓐ	ⓑ	ⓒ	ⓓ
20.	ⓐ	ⓑ	ⓒ	ⓓ
21.	ⓐ	ⓑ	ⓒ	ⓓ
22.	ⓐ	ⓑ	ⓒ	ⓓ
23.	ⓐ	ⓑ	ⓒ	ⓓ
24.	ⓐ	ⓑ	ⓒ	ⓓ
25.	ⓐ	ⓑ	ⓒ	ⓓ

Subtest 3: Word Knowledge

1.	ⓐ	ⓑ	ⓒ	ⓓ
2.	ⓐ	ⓑ	ⓒ	ⓓ
3.	ⓐ	ⓑ	ⓒ	ⓓ
4.	ⓐ	ⓑ	ⓒ	ⓓ
5.	ⓐ	ⓑ	ⓒ	ⓓ
6.	ⓐ	ⓑ	ⓒ	ⓓ
7.	ⓐ	ⓑ	ⓒ	ⓓ
8.	ⓐ	ⓑ	ⓒ	ⓓ
9.	ⓐ	ⓑ	ⓒ	ⓓ

10.	ⓐ	ⓑ	ⓒ	ⓓ
11.	ⓐ	ⓑ	ⓒ	ⓓ
12.	ⓐ	ⓑ	ⓒ	ⓓ
13.	ⓐ	ⓑ	ⓒ	ⓓ
14.	ⓐ	ⓑ	ⓒ	ⓓ
15.	ⓐ	ⓑ	ⓒ	ⓓ
16.	ⓐ	ⓑ	ⓒ	ⓓ
17.	ⓐ	ⓑ	ⓒ	ⓓ

18.	ⓐ	ⓑ	ⓒ	ⓓ
19.	ⓐ	ⓑ	ⓒ	ⓓ
20.	ⓐ	ⓑ	ⓒ	ⓓ
21.	ⓐ	ⓑ	ⓒ	ⓓ
22.	ⓐ	ⓑ	ⓒ	ⓓ
23.	ⓐ	ⓑ	ⓒ	ⓓ
24.	ⓐ	ⓑ	ⓒ	ⓓ
25.	ⓐ	ⓑ	ⓒ	ⓓ

Subtest 4: Math Knowledge

1.	ⓐ	ⓑ	ⓒ	ⓓ
2.	ⓐ	ⓑ	ⓒ	ⓓ
3.	ⓐ	ⓑ	ⓒ	ⓓ
4.	ⓐ	ⓑ	ⓒ	ⓓ
5.	ⓐ	ⓑ	ⓒ	ⓓ
6.	ⓐ	ⓑ	ⓒ	ⓓ
7.	ⓐ	ⓑ	ⓒ	ⓓ
8.	ⓐ	ⓑ	ⓒ	ⓓ
9.	ⓐ	ⓑ	ⓒ	ⓓ

10.	ⓐ	ⓑ	ⓒ	ⓓ
11.	ⓐ	ⓑ	ⓒ	ⓓ
12.	ⓐ	ⓑ	ⓒ	ⓓ
13.	ⓐ	ⓑ	ⓒ	ⓓ
14.	ⓐ	ⓑ	ⓒ	ⓓ
15.	ⓐ	ⓑ	ⓒ	ⓓ
16.	ⓐ	ⓑ	ⓒ	ⓓ
17.	ⓐ	ⓑ	ⓒ	ⓓ

18.	ⓐ	ⓑ	ⓒ	ⓓ
19.	ⓐ	ⓑ	ⓒ	ⓓ
20.	ⓐ	ⓑ	ⓒ	ⓓ
21.	ⓐ	ⓑ	ⓒ	ⓓ
22.	ⓐ	ⓑ	ⓒ	ⓓ
23.	ⓐ	ⓑ	ⓒ	ⓓ
24.	ⓐ	ⓑ	ⓒ	ⓓ
25.	ⓐ	ⓑ	ⓒ	ⓓ

Subtest 5: Instrument Comprehension

1.	ⓐ	ⓑ	ⓒ	ⓓ
2.	ⓐ	ⓑ	ⓒ	ⓓ
3.	ⓐ	ⓑ	ⓒ	ⓓ
4.	ⓐ	ⓑ	ⓒ	ⓓ
5.	ⓐ	ⓑ	ⓒ	ⓓ
6.	ⓐ	ⓑ	ⓒ	ⓓ
7.	ⓐ	ⓑ	ⓒ	ⓓ

8.	ⓐ	ⓑ	ⓒ	ⓓ
9.	ⓐ	ⓑ	ⓒ	ⓓ
10.	ⓐ	ⓑ	ⓒ	ⓓ
11.	ⓐ	ⓑ	ⓒ	ⓓ
12.	ⓐ	ⓑ	ⓒ	ⓓ
13.	ⓐ	ⓑ	ⓒ	ⓓ
14.	ⓐ	ⓑ	ⓒ	ⓓ

15.	ⓐ	ⓑ	ⓒ	ⓓ
16.	ⓐ	ⓑ	ⓒ	ⓓ
17.	ⓐ	ⓑ	ⓒ	ⓓ
18.	ⓐ	ⓑ	ⓒ	ⓓ
19.	ⓐ	ⓑ	ⓒ	ⓓ
20.	ⓐ	ⓑ	ⓒ	ⓓ

Subtest 6: Block Counting

1.	ⓐ	ⓑ	ⓒ	ⓓ
2.	ⓐ	ⓑ	ⓒ	ⓓ
3.	ⓐ	ⓑ	ⓒ	ⓓ
4.	ⓐ	ⓑ	ⓒ	ⓓ
5.	ⓐ	ⓑ	ⓒ	ⓓ
6.	ⓐ	ⓑ	ⓒ	ⓓ
7.	ⓐ	ⓑ	ⓒ	ⓓ

8.	ⓐ	ⓑ	ⓒ	ⓓ
9.	ⓐ	ⓑ	ⓒ	ⓓ
10.	ⓐ	ⓑ	ⓒ	ⓓ
11.	ⓐ	ⓑ	ⓒ	ⓓ
12.	ⓐ	ⓑ	ⓒ	ⓓ
13.	ⓐ	ⓑ	ⓒ	ⓓ
14.	ⓐ	ⓑ	ⓒ	ⓓ

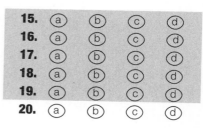

15.	ⓐ	ⓑ	ⓒ	ⓓ
16.	ⓐ	ⓑ	ⓒ	ⓓ
17.	ⓐ	ⓑ	ⓒ	ⓓ
18.	ⓐ	ⓑ	ⓒ	ⓓ
19.	ⓐ	ⓑ	ⓒ	ⓓ
20.	ⓐ	ⓑ	ⓒ	ⓓ

Subtest 7: Table Reading

1.	ⓐ	ⓑ	ⓒ	ⓓ
2.	ⓐ	ⓑ	ⓒ	ⓓ
3.	ⓐ	ⓑ	ⓒ	ⓓ
4.	ⓐ	ⓑ	ⓒ	ⓓ
5.	ⓐ	ⓑ	ⓒ	ⓓ
6.	ⓐ	ⓑ	ⓒ	ⓓ
7.	ⓐ	ⓑ	ⓒ	ⓓ
8.	ⓐ	ⓑ	ⓒ	ⓓ
9.	ⓐ	ⓑ	ⓒ	ⓓ
10.	ⓐ	ⓑ	ⓒ	ⓓ
11.	ⓐ	ⓑ	ⓒ	ⓓ
12.	ⓐ	ⓑ	ⓒ	ⓓ
13.	ⓐ	ⓑ	ⓒ	ⓓ
14.	ⓐ	ⓑ	ⓒ	ⓓ

15.	ⓐ	ⓑ	ⓒ	ⓓ
16.	ⓐ	ⓑ	ⓒ	ⓓ
17.	ⓐ	ⓑ	ⓒ	ⓓ
18.	ⓐ	ⓑ	ⓒ	ⓓ
19.	ⓐ	ⓑ	ⓒ	ⓓ
20.	ⓐ	ⓑ	ⓒ	ⓓ
21.	ⓐ	ⓑ	ⓒ	ⓓ
22.	ⓐ	ⓑ	ⓒ	ⓓ
23.	ⓐ	ⓑ	ⓒ	ⓓ
24.	ⓐ	ⓑ	ⓒ	ⓓ
25.	ⓐ	ⓑ	ⓒ	ⓓ
26.	ⓐ	ⓑ	ⓒ	ⓓ
27.	ⓐ	ⓑ	ⓒ	ⓓ
28.	ⓐ	ⓑ	ⓒ	ⓓ

29.	ⓐ	ⓑ	ⓒ	ⓓ
30.	ⓐ	ⓑ	ⓒ	ⓓ
31.	ⓐ	ⓑ	ⓒ	ⓓ
32.	ⓐ	ⓑ	ⓒ	ⓓ
33.	ⓐ	ⓑ	ⓒ	ⓓ
34.	ⓐ	ⓑ	ⓒ	ⓓ
35.	ⓐ	ⓑ	ⓒ	ⓓ
36.	ⓐ	ⓑ	ⓒ	ⓓ
37.	ⓐ	ⓑ	ⓒ	ⓓ
38.	ⓐ	ⓑ	ⓒ	ⓓ
39.	ⓐ	ⓑ	ⓒ	ⓓ
40.	ⓐ	ⓑ	ⓒ	ⓓ

Subtest 8: Aviation Information

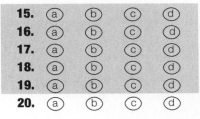

1.	ⓐ	ⓑ	ⓒ	ⓓ
2.	ⓐ	ⓑ	ⓒ	ⓓ
3.	ⓐ	ⓑ	ⓒ	ⓓ
4.	ⓐ	ⓑ	ⓒ	ⓓ
5.	ⓐ	ⓑ	ⓒ	ⓓ
6.	ⓐ	ⓑ	ⓒ	ⓓ
7.	ⓐ	ⓑ	ⓒ	ⓓ

8.	ⓐ	ⓑ	ⓒ	ⓓ
9.	ⓐ	ⓑ	ⓒ	ⓓ
10.	ⓐ	ⓑ	ⓒ	ⓓ
11.	ⓐ	ⓑ	ⓒ	ⓓ
12.	ⓐ	ⓑ	ⓒ	ⓓ
13.	ⓐ	ⓑ	ⓒ	ⓓ
14.	ⓐ	ⓑ	ⓒ	ⓓ

15.	ⓐ	ⓑ	ⓒ	ⓓ
16.	ⓐ	ⓑ	ⓒ	ⓓ
17.	ⓐ	ⓑ	ⓒ	ⓓ
18.	ⓐ	ⓑ	ⓒ	ⓓ
19.	ⓐ	ⓑ	ⓒ	ⓓ
20.	ⓐ	ⓑ	ⓒ	ⓓ

Subtest 9: General Science

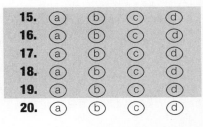

1.	ⓐ	ⓑ	ⓒ	ⓓ
2.	ⓐ	ⓑ	ⓒ	ⓓ
3.	ⓐ	ⓑ	ⓒ	ⓓ
4.	ⓐ	ⓑ	ⓒ	ⓓ
5.	ⓐ	ⓑ	ⓒ	ⓓ
6.	ⓐ	ⓑ	ⓒ	ⓓ
7.	ⓐ	ⓑ	ⓒ	ⓓ

8.	ⓐ	ⓑ	ⓒ	ⓓ
9.	ⓐ	ⓑ	ⓒ	ⓓ
10.	ⓐ	ⓑ	ⓒ	ⓓ
11.	ⓐ	ⓑ	ⓒ	ⓓ
12.	ⓐ	ⓑ	ⓒ	ⓓ
13.	ⓐ	ⓑ	ⓒ	ⓓ
14.	ⓐ	ⓑ	ⓒ	ⓓ

15.	ⓐ	ⓑ	ⓒ	ⓓ
16.	ⓐ	ⓑ	ⓒ	ⓓ
17.	ⓐ	ⓑ	ⓒ	ⓓ
18.	ⓐ	ⓑ	ⓒ	ⓓ
19.	ⓐ	ⓑ	ⓒ	ⓓ
20.	ⓐ	ⓑ	ⓒ	ⓓ

Subtest 10: Rotated Blocks

1.	ⓐ	ⓑ	ⓒ	ⓓ
2.	ⓐ	ⓑ	ⓒ	ⓓ
3.	ⓐ	ⓑ	ⓒ	ⓓ
4.	ⓐ	ⓑ	ⓒ	ⓓ
5.	ⓐ	ⓑ	ⓒ	ⓓ

6.	ⓐ	ⓑ	ⓒ	ⓓ
7.	ⓐ	ⓑ	ⓒ	ⓓ
8.	ⓐ	ⓑ	ⓒ	ⓓ
9.	ⓐ	ⓑ	ⓒ	ⓓ
10.	ⓐ	ⓑ	ⓒ	ⓓ

11.	ⓐ	ⓑ	ⓒ	ⓓ
12.	ⓐ	ⓑ	ⓒ	ⓓ
13.	ⓐ	ⓑ	ⓒ	ⓓ
14.	ⓐ	ⓑ	ⓒ	ⓓ
15.	ⓐ	ⓑ	ⓒ	ⓓ

Subtest 11: Hidden Figures

1.	ⓐ	ⓑ	ⓒ	ⓓ
2.	ⓐ	ⓑ	ⓒ	ⓓ
3.	ⓐ	ⓑ	ⓒ	ⓓ
4.	ⓐ	ⓑ	ⓒ	ⓓ
5.	ⓐ	ⓑ	ⓒ	ⓓ

6.	ⓐ	ⓑ	ⓒ	ⓓ
7.	ⓐ	ⓑ	ⓒ	ⓓ
8.	ⓐ	ⓑ	ⓒ	ⓓ
9.	ⓐ	ⓑ	ⓒ	ⓓ
10.	ⓐ	ⓑ	ⓒ	ⓓ

11.	ⓐ	ⓑ	ⓒ	ⓓ
12.	ⓐ	ⓑ	ⓒ	ⓓ
13.	ⓐ	ⓑ	ⓒ	ⓓ
14.	ⓐ	ⓑ	ⓒ	ⓓ
15.	ⓐ	ⓑ	ⓒ	ⓓ

Subtest 1: Verbal Analogies

Directions: The Verbal Analogies subtest measures your ability to reason and to see relationships between words. You are to choose the answer that best completes the analogy developed at the beginning of each question. The best way to approach this type of test is to look for patterns or comparisons between the first phrase and the choices available to you. You have eight (8) minutes to complete this subtest.

Questions: 25
Time: 8 minutes

For sample Verbal Analogies questions, see page 195.

1. *School* is to *principal* as *office* is to
   a. manager
   b. secretary
   c. computer
   d. teacher
   e. building

2. *Paint* is to *brush* as *clay* is to
   a. dough
   b. mold
   c. sculpture
   d. artist
   e. rock

3. *Knife* is to *slice* as *spoon* is to
   a. fork
   b. stab
   c. stir
   d. cereal
   e. handle

4. *Proud* is to *brag* as *despairing* is to
   a. sing
   b. exult
   c. sad
   d. depress
   e. weep

5. *Excited* is to *thrilled* as *angered* is to
   a. amused
   b. enraged
   c. disinterested
   d. sleepy
   e. delayed

6. *String* is to *guitar* as *key* is to
   a. score
   b. organ
   c. orchestra
   d. song
   e. drum

7. *Thesaurus* is to *synonyms* as *dictionary* is to
   a. words
   b. reference
   c. book
   d. volume
   e. definitions

8. *Pedestal* is to *bust* as *tripod* is to
   a. film
   b. figure
   c. leg
   d. adjust
   e. camera

9. *Beautician* is to *salon* as
   a. follicle is to hair
   b. musician is to concert hall
   c. scissors is to blow dryer
   d. cinematographer is to movie
   e. cosmetologist is to makeup

10. *Stall* is to *engine* as
    a. drive is to motor
    b. race is to heart
    c. block is to progress
    d. freeze is to computer
    e. mechanical is to functional

11. *Leave* is to *bolt* as
   a. dance is to shuffle
   b. toss is to hurl
   c. drive is to race
   d. play is to frolic
   e. shine is to glisten

12. *Disseminate* is to *gather* as
   a. puncture is to prod
   b. resist is to tempt
   c. distinct is to dissimilar
   d. rip is to mend
   e. adjoined is to conjoined

13. *Enjoy* is to *adore* as
   a. love is to desire
   b. spend is to waste
   c. burn is to sear
   d. care is to concern
   e. dislike is to loathe

14. *Gaggle* is to *goose* as
   a. leap is to kangaroo
   b. stripe is to tiger
   c. barracuda is to fish
   d. mane is to lion
   e. flock is to sheep

15. *Science fiction* is to *novel* as
   a. tale is to story
   b. horror is to frightening
   c. country is to western
   d. rhythm and blues is to album
   e. style is to book

16. *Carpenter* is to *constructive* as
   a. farmer is to crops
   b. conservationist is to environment
   c. employee is to duty
   d. critic is to judgmental
   e. instructor is to lesson

17. *Carelessness* is to *mistake* as
   a. destruction is to damage
   b. meticulous is to perfection
   c. process is to result
   d. watchfulness is to sight
   e. reflective is to intelligence

18. *Cautious* is to *heedless* as
   a. oblivious is to negligent
   b. wary is to trusting
   c. alert is to cagey
   d. shameful is to abhorrent
   e. scorn is to react

19. *Surprised* is to *jump* as
   a. relaxed is to seated
   b. amused is to chuckle
   c. stunned is to disturbed
   d. energy is to sprint
   e. perplexed is to wonder

20. *Brace* is to *bolster* as
   a. revert is to rectitude
   b. covert is to manifest
   c. accelerate is to hasten
   d. fulcrum is to level
   e. halt is to increase

21. *Spider* is to *arachnid* as
   a. lobster is to crustacean
   b. arthropod is to insect
   c. ant is to cricket
   d. octopus is to squid
   e. porpoise is to fish

22. *Psychology* is to *mind* as
   a. think is to cerebral cortex
   b. physiology is to science
   c. methodology is to study
   d. anatomy is to body
   e. cognizant is to perceptive

23. *Cardiologist* is to *heart* as
a. surgeon is to general practitioner
b. neurologist is to brain
c. epidermis is to endocrine system
d. orthodontist is to braces
e. dermatologist is to podiatrist

24. *Bushel* is to *peas* as
a. core is to apple
b. bunch is to bananas
c. skin is to grape
d. juice is to orange
e. stem is to carrot

25. *Apathy* is to *disinterest* as
a. tenacity is to resolve
b. insincerity is to candor
c. sobriety is to indulgence
d. affection is to relationship
e. believability is to reality

Subtest 2: Arithmetic Reasoning

Directions: The Arithmetic Reasoning subtest measures mathematical reasoning and problem solving. Each problem is followed by five possible answers. Decide which one of the five answers is most nearly correct. A method for attacking each of these questions is given in the answer block at the end of this chapter. You have twenty-nine (29) minutes to complete this subtest.

Questions: 25
Time: 29 minutes

For sample Arithmetic Reasoning questions, see page 196.

1. It costs $0.85 to make a single color copy at a copy center. At this price, how many copies can be purchased with $68.00?
a. 9
b. 45
c. 68
d. 72
e. 80

2. An aquarium has a base length of 12 inches and a width of 5 inches. If the aquarium is 10 inches tall, what is the total volume?
a. 480 cubic inches
b. 540 cubic inches
c. 600 cubic inches
d. 720 cubic inches
e. 920 cubic inches

3. A man turns a woman's handbag in to the Lost and Found Department of a large downtown store. The man informs the clerk in charge that he found the handbag on the floor beside an entranceway. The clerk estimates that the handbag is worth approximately $150. Inside, the clerk finds the following items: one leather makeup case valued at $65, one vial of perfume, unopened, valued at $75, one pair of earrings valued at $150, and $178 in cash.

The clerk is writing a report to be submitted along with the found property. What should he write as the total value of the found cash and property?

a. $468
b. $608
c. $618
d. $658
e. $718

Use the following information to answer questions 4 through 6.

The cost of movie theater tickets is $7.50 for adults and $5 for children ages 12 and under. On Saturday and Sunday afternoons until 4:00 P.M., there is a matinee price: $5.50 for adults and $3 for children ages 12 and under. Special group discounts are available for groups of 30 or more people.

4. Which of these can be determined from the information given in the above passage?
   a. how much it will cost a family of four to buy movie theater tickets on Saturday afternoon
   b. the difference between the cost of two movie theater tickets on Tuesday night and the cost of one ticket on Sunday at 3:00 P.M.
   c. how much movie theater tickets will cost each person if he or she is part of a group of 40 people
   d. the difference between the cost of a movie theater ticket for an adult on Friday night and a movie theater ticket for a 13-year-old on Saturday afternoon at 1:00 P.M.
   e. none of the above

5. Based on the passage, how much will movie theater tickets cost for two adults, one 15-year-old child, and one 10-year-old child at 7:00 P.M. on a Sunday night?
   a. $17.00
   b. $19.50
   c. $25.00
   d. $27.50
   e. $37.50

6. Using the passage, how can you find the difference in price between a movie theater ticket for an adult and a movie theater ticket for a child under the age of 12 if the tickets are for a show at 3:00 P.M. on a Saturday afternoon?
   a. Subtract $3 from $5.50.
   b. Subtract $5 from $7.50.
   c. Subtract $7.50 from $5.50.
   d. Add $5.50 and $3 and divide by 2.
   e. Add $7.50 and $5.50 and divide by 2.

7. It takes a typist 0.50 seconds to type one word. At this rate, how many words can be typed in 60 seconds?
   a. 2.25
   b. 50
   c. 90
   d. 120
   e. 220

8. If the average cadet burns 8.2 calories per minute while riding a bicycle, how many calories will the cadet burn if he or she rides for 35 minutes?
   a. 286
   b. 287
   c. 387
   d. 980
   e. 1,080

9. Dr. Drake charges $36 for an office visit, which is $\frac{3}{4}$ of what Dr. Jean charges. How much does Dr. Jean charge?
   a. $27
   b. $38
   c. $48
   d. $57
   e. $68

10. Thirty percent of the cadets at the Air Force Academy are involved in athletics. If 15% of the athletes play lacrosse, what percentage of the whole academy plays lacrosse?
a. 4.5%
b. 9.0%
c. 15%
d. 30%
e. 40%

Use the following information to answer questions 11 and 12.

Basic cable television service, which includes 16 channels, costs $15 a month. The initial labor fee to install the service is $25. A $65 deposit is required but will be refunded within two years if the customer's bills are paid in full. Other cable services may be added to the basic service: the movie channel service is $9.40 a month; the news channels are $7.50 a month; the arts channels are $5 a month; the sports channels are $4.80 a month.

11. A customer's cable television bill totaled $20 a month. Using the preceding passage, what portion of the bill was for basic cable service?
a. 25%
b. 33%
c. 50%
d. 75%
e. 85%

12. A customer's first bill after having cable television installed totaled $112.50. This customer chose basic cable and one additional cable service. Which additional service was chosen?
a. the news channels
b. the movie channels
c. the arts channels
d. the sports channels
e. none of the above

13. Out of every 200 shoppers polled, 60 said they buy fresh vegetables every week. How many shoppers out of 40,000 could be expected to buy fresh vegetables every week?
a. 3,600
b. 9,000
c. 12,000
d. 24,000
e. 36,000

Use the following pie chart to answer questions 14 and 15.

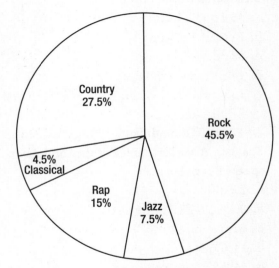

Songs Downloaded

14. If 400 total songs were downloaded, how many downloads were country music?
a. 11
b. 28
c. 55
d. 110
e. 270

15. Based on the pie chart, which types of music represent exactly half of the songs downloaded?
a. rock and jazz
b. classical and rock
c. rap, classical, and country
d. jazz, classical, and rap
e. jazz and rap

16. Last year, 220 people bought cars from a certain dealer. Of those, 60 percent reported that they were completely satisfied with their new cars. How many people reported being unsatisfied with their new car?
a. 36
b. 55
c. 88
d. 132
e. 155

17. Of 1,125 OTS candidates, 135 speak fluent Spanish. What percentage of the candidates speaks fluent Spanish?
a. 7.3%
b. 8.3%
c. 12%
d. 14%
e. 16%

18. The perimeter of a rectangle is 268 feet. Its two longest sides add up to 156 feet. What is the length of each of its two shortest sides?
a. 43 feet
b. 56 feet
c. 72 feet
d. 80 feet
e. 112 feet

19. A piece of wire 3 feet 4 inches long was divided into 5 equal parts. How long was each part?
a. 6 inches
b. 7.5 inches
c. 8 inches
d. 10 inches
e. 1 foot 2 inches

20. A middle school cafeteria has three different options for lunch. For $2, a student can get either a sandwich or two cookies. For $3, a student can get a sandwich and one cookie. For $4, a student can get either two sandwiches or a sandwich and two cookies. If Jimae has $6 to pay for lunch for her and her brother, which of the following is NOT a possible combination?
a. three sandwiches and one cookie
b. two sandwiches and two cookies
c. one sandwich and four cookies
d. three sandwiches and no cookies
e. three sandwiches and two cookies

21. A bed is 4 feet wide and 6 feet long. What is the area of the bed?
a. 10 square feet
b. 20 square feet
c. 24 square feet
d. 30 square feet
e. 36 square feet

22. Airman Beard's temperature is 98 degrees Fahrenheit. Using the formula $C = \frac{5}{9}(F - 32)$, what is his temperature in degrees Celsius?
a. 35.8
b. 36.7
c. 37.6
d. 41.1
e. 59.6

23. All of the rooms on the main floor of a barracks are rectangular, with 8-foot high ceilings. Captain Keira's office is 9 feet wide by 11 feet long. What is the combined surface area of the four walls of her office, including any windows and doors?
  a. 99 square feet
  b. 160 square feet
  c. 320 square feet
  d. 792 square feet
  e. 640 square feet

24. A recipe serves four people and calls for $1\frac{1}{2}$ cups of broth. If you want to serve six people, how much broth do you need?
  a. 2 cups
  b. $2\frac{1}{4}$ cups
  c. $2\frac{1}{3}$ cups
  d. $2\frac{1}{2}$ cups
  e. $2\frac{3}{4}$ cups

25. Fort Greenville is 120 miles west and 90 miles north of Fort Johnson. How long is a direct straight line route from Fort Greenville to Fort Johnson City?
  a. 100 miles
  b. 125 miles
  c. 150 miles
  d. 180 miles
  e. 195 miles

Subtest 3: Word Knowledge

Directions: The Word Knowledge subtest measures your vocabulary comprehension. For each question you are to choose the answer that most closely means the same as the italicized word. If you are somewhat familiar with the italicized word, you can quickly eliminate the options that you know are incorrect. You have five (5) minutes to complete this subtest.

Questions: 25
Time: 5 minutes

For sample Word Knowledge questions, see page 200.

1. *Preside*
  a. challenge
  b. alter
  c. confuse
  d. preview
  e. lead

2. *Liability*
  a. burden
  b. support
  c. effort
  d. ability
  e. link

3. *Diligent*
  a. angry
  b. hardworking
  c. hearty
  d. surprised
  e. dainty

4. *Agility*
  a. leadership
  b. difficulty
  c. slim
  d. fierce
  e. quickness

5. *Elicit*
  a. impair
  b. extract
  c. illegal
  d. sketch
  e. crave

6. *Proclamation*
  a. performance
  b. study
  c. contract
  d. announcement
  e. fad

7. *Pragmatic*
   a. forward
   b. tremendous
   c. sensible
   d. clumsy
   e. fearless

8. *Quandary*
   a. question
   b. stone
   c. problem
   d. jumble
   e. discovery

9. *Opulent*
   a. wealthy
   b. overweight
   c. sickly
   d. inexpensive
   e. fair

10. *Eloquent*
   a. elegant
   b. beautiful
   c. well spoken
   d. tidy
   e. sharp

11. *Fidelity*
   a. falsity
   b. love
   c. clarity
   d. loudness
   e. loyalty

12. *Limpid*
   a. bright
   b. long
   c. true
   d. slight
   e. strange

13. *Refute*
   a. agree
   b. contest
   c. respond
   d. fuse
   e. shock

14. *Vulnerable*
   a. creative
   b. old
   c. upset
   d. weak
   e. feisty

15. *Systematic*
   a. orderly
   b. institution
   c. mechanism
   d. computerized
   e. symbolically

16. *Sagacity*
   a. wisdom
   b. age
   c. size
   d. darkness
   e. humor

17. *Motley*
   a. ugly
   b. tough
   c. multicolor
   d. dangerous
   e. inspire

18. *Jaunt*
   a. joke
   b. trip
   c. bend
   d. exercise
   e. story

19. *Myriad*
  a. watery
  b. strong
  c. ethical
  d. absurd
  e. many

20. *Unison*
  a. single
  b. under
  c. mystery
  d. harmony
  e. truth

21. *Valor*
  a. smoothness
  b. swiftness
  c. popularity
  d. smarts
  e. courage

22. *Blatant*
  a. secretive
  b. terrible
  c. obvious
  d. humble
  e. dignified

23. *Construe*
  a. interpret
  b. make
  c. deceive
  d. suspect
  e. order

24. *Heinous*
  a. delightful
  b. monstrous
  c. hairy
  d. tiny
  e. depressing

25. *Gusto*
  a. hunger
  b. clarity
  c. pride
  d. enthusiasm
  e. sleepiness

Subtest 4: Math Knowledge

Directions: The Math Knowledge subtest measures your ability to use learned mathematical relationships. Each problem is followed by five possible answers. You must decide which one of the five answers is correct. The best method for attacking each of these questions is given in the answer block at the end of this chapter. When you take the actual test, scratch paper will be provided for working out the problems. You have twenty-two (22) minutes to finish this subtest.

Questions: 25
Time: 22 minutes

For sample Math Knowledge questions, see page 201.

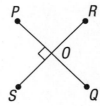

1. In this figure, angle *POS* measures 90°. What is the measure of angle *ROQ*?
  a. 45°
  b. 90°
  c. 180°
  d. 270°
  e. 360°

2. $4\frac{1}{5} + 1\frac{2}{5} + 3\frac{3}{10}$
  a. $8\frac{9}{10}$
  b. $9\frac{1}{10}$
  c. $8\frac{4}{5}$
  d. $8\frac{6}{15}$
  e. $9\frac{5}{10}$

3. $\frac{3}{4}$ is equal to
 a. 0.25
 b. 0.30
 c. 0.34
 d. 0.50
 e. 0.75

4. $76\frac{1}{2} + 11\frac{5}{6} =$
 a. $87\frac{1}{2}$
 b. $88\frac{1}{3}$
 c. $88\frac{2}{3}$
 d. $88\frac{5}{6}$
 e. 89

5. What is the decimal equivalent of $\frac{1}{6}$ rounded to the nearest thousandth?
 a. 0.165
 b. 0.666
 c. 0.123
 d. 0.167
 e. 0.176

6. $\frac{1}{6} + \frac{7}{12} + \frac{2}{3} =$
 a. $\frac{10}{24}$
 b. $2\frac{1}{6}$
 c. $1\frac{5}{6}$
 d. $1\frac{5}{12}$
 e. $2\frac{5}{6}$

7. Which of the following is equivalent to 202,436?
 a. $20,000 + 2,000 + 400 + 30 + 6$
 b. $2,000 + 40 + 300 + 6$
 c. $200,000 + 2,000 + 400 + 30 + 6$
 d. $200,000 + 2,000 + 4,000 + 300 + 6$
 e. $200,000 + 12,000 + 4,000 + 300 + 6$

8. What are the missing integers on this number line?
 a. −4 and 1
 b. −6 and 1
 c. −6 and −1
 d. 4 and 9
 e. 5 and 8

9. $1\frac{1}{2}$ is equal to
 a. 0.50
 b. 1.25
 c. 2.50
 d. 1.50
 e. .150

10. If $\frac{x}{54} = \frac{2}{9}$, then x is
 a. 12
 b. 14
 c. 18
 d. 108
 e. 118

11. Which of the following is divisible by both 7 and by 8?
 a. 63
 b. 106
 c. 114
 d. 112
 e. 78

12. What is $\frac{3}{8}$ equal to?
 a. 0.25
 b. 0.333
 c. 0.60
 d. 0.375
 e. 3.80

13. What is another way to write $4 \times 4 \times 4$?

  a. 3×4

  b. 8×4

  c. 4^3

  d. 3^4

  e. 8^3

14. Which of the following choices completes this number sentence? $5\rule{1cm}{0.4pt} = (10 \times 2) + (5 \times 3)$

  a. $\times (5 + 2)$

  b. $+ (5 + 2)$

  c. $\times (5 \times 2)$

  d. $+ (5 \times 2)$

  e. $+ (5 \times 3)$

15. Which of these is equivalent to 20°C?

  $(F = \frac{9}{5}C + 32)$

  a. 68°F

  b. 95°F

  c. 45°F

  d. 19°F

  e. 70°F

16. What is the volume of a pyramid that has a rectangular base 5 feet by 3 feet and a height of 8 feet? $(V = \frac{1}{3}lwh)$

  a. 16 feet^3

  b. 30 feet^3

  c. 40 feet^3

  d. 120 feet^3

  e. 220 feet^3

17. What is another way to write 7.25×10^3?

  a. 72.5

  b. 725

  c. 7,250

  d. 72,500

  e. 720,500

18. How many inches are there in $3\frac{1}{3}$ yards?

  a. 126

  b. 120

  c. 160

  d. 168

  e. 313

19. $\frac{3}{5} =$

  a. 0.60

  b. 0.20

  c. 0.50

  d. 0.80

  e. 0.90

20. 0.97 is equal to

  a. 97%

  b. 9.7%

  c. 0.97%

  d. 0.097%

  e. 0.0097%

21. In a triangle, angle A is 70 degrees and angle B is 30 degrees. What is the measure of angle C?

  a. 90 degrees

  b. 70 degrees

  c. 80 degrees

  d. 100 degrees

  e. 120 degrees

22. Which value of x will make the number sentence $x + 32 \leq 14$ true?

  a. −16

  b. −21

  c. 12

  d. 38

  e. none of the above

23. What is the length of a rectangle if its width is 6 feet and its area is 108 square feet?

  a. 1.8 feet

  b. 10.5 feet

  c. 18 feet

  d. 16 feet

  e. 68 feet

24. 37.5 percent is equal to

  a. $\frac{3}{8}$

  b. $\frac{5}{8}$

  c. $4\frac{3}{4}$

  d. $6\frac{3}{4}$

  e. $3\frac{7}{5}$

25. 0.15 is equal to

  a. $\frac{2}{5}$

  b. $\frac{3}{20}$

  c. $\frac{2}{10}$

  d. $\frac{1}{20}$

  e. $\frac{1.5}{20}$

Subtest 5: Instrument Comprehension

Directions: The Instrument Comprehension subtest measures your ability to determine the position of an aircraft in flight by reading instruments showing its compass heading, its amount of climb or dive, and its degree of bank to right or left. In each test item, the left-hand dial is labeled *artificial horizon*. The small aircraft silhouette remains stationary in the center of this dial, while the positions of the heavy black line and the black pointer vary with the changes in the position of the aircraft in which the instrument is located.

The heavy black line represents the *horizon line* and the black pointer shows the degree of *bank* to right or left. If the aircraft is neither climbing nor diving, the horizon line is directly on the silhouette's fuselage. If the aircraft has no bank, the black pointer will point to zero (Dial 1).

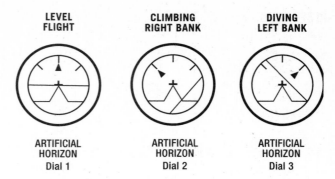

If the aircraft is climbing, the fuselage silhouette is seen between the horizon line and the pointer. The greater the amount of climb, the greater the distance between the horizon line and the fuselage silhouette. If the aircraft is banked to the pilot's right, the pointer will point to the left of zero (Dial 2).

If the aircraft is diving, the horizon line is between the fuselage silhouette and the pointer. The greater the amount of dive, the greater the distance between the horizon line and the fuselage silhouette. If the aircraft is banked to the pilot's left, the pointer will point to the right of zero (Dial 3).

The *horizon line* tilts as the aircraft is banked. It is always at a right angle to the pointer.

In each test item, the right-hand dial is the *compass*. This dial shows the direction in which the aircraft is headed. Dial 4 shows north, Dial 5 is west, and Dial 6 is northwest.

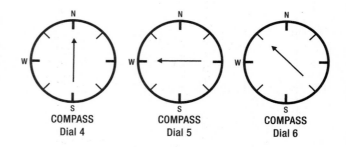

Each item in this test consists of two dials and four silhouettes of aircraft in flight. Your task is to determine which of the four aircraft is closest to the position indicated by the two dials. Remember, you are always looking *north* at the same altitude as each plane. East is always to the *right* as you look at the page. (*Note:* B in Question 2 is the rear view of the aircraft, and B in Question 4 is the front view.) You have nine (9) minutes to complete this subtest.

Questions: 20
Time: 9 minutes

For sample Instrument Comprehension questions, see page 205.

1.

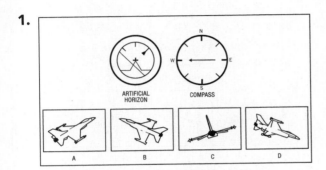

2.

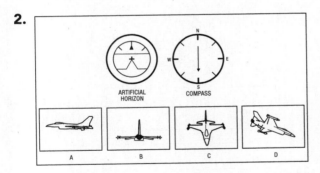

3.

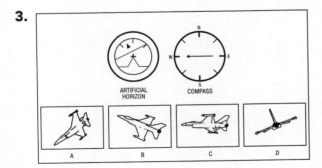

4.

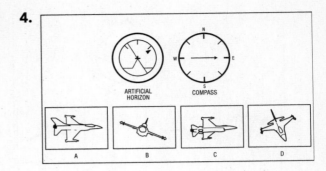

5.

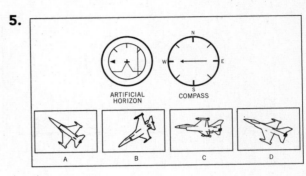

6.

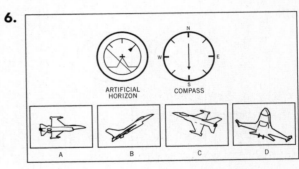

7.

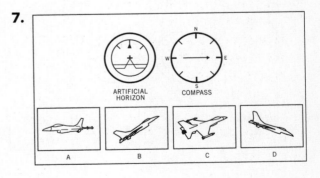

8.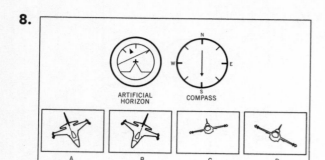

9.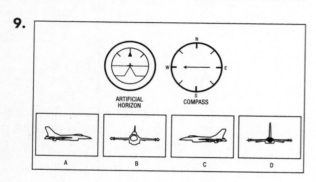

10.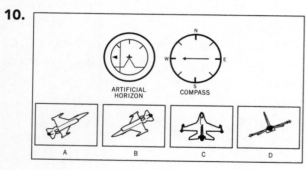

11.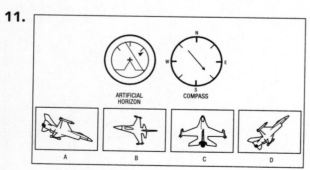

12.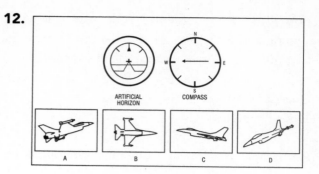

13.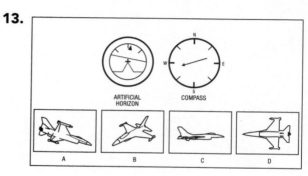

14.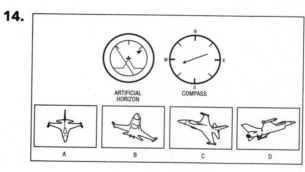

15.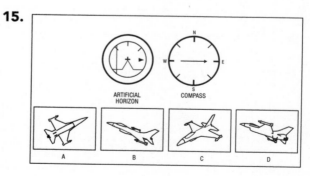

16.

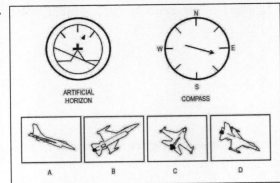

17.

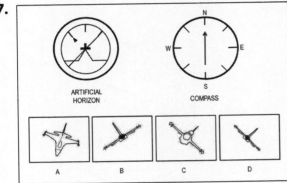

18.

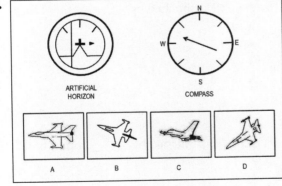

19.

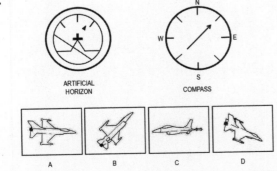

20.

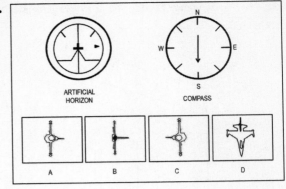

Subtest 6: Block Counting

Directions: The Block Counting subtest measures your ability to see into a three-dimensional stack of blocks to determine how many pieces are touched by the numbered blocks. It is also a test of your abilities to observe and deduce what you cannot specifically see. Closely study the way in which the blocks are stacked. You may find it helpful to remember that all of the blocks in a pile are the same size and shape. Each stack of blocks is followed by five questions pertaining only to that stack. You have three (3) minutes to complete this subtest.

Questions: 20
Time: 3 minutes

For sample Block Counting questions, see page 210.

Use the following figure to answer questions 1 through 5.

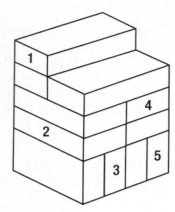

1. Block 1 is touched by _____ other blocks.
   a. 1
   b. 2
   c. 3
   d. 4
   e. 5

2. Block 2 is touched by _____ other blocks.
   a. 2
   b. 3
   c. 4
   d. 5
   e. 6

3. Block 3 is touched by _____ other blocks.
   a. 2
   b. 3
   c. 4
   d. 5
   e. 6

4. Block 4 is touched by _____ other blocks.
   a. 1
   b. 2
   c. 3
   d. 4
   e. 5

5. Block 5 is touched by _____ other blocks.
   a. 2
   b. 3
   c. 4
   d. 5
   e. 6

Use the following figure to answer questions 6 through 10.

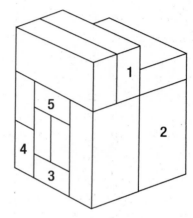

6. Block 1 is touched by _____ other blocks.
   a. 3
   b. 4
   c. 5
   d. 6
   e. 7

7. Block 2 is touched by _____ other blocks.
   a. 1
   b. 2
   c. 3
   d. 4
   e. 5

8. Block 3 is touched by _____ other blocks.
   a. 1
   b. 2
   c. 3
   d. 4
   e. 5

9. Block 4 is touched by _____ other blocks.

    a. 3

    b. 4

    c. 5

    d. 6

    e. 7

10. Block 5 is touched by _____ other blocks.

    a. 4

    b. 5

    c. 6

    d. 7

    e. 8

Use the following figure to answer questions 11 through 15.

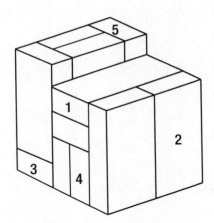

11. Block 1 is touched by _____ other blocks.

    a. 4

    b. 5

    c. 6

    d. 7

    e. 8

12. Block 2 is touched by _____ other blocks.

    a. 1

    b. 2

    c. 3

    d. 4

    e. 5

13. Block 3 is touched by _____ other blocks.

    a. 4

    b. 5

    c. 6

    d. 7

    e. 8

14. Block 4 is touched by _____ other blocks.

    a. 2

    b. 3

    c. 4

    d. 5

    e. 6

15. Block 5 is touched by _____ other blocks.

    a. 2

    b. 3

    c. 4

    d. 5

    e. 6

Use the following figure to answer questions 16 through 20.

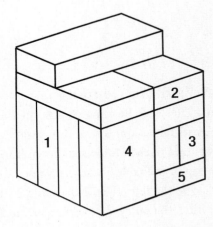

16. Block 1 is touched by _____ other blocks.

    a. 2

    b. 3

    c. 4

    d. 5

    e. 6

17. Block 2 is touched by _____ other blocks.
  a. 2
  b. 3
  c. 4
  d. 5
  e. 6

18. Block 3 is touched by _____ other blocks.
  a. 3
  b. 4
  c. 5
  d. 6
  e. 7

19. Block 4 is touched by _____ other blocks.
  a. 3
  b. 4
  c. 5
  d. 6
  e. 7

20. Block 5 is touched by _____ other blocks.
  a. 2
  b. 3
  c. 4
  d. 5
  e. 6

Subtest 7: Table Reading

Directions: The Table Reading subtest measures your ability to read tables quickly and accurately. Notice that the X values in each table are shown horizontally across the top of the table and the Y values are shown vertically along the left edge of the table. In this test, you are to find the entry that occurs at the intersection of the row and the column corresponding to the values given. On your answer sheet, fill in the letter that corresponds with the number at the intersection of the X and Y values. You have seven (7) minutes to complete this subtest.

Questions: 40
Time: 7 minutes

For sample Table Reading questions, see page 212.

Use the following table to determine the correct value for the X and Y values given in questions 1 through 5.

		X VALUE						
		−3	−2	−1	0	1	2	3
Y V A L U E	−3	76	47	65	88	93	20	22
	−2	57	43	74	77	37	57	46
	−1	43	85	94	22	13	11	35
	0	48	30	68	67	48	58	56
	1	98	42	76	84	10	84	57
	2	76	35	10	62	93	37	43
	3	56	86	40	41	95	99	68

1. −3,0
  a. 85
  b. 48
  c. 76
  d. 40
  e. 56

2. −1,1
  a. 42
  b. 99
  c. 35
  d. 88
  e. 76

3. 2,0
  a. 58
  b. 35
  c. 20
  d. 37
  e. 10

4. 1,2
   a. 10
   b. 62
   c. 37
   d. 93
   e. 95

5. –2,2
   a. 98
   b. 42
   c. 35
   d. 86
   e. 40

Use the following table to determine the correct value for the X and Y values given in questions 6 through 10.

			X VALUE				
		–3	–2	–1	0	1	2	3
Y V A L U E	–3	23	34	35	36	49	74	58
	–2	91	45	47	24	20	34	43
	–1	82	36	56	35	29	55	23
	0	73	27	65	36	39	67	54
	1	74	18	64	47	48	88	65
	2	65	20	52	58	50	79	74
	3	12	39	13	69	68	60	37

6. –3,0
   a. 82
   b. 73
   c. 74
   d. 27
   e. 36

7. –2,1
   a. 27
   b. 74
   c. 64
   d. 18
   e. 13

8. 1,1
   a. 48
   b. 49
   c. 20
   d. 29
   e. 68

9. 0,3
   a. 58
   b. 47
   c. 69
   d. 13
   e. 60

10. 2, 0
   a. 36
   b. 67
   c. 39
   d. 54
   e. 48

Use the following table to determine the correct value for the X and Y values given in questions 11 through 15.

		X VALUE					
		−3	−2	−1	0	1	2	3
Y VALUE	−3	43	35	19	21	24	90	83
	−2	46	46	59	10	35	98	49
	−1	57	54	48	99	43	78	30
	0	68	76	37	88	45	67	36
	1	79	58	24	77	65	87	38
	2	10	49	11	66	67	56	48
	3	34	22	50	55	87	76	74

11. −1,2
  a. 37
  b. 24
  c. 87
  d. 50
  e. 11

12. 3,−1
  a. 83
  b. 49
  c. 30
  d. 57
  e. 50

13. −2,3
  a. 22
  b. 10
  c. 29
  d. 11
  e. 49

14. 0,0
  a. 88
  b. 99
  c. 77
  d. 66
  e. 55

15. 0,3
  a. 50
  b. 87
  c. 76
  d. 55
  e. 74

Use the following table to determine the correct value for the X and Y values given in questions 16 through 20.

		X VALUE					
		−3	−2	−1	0	1	2	3
Y VALUE	−3	84	21	22	79	24	70	99
	−2	58	25	34	86	35	60	87
	−1	95	34	35	58	46	56	67
	0	60	64	36	46	57	77	57
	1	70	56	47	58	54	43	46
	2	74	45	54	69	32	55	43
	3	83	37	38	70	12	78	22

16. 1,−3
  a. 12
  b. 78
  c. 32
  d. 24
  e. 70

17. 2,3
   a. 32
   b. 78
   c. 22
   d. 77
   e. 56

18. 2,–2
   a. 55
   b. 60
   c. 45
   d. 25
   e. 38

19. 1,0
   a. 79
   b. 95
   c. 57
   d. 87
   e. 36

20. 0,–2
   a. 25
   b. 69
   c. 77
   d. 86
   e. 54

Use the following table to determine the correct value for the X and Y values given in questions 21 through 25.

				X VALUE			
	–3	**–2**	**–1**	**0**	**1**	**2**	**3**
Y **–3**	38	33	87	34	13	54	54
V A **–2**	94	21	68	35	14	75	36
L U **–1**	58	31	69	64	25	86	47
E **0**	66	41	80	58	36	93	85
1	77	54	88	61	47	20	77
2	58	36	65	91	58	41	65
3	45	47	43	92	66	55	45

21. 0,2
   a. 93
   b. 91
   c. 61
   d. 92
   e. 66

22. 1,1
   a. 47
   b. 69
   c. 33
   d. 77
   e. 58

23. –1,–1
   a. 36
   b. 65
   c. 54
   d. 68
   e. 69

24. 3,2
   a. 54
   b. 55
   c. 20
   d. 47
   e. 65

25. −3,−3
   a. 45
   b. 54
   c. 36
   d. 38
   e. 93

Use the following table to determine the correct value for the X and Y values given in questions 26 through 30.

	X VALUE						
	−3	−2	−1	0	1	2	3
−3	92	57	37	83	33	48	50
−2	84	65	55	94	20	59	33
−1	84	68	68	85	82	60	42
0	10	69	77	86	92	17	35
1	29	40	99	62	74	63	46
2	39	42	80	73	85	48	47
3	44	36	75	32	55	94	58

(Y VALUE shown along left side)

26. −3,3
   a. 58
   b. 50
   c. 92
   d. 84
   e. 44

27. 0,1
   a. 86
   b. 62
   c. 77
   d. 92
   e. 74

28. 2,0
   a. 17
   b. 80
   c. 94
   d. 58
   e. 75

29. 3,0
   a. 46
   b. 85
   c. 35
   d. 32
   e. 75

30. 3,1
   a. 39
   b. 37
   c. 46
   d. 29
   e. 69

Use the following table to determine the correct value for the X and Y values given in questions 31 through 35.

	X VALUE						
	−3	−2	−1	0	1	2	3
−3	66	24	97	11	12	91	21
−2	77	43	67	22	31	82	23
−1	88	44	68	33	23	73	34
0	99	56	56	55	41	64	53
1	10	67	47	65	62	55	64
2	12	69	33	76	63	45	75
3	13	87	42	89	47	36	83

(Y VALUE shown along left side)

31. −2,−2
   a. 82
   b. 45
   c. 12
   d. 43
   e. 24

32. −2,3
   a. 91
   b. 36
   c. 87
   d. 24
   e. 69

33. 0,−3
   a. 22
   b. 67
   c. 76
   d. 65
   e. 11

34. 1,−3
   a. 12
   b. 47
   c. 97
   d. 13
   e. 21

35. 1,1
   a. 55
   b. 52
   c. 33
   d. 99
   e. 23

Use the following table to determine the correct value for the X and Y values given in questions 36 through 40.

		X VALUE						
		−3	−2	−1	0	1	2	3
Y	−3	44	13	83	35	45	99	33
	−2	65	24	25	46	65	89	44
V A	−1	76	32	47	57	43	70	56
L	0	83	53	65	68	27	67	57
U	1	46	28	43	97	56	60	69
E	2	57	91	78	66	33	61	80
	3	45	28	97	54	43	23	43

36. −3,0
   a. 13
   b. 35
   c. 83
   d. 25
   e. 24

37. 0,2
   a. 67
   b. 66
   c. 53
   d. 91
   e. 78

38. −2,−1
   a. 70
   b. 32
   c. 60
   d. 28
   e. 53

39. 0,−1
   a. 57
   b. 46
   c. 27
   d. 66
   e. 43

40. 1,3
   a. 43
   b. 69
   c. 56
   d. 76
   e. 46

Subtest 8: Aviation Information

Directions: The Aviation Information subtest measures your knowledge of aviation. This subtest is common to all three service selection tests, although the number of questions varies from one service to another. Each of the questions or incomplete statements is followed by five choices. You must decide which one of the choices best completes the statement or answers the question. Eliminating any obviously incorrect choices first will increase your chances of selecting the correct answer. You have eight (8) minutes to complete this subtest.

Questions: 20
Time: 8 minutes

For sample Aviation Information questions, see page 212.

1. An example of a high lift device would be
   a. flaps.
   b. slats.
   c. leading edge extensions.
   d. all the above.
   e. none of the above.

2. Aircraft performance increases in cold weather because
   a. cold air improves fuel flow.
   b. cold air is more dense.
   c. cold air is less dense.
   d. the engine exhaust is hotter than the surrounding air.
   e. none of the above.

3. If you wanted to roll the aircraft about its longitudinal axis, what flight control movement would accomplish this?
   a. aft stick movement
   b. trim tabs
   c. aileron deflection
   d. vertical stabilizer movement
   e. forward stick movement

4. The standard altimeter setting used in Class A airspace would be
   a. obtained from the nearest airfield.
   b. 30.00 in Hg.
   c. 29.92 in Hg.
   d. calculated from an air computer.
   e. none of the above.

5. During the execution of an aerobatic loop, what sort of energy will an aircraft have at the top of a loop?
  a. kinetic
  b. potential
  c. forced
  d. assumed
  e. none of the above

6. Airfield runways are numbered in accordance with
  a. their compass headings.
  b. FAA directives.
  c. airfield altitude.
  d. average relative wind.
  e. runway length.

7. In which of the following takeoff or landing situations would you be most concerned about aircraft performance?
  a. low altitude airport on a hot day
  b. low altitude airport on a cold day
  c. high altitude airport on a hot day
  d. high altitude airport on a cold day
  e. low altitude airport located next to water

8. Lights that outline an airport taxiway are _____ in color.
  a. red
  b. blue
  c. green
  d. white
  e. alternating red and white

9. Extending wing flaps produces an increase in both lift and
  a. thrust.
  b. angle of attack.
  c. pressure.
  d. drag.
  e. energy.

10. The very thin layer of air flowing over the surface of an aircraft wing, an airfoil, or over the entire fuselage is called
  a. free-stream velocity air.
  b. the boundary layer.
  c. the slipstream.
  d. wake turbulence.
  e. wing drop.

11. If your cockpit turn and bank indicator shows a perfectly centered ball,
  a. the aircraft is in aerodynamically balanced flight.
  b. the aircraft weight and balance criteria have been met.
  c. the aircraft thrust-to-weight ratio is equal.
  d. the aircraft is pointed directly ahead.
  e. none of the above.

12. What effect do wing spoilers have when they are employed?
  a. true air speed is increased
  b. they aid in the production of lift by increasing effective wing area
  c. they disrupt the boundary layer airflow, increasing lift and reducing drag
  d. they disrupt the boundary layer airflow, reducing lift and increasing drag
  e. they augment boundary layer air to increase lift

13. The aircraft instrument that transmits signals that identify various aircraft parameters to air traffic control and flight monitoring organizations is the
  a. altimeter.
  b. attitude indicator.
  c. transponder.
  d. tachometer.
  e. UHF radio.

14. How would taking off into a headwind affect your aircraft?
   a. Your takeoff distance would be unchanged.
   b. Your takeoff distance would be longer with little to no increase in climb angle.
   c. Your takeoff distance would be shorter with an increased climb angle.
   d. Your takeoff distance would be shorter and your available engine power would be unchanged.
   e. None of the above.

15. The acronym VSI stands for
   a. variable situational index.
   b. velocity and speed instrument.
   c. vertical speed indicator.
   d. vertical stability index.
   e. variable speed instrument.

16. The VSI instrument indicates
   a. rate of climb.
   b. rate of descent.
   c. level flight.
   d. all of the above.
   e. none of the above.

17. If one end of a runway is numbered 33, what would the other end be numbered?
   a. 15
   b. 33
   c. 24
   d. 66
   e. There is not enough information provided.

18. Ground speed can be affected by which of the following?
   a. pressure
   b. altitude
   c. wind
   d. heat
   e. rain

19. The two main types of drag an aircraft experiences in flight are
   a. parasite and induced.
   b. controlled and unlimited.
   c. supersonic and transonic.
   d. kinetic and potential.
   e. uncontrolled and limited.

20. Bernoulli's Principle states that
   a. a body that is at rest will stay at rest unless acted upon by an outside force.
   b. when there is an increase in pressure, there must be a decrease in temperature.
   c. when there is an increase in velocity there must be a decrease in pressure.
   d. force times mass equals acceleration.
   e. air will circulate counterclockwise in the northern hemisphere.

Subtest 9: General Science

Directions: The General Science subtest measures your knowledge in the area of science. Each of the questions or incomplete statements is followed by five choices. You must decide which one of the choices best answers the question or completes the statement. Again, if you are unsure of an answer, use the process of elimination. Remember, there are no penalties for guessing. You have ten (10) minutes to complete this subtest.

Questions: 20
Time: 10 minutes

For sample General Science questions, see page 215.

1. An element's location on the periodic table is determined by its number of
   a. electrons.
   b. neutrons.
   c. protons.
   d. nuclei.
   e. radons.

2. What are atoms of the same element that have different numbers of neutrons called?
   a. alloys
   b. isotopes
   c. alkali metals
   d. ions
   e. neurons

3. Marine biology is most closely associated with which field of science?
   a. geography
   b. botany
   c. oceanography
   d. geology
   e. seismology

4. Which of the following symbols represents a molecule of carbon dioxide?
   a. C
   b. O
   c. CO
   d. CO_2
   e. C_2O

5. The driver of a car you are riding in loses control in a snowstorm. The car spins 360 degrees and you are thrown against the car door. Which of the following is the best description of what you are experiencing?
   a. fundamental forces
   b. center of mass
   c. centrifugal force
   d. Coriolis effect
   e. center of gravity

6. If particles of food coloring are dropped into a glass of hot water, they will spread rapidly. This is an example of
   a. osmosis.
   b. respiration
   c. evaporation.
   d. active transport.
   e. diffusion.

7. Which of the following represents a chemical change?
   a. tearing a piece of paper
   b. melting an ice cube
   c. cooking a hamburger
   d. dissolving sugar in water
   e. the wind blowing

8. Carbohydrates are much better foods for quick energy than fats because they
   a. are digested more easily and absorbed more quickly.
   b. supply essential amino acids, which provide energy.
   c. are high in both protein and iron.
   d. carry oxygen to the blood.
   e. all of the above.

9. Which of the following atmospheric levels is closest to the Earth's surface?
   a. mesosphere
   b. stratosphere
   c. thermosphere
   d. troposphere
   e. necrosphere

10. All of the following are characteristics of reptiles *except*
   a. cold blood.
   b. lungs.
   c. land-dwelling adults.
   d. scaly skin.
   e. internal development of eggs.

11. Which of the following is a vertebrate?
   a. a sponge
   b. a starfish
   c. an octopus
   d. a snake
   e. an oyster

12. The process by which an organism adapts physiologically to the rigors of a new environment is known as
  a. natural selection.
  b. acclimatization.
  c. evolution.
  d. mutation.
  e. gestation.

13. Which of the following is the best description of what an omnivore eats?
  a. animal matter only
  b. vegetable matter only
  c. detritus only
  d. decomposing matter only
  e. both animal and vegetable matter

14. Which of the following has the shortest wavelength?
  a. ultraviolet
  b. x-rays
  c. microwave
  d. infrared
  e. visible

15. The fundamental force that is the natural force of attraction acting between objects with mass is which of the following?
  a. electromagnetism
  b. strong nuclear force
  c. weak nuclear force
  d. gravity
  e. radiomagnetism

16. Where is most of the mass of our solar system?
  a. Sun
  b. Earth
  c. Venus
  d. Jupiter
  e. Mercury

17. Absolute zero is equal to which of the following?
  a. 0° Fahrenheit
  b. 30° Fahrenheit
  c. 30° Kelvin
  d. −30° Kelvin
  e. −273° Celsius

18. Our solar system is made up of the Sun and how many planets?
  a. eight
  b. nine
  c. ten
  d. eleven
  e. twelve

19. A cell containing chloroplasts would most likely belong to which organism?
  a. rabbit
  b. fern
  c. roach
  d. lizard
  e. shark

20. In animal cells, what organelle contains the DNA?
  a. nucleus
  b. cytoplasm
  c. Golgi apparatus
  d. ribosomes
  e. endoplasmic reticulum

Subtest 10: Rotated Blocks

Directions: The Rotated Blocks subtest measures your ability to visualize and manipulate objects in space. For each question in this test, you will be shown a picture of a block. You must find a second block that is identical to the first. You have thirteen (13) minutes to complete this subtest.

Questions: 15
Time: 13 minutes

For sample Rotated Block questions, see page 202.

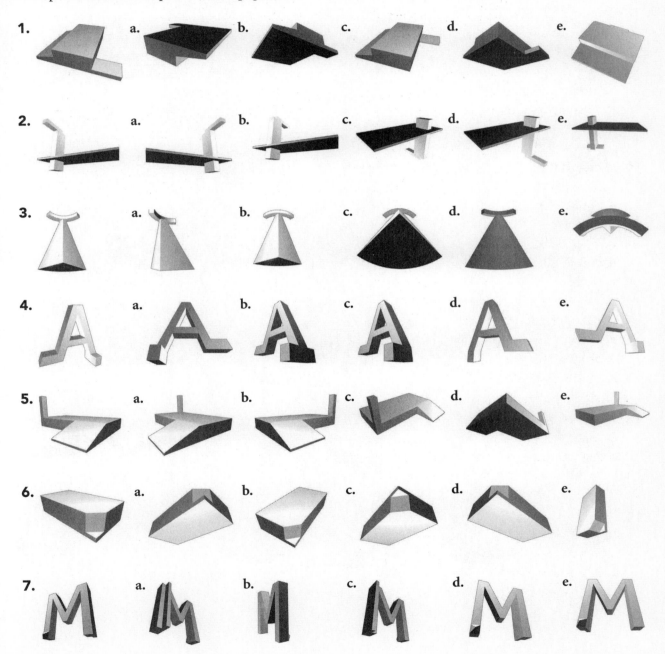

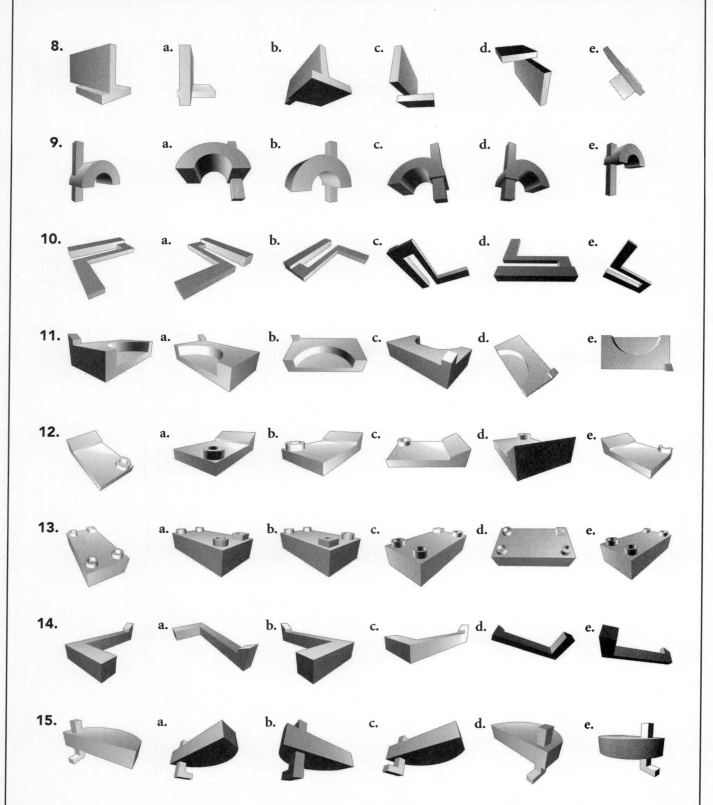

Subtest 11: Hidden Figures

Directions: The Hidden Figures subtest measures your ability to see a simple figure in a complex drawing. Above each group of questions are five figures, lettered A, B, C, D, and E. Below this set of figures are several numbered drawings. You are to determine which lettered figure is contained in each of the numbered drawings. Each numbered drawing contains only *one* of the lettered figures. The correct figure in each drawing will always be of the same size and in the same position as it appears in the top set of figures. Look at each numbered drawing and decide which one of the five lettered figures is contained in it. You have eight (8) minutes to complete this subtest.

Questions: 15
Time: 8 minutes

For sample Hidden Figures questions, see page 217.

Use the following figure to answer questions 1 through 5.

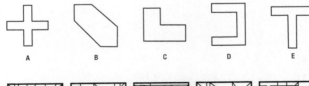

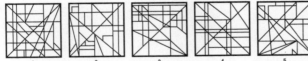

1. The hidden figure in block 1 is _____.
   a. A
   b. B
   c. C
   d. D
   e. E

2. The hidden figure in block 2 is _____.
   a. A
   b. B
   c. C
   d. D
   e. E

3. The hidden figure in block 3 is _____.
   a. A
   b. B
   c. C
   d. D
   e. E

4. The hidden figure in block 4 is _____.
   a. A
   b. B
   c. C
   d. D
   e. E

5. The hidden figure in block 5 is _____.
   a. A
   b. B
   c. C
   d. D
   e. E

Use the following figure to answer questions 6 through 10.

6. The hidden figure in block 6 is _____.
   a. A
   b. B
   c. C
   d. D
   e. E

7. The hidden figure in block 7 is _____.
- **a.** A
- **b.** B
- **c.** C
- **d.** D
- **e.** E

8. The hidden figure in block 8 is _____.
- **a.** A
- **b.** B
- **c.** C
- **d.** D
- **e.** E

9. The hidden figure in block 9 is _____.
- **a.** A
- **b.** B
- **c.** C
- **d.** D
- **e.** E

10. The hidden figure in block 10 is _____.
- **a.** A
- **b.** B
- **c.** C
- **d.** D
- **e.** E

11. The hidden figure in block 11 is _____.
- **a.** A
- **b.** B
- **c.** C
- **d.** D
- **e.** E

12. The hidden figure in block 12 is _____.
- **a.** A
- **b.** B
- **c.** C
- **d.** D
- **e.** E

13. The hidden figure in block 13 is _____.
- **a.** A
- **b.** B
- **c.** C
- **d.** D
- **e.** E

14. The hidden figure in block 14 is _____.
- **a.** A
- **b.** B
- **c.** C
- **d.** D
- **e.** E

15. The hidden figure in block 15 is _____.
- **a.** A
- **b.** B
- **c.** C
- **d.** D
- **e.** E

Use the following figure to answer questions 11 through 15.

Answer Key

Subtest 1: Verbal Analogies

1. a. The head of a school is its *principal* and the head of an office is its *manager*. Although a secretary works in an office, he or she is not the head of the office, so choice **b** is incorrect. Choice **c** is incorrect because a computer is a tool used in an office. Choice **d** is incorrect because a teacher works in a school, not an office, and is not the head of either. A building is where schools and offices are located and does not explain who the head of an office is, so choice **e** is incorrect.

2. b. A painter manipulates paint by *brushing* it and a sculptor manipulates clay by *molding* it. Choices **a** and **e** are incorrect because they describe other substances a sculptor can mold. Choice **c** is wrong because it describes the end result of molding clay but fails to address how the clay is manipulated. Choice **d** is incorrect because it describes the person who works with clay.

3. c. A function of a knife is to *slice* and a function of a spoon is to *stir*. Choice **a** is incorrect because a fork is just another kind of kitchen utensil. Choice **b** is wrong because it just describes another function of a knife. Choice **d** is something one might eat with a spoon and choice **e** is a part of a spoon, so these are incorrect as well.

4. e. *Brag* is the action of a person who is proud and *weep* is the action of a person who is despairing. A person who is despairing, or sad, is not likely to sing (**a**) or to exult (**b**). Choice **c** is incorrect because sad has a similar meaning to despairing but does not describe what a despairing person does. To depress is to have a despairing effect on someone, so choice **d** is incorrect.

5. b. *Thrilled* is an intensified form of *excited* and *enraged* is an intensified form of *angered*. Choices **a**, **c**, **d**, and **e** are incorrect because they do not describe intensified forms of angered.

6. b. The *string* is the part of the *guitar* that produces sound and the *key* is the part of the *organ* that produces sound. Choices **a**, **c**, **d**, and **e** all refer to music without specifying the instrument that uses keys to produce its sound.

7. e. A *thesaurus* is a book of *synonyms* and a *dictionary* is a book of *definitions*. Both books focus on words and both are reference books, so a more specific answer than choices **a**, **b**, **c**, and **d** is required.

8. e. A *bust* sits atop a *pedestal* and a *camera* sits atop a *tripod*. Choices **a**, **b**, **c**, and **d** are incorrect because none of them explain what sits atop a tripod.

9. b. A *beautician* works in a *salon*; a *musician* works in a *concert hall*.

10. d. An *engine stalls* when it ceases to function; a *computer freezes* when it ceases to function.

11. c. To *bolt* is to *leave quickly*; to *race* is to *drive quickly*.

12. d. *Disseminate* and *gather* are antonyms; *rip* and *mend* are antonyms.

13. e. *Adore* is an intensified form of *enjoy*; *loathe* is an intensified form of *dislike*.

14. e. A group of geese is a *gaggle*; a group of sheep is a *flock*.

15. d. Science fiction is a genre of literature one might read in a *novel*; rhythm and blues is a genre of music one might listen to on an *album*.

16. d. *Constructive* is a trait of a *carpenter*; *judgmental* is a trait of a *critic*.

17. b. *Carelessness* can lead to a *mistake*; *meticulousness* can lead to *perfection*.

18. b. *Cautious* and *heedless* are antonyms; *wary* and *trusting* are antonyms.

19. b. To *jump* is the physical reaction to being *surprised*; to *chuckle* is the physical reaction to being *amused*.

20. c. *Brace* and *bolster* are synonyms; *accelerate* and *hasten* are synonyms.

21. a. A *spider* is a kind of *arachnid*; a *lobster* is a kind of *crustacean*.

22. d. *Psychology* is the study of the *mind*; *anatomy* is the study of the *body*.

23. b. A *cardiologist* is a doctor specializing in the *heart*; a *neurologist* is a doctor specializing in the *brain*.

24. b. A group of *peas* is a *bushel*; a group of *bananas* is a *bunch*.

25. a. *Apathy* and *disinterest* are synonyms; *tenacity* and *resolve* are synonyms.

Subtest 2: Arithmetic Reasoning

1. e. Since the price per copy is $0.85, divide 68 by .85 to find the total number that can be purchased with $68; $68 ÷ .85 = 80$ copies that can be purchased.

2. c. The volume of the aquarium can be found by using the formula $V = l \times w \times h$. Since the length is 12 inches, the width is 5 inches and the height is 10 inches, multiply $V = 12 \times 5 \times 10$ to get a volume of 600 cubic inches.

3. c. The value of the handbag ($150) must be included in the total.

4. d. Both choices **a** and **b** can be ruled out because there is no way to determine how many tickets are for adults or for children. Choice **c** can be ruled out because the price of group tickets is not given.

5. d. Because the 15-year-old requires an adult ticket, there are 3 adult tickets at $7.50 each and one child's ticket at $5.

6. a. The adult price on Saturday afternoon is $5.50; the child's price is $3.00.

7. d. This problem is solved by dividing 60 by 0.50. $60 ÷ .50 = 120$.

8. b. This problem is solved by multiplying 35 times 8.2.

9. c. You know the ratio of Drake's charge to Jean's charge is 3 to 4, or $\frac{3}{4}$. To find what Jean charges, you use the equation $\frac{3}{4} = \frac{36}{x}$, or $3x = 4(36)$; $(4)(36) = 144$, which is then divided by 3 to arrive at $x = 48$.

10. a. In this question, you need to find 15% of the 30% of cadet athletes that play lacrosse. To find 15% of 30%, change the percents to decimal form and multiply. Since 30% = 0.30 and 15% = 0.15, multiply $(0.30)(0.15) = 0.045$. As a decimal, this is equivalent to 4.5%.

11. d. The basic cable service fee of $15 is 75% of $20.

12. a. The labor fee ($25) plus the deposit ($65) plus the basic service ($15) equals $105. The difference between the total bill, $112.50, and $105 is $7.50, the cost of the news channels.

13. c. 60 out of 200 is 30%. Thirty percent of 40,000 is 12,000.

14. d. 27.5% of 400 is 110.

15. b. Rock is 45.5%; when we add 4.5% for classical we arrive at 50%.

16. c. If 60% of the people were satisfied with their new car, 40% were unsatisfied; 40% of 220 is 88.

17. c. Divide 135 Spanish-speaking candidates by 1,125 total number of candidates to arrive at .12 or 12%.

18. b. The first step in solving the problem is to subtract 156 from 268. $268 - 156 = 112$. The remainder, 112, is then divided by 2. $112 ÷ 2 = 56$.

19. c. Three feet 4 inches equals 40 inches; 40 divided by 5 is 8.

20. a. It will cost $3 for a sandwich and a cookie. To get two additional sandwiches, it would cost another $4. Therefore, it would cost $7 to get three sandwiches and a cookie. Since she only has $6 to spend, this combination is not possible.

21. c. Area = width × length. In this case, $4 \times 6 = 24$ square feet.

22. b. Use the formula beginning with the operation in parentheses: $98 - 32 = 66$. Then multiply 66 by $\frac{5}{9}$, first multiplying 66 by 5 to get 330; 330 divided by 9 is 36.66667, which is rounded up to 36.7.

23. c. Each 9-foot wall has an area of 9×8 or 72 square feet. There are two such walls, so those two walls combined have an area of 72×2 or 144 square feet. Each 11-foot wall has an area of 11×8 or 88 square feet, and again there are two such walls: $88 \times 2 = 176$. To find the total surface area, add 144 and 176 to get 320 square feet.

24. b. $1\frac{1}{2}$ cups equals $\frac{3}{2}$ cups. The ratio is 6 people to 4 people, which is equal to the ratio of x to $\frac{3}{2}$. By cross-multiplying, we get $6(\frac{3}{2})$ equals $4x$, or 9 equals $4x$. Dividing both sides by 4, we get $\frac{9}{4}$, or $2\frac{1}{4}$ cups.

25. c. The distance between Fort Greenville and Fort Johnson is the hypotenuse of a right triangle with sides of length 90 and 120. The length of the hypotenuse equals the square root of the sum of the other two sides squared. $90^2 + 120^2 = \sqrt{22,500} = 150$ miles.

Subtest 3: Word Knowledge

1. e. To *preside* over a group or person is to *lead* that group or person.

2. a. Something that is a *liability* is a *burden* to someone.

3. b. Someone who is *diligent* is *hardworking*.

4. e. To possess *agility* is to be able to move in a *quick, graceful* manner.

5. b. To *elicit* means to *extract*.

6. d. A *proclamation* is an *announcement*.

7. c. Someone who is *pragmatic* is *sensible*.

8. c. A *quandary* is a serious *problem*.

9. a. An *opulent* person is a *wealthy* one.

10. c. Someone who is *eloquent* is very *well spoken*.

11. e. To have *fidelity* is to have great *loyalty*.

12. a. *Limpid* means the same thing as *bright*.

13. b. To *refute* an idea or statement means to *contest* its accuracy.

14. d. When something or someone is *vulnerable*, that thing or person is *weak*.

15. a. To perform a task in a *systematic* way is to do it in an *orderly* fashion.

16. a. Someone with great *sagacity* possesses great *wisdom*.

17. c. *Motley* means *multicolor*.

18. b. To take a *jaunt* is to take a *trip*.

19. e. To have *myriad* reasons for doing something is to have *many* reasons.

20. d. To be in *unison* about an issue is to be in *harmony* about it.

21. e. To possess *valor* is to possess *courage*.

22. c. To be *blatant* is to be *obvious*.

23. a. To *construe* means to *interpret*.

24. b. Something that is *heinous* is *monstrous*.

25. d. To do something with *gusto* is to do it with great *enthusiasm*.

Subtest 4: Math Knowledge

1. b. *PQ* and *RS* are intersecting lines. The fact that angle *POS* is a 90-degree angle means that *PQ* and *RS* are perpendicular, indicating that all the angles formed by their intersection, including *ROQ*, measure 90 degrees.

2. a. Incorrect answers include adding both the numerator and the denominator and not converting fifths to tenths properly.

3. e. To convert a fraction to a decimal, divide the numerator, 3, by the denominator, 4. $3 \div 4 = 0.75$.

4. b. The correct answer is $88\frac{1}{3}$.

5. d. Divide the numerator by the denominator: $1 \div 6 = 0.166667$. Round the answer to the thousandths place (three decimal places) to get the answer 0.167.

6. d. You have to convert all three fractions to twelfths before adding them.

7. c. Choice **a** totals 22,436; choice **b** totals 2,346; choice **d** totals 206,306, and choice **e** totals 216,306.

8. a. The first box is one greater than –5; the second is one greater than 0.

9. d. $1\frac{1}{2}$ is a mixed number. To convert this into a decimal, first take the whole number (in this case, 1) and place it to the left of the decimal point. Then, take the fraction (in this case, $\frac{1}{2}$) and convert it to a decimal by dividing the numerator by the denominator, yielding .50.

10. a. Raise the fraction $\frac{2}{9}$ to 54ths by multiplying both numerator and denominator by 6.

11. d. $7(8)(2) = 112$.

12. d. Divide 3 by 8 in order to convert the fraction into a decimal. $3 \div 8 = 0.375$.

13. c. The meaning of 4^3 is 4 times itself 3 times.

14. a. The total on the right is 35. On the left, you need an operation you can do on 5 to get 35. Multiplying by $(5 + 2)$ does the trick.

15. a. Using 20 for C: $F = (\frac{9}{5} \times 20) + 32$. Therefore $F = 36 + 32$, or 68.

16. c. $5(3)(8) = 120$; $120 \div 3 = 40$.

17. c. $10(10)(10) = 1,000$; $1,000(7.25) = 7,250$.

18. b. To solve this problem, you must first convert yards to inches. There are 36 inches in a yard; and $\frac{1}{3}$ of a yard is 12 inches; $36 \times 3 = 108 + 12 = 120$.

19. a. Divide 3 by 5 to convert from a fraction into a decimal: $3 \div 5 = 0.60$.

20. a. 0.97 multiplied by 100 is 97.

21. c. The sum of the measure of the angles in a triangle is 180°; $70° + 30° = 100°$; $180° - 100° = 80°$.

22. b. Since the solution to the problem $x + 32 = 14$, $x = -18$. Choices **a**, **c**, and **d** are all too large to be correct.

23. c. Use the formula $A = lw$. or $108 = l \times 6$. Since the area is the length × the width of the rectangle, then *dividing* the area (108) by the width (6) will give you the length, 18 feet.

24. a. 37.5% is the same as $\frac{37.5}{100}$. Multiply both the numerator and the denominator by 10 to move the decimal point, resulting in $\frac{375}{1,000}$. Next, factor both the numerator and denominator to find out how far you can reduce the fraction: $\frac{5 \times 5 \times 5 \times 3}{5 \times 5 \times 5 \times 8}$. If you cancel the three 5s that are in both the numerator and the denominator, you get $\frac{3}{8}$.

25. b. In the decimal, 0.15, the 5 falls in the hundredths place (two places to the right of the decimal). To convert this to a fraction, the 15 is placed over 100. Reduce, which gives you $\frac{3}{20}$.

Subtest 5: Instrument Comprehension

QUESTION	ANSWER	HEADING	PITCH	ROLL
1.	B	270° west	up	left
2.	C	180° south	down	none
3.	A	270° west	down	right
4.	C	090° east	none	left
5.	A	270° west	up	right
6.	D	180° south	up	left
7.	B	090° east	up	none
8.	A	180° south	down	right
9.	C	270° west	none	none
10.	B	270° west	down	right
11.	A	135° southeast	down	left

12.	C	270° west	up	none
13.	B	260° west-southwest	down	left
14.	C	255° west-southwest	up	left
15.	A	090° east	up	left
16.	B	100° east-southeast	up	left
17.	D	360° north	none	right
18.	B	285° west-northwest	up	left
19.	B	045° northeast	up	left
20.	A	180° south	none	left

Subtest 6: Block Counting

1. a. Block 1 touches only the block directly below it.

2. c. Block 2 touches the two blocks below it and the one above it, as well as the one to the right.

3. b. Block 3 touches the blocks to the left and to the right of it, as well as block 2.

4. d. Block 4 touches the block below it and above it, as well as the block to the left and the block below block 1.

5. a. Block 5 touches the block above it and the one to its left.

6. c. Block 1 touches the blocks to its left and right, as well as block 5 and the blocks to the left and right of block 5.

7. e. Block 2 touches the block above it and the block to its left, as well as block 5 and block 3, as well as the block between them.

8. e. Block 3 touches the two blocks above it, the one to its right, block 4, and block 2.

9. a. Block 4 touches the block above it, the block to its right, and block 3.

10. e. Block 5 touches the two blocks below it, the blocks to its left and right, block 2, the blocks to the left and right of block 1, and block 1.

11. c. Block 1 touches the block below it, the three blocks to its left including block 5, and the two blocks to its right including block 2.

12. d. Block 2 touches the block to its left, block 1 and block 4, and the block between block 1 and block 4.

13. b. Block 3 touches the block to its right and the 4 blocks above it including block 5.

14. c. Block 4 touches the block above it, the block to its left, and the two blocks to its right including block 2.

15. d. Block 5 touches the two blocks to its left, block 1, the block under block 1, and the block to the right of block 3.

16. e. Block 1 touches the blocks to its left and right, the block above it, the block below block 2, the block above block 5, and block 5.

17. b. Block 2 touches the block to its left, and the blocks above and below it.

18. a. Block 3 touches the block above it, the block to its left, and block 5.

19. c. Block 4 touches the block above it, the block to its left, the block below block 2, the block above block 5, and block 5.

20. e. Block 5 touches the block to the left and right of block 1, block 1, block 4, and the two blocks above it including block 3.

Subtest 7: Table Reading

1. b. Finding the intersection of the −3 column with the 0 row yields an answer of 48.

2. e. Finding the intersection of the −1 column with the 1 row yields an answer of 76.

3. a. Finding the intersection of the −2 column with the 0 row yields an answer of 58.

4. d. Finding the intersection of the 1 column with the 2 row yields an answer of 93.

5. c. Finding the intersection of the –2 column with the 2 row yields an answer of 35.

6. b. Finding the intersection of the –3 column with the 0 row yields an answer of 73.

7. d. Finding the intersection of the –2 column with the 1 row yields an answer of 18.

8. a. Finding the intersection of the 1 column with the 1 row yields an answer of 48.

9. c. Finding the intersection of the 0 column with the 3 row yields an answer of 69.

10. b. Finding the intersection of the 2 column with the 0 row yields an answer of 67.

11. e. Finding the intersection of the –1 column with the 2 row yields an answer of 11.

12. c. Finding the intersection of the 3 column with the –1 row yields an answer of 30.

13. a. Finding the intersection of the –2 column with the 3 row yields an answer of 22.

14. a. Finding the intersection of the 0 column with the 0 row yields an answer of 88.

15. d. Finding the intersection of the 0 column with the 3 row yields an answer of 55.

16. d. Finding the intersection of the 1 column with the –3 row yields an answer of 24.

17. b. Finding the intersection of the 2 column with the 3 row yields an answer of 78.

18. b. Finding the intersection of the 2 column with the –2 row yields an answer of 60.

19. c. Finding the intersection of the 1 column with the 0 row yields an answer of 57.

20. d. Finding the intersection of the 0 column with the –2 row yields an answer of 86.

21. b. Finding the intersection of the 0 column with the 2 row yields an answer of 91.

22. a. Finding the intersection of the 1 column with the 1 row yields an answer of 47.

23. e. Finding the intersection of the –1 column with the –1 row yields an answer of 69.

24. e. Finding the intersection of the 3 column with the 2 row yields an answer of 65.

25. d. Finding the intersection of the –3 column with the –3 row yields an answer of 38.

26. e. Finding the intersection of the –3 column with the 3 row yields an answer of 44.

27. b. Finding the intersection of the 0 column with the 1 row yields an answer of 62.

28. a. Finding the intersection of the 2 column with the 0 row yields an answer of 17.

29. c. Finding the intersection of the 3 column with the 0 row yields an answer of 35.

30. c. Finding the intersection of the 3 column with the 1 row yields an answer of 46.

31. d. Finding the intersection of the –2 column with the –2 row yields an answer of 43.

32. c. Finding the intersection of the –2 column with the 3 row yields an answer of 87.

33. e. Finding the intersection of the 0 column with the –3 row yields an answer of 11.

34. a. Finding the intersection of the 1 column with the –3 row yields an answer of 12.

35. b. Finding the intersection of the 1 column with the 1 row yields an answer of 62.

36. c. Finding the intersection of the –3 column with the 0 row yields an answer of 83.

37. b. Finding the intersection of the 0 column with the 2 row yields an answer of 66.

38. b. Finding the intersection of the –2 column with the –1 row yields an answer of 32.

39. a. Finding the intersection of the 0 column with the –1 row yields an answer of 57.

40. a. Finding the intersection of the 1 column with the 3 row yields an answer of 43.

Subtest 8: Aviation Information

1. d. All the examples given are high lift devices that increase the effective wing area. This increases the distance air has to travel over and under the wing, creating a larger pressure differential, which will increase lift at lower airspeeds.

2. b. As the outside air temperature drops, the movement of air molecules in the atmosphere slows down. This results in an increase in air density, resulting in a corresponding increase in aircraft performance because of the more dense atmospheric medium it will operate in.

3. c. The longitudinal axis extends the length of the aircraft, from the nose directly aft through the tail. Any movement about this axis is called roll. The ailerons are located on the wings, and when deflected into the airstream they alter lift on that wing, causing it to drop, resulting in a rolling motion. The other answers involve aircraft control mechanisms that affect other aircraft movements.

4. c. Class A airspace is that airspace from Flight Level (FL) 180 or 18,000 feet to FL 600 or 60,000. Pilots are required to change the altimeter setting from the local altimeter they have been using to 29.92. This ensures all aircraft flying in Class A airspace have the same altimeter setting and will have proper altitude separation.

5. b. In aeronautics, potential energy is energy stored in an aircraft by virtue of its position in space. An aircraft at the top of a loop has significant potential energy that can be reclaimed by pointing the nose down and gaining speed. At the bottom of the loop, that potential energy is converted to kinetic energy, or energy that exists because of an object's motion.

6. a. Runways are numbered by the compass heading they are aligned toward.

7. c. Air becomes less dense with altitude and hot weather, significantly degrading aircraft performance. Therefore a high altitude airport on a hot day poses a takeoff or landing challenge for a pilot.

8. b. Runway taxi lights are blue in color. Different colors are used to identify all airfield areas where aircraft must operate while on the ground.

9. d. Lowering wing flaps will change the shape of the wing, which increases lift. This increased wing area resulting from lowered flaps, however, will also increase drag.

10. b. Boundary layer airflow is the thin layer of air that passes directly along the surface of a wing or an airfoil. Its thickness is measured in molecules. Smooth boundary layer air is known as laminar flow, while boundary layer air that becomes less smooth and stable as it moves along the larger upper surface of a wing or airfoil becomes thicker and eventually detached from the surface and is then known as turbulent flow.

11. a. If your cockpit turn and bank indicator shows a perfectly centered ball, all aerodynamic parameters of the aircraft are in balance.

12. d. Spoilers are small control surfaces on the wings. When deployed, or raised into an *up* position, they disrupt the boundary layer airflow over the wing which decreases lift on that wing and increases drag.

13. c. The transponder, also called an *identification, friend or foe* (IFF) device in the military, can provide a wide variety of aircraft information to a ground unit or to another airborne unit.

14. c. A headwind during takeoff would provide your aircraft with more wind over your wings, increasing lift earlier in your takeoff roll, resulting in a shorter takeoff distance. Likewise, this increased lift during takeoff would translate into an increased climb angle to the increased efficiency of a headwind takeoff.

15. c. VSI stands for *vertical speed indicator* and measures aircraft speed in feet per minute during a climb or a descent.

16. d. The vertical speed indicator measures how fast you are climbing in altitude (rate of climb), how fast you are descending in altitude (rate of descent), or whether you are in level flight (zero rate of climb or descent).

17. a. Remember that runways are numbered based on an two-digit abbreviation of their compass headings, so when one end of a runway is numbered 33 (based on a 330 heading), the opposite end will be 18 degrees (or 180 degrees) opposite, or 15 (based on a 150 heading).

18. c. Ground speed (GS) is the actual speed of the aircraft over the ground. The GS component is not affected by air density, temperature, or any atmospheric effect other than wind, which will physically slow down the aircraft with a headwind or speed up the aircraft with a tailwind, affecting the aircraft's physical speed over the ground.

19. a. While there are many components that make up drag, total drag can be classified as either parasite or induced. Parasite drag is the result of the skin friction, roughness, and pressure drag of the major components of the aircraft. Induced drag is that aerodynamic effect that results from the development and production of lift. For example, lowering wing flaps would result in an increase in induced drag since there is more wing area in the relative wind.

20. c. Bernoulli's Principle uses the laws of physics to demonstrate how an aircraft wing produces lift. The curvature of the upper portion of a wing creates a larger area for air to pass over, resulting in an increase in the speed of the airflow, and thereby decreasing pressure. The bottom portion of a wing is not curved at all or as much, resulting in the air passing over at a slower rate, increasing pressure. A moving body will always move in the direction of lower pressure, resulting in lift on an airfoil or wing.

Subtest 9: General Science

1. c. An element's number of protons determines its location on the periodic table. For instance, hydrogen (H) has one proton, helium (He) has two protons, and lithium (Li) has three protons, so H, He, and Li are numbers 1, 2, and 3 on the periodic table.

2. b. Isotopes are atoms of the same element with varying atomic masses depending on how many neutrons are in the nucleus.

3. c. Marine biology is the study of the plants, animals, and microbes found under water and is a branch of the larger encompassing field of oceanography.

4. d. A single molecule of any substance must contain the same elements in the same proportions as a larger amount of that substance. Therefore, a molecule of carbon dioxide (CO_2) must have 1 carbon atom and 2 oxygen atoms.

5. c. The concept of centrifugal force suggests that the mass of an object will be pushed in an outward direction when it is spinning in a circular motion. Fundamental forces usually refer to forces between elementary particles such as electromagnetism or gravity. The Coriolis effect is caused by the rotation of the Earth on its axis.

6. e. The food coloring spreading out into the water is an example of diffusion, which is the spreading out of the molecules of a substance from places of greater molecular concentration to places of lower concentration.

7. c. Cooking a hamburger involves a chemical change. The other choices involve physical changes.

8. a. Carbohydrates are digested more easily and absorbed more quickly than fats. Choice **b** is incorrect because amino acids are the building blocks of proteins. Choices **c** and **d** are not true of carbohydrates.

9. d. The troposphere is closest to the Earth's surface, then the stratosphere, the mesosphere, and finally the thermosphere. There is no such thing as the necrosphere.

10. e. Reptiles lay their eggs on land, so they do not have internal development of eggs.

11. d. The snake is the only vertebrate—that is, it is the only one of the four animals that has a backbone.

12. b. A single organism may acclimate itself to the stresses associated with a new environment. Evolution and the process of natural selection occur over several generations.

13. e. Omnivores eat many types of food, including plants and flesh.

14. b. The electromagnetic spectrum contains these wavelengths, from shortest to longest: gamma rays, x-rays, ultraviolet, visible, infrared, microwave, radio.

15. d. Gravity is the weakest of the four fundamental forces. Gravity controls the movement of planets, stars, and galaxies, as well as holding objects on Earth.

16. a. The Sun is a star in the center of the solar system; it is almost 110 times the diameter of the Earth. Venus is slightly smaller than the Earth. Jupiter is the largest planet in the Solar System (with a diameter 11 times that of the Earth), but it only contains 0.1 percent of a solar mass.

17. e. Absolute zero, when all atoms in solid matter stop vibrating, is −273° Celsius or 0° Kelvin.

18. a. Our solar system contains eight planets: Mercury, Venus, Earth, Mars, Jupiter, Saturn, Uranus, and Neptune.

19. b. Only a plant or algae cell contains chloroplasts, the site of photosynthesis in plants and algae. Therefore, fern (a plant) is the only possible answer.

20. a. Deoxyribonucleic acid (DNA), the genetic blueprint of cells, is located in the nucleus of animal cells.

Subtest 10: Rotated Blocks

1. b.
2. d.
3. e.
4. c.
5. c.
6. a.
7. c.
8. b.
9. c.
10. e.
11. e.
12. a.
13. b.
14. a.
15. c.

Subtest 11: Hidden Figures

1. c
2. b
3. a
4. d
5. e
6. a
7. b
8. d
9. e
10. c
11. c
12. d
13. b
14. a
15. e

For information on how the official AFOQT is scored, see Chapter 3.

DIAGNOSTIC TEST FOR THE AVIATION SELECTION TEST BATTERY

CHAPTER SUMMARY

This is the first of two sample Aviation Selection Test Batteries (ASTBs) in this book. On the official Aviation Selection Test Battery, you will be tested on mathematical and verbal reasoning, mechanical comprehension, spatial apperception, and aviation and nautical knowledge. Please note that this diagnostic ASTB does not contain the Aviation Supplemental Test (AST).

Math Skills Test (MST)

1.	a	b	c	d	11.	a	b	c	d	21.	a	b	c	d
2.	a	b	c	d	12.	a	b	c	d	22.	a	b	c	d
3.	a	b	c	d	13.	a	b	c	d	23.	a	b	c	d
4.	a	b	c	d	14.	a	b	c	d	24.	a	b	c	d
5.	a	b	c	d	15.	a	b	c	d	25.	a	b	c	d
6.	a	b	c	d	16.	a	b	c	d	26.	a	b	c	d
7.	a	b	c	d	17.	a	b	c	d	27.	a	b	c	d
8.	a	b	c	d	18.	a	b	c	d	28.	a	b	c	d
9.	a	b	c	d	19.	a	b	c	d	29.	a	b	c	d
10.	a	b	c	d	20.	a	b	c	d	30.	a	b	c	d

Reading Skills Test (RST)

1.	a	b	c	d	11.	a	b	c	d	21.	a	b	c	d
2.	a	b	c	d	12.	a	b	c	d	22.	a	b	c	d
3.	a	b	c	d	13.	a	b	c	d	23.	a	b	c	d
4.	a	b	c	d	14.	a	b	c	d	24.	a	b	c	d
5.	a	b	c	d	15.	a	b	c	d	25.	a	b	c	d
6.	a	b	c	d	16.	a	b	c	d	26.	a	b	c	d
7.	a	b	c	d	17.	a	b	c	d	27.	a	b	c	d
8.	a	b	c	d	18.	a	b	c	d					
9.	a	b	c	d	19.	a	b	c	d					
10.	a	b	c	d	20.	a	b	c	d					

Mechanical Comprehension Test (MCT)

1.	a	b	c	d	11.	a	b	c	d	21.	a	b	c	d
2.	a	b	c	d	12.	a	b	c	d	22.	a	b	c	d
3.	a	b	c	d	13.	a	b	c	d	23.	a	b	c	d
4.	a	b	c	d	14.	a	b	c	d	24.	a	b	c	d
5.	a	b	c	d	15.	a	b	c	d	25.	a	b	c	d
6.	a	b	c	d	16.	a	b	c	d	26.	a	b	c	d
7.	a	b	c	d	17.	a	b	c	d	27.	a	b	c	d
8.	a	b	c	d	18.	a	b	c	d	28.	a	b	c	d
9.	a	b	c	d	19.	a	b	c	d	29.	a	b	c	d
10.	a	b	c	d	20.	a	b	c	d	30.	a	b	c	d

Spatial Apperception Test (SAT)

1.	ⓐ	ⓑ	ⓒ	ⓓ	10.	ⓐ	ⓑ	ⓒ	ⓓ	18.	ⓐ	ⓑ	ⓒ	ⓓ
2.	ⓐ	ⓑ	ⓒ	ⓓ	11.	ⓐ	ⓑ	ⓒ	ⓓ	19.	ⓐ	ⓑ	ⓒ	ⓓ
3.	ⓐ	ⓑ	ⓒ	ⓓ	12.	ⓐ	ⓑ	ⓒ	ⓓ	20.	ⓐ	ⓑ	ⓒ	ⓓ
4.	ⓐ	ⓑ	ⓒ	ⓓ	13.	ⓐ	ⓑ	ⓒ	ⓓ	21.	ⓐ	ⓑ	ⓒ	ⓓ
5.	ⓐ	ⓑ	ⓒ	ⓓ	14.	ⓐ	ⓑ	ⓒ	ⓓ	22.	ⓐ	ⓑ	ⓒ	ⓓ
6.	ⓐ	ⓑ	ⓒ	ⓓ	15.	ⓐ	ⓑ	ⓒ	ⓓ	23.	ⓐ	ⓑ	ⓒ	ⓓ
7.	ⓐ	ⓑ	ⓒ	ⓓ	16.	ⓐ	ⓑ	ⓒ	ⓓ	24.	ⓐ	ⓑ	ⓒ	ⓓ
8.	ⓐ	ⓑ	ⓒ	ⓓ	17.	ⓐ	ⓑ	ⓒ	ⓓ	25.	ⓐ	ⓑ	ⓒ	ⓓ
9.	ⓐ	ⓑ	ⓒ	ⓓ										

Aviation and Nautical Information Test (ANIT)

1.	ⓐ	ⓑ	ⓒ	ⓓ	11.	ⓐ	ⓑ	ⓒ	ⓓ	21.	ⓐ	ⓑ	ⓒ	ⓓ
2.	ⓐ	ⓑ	ⓒ	ⓓ	12.	ⓐ	ⓑ	ⓒ	ⓓ	22.	ⓐ	ⓑ	ⓒ	ⓓ
3.	ⓐ	ⓑ	ⓒ	ⓓ	13.	ⓐ	ⓑ	ⓒ	ⓓ	23.	ⓐ	ⓑ	ⓒ	ⓓ
4.	ⓐ	ⓑ	ⓒ	ⓓ	14.	ⓐ	ⓑ	ⓒ	ⓓ	24.	ⓐ	ⓑ	ⓒ	ⓓ
5.	ⓐ	ⓑ	ⓒ	ⓓ	15.	ⓐ	ⓑ	ⓒ	ⓓ	25.	ⓐ	ⓑ	ⓒ	ⓓ
6.	ⓐ	ⓑ	ⓒ	ⓓ	16.	ⓐ	ⓑ	ⓒ	ⓓ	26.	ⓐ	ⓑ	ⓒ	ⓓ
7.	ⓐ	ⓑ	ⓒ	ⓓ	17.	ⓐ	ⓑ	ⓒ	ⓓ	27.	ⓐ	ⓑ	ⓒ	ⓓ
8.	ⓐ	ⓑ	ⓒ	ⓓ	18.	ⓐ	ⓑ	ⓒ	ⓓ	28.	ⓐ	ⓑ	ⓒ	ⓓ
9.	ⓐ	ⓑ	ⓒ	ⓓ	19.	ⓐ	ⓑ	ⓒ	ⓓ	29.	ⓐ	ⓑ	ⓒ	ⓓ
10.	ⓐ	ⓑ	ⓒ	ⓓ	20.	ⓐ	ⓑ	ⓒ	ⓓ	30.	ⓐ	ⓑ	ⓒ	ⓓ

Math Skills Test

Directions: The Math Skills Test measures your mathematical reasoning, that is, your ability to arrive at solutions to problems. Each problem is followed by four possible answers. Decide which one of the answers is most nearly correct. A method for attacking each of these questions is given in the answer block at the end of this chapter. You have twenty-five (25) minutes to complete this subtest.

Questions: 30
Time: 25 minutes

1. Choose the answer to the following problem:

   $\frac{5}{12} \times \frac{1}{6} \times \frac{2}{3} =$

   a. $\frac{10}{12}$
   b. $\frac{5}{6}$
   c. $\frac{5}{108}$
   d. $\frac{5}{216}$

2. In which of the following are the diagonals of the figure always congruent and perpendicular?
   a. isosceles trapezoid
   b. square
   c. isosceles triangle
   d. rhombus

3. Which of the following expressions is equal to 40,503?
   a. 400 + 50 + 3
   b. 4,000 + 500 + 3
   c. 40,000 + 50 + 3
   d. 40,000 + 500 + 3

4. If the perimeter of a rectangle is 40 centimeters and the shorter sides are 4 centimeters, what is the length of the longer sides?
   a. 12 centimeters
   b. 10 centimeters
   c. 18 centimeters
   d. 16 centimeters

5. A straight angle is
   a. exactly 180°.
   b. between 90° and 180°.
   c. exactly 90°.
   d. less than 90°.

6. 3 hours 20 minutes − 1 hour 48 minutes =
   a. 5 hours 8 minutes
   b. 4 hours 8 minutes
   c. 2 hours 28 minutes
   d. 1 hour 32 minutes

7. A distance of 3 inches on a topographical map is equivalent to 100 miles. The distance between two mountain peaks on the map is 5 inches. Which is the most accurate length of the distance between the two mountain peaks?
   a. 60 miles
   b. 102 miles
   c. 160 miles
   d. 167 miles

8. If the circumference of a circle is 100π centimeters, the radius of the circle is
  a. 10 centimeters
  b. 50 centimeters
  c. 100 centimeters
  d. 50π centimeters

9. What is the area of this shaded triangle?

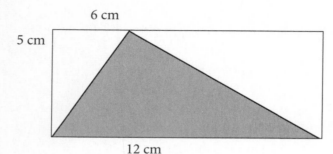

  a. 30 sq. cm
  b. 36 sq. cm
  c. 60 sq. cm
  d. 72 sq. cm

10. There are three different colored pens in Ming's drawer. The ratio of black to blue to red pens is 5:2:1, respectively. If there are a total of 40 pens in his drawer, how many blue pens does Ming have?
  a. 2
  b. 5
  c. 10
  d. 20

11. A lighthouse flashes every 6 seconds. Robert's watch is set to beep every 10 seconds. Robert's watch beeps and the lighthouse flashes at the exact same time. How much later will Robert's watch beep and the lighthouse flash at the same time?
  a. 2 seconds
  b. 16 seconds
  c. 30 seconds
  d. 1 minute

12. The following numbers are the first four terms of a number pattern, 1, 2, 3, 5, . . . The pattern is created by finding the sum of the previous two terms. What will be the *seventh* term in the pattern?
  a. 8
  b. 13
  c. 19
  d. 21

13. A game player rolls a pair of number cubes that are each numbered from 1 through 6. The player needs the cubes to land in such a way that their sum is equal to 3. What is the probability that this will happen?
  a. $\frac{1}{36}$
  b. $\frac{1}{18}$
  c. $\frac{1}{12}$
  d. $\frac{1}{8}$

14. If $2m + 22 = 6n$, what is the value of m in terms of n?
  a. $3n + 11$
  b. $6n - 11$
  c. $6n + 22$
  d. $3n - 11$

15. Which digit is in the tenths place in the decimal 174.56?
  a. 4
  b. 5
  c. 6
  d. 7

16. Which of the following is not less than $\frac{2}{5}$?
  a. $\frac{1}{3}$
  b. 0.04
  c. $\frac{3}{8}$
  d. $\frac{3}{7}$

17. A satellite orbits Earth the same number of times each day. After five days the satellite will have orbited Earth a total of 90 times. How many times will the satellite orbit Earth after one full seven-day week?

a. 36
b. 92
c. 108
d. 126

18. One inch on a map is equivalent to 50 feet. A rectangular farm on the map has a length of 8 inches and a width of 0.5 inches. What is the area of the farm, in square feet?

a. 4
b. 850
c. 1,000
d. 10,000

19. A standard deck of cards has 52 cards, 26 of which are red and 26 of which are black. What is the probability that a red card will be drawn from the deck three consecutive times, if the card is replaced in the deck after each time a card is drawn?

a. $\frac{1}{78}$
b. $\frac{1}{8}$
c. $\frac{1}{6}$
d. $\frac{1}{3}$

20. What is the value of the expression $-2x^2 + 3x - 7$ when $x = -3$?

a. −34
b. −27
c. −16
d. −10

21. What is the value of 2^6?

a. 26
b. 32
c. 36
d. 64

22. The gray rectangle in the figure below is three-quarters the height and three-quarters the width of the surrounding rectangle. If the length of the white rectangle is 12 inches and its width is 6 inches, what is the perimeter of the gray rectangle, in inches?

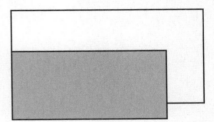

a. 26
b. 27
c. 36
d. 40.5

23. An aquarium has a base length of 12 inches and a width of 5 inches. If the aquarium is 10 inches tall, what is the total volume?

a. 480 cubic inches
b. 540 cubic inches
c. 600 cubic inches
d. 720 cubic inches

24. In this figure, if angle 1 is 30°, and angle 2 is a right angle, what is the measure of angle 5?

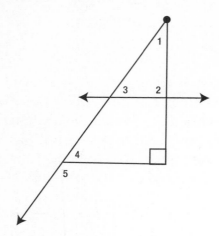

a. 30°

b. 60°

c. 120°

d. 180°

25. A circle drawn on a gymnasium floor for a basketball court has an area of 78.5 square feet. What is the length of the diameter of this circle? Use $\pi = 3.14$.

a. 25 feet

b. 15 feet

c. 12.5 feet

d. 10 feet

26. A certain county has an annual spending budget of about $490,000. The largest area of allocation is regional transportation, on which the county spends about $98,000 per year. Which fraction most accurately indicates the portion the county spends on regional transportation compared to its total annual budget?

a. $\frac{1}{5}$

b. $\frac{1}{4}$

c. $\frac{2}{9}$

d. $\frac{3}{4}$

27. Which of the following is NOT equivalent to the others?

a. $3(21 + 55) - 10$

b. $3(55 + 21) - 10$

c. $3 \times 55 + 3 \times 21 - 10$

d. $10 - 3(21 + 55)$

28. Given a polygon with four congruent sides, which of the following does NOT contradict the statement *If a polygon has four congruent sides, then the polygon is a square*?

a. The polygon has five congruent sides.

b. The polygon does not have four congruent sides.

c. The polygon has exactly one pair of parallel sides.

d. The polygon is also a rhombus.

29. At a baseball game, Deanna bought food for herself and her sister Jamie: one jumbo box of popcorn to share at $7 a box, two hot dogs for each of them (four total) at $3 a dog, and one soda for each at $4 apiece. Jamie paid for their tickets at $13 a ticket. Who spent more money and by how much?

a. Deanna, by $1

b. Deanna, by $3

c. Jamie, by $1

d. Jamie, by $2

30. A triangle has two sides that measure 14 cm and 17 cm, respectively. Which of the following could be the length of the triangle's third side?

a. 33 cm

b. 31 cm

c. 25 cm

d. 44 cm

Reading Skills Test

Directions: The Reading Skills Test measures your ability to read and understand paragraphs. For each question, choose the answer that best completes the meaning of the paragraph. Pay close attention as you read, and try to find the point that the author was trying to make. Once you have read the paragraph all the way through, you will find that one or two of the possible answers can quickly be eliminated based on the context. You have twenty-five (25) minutes to complete this subtest.

Questions: 27
Time: 25 minutes

Many lives are lost every year through drowning, and the majority of drowning victims could have been saved if they or someone nearby had only known the simple rules of water safety. The first and most important rule is to remain calm. Panic is the swimmer's worst enemy! When swimmers allow fear to overwhelm them, they stop making rational decisions and begin to *flounder*. That is the first step in drowning. When fear strikes, the swimmer must choose to remain calm and focused, thinking deliberately about how to escape from the situation.

1. According to this passage, what is the first step in drowning?
- **a.** going underwater
- **b.** giving in to fear
- **c.** not wearing a life preserver
- **d.** not knowing how to swim

2. The word *flounder*, as used in this passage, most nearly means
- **a.** a fish.
- **b.** a building foundation.
- **c.** to splash about helplessly.
- **d.** to float.

3. According to the passage, the best way to prevent drowning is to
- **a.** stay out of the water.
- **b.** learn how to swim.
- **c.** have a buddy nearby.
- **d.** remain calm.

Braille is a special *tactile* form of printing that enables blind people to read. It consists of a series of raised dots that can be felt with the fingertips; each letter of the alphabet is represented by one to six dots. The six dots form a rectangle if all are present, but most letters use only some of the dots. The letter *A*, for example, is one dot in the upper left corner of the rectangle. The Braille system was actually a by-product of the Napoleonic wars of the nineteenth century. Napoleon wanted to devise a code that could be read at night, and a soldier invented a system of raised dots. Napoleon rejected it as too complicated, but Louis Braille simplified it for use by the blind. It is still used today.

4. Napoleon was interested in Braille because
- **a.** he was blind.
- **b.** he wanted to help the blind.
- **c.** he could not read.
- **d.** he wanted a code that could be read at night.

5. The word *tactile*, as used in this passage, most nearly means
- **a.** a sharp object.
- **b.** words on a printed page.
- **c.** something that is sticky.
- **d.** something that can be felt with the fingers.

6. How many raised dots are used to form each letter of the alphabet in Braille?
- **a.** three
- **b.** six
- **c.** from one to six
- **d.** none

7. What was Louis Braille's contribution to the invention of this reading system?
    a. He taught blind people how to read.
    b. He urged Napoleon to have it developed.
    c. He named it.
    d. He simplified someone else's complicated idea.

One New York publisher has estimated that 50,000 to 60,000 people in the United States want an *anthology* that includes the complete plays of William Shakespeare. What accounts for this renewed interest in Shakespeare? As scholars point out, the psychological insights that he portrays in both male and female characters are amazing even today.

8. This paragraph best supports the statement that
    a. Shakespeare's characters are more interesting than fictional characters today.
    b. people today are interested in Shakespeare's work because of the characters.
    c. academic scholars are putting together an anthology of Shakespeare's work.
    d. New Yorkers have a renewed interested in the work of Shakespeare.

9. As used in the passage, *anthology* most nearly means
    a. a collection of literature.
    b. a phrase that compares two things.
    c. the history of the human race.
    d. a television program.

People have used mechanical devices to keep track of time throughout history. The hourglass, for example, uses sand falling through a glass tube to count minutes and hours. During the 1500s, however, clock makers created a revolutionary new idea in timekeeping when they invented the pendulum clock. A pendulum is basically a long stick with a weight at the end of it that swings back and forth in a regular rhythm, powered by a spring. The pendulum moves gears inside the clock that count the seconds and minutes and hours, since the pendulum's movement is very stable and consistent. For example, a pendulum that is 10 inches long will swing back and forth once per second, making it easy for the gears to track the passage of seconds and convert them into minutes and hours.

Another major breakthrough occurred in the late twentieth century with the invention of the quartz timekeeping mechanism. When electricity is passed through a small piece of quartz, the crystal *oscillates* at a very predictable rate, vibrating back and forth exactly 32,768 times per second. Modern quartz watches have a *rudimentary* computer inside, which simply counts the number of vibrations, converting the quartz crystal's movement into the passage of time. And best of all, quartz is a very common mineral and very inexpensive to work with, far less complicated than manmade mechanical pendulums.

10. Which of the following would be the best title for this passage?
    a. The Development of the Pendulum
    b. What Time Is It?
    c. Timekeeping through History
    d. The Many Uses of Quartz

11. As used in the passage, *oscillates* most nearly means
    a. opens like a clamshell.
    b. vibrates back and forth.
    c. makes a ticking noise.
    d. sits very still.

12. You can infer from this passage that
- **a.** quartz clocks are less expensive to make than pendulum clocks.
- **b.** pendulum clocks look nicer than quartz clocks.
- **c.** timekeeping today is more accurate than ever before.
- **d.** quartz clocks are waterproof.

13. As used in the passage, *rudimentary* most nearly means
- **a.** chewing the cud.
- **b.** written in runes.
- **c.** alien.
- **d.** basic.

The Fourth Amendment to the Constitution protects citizens against unreasonable searches and seizures. No search of a person's home or personal effects may be conducted without a written search warrant issued on probable cause. This means that a neutral judge must approve the factual basis justifying a search before it can be conducted.

14. This paragraph best supports the statement that the police cannot search a person's home or private papers unless they have
- **a.** legal authorization.
- **b.** direct evidence of a crime.
- **c.** read the person his or her constitutional rights.
- **d.** a reasonable belief that a crime has occurred.

15. Which of the following would be considered "probable cause" for a search warrant, according to this passage?
- **a.** a reasonable belief that a crime has occurred
- **b.** sworn testimony of the police
- **c.** direct evidence of a crime
- **d.** a judge's decision

Monday, Tuesday, Wednesday, Thursday. . . . We all know the days of the week, but have you ever wondered where their names came from? The answer dates back to the ancient Greeks, who decided to name the weekdays after their *pantheon* of gods. Two of their primary gods were the Sun and the Moon, so they named the first two days of the week after them; these names survive in modern English as Sun-day and Moon-day (Sunday and Monday).

Other day names are not quite so obvious to the modern person, however. This is because English is a Germanic language, influenced by the ancient German peoples, who translated the Greek and Norse gods into their own language. The Greeks, for example, named the third day after Mars, their god of war; the ancient Germanic peoples named it after Tiw (also known as Tyr), their god of war—giving us Tuesday (Tiw's Day). Wednesday is named after Woden, the ancient Germanic god of musical inspiration. Thursday is named for Thor, the Germanic thunder god, while Friday is named for Frigga, Germanic goddess of love (like the Roman goddess Venus). Finally, Saturday is named after Saturn, ancient god of the harvest.

16. What is the main idea of this passage?
- **a.** The days of the week are named after the sun, the moon, and ancient gods.
- **b.** English is a Germanic language.
- **c.** The ancient Germans had gods that were like the Greeks' gods.
- **d.** Thursday is named after Thor.

17. According to the passage, Wednesday is named after
- **a.** the god of speed.
- **b.** the god of war.
- **c.** the god of musical inspiration.
- **d.** the god of love.

18. As used in the passage, *pantheon* most nearly
means
   a. a sports coliseum.
   b. a wild animal.
   c. the days of the week.
   d. a list of ancient gods.

19. From this passage, you can infer that
   a. ancient mythology played a role in the
development of modern English.
   b. the Greeks worshiped different gods from
the Romans.
   c. ancient Germans spoke English.
   d. Mercury is similar to Thor.

Linoleum was invented in 1860 by a British
man named Frederick Walton. It is actually a
natural compound made from linseed oil, pine
rosin, and pine flour. To that mixture is added
wood pulp or other fibers to give it a stiff
consistency. Walton named his invention
linoleum from the Latin word *linum*, meaning
flax (from which linseed oil is made) and
oleum, meaning oil. Linoleum is still widely
used around the world today for floor coverings
and countertops.

20. Linoleum got its name from
   a. Latin words meaning *flax oil*.
   b. Greek words meaning *floor covering*.
   c. the inventor's imagination.
   d. the British patent office.

21. The main idea of this passage is
   a. that Latin is used in naming inventions.
   b. the many uses of linoleum.
   c. why linoleum is used around the world.
   d. the history of linoleum.

Today's postal service is more efficient than
ever. Mail that once took months to move by
horse and foot now moves around the country

in days or hours by truck, train, and plane. If
your letter or package is urgent, the U.S. Postal
Service offers Priority Mail and Express Mail
services. Priority Mail is guaranteed to go
anywhere in the United States in two days or
less, while Express Mail will get your package
there overnight.

22. The main idea of this paragraph is that
   a. more people use the post office for urgent
deliveries than any other delivery service.
   b. Express Mail is a good way to send urgent
mail.
   c. Priority Mail usually takes two days or less.
   d. mail service today is more effective and
dependable.

23. According to the passage, Priority Mail will get
a package delivered
   a. overnight.
   b. in two days or less.
   c. within a week.
   d. in three hours.

Paper clips are such an everyday item that most
of us don't even notice them. We use them to
get stuck disks out of computers, to clean dirt
from tiny *crevices*, to fix our eyeglasses, and a
million other things—and sometimes we even
use them to clip papers together! But if you
think about it, you'll realize that somebody had
to invent the paper clip; it didn't suddenly drop
out of the sky one day. That inventor was a
Norwegian named Johan Vaaler who registered
his idea with the German patent office in 1899
for a "rectangular, triangular, or otherwise
shaped hoop" that could be used to fasten
papers together. Previously, people had used
ribbons, pins, and even string to bind paper,
but Vaaler's simple idea changed that forever.

24. The author of this passage thinks that paper clips
  a. are funny.
  b. are a useful invention.
  c. fell from the sky.
  d. should be used for other things besides clipping paper.

25. As used in the passage, *crevices* most nearly means
  a. small cracks.
  b. ceiling paint.
  c. fast-moving water.
  d. tiny bumps.

26. According to the passage, which of the following was once used to bind papers together?
  a. tape
  b. hairpins
  c. string
  d. glue

27. Where was the first paper clip patented, according to the passage?
  a. Norway
  b. Germany
  c. United States
  d. not stated

Mechanical Comprehension Test

Directions: The Mechanical Comprehension subtest assesses your ability to learn and reason with mechanical terms. Included in this part of the test are diagrams showing various mechanical devices. Following each diagram are several questions or incomplete statements. Study each diagram carefully, as details do make a difference in how each device operates, and then select the choice that best answers the question or completes the statement. You have fifteen (15) minutes to complete this subtest.

Questions: 30
Time: 15 minutes

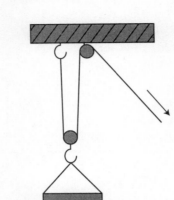

1. Using the pulley system shown here, how much force is required to lift a 276-pound load?
  a. 49 pounds
  b. 92 pounds
  c. 138 pounds
  d. 276 pounds

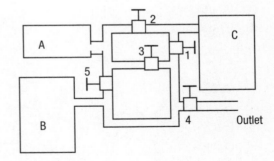

2. The water system in tank A has been contaminated. In what order can the valves be opened to empty tank A through the outlet and then refill it from tank C?
  a. open 4, then open 2
  b. open 5 and 4, then open 3
  c. open 5 and 3, then open 2
  d. open 3 and 4, then open 2

3. Ice cubes float on top of water because
   a. ice is a solid.
   b. ice is hollow.
   c. ice is denser than water.
   d. ice is less dense than water.

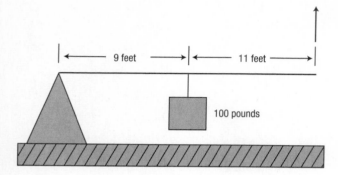

4. In the diagram shown here, Shannon wants to lift a 100-pound block using a lever. If the block is 9 feet from the pivot point and Shannon is 11 feet beyond that, how much force must she apply to lift the block?
   a. 45 pounds
   b. 99 pounds
   c. 100 pounds
   d. 109 pounds

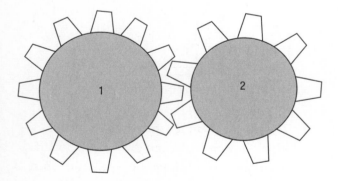

5. Gear 1 in this figure has 12 teeth and gear 2 has 9. If gear 2 turns at 60 rpm, how fast will gear 1 turn?
   a. 15 rpm
   b. 30 rpm
   c. 45 rpm
   d. 60 rpm

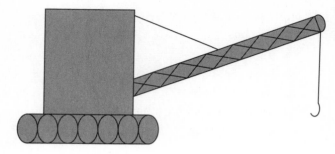

6. The arm of this crane is 16 feet long, and the cable used to lift the arm is attached 10 feet from the crane body. For the crane to lift an object weighing 600 pounds, how much force must be applied by the cable?
   a. 160 pounds
   b. 600 pounds
   c. 960 pounds
   d. 1,600 pounds

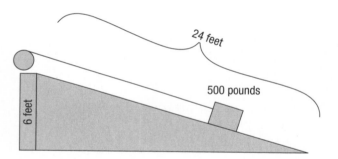

7. This figure shows a 500-pound block being pulled up an incline by a pulley. The incline is 24 feet long and rises 6 feet. Neglecting friction, how much force is necessary to move the block up the incline?
   a. 125 pounds
   b. 500 pounds
   c. 144 pounds
   d. 476 pounds

8. Jill leaves her house in a car and travels north at 40 mph. Alex leaves from the same place one hour later and follows the same route at 60 mph. How long will Alex have to drive before he overtakes Jill?

a. 40 minutes

b. 1 hour

c. 2 hours

d. 3 hours

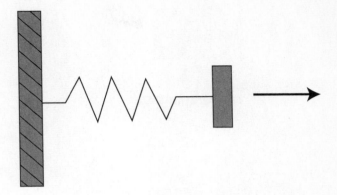

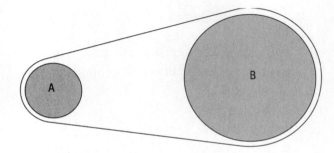

9. Pulley B in this figure has twice the circumference of pulley A. If pulley A rotates at 20 revolutions per minute (rpm), how fast must pulley B rotate?

a. 10 rpm

b. 20 rpm

c. 40 rpm

d. 200 rpm

10. The spring shown here has a force constant of 2.5 pounds per inch. How much force is required to move the spring 10 inches?

a. 4 pounds

b. 12.5 pounds

c. 25 pounds

d. 50 pounds

11. Styrofoam cups do well at keeping coffee warm because they

a. are good insulators.

b. are poor insulators.

c. absorb light and convert it to heat.

d. transfer heat from your hand to the coffee.

12. A screw has 20 threads per inch. How many full turns of the nut are required for the nut to travel 1.5 inches?

a. 15 turns

b. 20 turns

c. 25 turns

d. 30 turns

13. When oil and water are mixed together, the oil forms a layer at the top, and the water sinks to the bottom because

a. oil is less dense than water.

b. oil is denser than water.

c. oil is more acidic than water.

d. oil is less acidic than water.

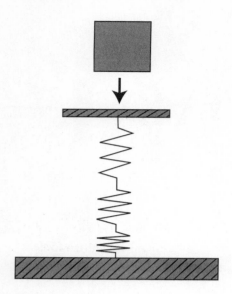

14. This figure shows a series of springs with force constants of 2, 3, and 6 pounds per inch supporting a platform. When a 6-pound block is lowered onto it, how many inches does the platform compress?

   a. 4 inches

   b. 5 inches

   c. 6 inches

   d. 7 inches

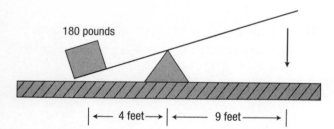

15. In the diagram shown here, Dave wants to lift a 180-pound block using a lever. If the block is 4 feet from the pivot point and Dave is 9 feet from the pivot point, how much force must he apply to lift the block?

   a. 36 pounds

   b. 80 pounds

   c. 120 pounds

   d. 180 pounds

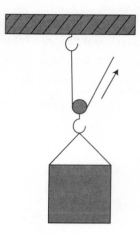

16. Using the pulley system shown here, how much force is required to lift a 200-pound weight?

   a. 50 pounds

   b. 100 pounds

   c. 150 pounds

   d. 200 pounds

17. An ax is a form of what simple machine?

   a. a lever

   b. a pulley

   c. an inclined plane

   d. a gear

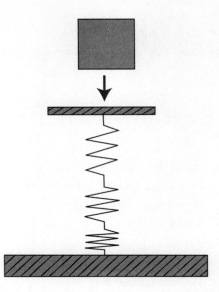

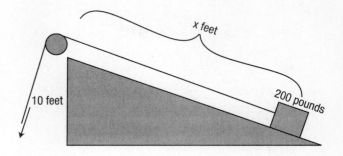

18. What is the mechanical advantage of the pulley system shown here?
   a. 1
   b. 2
   c. 3
   d. 4

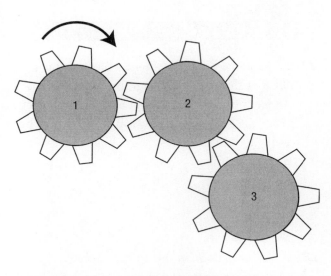

19. If gear 1 in this figure turns clockwise, which other gear(s), if any, will also turn clockwise?
   a. 2 only
   b. 3 only
   c. 2 and 3
   d. none

20. This figure shows a 200-pound block being pulled up an incline by a pulley. The incline rises 10 feet. Neglecting friction, if 50 pounds of force is necessary to move the block up the incline, how long is the incline?
   a. 30 feet
   b. 20 feet
   c. 40 feet
   d. 100 feet

21. A single-speed bicycle has a front chain ring with 48 teeth. The back gear has 16 teeth. If the bicycle is pedaled for 3 revolutions, how many complete revolutions will the rear wheel make?
   a. 3
   b. 9
   c. 16
   d. 48

22. What causes the pistons in an engine to move when the fuel–air mixture is ignited in the combustion chamber?
   a. The heat from the explosion gives the pistons energy.
   b. The high pressure created from the ignition forces the piston down.
   c. Electrical energy moves the piston.
   d. The piston is moved by momentum from the other pistons.

23. Which material would be optimal for constructing a boat anchor?

a. wood

b. metal

c. glass

d. plastic

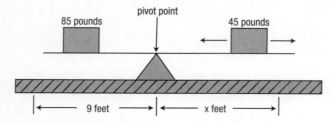

24. In this diagram, Nadine wants to balance two blocks on either side of a lever. One block weighs 85 pounds, and the other weighs 45 pounds. If the 85-pound block is 9 feet to the left of the pivot point, how far to the right of the pivot point should the 45-pound block be placed?

a. 15 feet

b. 9 feet

c. 18 feet

d. 17 feet

25. A bicycle has one front chain ring with 48 teeth and two possible gears on the back wheel: one with 16 teeth and one with 12 teeth. If the bike with the 16-tooth cog is pedaled at 80 rpm, how fast would the bike with the 12-tooth cog have to be pedaled to go the same speed?

a. 60 rpm

b. 80 rpm

c. 100 rpm

d. 120 rpm

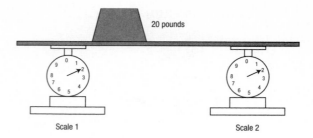

26. According to this figure, assuming the board connecting scales 1 and 2 has no weight, how many pounds will scale 1 register?

a. less than 10 pounds

b. 10 pounds

c. more than 10 pounds

d. impossible to determine

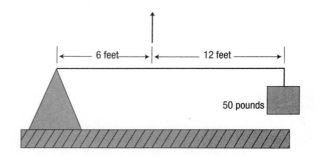

27. Todd wants to lift a 50-pound block using a lever as shown in this diagram. If the block is 18 feet from the pivot point and Todd is 6 feet from the pivot point, how much force must he apply to lift the block?

a. 100 pounds

b. 72 pounds

c. 150 pounds

d. 50 pounds

28. A hot air balloon is able to float because

a. the hot air acts as a jet.

b. hot air is less dense than the outside air.

c. hot air is more dense than the outside air.

d. it is filled with helium.

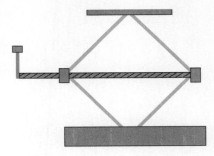

29. To change a tire, a person is able to take advantage of the mechanical advantage of a jack to lift a car. Each complete turn of the screw raises the car $\frac{1}{4}$ inch. If the handle travels 3 feet per revolution, what is the mechanical advantage of this jack?
   a. 12
   b. 36
   c. 14
   d. 144

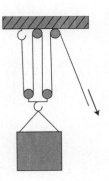

30. Bryan is strong enough to pull a rope with 150 pounds of force. Using the pulley system shown here, what is the maximum weight he can lift?
   a. 50 pounds
   b. 300 pounds
   c. 450 pounds
   d. 600 pounds

Spatial Apperception Test

Directions: The Spatial Apperception subtest measures your ability to determine the position of an aircraft in flight in relation to a ship on the water. You are to determine whether it is climbing, diving, banking to right or left, or in level flight. For each question, select the choice that most nearly represents the aircraft's position in relation to the position of the ship. You have ten (10) minutes to complete this subtest.

Questions: 25
Time: 10 minutes

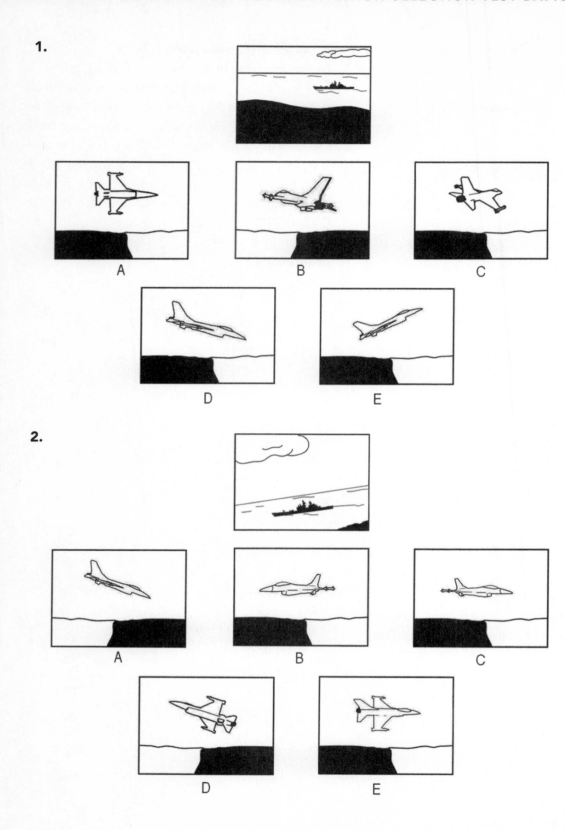

3.

A   B   C

D   E

4.

A   B   C

D   E

5.

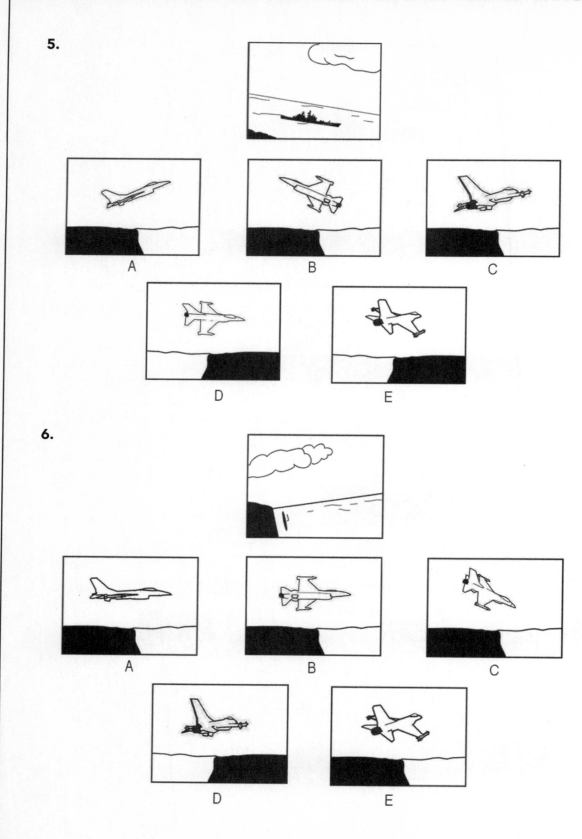

6.

7.

8.

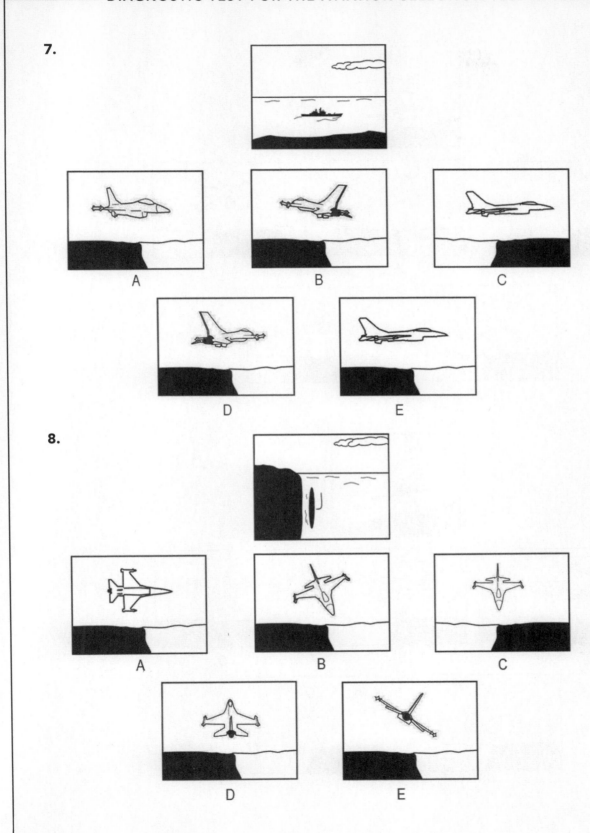

9.

10.

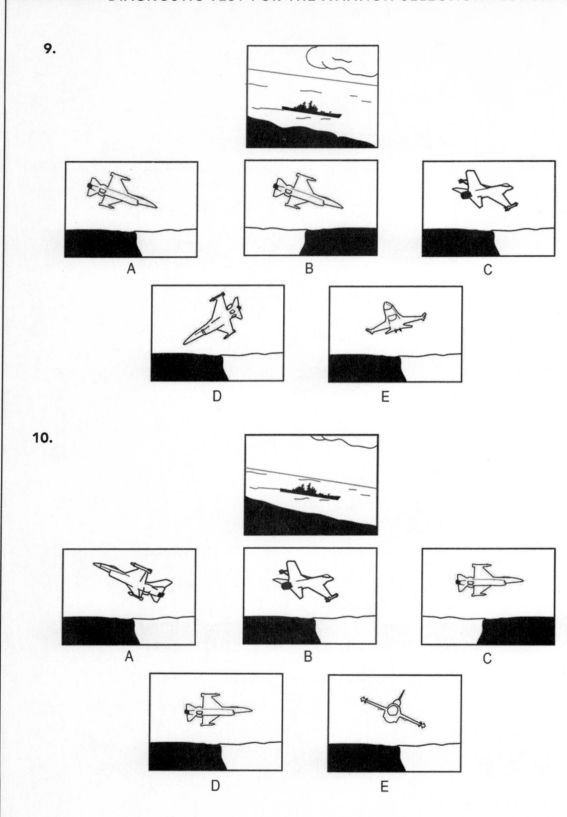

11.

12.

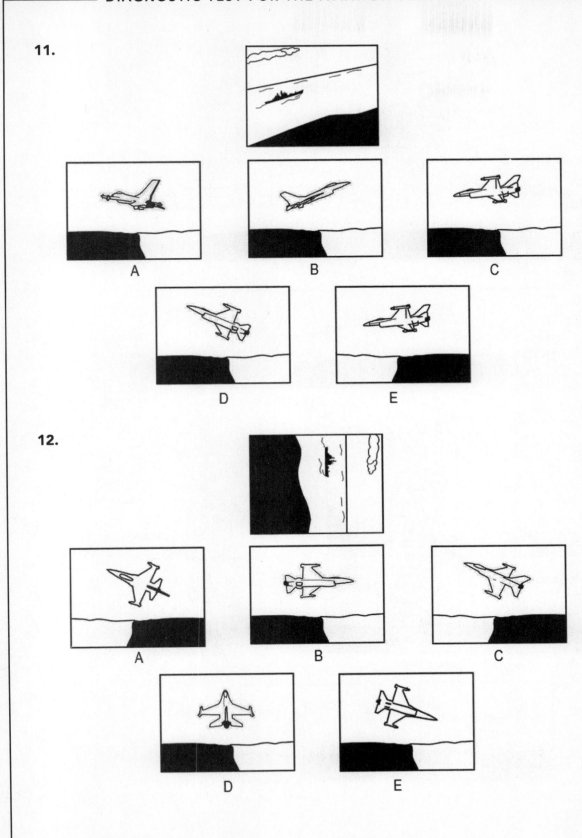

13.

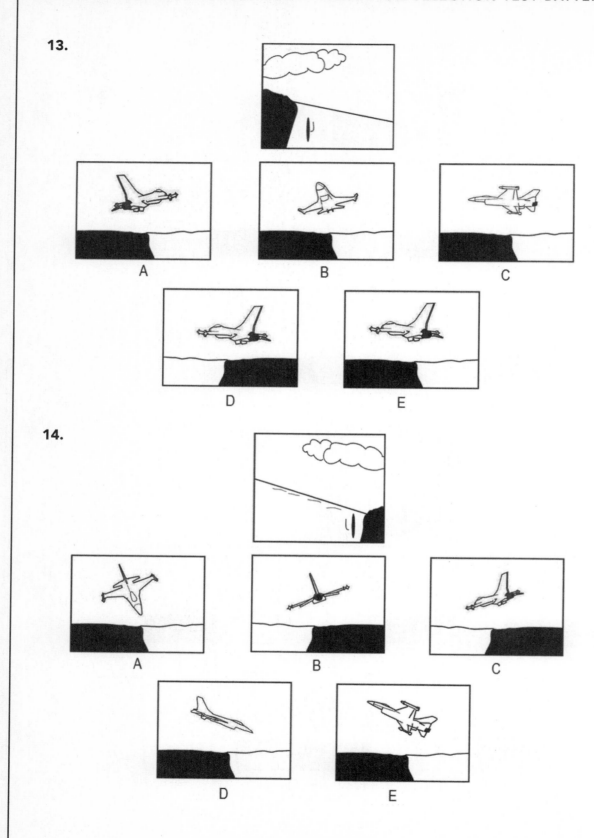

14.

15.

16.

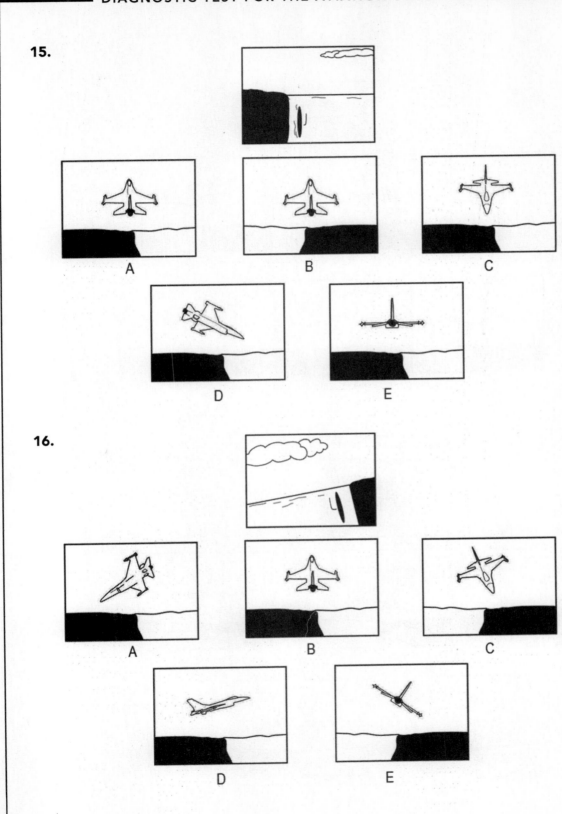

17.

18.

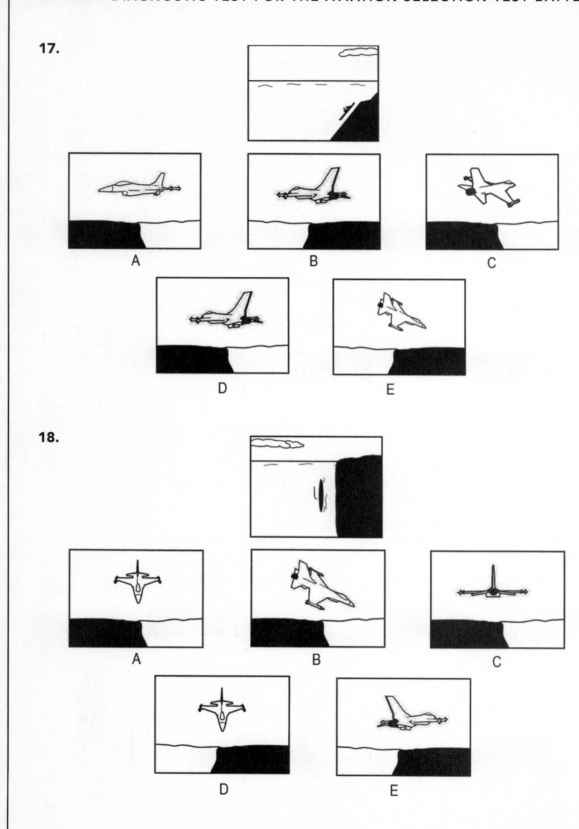

19.

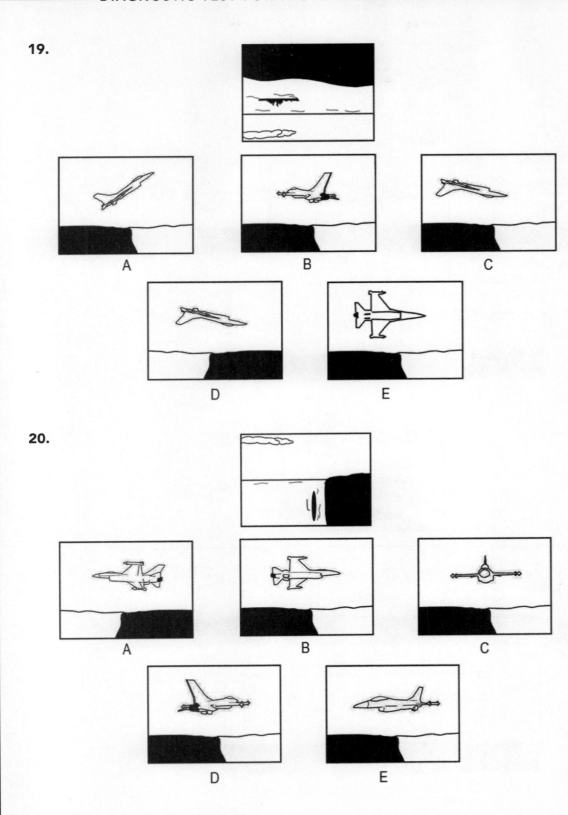

A

B

C

D

E

20.

A

B

C

D

E

21.

22.

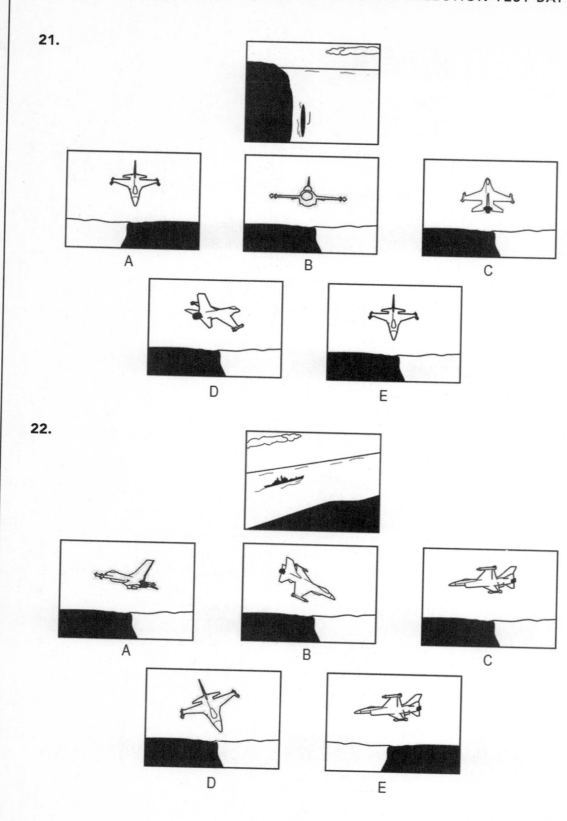

23.

24.

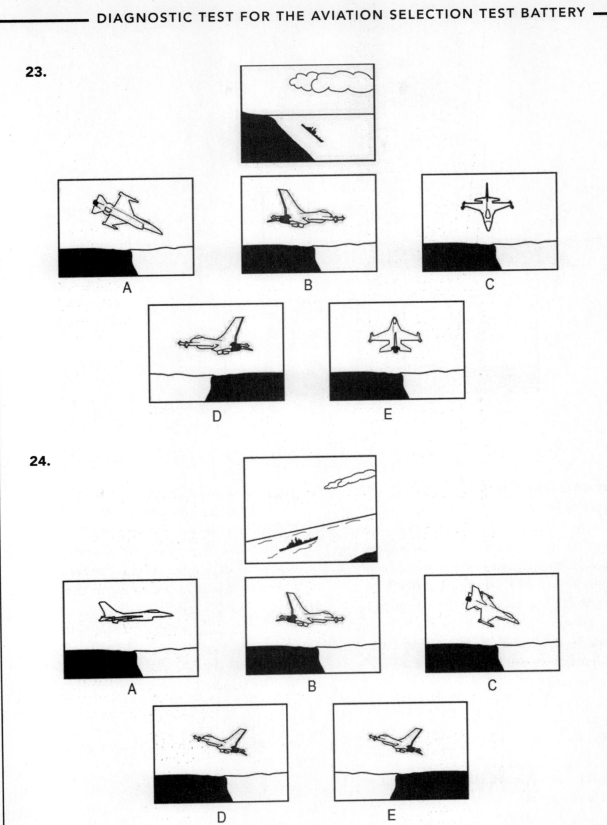

25.

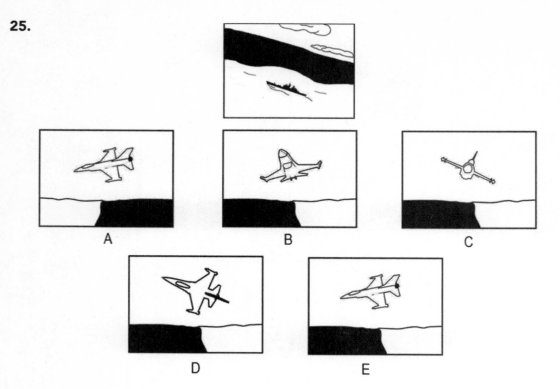

A   B   C

D   E

Aviation and Nautical Information Test

Directions: The Aviation and Nautical Information subtest measures your aviation and nautical knowledge. Each of the questions or incomplete statements is followed by five choices. You must decide which one of the choices best completes the statement or answers the question. Eliminating any obviously incorrect choices first will increase your chances of selecting the right answer. You have fifteen (15) minutes to complete this subtest.

Questions: 30
Time: 15 minutes

1. All motions of an aircraft take place around
  a. the landing gear.
  b. the longitudinal axis.
  c. the vertical axis.
  d. the center of gravity.
  e. the empennage.

2. The term *abeam* refers to
  a. anything aft of amidships.
  b. anything forward of amidships.
  c. 90° or 270° relative to one's own ship.
  d. directly ahead of or behind one's own ship.
  e. the depth of the water under the keel.

3. A _____ would be an example of a deck fitting.
  a. bulkhead
  b. marlinespike
  c. cleat
  d. watertight hatch
  e. quarterdeck

4. What three components make up the structure of an aircraft?
  a. nose, wings, and tail
  b. cockpit, passenger compartment, and empennage
  c. wings, fuselage, and empennage
  d. bow, keel, and stern
  e. flaps, stabilizer, and landing gear

5. A _____ is a horizontal cylinder usually turned by a motor upon which cable, rope, or chain is wound.
  a. windlass
  b. forecastle
  c. hand crank
  d. jumbo sheet
  e. half-hitch

6. When discussing aircraft movement, what is yaw?
  a. side-to-side movement of the nose
  b. up-and-down movement of the nose
  c. rotational movement of the fuselage
  d. using main-gear steering to move the aircraft while on the ground
  e. oscillation during high-speed flight

7. The term _____ refers to that part of a ship or island that is sheltered or away from the relative wind.
  a. downwind
  b. windward
  c. leeward
  d. starboard
  e. port

8. When discussing aircraft movement, what is pitch?
  a. the side-to-side movement of the nose
  b. an up or down movement of the nose
  c. the rotational movement of the fuselage
  d. the roll about the vertical axis
  e. using differential braking to move the aircraft while on the ground

9. The term _____ refers to the direction from which the wind blows.
  a. downwind
  b. windward
  c. leeward
  d. port
  e. starboard

10. An aircraft engine cowling provides what advantages?
  a. It allows for cooling air to reach the power plant.
  b. It protects the engine from external objects.
  c. It provides an aerodynamic union between the engine and the aircraft fuselage or wing.
  d. All the above.
  e. None of the above.

11. Any position on a nautical chart can be located or expressed in terms of _____ and _____.
  a. fathoms and depth.
  b. reefs and shoals.
  c. miles and kilometers.
  d. latitude and longitude.
  e. X and Y axes.

12. In aeronautics, the term *chord* refers to
  a. the straight-line distance between the leading edge and the trailing edge of a wing.
  b. the overall length of the fuselage.
  c. the effective wing area.
  d. the straight-line distance between either wingtip and the nose of the aircraft.
  e. the speed at which air compression is at its maximum.

13. The Beaufort Scale is used to describe
  a. wind speed.
  b. cloud cover.
  c. amount of precipitation.
  d. the depth of the water.
  e. the length of a ship.

14. What happens to atmospheric pressure with an increase in altitude?

   a. Atmospheric pressure is not affected by an altitude increase.

   b. Atmospheric pressure increases as altitude increases.

   c. Atmospheric pressure decreases as altitude increases.

   d. Atmospheric pressure is affected only by aircraft speed.

   e. Atmospheric pressure does not affect aircraft.

15. If a ship is secured by a single anchor, it is said to be *anchored*. If a ship is secured by two anchors, it is said to be

   a. double anchored.

   b. moored.

   c. held fast.

   d. hove to.

   e. quartered.

16. What happens to temperature as altitude increases?

   a. Temperature is not affected by an altitude increase.

   b. Temperature decreases as altitude increases.

   c. Temperature increases as altitude increases.

   d. Temperature is affected only by aircraft speed.

   e. Temperature does not affect aircraft.

17. *Slanted lettering* on a nautical chart indicates

   a. updated data since the previous chart was issued.

   b. information more than six months old.

   c. all names and designations for restricted areas.

   d. all information about objects that are affected by tidal changes and currents.

   e. nothing (slanted lettering is only for emphasis)

18. The initials VFR stand for

   a. velocity of flight restrictions.

   b. variable flight regime.

   c. visual flight requirements.

   d. visual flight rules.

   e. VHF flight radio.

19. A *port quartering sea* would describe

   a. seas that are arriving at an angle on the right side of the stern.

   b. seas that are arriving at an angle on the left side of the stern.

   c. seas that are arriving at an angle from the left side of the bow.

   d. seas that are arriving as the ship enters port.

   e. waves between 4 and 6 feet.

20. Adding corrections for temperature and pressure to calibrated airspeed (CAS) gives you

   a. ground speed.

   b. true airspeed.

   c. equivalent airspeed.

   d. mach number.

   e. aircraft never-exceed speed.

21. The program that issues information and updates by the U.S. Coast Guard to aid in updating nautical charts and other publications is called

   a. Seamanship Weekly.

   b. The Coast Guard Monthly.

   c. Notice to Mariners.

   d. The Sailor's Report.

   e. The Maritime Daily Report.

22. The United Nations–based organization that organizes aeronautical standards and recommended practices concerning international air navigation and operations is
 a. the Civil Aviation Safety Authority.
 b. the International Civil Aviation Organization.
 c. the Federal Aviation Administration.
 d. the Airline Pilots Organization.
 e. none of the above.

23. You have just been ordered to *take the helm*. You would be expected to
 a. set the anchor detail.
 b. make an entry into the deck log.
 c. assume the watch.
 d. steer the ship.
 e. empty the ballast tanks.

24. The aerodynamic force that acts perpendicular to the direction of relative motion is
 a. weight.
 b. thrust.
 c. drag.
 d. lift.
 e. pressure.

25. To determine the swinging radius of a ship at anchor to avoid hitting other ships in your anchorage, what is one of the important factors to know?
 a. The overall length of your own ship.
 b. The amount of anchor line out.
 c. The depth of the water you are anchored in.
 d. All the above.
 e. None of the above.

26. With regard to landing distance, what happens at a high-altitude airport?
 a. Landing distance is not affected by altitude.
 b. Landing distance decreases.
 c. Landing distance increases.
 d. Landing distance is only a factor of aircraft speed.
 e. The aircraft landing gear is less limited by landing speed.

27. The _____ is that part of a ship that is reserved for official and ceremonial functions.
 a. orlop deck
 b. poop deck
 c. quarterdeck
 d. forecastle
 e. bilge

28. With regard to takeoff distance, what happens in conditions of high temperature?
 a. Takeoff distance increases.
 b. Takeoff distance decreases.
 c. Takeoff distance does not change.
 d. Takeoff distance is only a factor of aircraft speed.
 e. Standard takeoff distance is halved.

29. A _____ is a pier or dock providing shipside access for passengers and cargo.
 a. quay
 b. davit
 c. brow
 d. gunwale
 e. bollard

30. One mechanism that is used to increase aircraft lift in a slow-speed environment would be
 a. a horizontal stabilizer.
 b. a vertical stabilizer.
 c. wing flaps.
 d. a pitot static system.
 e. a landing gear extension.

Answer Key

Math Skills Test

1. c. Multiply across: $\frac{10}{216}$. Then reduce to lowest terms to get the answer: $\frac{5}{108}$.

2. b. Both the isosceles trapezoid and the square have congruent diagonals, but only the square has diagonals that are both congruent and perpendicular.

3. d. Use the place value of each of the nonzero numbers. The four is in the ten thousands place, so it is equal to 40,000, the five is in the hundreds place, so it is equal to 500, and the three is in the ones place, so it is equal to 3; 40,000 + 500 + 3 = 40,503.

4. d. If the shorter sides are each 4 centimeters, then the longer sides must each equal $40 - 8 \div 2$; therefore, the length of each of the longer sides is 16 centimeters.

5. a. A straight angle is exactly 180°.

6. d. You must borrow 60 minutes from the three hours in order to be able to subtract.

7. d. The easiest way to solve this scale problem is to set up a proportion. To correctly set up the proportion, you need to compare the known relationship of 3 inches : 100 miles to 5 inches : x miles.

$$\frac{3 \text{ inches}}{100 \text{ miles}} = \frac{5 \text{ inches}}{x \text{ miles}}$$

Once the proportion is set up, you can cross-multiply to get 3 inches × x miles = 5 inches × 100 miles. This is equivalent to $3x = 500$. Then dividing both sides of the equation by 3 provides the answer. The most accurate length in the answer choices is 167 miles, choice **d**.

8. b. The formula for the circumference of a circle is $C = 2r\pi$ or $d\pi$. Therefore, to find the radius of a circle from its circumference, you can divide the circumference by 2π. Because 100π centimeters $\div 2\pi = $ 50 centimeters, choice **b** is correct. If the area of the circle were 100π square centimeters, then its radius would be 10 centimeters, choice **a**. The diameter of the circle would be 100 centimeters, choice **c**. If you selected choice **d**, you forgot to divide by π ($\pi = 3.14$) to determine the radius.

9. a. The formula for the area of a triangle is, $\frac{1}{2}bh$, where b is the base of the triangle and h is its height. In the given figure, the base of the triangle is 12 cm and its height is 5 cm. (The side labeled 6 cm does *not* represent the height.) The area of the triangle is therefore, $\frac{1}{2}(5)(12)$, which is 30 sq. cm.

10. c. The ratio of black to blue to red pens in Ming's drawer is 5:2:1. That means for every 5 black pens, there are 2 blue pens and 1 red pen. Another way to consider that is for every 8 pens, there are 5 black pens, 2 blue pens, and 1 red pen. If the ratio of blue pens is 2 out of every 8, you can set up a proportion to find how many blue pens he has out of 40. Use x for the unknown number of blue pens out of 40:

$$\frac{2}{8} = \frac{x}{40}$$

By cross-multiplying, you will find that $8x = 80$, which means that $x = 10$. There are 10 blue pens in Ming's drawer.

11. c. The lighthouse flashes every 6 seconds. Robert's watch beeps every 10 seconds. They beep and flash at the same time. To find the next time when this will happen, you need to find the least common denominator (LCD) of the two numbers. The LCD of 6 and 10 is 30, which means that the watch will beep and the lighthouse will flash together the next time in 30 seconds. Choice **a**, 2 seconds, represents the greatest common factor (GCF) of the two numbers, which would not be useful in identifying the next time a repeated event will occur. While Robert's watch *will* beep and the lighthouse flash together in 60 seconds, or 1 minute, choice **d** does not represent the *next* time that this will happen. It will happen earlier, at 30 seconds.

12. d. The fifth term in the pattern will be the sum of the two previous terms: 3 and 5. Because 3 + 5 = 8, the fifth term will be 8, choice **a**. The sixth term will then be the sum of the two previous terms: 5 and 8. Therefore, the sixth term will be 5 + 8, or 13, choice **b**. The seventh term is the sum of the fifth and sixth terms, 8 and 13, which is 21, choice **d**.

13. b. There are 36 possible distinct outcomes when two number cubes are rolled. That is because each number cube has 6 different numbers, and the possibilities are multiplied when they are rolled together. There are two possible outcomes for the sum of the number cubes to equal 3: One cube can show a 2 and the other can show a 1 or one cube can show a 1 and the other can show a 2. Any probability is found using the fraction

$$\frac{\text{number of successful options}}{\text{total number of possibilities}}$$

In this case, the probability is $\frac{2}{36}$, which can be reduced to $\frac{1}{18}$.

14. d. To find the value of m in terms of n, you need to isolate m on one side of the equation. To do that, you need to subtract 22 from both sides of the equation and then divide both sides by 2, as shown.

$2m + 22 = 6n$

$2m + 22 - 22 = 6n - 22$

$2m = 6n - 22$

$\frac{2m}{2} = \frac{6n - 22}{2}$

$m = 3n - 11$

Because the value of m is identified as $3n - 11$, the answer is choice **d**.

15. b. The tenths place in a decimal is the digit directly to the right of the decimal point. In the number 174.56, the digit 5 is in the tenths place. The tens place is 7, choice **d**. The ones place is 4, choice **a**. The hundredths place is 6, choice **c**.

16. d. Note that $\frac{2}{5} = 0.40$ and $\frac{3}{7} \approx 0.42857$. So, $\frac{3}{7}$ is not less than $\frac{2}{5}$.

17. d. The satellite orbits Earth 90 times in five days. Because it orbits Earth the same number of times each day, you can determine how many times it orbits each day by dividing 90 by 5, thus $90 \div 5 = 18$. You can find out the number of times it will orbit Earth in 7 days by multiplying 18 by 7; the correct answer is 126, choice **d**. Another way to solve this problem is to set up a proportion as follows:

$\frac{90}{5} = \frac{x}{7}$

You can then cross-multiply to find that $5x = 630$, which simplifies to $x = 126$.

18. d. According to the map's scale, one inch is equivalent to 50 feet. Therefore, the length of the rectangular farm, 8 inches on the map, is equivalent to 8 × 50 ft = 400 ft. The width of the map, 0.5 inches on the map, is equivalent to 0.5 × 50 ft = 25 ft. To calculate the area of any rectangle, multiply the length by the width. In the case of this farm, that would be 400 ft × 25 ft = 10,000 sq. ft. Choice **b**, 850 ft, would be the perimeter of the farm.

19. b. The probability of picking a red card at random from the deck of cards is $\frac{26}{52}$, or exactly $\frac{1}{2}$. As long as the card is replaced after each pick, the probability will not change. Therefore, you can determine the probability of picking three consecutive red cards by multiplying $\frac{1}{2} \times \frac{1}{2} \times \frac{1}{2}$. The product, $\frac{1}{8}$, is the correct answer.

20. a. Apply the order of operations, as follows: $-2(-3)^2 + 3(-3) - 7 = -2(9) - 9 - 7 = -18 - 9 - 7 = -34$

21. d. To find the value of 2^6, you need to multiply 2 by itself 6 times. $2 \times 2 \times 2 \times 2 \times 2 \times 2 = 64$. If you chose choice **c**, you found the value of 6^2, which is equivalent to 6 × 6, or 36.

22. b. The dimensions of the gray rectangle are exactly three-quarters that of the white rectangle. The length of the white rectangle is 12 inches. The length of the gray rectangle must therefore be equal to $\frac{3}{4} \times 12$, which is 9 inches. The width of the white rectangle is 6 inches. The width of the gray rectangle must therefore be equal to $\frac{3}{4} \times 6$ inches, which is 4.5 inches. Knowing the length and width of the gray rectangle, you can find the sum of the sides (9 + 9 + 4.5 + 4.5 = 27) to find its perimeter.

23. c. The volume of the aquarium can be found by using the formula $V = l \times w \times h$. Because the length is 12 inches, the width is 5 inches, and the height is 10 inches, multiply $V = 12 \times 5 \times 10$ to get a volume of 600 cubic inches.

24. c. If angle 1 is 30° and angle 2 is a right angle (90°), then angle 3 must be 60° because the sum of the angles in a triangle is 180°. Angles 3 and 4 are formed by parallel lines, so angle 4 also 60°. A straight line (which forms angles 4 and 5) is 180°. Subtract 60° from 180° to get the answer: 120°.

25. d. The area of a circle is calculated with the formula $A = \pi r^2$, where r is the radius of the circle. In this problem, $A = 78.5$ and $\pi = 3.14$, therefore $78.5 = 3.14r^2$. Divide each side of the equation by 3.14 to get $25 = r^2$. Take the square root of each side to get $r = 5$ feet. The diameter is twice the radius, in this case, 10 feet.

26. a. Rounding to compatible numbers can help solve this problem: 490,000 rounds to 500,000 and 98,000 rounds to 100,000. The question now becomes 100,000 compared to 500,000, or $\frac{100,000}{500,000}$, which reduces to $\frac{1}{5}$.

27. d. In each of the answer choices, the numbers remain the same but the order changes. The commutative property changes the order but the result is the same. This property is true when used with addition or multiplication, but does not hold for subtraction. Because the terms surrounding the subtraction sign in choice **d** are switched, this expression will most likely not have the same value as the others. To check, evaluate each expression to see which one results in a different value than the others. Be sure to use the correct order of operations (PEMDAS) when evaluating expressions. When evaluated, each answer choice gives a result of 218 except for choice **d**. Choice **d** evaluated becomes 10 − 3(76) = 10 − 228 = −218.

28. d. "The polygon is also a rhombus" is the only statement that does not contradict the original statement because a square is a special rhombus.

29. a. This problem has multiple steps. First, figure out what Deanna spent: $7 for popcorn, 2 hot dogs × 2 girls × $3 each = $12, 2 sodas × $4 = $8. Then add them up: $7 + $12 + $8 = $27. Next, figure out what Jamie spent: $13 × 2 = $26. Last, subtract the two numbers: $27 − $26 = $1. Deanna spent $1 more.

30. c. The third side of the triangle must be less than the sum of the other two sides (17 + 14) and greater than their difference (17 − 14). This means that the third side must be less than 31 and greater than 3. Only choice **c** fits these criteria.

Reading Skills Test

1. b. The passage states that fear leads a swimmer to stop making rational decisions, the first step in drowning.

2. c. To *flounder* in the water is to splash about helplessly.

3. d. The author does not discourage the reader from going in the water, nor does the author urge the reader to learn to swim. Having someone nearby is mentioned, but the focus of the passage is the importance of remaining calm when trouble strikes.

4. d. Napoleon wanted to devise a code that could be read at night, and one of his soldiers invented a system of raised dots that later became Braille.

5. d. The word *tactile* refers to something that can be felt with one's hands.

6. c. The passage states that each letter of the alphabet is represented in Braille by raised dots, each letter using from one to six dots. Some letters may indeed use one dot or six, or even none—but the question asks about the alphabet as a whole, not about any individual letters.

7. d. Napoleon rejected a soldier's idea for a code that could be read at night because it was too complicated. Louis Braille took that idea and simplified it so that blind people could read.

8. b. The last sentence in the paragraph clearly supports the idea that the renewed interest in Shakespeare is due to the development of his characters. Choice **a** is incorrect because the writer never makes this type of comparison. Choice **c** is wrong because, even though scholars are mentioned in the paragraph, there is no indication that the scholars are compiling the anthology. Choice **d** is wrong because there is no support to show that most New Yorkers are interested in this work.

9. a. An *anthology* is a collection of many different pieces of literature, often spanning a historical period. An *anthology* of British poetry, for example, is a book containing a selection of poems written by British writers.

10. c. The passage discusses several mechanical timekeeping devices, including the hourglass, the pendulum clock, and the quartz watch. The information is arranged chronologically, so a title describing the history of timekeeping is most appropriate.

11. b. The word *oscillate* means to vibrate back and forth. The word is also defined in the same sentence of the passage.

12. a. The passage concludes by stating that quartz is "very inexpensive to work with" and "far less complicated" than other types of timekeeping. You might safely infer, then, that quartz clocks cost less to manufacture than traditional pendulum styles. Any of the other choices might be true, but they are not addressed in the passage.

13. d. Something that is *rudimentary* is very basic and simple.

14. a. The second and third sentence combine to give support to choice **a**. The statement stresses that there must be a judge's approval (that is, legal authorization) before a search can be conducted. Choices **b** and **d** are wrong because it is not enough for the police to have direct evidence or a reasonable belief—a judge must authorize the search for it to be legal. Choice **c** is not mentioned in the passage.

15. c. This question refers to what the judge needs before issuing a search warrant: direct factual evidence of a crime. Neither a reasonable suspicion nor the sworn testimony of the police is enough, according to the passage. The judge's decision must be based on factual evidence.

16. a. Each of the choices is mentioned in the passage, but only **a** states the overall theme or central idea of the passage. The other choices are details of that central idea.

17. c. The passage states that Wednesday is named after Woden, a god associated with musical inspiration. The other choices are not supported in the passage.

18. d. The word *pantheon* comes from the Greek words *pan*, meaning *all*, and *theos*, meaning *gods*. Thus, *pantheon* means *all gods*, and refers to a list of ancient deities.

19. a. The passage addresses the names of weekdays, demonstrating that they are drawn from the names of ancient gods. Therefore, one can safely conclude that mythology played a role in the development of the English language. The other choices may or may not be true, but they are not sufficiently addressed in the passage to draw an accurate inference.

20. a. The passage states that the word *linoleum* comes from the Latin words *linum* (flax) and *oleum* (oil).

21. d. The passage does mention that linoleum is used around the world and that it is named from Latin words, but the main idea is to discuss the floor covering's history.

22. d. Choices **a** and **c** are not supported by the paragraph. Choice **b** only tells us about particular parts of the paragraph and is too specific to be the main idea. Choice **d**, however, is general enough to encompass all the sentences and the paragraph as a whole. Every sentence supports the idea asserted in choice **d**.

23. b. The last sentence states that Priority Mail will deliver a package in two days or less. Express Mail gets a package delivered overnight, while the other options are not addressed in the passage.

24. b. The author does not specifically state that paper clips are a useful invention, but the enthusiastic tone of the passage suggests it. The author's list of uses for paper clips reinforces this tone.

25. a. The word *crevice* refers to a crack or fracture, such as crevices in rocks.

26. c. The last sentence of the passage lists several things, including string, that people once used to bind papers together. The other items are not listed.

27. b. The second paragraph does state that Vaaler was a Norwegian, but he patented his idea with the German patent office, so choice **b** is the correct answer.

Mechanical Comprehension Test

1. c. The mechanical advantage of this pulley system is 2. The force required to lift the 276 pound load is 276 pounds ÷ 2 = 138 pounds.

2. d. Valves 3 and 4 allow liquid from tank A to flow to the outlet, while opening 2 provides a direct route for liquid to travel from C to A.

3. d. When water freezes into ice, it expands, meaning that it becomes less dense than water. Objects that are less dense than the fluid they are in will float.

4. a. $w_1 \times d_1 = w_2 \times d_2$. Shannon is 20 feet away from the pivot point. 100 pounds × 9 feet = 20 feet × w_2. Solving for w_2 gives 45 pounds.

5. c. For every 1 rotation of gear 2, gear 1 turns 9 teeth ÷ 12 teeth = $\frac{3}{4}$ times. If gear 2 turns at 60 rpm, then gear 1 will turn at 60 rpm × $\frac{3}{4}$ = 45 rpm.

6. c. $w_1 \times d_1 = w_2 \times d_2$. The crane shown is a special type of lever. The weight is 16 feet away from the pivot point, and the lifting cable is 10 feet from the pivot point. 600 pounds × 16 feet = 10 feet × w_2. Solving for w_2 gives 960 pounds.

7. a. The mechanical advantage (MA) of a ramp is determined by the length of the ramp, l, divided by the height gained, h. In this case, MA = $\frac{l}{h}$ = 24 feet ÷ 6 feet = 4. The force required to pull a 500-pound block up a ramp is 500 pounds ÷ 4 = 125 pounds.

8. c. When Alex departs, Jill is 40 miles ahead. After 1 hour, Alex has traveled 60 miles and Jill 80 miles. After 2 hours, both Alex and Jill will have traveled 120 miles.

9. a. Since the circumference of B is twice that of A, A will have to complete 2 revolutions per 1 revolution of B. Therefore, B must rotate at 10 rpm.

10. c. The force required to stretch a spring is equal to its force constant multiplied by the distance stretch ($F = kx$). The force required to move a spring with a force constant of 2.5 pounds per inch a distance of 10 inches is 2.5 × 10 = 25 pounds.

11. a. Styrofoam is an excellent insulator, meaning that it prevents heat from flowing from the coffee to the surrounding environment. It also keeps one's hands from being burned by hot coffee.

12. d. The nut will move 1 inch down the screw every 20 turns. To travel 1.5 inches, the nut must be turned 1.5 inches × 20 turns per inch = 30 turns.

13. a. Oil is less dense than water. When two immiscible liquids of different density combine, the one that is less dense will always float to the top.

14. c. The 6-pound weight will compress the first spring: 6 pounds ÷ 2 pounds per inch = 3 inches. The second spring compresses 6 pounds ÷ 3 pounds per inch = 2 inches. The third spring compresses 6 pounds ÷ 6 pounds per inch = 1 inch. The total amount the platform compresses is therefore 3 + 2 + 1 = 6 inches.

15. b. $w_1 \times d_1 = w_2 \times d_2$. 180 pounds × 4 feet = w_2 × 9 feet. Solving for w_2 gives 80 pounds.

16. b. A pulley system of this type has a mechanical advantage of 2. So, lifting a 200-pound weight will require 200 pounds ÷ 2 = 100 pounds.

17. c. An ax head is a wedge used to split a piece of wood. It can be thought of as two ramps pressed together.

18. c. In this pulley system, the weight of the box is shared by 3 cables. It therefore has a mechanical advantage of 3.

19. b. If gear 1 turns clockwise, it will cause gear 2 to turn counterclockwise, and gear 3 will turn clockwise.

20. c. Mechanical advantage (MA) is the factor by which a simple machine multiplies for the force put into it. In this case, 50 pounds of force is used to move a 200-pound block, so MA = $200 \div 50 = 4$. The MA of a ramp is determined by the length of the ramp, l, divided by the height gained, h. In this case, MA $= 4 = \frac{l}{h} = \frac{l}{10}$ feet. Solving for l tells us the ramp is 40 feet long.

21. b. Each full turn of the pedals will turn the rear wheel $48 \div 16 = 3$ revolutions; 3 turns of the pedals will turn the rear wheel $3 \times 3 = 9$ revolutions.

22. b. Combustion creates a dense, high-pressure gas that rapidly expands and pushes the piston downward.

23. b. Metal boat anchors offer the advantages of being dense and strong.

24. d. $w_1 \times d_1 = w_2 \times d_2$. Solving for d_2 gives 17 feet.

25. a. For the 16-tooth cog, the bike travels $48 \div 12 = 4$ revolutions per pedal stroke, and $48 \div 16 = 3$ revolutions per pedal stroke for the 12-tooth cog. At 80 turns of the pedal per minute, the bike wheel completes $80 \times 3 = 240$ rpm. In order to match that speed using the 12-tooth cog, one must pedal 240 rpm $\div 4 = 60$ rpm.

26. c. The 20-pound block is located closer to scale 1 than scale 2. Scale 1 will support more than half the weight of the block.

27. c. $w_1 \times d_1 = w_2 \times d_2$. Todd is 6 feet away from the pivot point, and the block is 18 feet away. 50×18 feet = 6 feet $\times w_2$. Solving for w_2 gives 150 pounds.

28. b. When air is heated it expands and becomes less dense than cold air, making the entire balloon buoyant and allowing it to float.

29. d. Mechanical advantage describes the factor that force is multiplied by a simple machine. Here, by moving the screw handle 3 feet (3 feet $\times$ 12 inches per foot = 36 inches), the jack is raised $\frac{1}{4}$ inch. Thus the mechanical advantage of the jack is $36 \div \frac{1}{4} = 144$.

30. d. A pulley system of this type has a mechanical advantage of 4. So, if Bryan can pull a rope with 150 pounds of force, he will be able to lift a weight of 150 pounds $\times 4 = 600$ pounds.

Spatial Apperception Test

QUESTION	ANSWER	PITCH	ROLL	DIRECTION
1.	D	nose low	no bank	flying out to sea
2.	D	nose up	banking right	flying out to sea
3.	B	nose low	banking right	flying out to sea
4.	A	nose low	no bank	flying out to sea

5.	C	nose slightly high	banking left	flying at an angle out to sea, coast on left
6.	E	nose slightly high	banking right	coastline on left
7.	E	level	no bank	flying out to sea
8.	C	nose low	no bank	flying along the coast, coast on left
9.	A	nose low	banking left	flying out to sea
10.	D	level	banking left	flying out to sea
11.	E	nose low	banking right	flying at a slight angle out to sea
12.	A	nose high	90° angle of bank	flying out to sea
13.	A	level	banking slightly left	flying out to sea
14.	C	nose low	banking left	flying at a slight angle out to sea
15.	E	level	no bank	flying parallel to the coast on the left
16.	E	level	banking right	flying parallel to the coast on the right
17.	B	level	no bank	flying at an angle out to sea
18.	A	nose low	no bank	flying parallel to the coast on the right
19.	C	nose low	inverted	flying out to sea
20.	C	level	no bank	flying parallel to the coast on the right
21.	A	nose low	no bank	flying parallel to the coast on the left
22.	B	nose low	banking right	flying out to sea
23.	B	level	no bank	flying at an angle out to sea
24.	E	nose high	banking right	flying at an angle out to sea
25.	E	nose low	banking left	flying inland

Aviation and Nautical Information Test

1. **d.** The aircraft center of gravity is a specific point in the aircraft where all weight would be evenly distributed. If the aircraft could be hung by a very strong string from this point, it would be perfectly balanced. All movement of an aircraft in flight take place around this central point.

2. **c.** *Abeam* means anything on a 90° or 270° relative direction from one's own or a reference ship.

3. **c.** A cleat would be an example of a deck fitting.

4. **c.** The wings, fuselage, and empennage make up the three main parts of an aircraft. Other elements, such as the engines or landing gear, are attached to one of these three elements. *Empennage* comes from the French word meaning *feathers on an arrow* and is used to denote the rear part of the aircraft comprising the horizontal and vertical stabilizers, the elevators, and the rudder.

5. **a.** A windlass is a horizontal cylinder usually turned by a motor upon which cable, rope, or chain is wound.

6. **a.** Yaw is the side-to-side movement of the nose, caused by pushing on the rudder pedals inside the cockpit.

7. **c.** The term leeward refers to that part of a ship or island that is sheltered or away from the relative wind.

8. **b.** Pitch is an up or down movement of the nose of the aircraft, caused by deflection forward or aft of the control stick.

9. **b.** The term windward refers to the direction from which the wind blows.

10. **d.** The engine cowling covers the engine and provides protection from things such as hail or bird impacts. It also allows outside ambient air to circulate through the engine, helping to cool it, and it creates an aerodynamic covering to the mechanical and nonaerodynamic parts of an engine to aid in the smooth flow of air over the area.

11. **d.** Any position on a nautical chart can be located or expressed in terms of latitude and longitude.

12. **a.** In aeronautics, *chord* is the straight-line distance between the leading edge and the trailing edge of a wing. This calculation, also known as the mean aerodynamic chord, helps determine the lift characteristics of an airfoil or a wing.

13. **a.** The Beaufort Scale is used to describe wind speed.

14. **c.** Remember that as you increase altitude, the air molecules get farther apart, meaning that atmospheric pressure is less dense and will decrease. There simply is not as much air mass above you to maintain the same atmospheric pressure as there is when you are at a lower altitude.

15. **b.** If a ship is secured by a single anchor, it is said to be *anchored*. If a ship is secured by two anchors, it is said to be *moored*.

16. **b.** Solar energy heats up the earth's surface and that heat is recirculated into the atmosphere via conduction and convection. The thick atmosphere at the earth's surface helps to retain that heat. As altitude increases, there is less and less atmospheric pressure to help retain the solar energy and there is no conduction and convection to reflect and return the heat to the atmosphere. This heat loss is called the *lapse rate* and can be calculated to be about 2° F per 1,000 feet of altitude.

17. d. *Slanted lettering* is used to denote all information about objects that are affected by tidal changes and currents.

18. d. VFR stands for visual flight rules. VFR flight operations are controlled by a set of regulations set down by the U.S. Civil Aeronautics Board to govern the operational control of aircraft during visual flight.

19. b. Seas that are arriving at an angle on the left side of the stern are known as port quartering seas.

20. b. True airspeed (TAS) is the airspeed of an aircraft relative to undisturbed air. The data required to determine true airspeed are outside air temperature (OAT), pressure altitude, and calibrated airspeed (CAS).

21. c. Notice to Mariners is the weekly information update put out by the U.S. Coast Guard to aid in updating nautical charts and other publications.

22. b. The International Civil Aviation Organization (ICAO) is based in Montreal, Quebec, and has been setting standards and procedures for international air flight since its inception in 1947. It was born out of the Convention on International Civil Aviation held in Chicago in 1944. The Civil Aviation Safety Authority is based in and covers Australia only and the Federal Aviation Administration is a United States–only organization.

23. d. An order for you to *take the helm* means you will be responsible for steering the ship.

24. d. Of the four components that act on an aircraft (lift, drag, thrust, and weight), lift works perpendicular to the relative motion of the aircraft.

25. d. All the listed answers are required to determine the swinging radius of a ship at anchor. In addition, you need to know the distance at the bow pulpit from the deck to the water.

26. c. When an aircraft is landing at a high-altitude airport, the air is less dense, which means that the aircraft must fly faster to maintain enough air over the wings to generate lift. This translates to a required increase in landing speed, meaning that a longer runway is necessary for an aircraft to land.

27. c. The quarterdeck is that part of a ship that is reserved for official and ceremonial functions.

28. a. In conditions of high temperature, the distance an aircraft needs to take off increases. Warm air is less dense than cold air because there are fewer air molecules in a given volume of warm air than in the same volume of cooler air. A takeoff in conditions of warm or hot temperatures means the aircraft will need more distance to take off and its rate of climb will be reduced.

29. a. A quay is a pier or dock providing shipside access for passengers and cargo.

30. c. When wing flaps are lowered, the camber (tilt) of the wing increases and this alters the distance that air must travel over and under the wing. This in turn changes the relative pressure differentials on the wing, resulting in increased lift. The other answer choices are mechanisms that provide aircraft movement or airspeed data.

For information on how the official ASTB is scored, see Chapter 3.

CHAPTER

7

DIAGNOSTIC TEST FOR THE ARMED SERVICES VOCATIONAL APTITUDE BATTERY

CHAPTER SUMMARY

This diagnostic test is based on the actual Armed Services Vocational Aptitude Battery (ASVAB). Use it to see how you would do today and to determine your strengths and weaknesses as you plan your study schedule. Information on official ASVAB scoring can be found in Chapter 3.

Subtest 1: General Science (GS)

1.	ⓐ	ⓑ	ⓒ	ⓓ
2.	ⓐ	ⓑ	ⓒ	ⓓ
3.	ⓐ	ⓑ	ⓒ	ⓓ
4.	ⓐ	ⓑ	ⓒ	ⓓ
5.	ⓐ	ⓑ	ⓒ	ⓓ
6.	ⓐ	ⓑ	ⓒ	ⓓ
7.	ⓐ	ⓑ	ⓒ	ⓓ
8.	ⓐ	ⓑ	ⓒ	ⓓ
9.	ⓐ	ⓑ	ⓒ	ⓓ

10.	ⓐ	ⓑ	ⓒ	ⓓ
11.	ⓐ	ⓑ	ⓒ	ⓓ
12.	ⓐ	ⓑ	ⓒ	ⓓ
13.	ⓐ	ⓑ	ⓒ	ⓓ
14.	ⓐ	ⓑ	ⓒ	ⓓ
15.	ⓐ	ⓑ	ⓒ	ⓓ
16.	ⓐ	ⓑ	ⓒ	ⓓ
17.	ⓐ	ⓑ	ⓒ	ⓓ

18.	ⓐ	ⓑ	ⓒ	ⓓ
19.	ⓐ	ⓑ	ⓒ	ⓓ
20.	ⓐ	ⓑ	ⓒ	ⓓ
21.	ⓐ	ⓑ	ⓒ	ⓓ
22.	ⓐ	ⓑ	ⓒ	ⓓ
23.	ⓐ	ⓑ	ⓒ	ⓓ
24.	ⓐ	ⓑ	ⓒ	ⓓ
25.	ⓐ	ⓑ	ⓒ	ⓓ

Subtest 2: Arithmetic Reasoning (AR)

1.	ⓐ	ⓑ	ⓒ	ⓓ
2.	ⓐ	ⓑ	ⓒ	ⓓ
3.	ⓐ	ⓑ	ⓒ	ⓓ
4.	ⓐ	ⓑ	ⓒ	ⓓ
5.	ⓐ	ⓑ	ⓒ	ⓓ
6.	ⓐ	ⓑ	ⓒ	ⓓ
7.	ⓐ	ⓑ	ⓒ	ⓓ
8.	ⓐ	ⓑ	ⓒ	ⓓ
9.	ⓐ	ⓑ	ⓒ	ⓓ
10.	ⓐ	ⓑ	ⓒ	ⓓ

11.	ⓐ	ⓑ	ⓒ	ⓓ
12.	ⓐ	ⓑ	ⓒ	ⓓ
13.	ⓐ	ⓑ	ⓒ	ⓓ
14.	ⓐ	ⓑ	ⓒ	ⓓ
15.	ⓐ	ⓑ	ⓒ	ⓓ
16.	ⓐ	ⓑ	ⓒ	ⓓ
17.	ⓐ	ⓑ	ⓒ	ⓓ
18.	ⓐ	ⓑ	ⓒ	ⓓ
19.	ⓐ	ⓑ	ⓒ	ⓓ
20.	ⓐ	ⓑ	ⓒ	ⓓ

21.	ⓐ	ⓑ	ⓒ	ⓓ
22.	ⓐ	ⓑ	ⓒ	ⓓ
23.	ⓐ	ⓑ	ⓒ	ⓓ
24.	ⓐ	ⓑ	ⓒ	ⓓ
25.	ⓐ	ⓑ	ⓒ	ⓓ
26.	ⓐ	ⓑ	ⓒ	ⓓ
27.	ⓐ	ⓑ	ⓒ	ⓓ
28.	ⓐ	ⓑ	ⓒ	ⓓ
29.	ⓐ	ⓑ	ⓒ	ⓓ
30.	ⓐ	ⓑ	ⓒ	ⓓ

Subtest 3: Word Knowledge (WK)

1.	ⓐ	ⓑ	ⓒ	ⓓ
2.	ⓐ	ⓑ	ⓒ	ⓓ
3.	ⓐ	ⓑ	ⓒ	ⓓ
4.	ⓐ	ⓑ	ⓒ	ⓓ
5.	ⓐ	ⓑ	ⓒ	ⓓ
6.	ⓐ	ⓑ	ⓒ	ⓓ
7.	ⓐ	ⓑ	ⓒ	ⓓ
8.	ⓐ	ⓑ	ⓒ	ⓓ
9.	ⓐ	ⓑ	ⓒ	ⓓ
10.	ⓐ	ⓑ	ⓒ	ⓓ
11.	ⓐ	ⓑ	ⓒ	ⓓ
12.	ⓐ	ⓑ	ⓒ	ⓓ

13.	ⓐ	ⓑ	ⓒ	ⓓ
14.	ⓐ	ⓑ	ⓒ	ⓓ
15.	ⓐ	ⓑ	ⓒ	ⓓ
16.	ⓐ	ⓑ	ⓒ	ⓓ
17.	ⓐ	ⓑ	ⓒ	ⓓ
18.	ⓐ	ⓑ	ⓒ	ⓓ
19.	ⓐ	ⓑ	ⓒ	ⓓ
20.	ⓐ	ⓑ	ⓒ	ⓓ
21.	ⓐ	ⓑ	ⓒ	ⓓ
22.	ⓐ	ⓑ	ⓒ	ⓓ
23.	ⓐ	ⓑ	ⓒ	ⓓ
24.	ⓐ	ⓑ	ⓒ	ⓓ

25.	ⓐ	ⓑ	ⓒ	ⓓ
26.	ⓐ	ⓑ	ⓒ	ⓓ
27.	ⓐ	ⓑ	ⓒ	ⓓ
28.	ⓐ	ⓑ	ⓒ	ⓓ
29.	ⓐ	ⓑ	ⓒ	ⓓ
30.	ⓐ	ⓑ	ⓒ	ⓓ
31.	ⓐ	ⓑ	ⓒ	ⓓ
32.	ⓐ	ⓑ	ⓒ	ⓓ
33.	ⓐ	ⓑ	ⓒ	ⓓ
34.	ⓐ	ⓑ	ⓒ	ⓓ
35.	ⓐ	ⓑ	ⓒ	ⓓ

Subtest 4: Paragraph Comprehension (PC)

1.	ⓐ	ⓑ	ⓒ	ⓓ
2.	ⓐ	ⓑ	ⓒ	ⓓ
3.	ⓐ	ⓑ	ⓒ	ⓓ
4.	ⓐ	ⓑ	ⓒ	ⓓ
5.	ⓐ	ⓑ	ⓒ	ⓓ

6.	ⓐ	ⓑ	ⓒ	ⓓ
7.	ⓐ	ⓑ	ⓒ	ⓓ
8.	ⓐ	ⓑ	ⓒ	ⓓ
9.	ⓐ	ⓑ	ⓒ	ⓓ
10.	ⓐ	ⓑ	ⓒ	ⓓ

11.	ⓐ	ⓑ	ⓒ	ⓓ
12.	ⓐ	ⓑ	ⓒ	ⓓ
13.	ⓐ	ⓑ	ⓒ	ⓓ
14.	ⓐ	ⓑ	ⓒ	ⓓ
15.	ⓐ	ⓑ	ⓒ	ⓓ

Subtest 5: Math Knowledge (MK)

1.	ⓐ	ⓑ	ⓒ	ⓓ
2.	ⓐ	ⓑ	ⓒ	ⓓ
3.	ⓐ	ⓑ	ⓒ	ⓓ
4.	ⓐ	ⓑ	ⓒ	ⓓ
5.	ⓐ	ⓑ	ⓒ	ⓓ
6.	ⓐ	ⓑ	ⓒ	ⓓ
7.	ⓐ	ⓑ	ⓒ	ⓓ
8.	ⓐ	ⓑ	ⓒ	ⓓ
9.	ⓐ	ⓑ	ⓒ	ⓓ

10.	ⓐ	ⓑ	ⓒ	ⓓ
11.	ⓐ	ⓑ	ⓒ	ⓓ
12.	ⓐ	ⓑ	ⓒ	ⓓ
13.	ⓐ	ⓑ	ⓒ	ⓓ
14.	ⓐ	ⓑ	ⓒ	ⓓ
15.	ⓐ	ⓑ	ⓒ	ⓓ
16.	ⓐ	ⓑ	ⓒ	ⓓ
17.	ⓐ	ⓑ	ⓒ	ⓓ

18.	ⓐ	ⓑ	ⓒ	ⓓ
19.	ⓐ	ⓑ	ⓒ	ⓓ
20.	ⓐ	ⓑ	ⓒ	ⓓ
21.	ⓐ	ⓑ	ⓒ	ⓓ
22.	ⓐ	ⓑ	ⓒ	ⓓ
23.	ⓐ	ⓑ	ⓒ	ⓓ
24.	ⓐ	ⓑ	ⓒ	ⓓ
25.	ⓐ	ⓑ	ⓒ	ⓓ

Subtest 6: Electronics Information (EI)

1.	ⓐ	ⓑ	ⓒ	ⓓ
2.	ⓐ	ⓑ	ⓒ	ⓓ
3.	ⓐ	ⓑ	ⓒ	ⓓ
4.	ⓐ	ⓑ	ⓒ	ⓓ
5.	ⓐ	ⓑ	ⓒ	ⓓ
6.	ⓐ	ⓑ	ⓒ	ⓓ
7.	ⓐ	ⓑ	ⓒ	ⓓ

8.	ⓐ	ⓑ	ⓒ	ⓓ
9.	ⓐ	ⓑ	ⓒ	ⓓ
10.	ⓐ	ⓑ	ⓒ	ⓓ
11.	ⓐ	ⓑ	ⓒ	ⓓ
12.	ⓐ	ⓑ	ⓒ	ⓓ
13.	ⓐ	ⓑ	ⓒ	ⓓ
14.	ⓐ	ⓑ	ⓒ	ⓓ

15.	ⓐ	ⓑ	ⓒ	ⓓ
16.	ⓐ	ⓑ	ⓒ	ⓓ
17.	ⓐ	ⓑ	ⓒ	ⓓ
18.	ⓐ	ⓑ	ⓒ	ⓓ
19.	ⓐ	ⓑ	ⓒ	ⓓ
20.	ⓐ	ⓑ	ⓒ	ⓓ

Subtest 7: Auto and Shop Information (AS)

1.	ⓐ	ⓑ	ⓒ	ⓓ
2.	ⓐ	ⓑ	ⓒ	ⓓ
3.	ⓐ	ⓑ	ⓒ	ⓓ
4.	ⓐ	ⓑ	ⓒ	ⓓ
5.	ⓐ	ⓑ	ⓒ	ⓓ
6.	ⓐ	ⓑ	ⓒ	ⓓ
7.	ⓐ	ⓑ	ⓒ	ⓓ
8.	ⓐ	ⓑ	ⓒ	ⓓ
9.	ⓐ	ⓑ	ⓒ	ⓓ

10.	ⓐ	ⓑ	ⓒ	ⓓ
11.	ⓐ	ⓑ	ⓒ	ⓓ
12.	ⓐ	ⓑ	ⓒ	ⓓ
13.	ⓐ	ⓑ	ⓒ	ⓓ
14.	ⓐ	ⓑ	ⓒ	ⓓ
15.	ⓐ	ⓑ	ⓒ	ⓓ
16.	ⓐ	ⓑ	ⓒ	ⓓ
17.	ⓐ	ⓑ	ⓒ	ⓓ

18.	ⓐ	ⓑ	ⓒ	ⓓ
19.	ⓐ	ⓑ	ⓒ	ⓓ
20.	ⓐ	ⓑ	ⓒ	ⓓ
21.	ⓐ	ⓑ	ⓒ	ⓓ
22.	ⓐ	ⓑ	ⓒ	ⓓ
23.	ⓐ	ⓑ	ⓒ	ⓓ
24.	ⓐ	ⓑ	ⓒ	ⓓ
25.	ⓐ	ⓑ	ⓒ	ⓓ

Subtest 8: Mechanical Comprehension (MC)

1.	ⓐ	ⓑ	ⓒ	ⓓ
2.	ⓐ	ⓑ	ⓒ	ⓓ
3.	ⓐ	ⓑ	ⓒ	ⓓ
4.	ⓐ	ⓑ	ⓒ	ⓓ
5.	ⓐ	ⓑ	ⓒ	ⓓ
6.	ⓐ	ⓑ	ⓒ	ⓓ
7.	ⓐ	ⓑ	ⓒ	ⓓ
8.	ⓐ	ⓑ	ⓒ	ⓓ
9.	ⓐ	ⓑ	ⓒ	ⓓ

10.	ⓐ	ⓑ	ⓒ	ⓓ
11.	ⓐ	ⓑ	ⓒ	ⓓ
12.	ⓐ	ⓑ	ⓒ	ⓓ
13.	ⓐ	ⓑ	ⓒ	ⓓ
14.	ⓐ	ⓑ	ⓒ	ⓓ
15.	ⓐ	ⓑ	ⓒ	ⓓ
16.	ⓐ	ⓑ	ⓒ	ⓓ
17.	ⓐ	ⓑ	ⓒ	ⓓ

18.	ⓐ	ⓑ	ⓒ	ⓓ
19.	ⓐ	ⓑ	ⓒ	ⓓ
20.	ⓐ	ⓑ	ⓒ	ⓓ
21.	ⓐ	ⓑ	ⓒ	ⓓ
22.	ⓐ	ⓑ	ⓒ	ⓓ
23.	ⓐ	ⓑ	ⓒ	ⓓ
24.	ⓐ	ⓑ	ⓒ	ⓓ
25.	ⓐ	ⓑ	ⓒ	ⓓ

Subtest 9: Assembling Objects (AO)

1.	ⓐ	ⓑ	ⓒ	ⓓ
2.	ⓐ	ⓑ	ⓒ	ⓓ
3.	ⓐ	ⓑ	ⓒ	ⓓ
4.	ⓐ	ⓑ	ⓒ	ⓓ
5.	ⓐ	ⓑ	ⓒ	ⓓ
6.	ⓐ	ⓑ	ⓒ	ⓓ
7.	ⓐ	ⓑ	ⓒ	ⓓ
8.	ⓐ	ⓑ	ⓒ	ⓓ
9.	ⓐ	ⓑ	ⓒ	ⓓ

10.	ⓐ	ⓑ	ⓒ	ⓓ
11.	ⓐ	ⓑ	ⓒ	ⓓ
12.	ⓐ	ⓑ	ⓒ	ⓓ
13.	ⓐ	ⓑ	ⓒ	ⓓ
14.	ⓐ	ⓑ	ⓒ	ⓓ
15.	ⓐ	ⓑ	ⓒ	ⓓ
16.	ⓐ	ⓑ	ⓒ	ⓓ
17.	ⓐ	ⓑ	ⓒ	ⓓ

18.	ⓐ	ⓑ	ⓒ	ⓓ
19.	ⓐ	ⓑ	ⓒ	ⓓ
20.	ⓐ	ⓑ	ⓒ	ⓓ
21.	ⓐ	ⓑ	ⓒ	ⓓ
22.	ⓐ	ⓑ	ⓒ	ⓓ
23.	ⓐ	ⓑ	ⓒ	ⓓ
24.	ⓐ	ⓑ	ⓒ	ⓓ
25.	ⓐ	ⓑ	ⓒ	ⓓ

Subtest 1: General Science

Questions: 25
Time: 11 minutes

1. Some of the world's land is unusable because it's desert, ice, or rock. Another fraction of the world's land is already used for crops and grazing. About how much, after accounting for these two categories, of the world's land could still be developed exclusively for human use?
   a. half
   b. a third
   c. one-eighth
   d. one-twentieth

2. Why might angiosperms recover faster than conifers from a devastating environmental phenomenon?
   a. Conifers require more sunlight.
   b. Angiosperms reproduce more quickly.
   c. Angiosperms depend on mammals to spread seeds.
   d. Conifers have tougher seeds.

3. Blood moving through the pulmonary vein is
   a. oxygenated.
   b. not oxygenated.
   c. mixed oxygenated and nonoxygenated blood.
   d. full of carbon dioxide.

4. The last column of the periodic table is the family of noble gases. Which of the following characteristics is NOT true?
   a. They have low boiling points.
   b. They are inert.
   c. They have full valence orbitals.
   d. They are highly reactive.

5. What do nuclear power plants do to control nuclear fission reactions to safely produce electricity?
   a. They use only small amounts of radioactive materials.
   b. Radioactive waste is securely contained.
   c. Materials are used to slow down the flow of neutrons.
   d. Fission reactors are located deep underground.

6. Which of the following is a mixture?
   a. sodium chloride
   b. rice and bean
   c. magnesium sulfate
   d. water

7. The specialized organ system that is responsible for filtering out impurities from the blood and excreting them is the
   a. renal system.
   b. respiratory system.
   c. circulatory system.
   d. endocrine system.

8. Mammalian mothers provide nutrients to the developing embryo through the
   a. fallopian tube.
   b. uterus.
   c. placenta.
   d. ovaries.

9. When light travels from a vacuum into air it is expected to undergo
   a. reflection.
   b. a change in wavelength.
   c. a change in frequency.
   d. refraction.

10. Nucleic acids are large molecules made up of smaller molecules called
   a. amino acids.
   b. nucleotides.
   c. lipids.
   d. carbohydrates.

11. The dinosaurs became extinct due to an impact from space
   a. 65 million years ago, which left a chemical imprint of radium.
   b. 65 million years ago, which left a chemical imprint of iridium.
   c. 540 million years ago, which left a chemical imprint of radium.
   d. 540 million years ago, which left a chemical imprint of iridium.

12. Which of the following atoms or ions is largest?
   a. Kr
   b. Br^-
   c. Ca^{2+}
   d. N^{2-}

13. All the following are forms of connective tissue *except*
   a. tendons.
   b. adipose.
   c. blood.
   d. nerves.

14. A sample of 7 g of CO_2 contains
   a. 0.75 g of carbon.
   b. 1.5 g of carbon.
   c. 3.0 g of carbon.
   d. 7.0 g of carbon.

15. What type of rock is expected to be found at a site of extreme pressure and temperature?
   a. igneous
   b. metamorphic
   c. stratified
   d. sedimentary

16. The population of species will continue to increase until it reaches the habitat's carrying capacity, which will limit the population. All the following are limiting factors of population in a habitat *except*
   a. limited water supply.
   b. excessive food supply.
   c. food web relationships.
   d. competition.

17. You find a unique species of ants living in tunnels formed by termites in a specific tree. The tree is lush and appears healthy. When you put your hand on the tree for a closer look, the ants race out of the tree to attack your hand. This is an example of
   a. predator-prey.
   b. parasitism.
   c. mutualism.
   d. commensalism.

18. Which is an example of an endothermic change?
   a. condensation
   b. combustion
   c. freezing
   d. sublimation

19. Sickle cell anemia is a recessive genetic disorder that decreases the amount of oxygen carried by red blood cells. Individuals have painful attacks and their life expectancy is shortened. Which of the following statements is true?
   a. Both parents must pass the defective allele to offspring with the disease.
   b. The allele should disappear from the gene pool in the future.
   c. One parent must show symptoms of the disorder.
   d. The mutation is not useful at all.

20. The isomers butane and isobutane are expected to have different properties *except* for which of the following?

   a. molecular weight

   b. freezing point

   c. vapor pressure

   d. shape

21. A cell experiences a genetic mutation and is unable to deliver the appropriate amino acids according to the genetic code. Which of the following is affected?

   a. DNA

   b. mRNA

   c. rRNA

   d. tRNA

22. How many grams of sugar are needed to make 500 mL of a 5% (weight/volume) solution of sugar?

   a. 20

   b. 25

   c. 50

   d. 10

23. Masses of ice, dust, and small rock particles orbiting the solar system and seen as patches of light with long tails are

   a. meteors.

   b. asteroids.

   c. meteor showers.

   d. comets.

24. Which of the following groups of organisms use flowers for reproduction?

   a. angiosperms

   b. gymnosperms

   c. mosses

   d. fungi

25. A gas that follows the ideal gas law is contained in a sealed piston at 25°C and 1 atm. What would you expect to happen if the temperature were increased to 35°C?

   a. The volume would decrease.

   b. The pressure would decrease.

   c. The volume and the pressure would decrease.

   d. The volume would increase.

Subtest 2: Arithmetic Reasoning

Questions: 30

Time: 36 minutes

1. In New York City, two out of every five people surveyed bicycle to work. Out of a population sample of 200,000 people, how many bicycle to work?

   a. 4,000

   b. 8,000

   c. 40,000

   d. 80,000

2. Serena has to choose between two jobs. One is at Books R Us and pays $18,000 with yearly raises of $800. The other, at Readers Galore, pays $16,400 per year with yearly raises of $1,200. In how many years will the two yearly salaries be equal?

   a. 6

   b. 5

   c. 4

   d. 3

Use the following pie chart to answer questions 3 through 5.

Ricardo's Budget
(cents per $1.00)

3. For which item does Ricardo spend half as much as he puts in his savings account?
   a. his car
   b. clothes
   c. housing
   d. food

4. For which two items does Ricardo spend 50% of each budgeted dollar?
   a. savings and housing
   b. clothes and housing
   c. car and medical
   d. medical and food

5. Last year, Ricardo made $46,500. About how much more did he spend on housing during the year than he put away in savings?
   a. $2,000
   b. $2,600
   c. $2,800
   d. $3,000

6. The number of red blood corpuscles in one cubic millimeter is about 5,000,000, and the number of white blood corpuscles in one cubic millimeter is about 8,000. What, then, is the ratio of white blood corpuscles to red blood corpuscles?
   a. 1:625
   b. 1:40
   c. 4:10
   d. 5:1,250

7. The living room in Donna's home is 182 square feet. How many square yards of carpet should she purchase to carpet the room?
   a. 9 square yards
   b. 1,638 square yards
   c. 61 square yards
   d. 21 square yards

8. During a basketball game, Jack has made 20 free-throw shots out of his 50 tries. How many of his next 25 free-throw attempts is Jack most likely to make?
   a. 5
   b. 10
   c. 15
   d. 20

9. Twelve people entered a room. Three more than two-thirds of these people then left. How many people remain in the room?
   a. 0
   b. 1
   c. 2
   d. 7

10. A map of Nevada has the following scale: 0.5 inches = 15 miles. Which expression tells the actual distance, *d*, between points that are 5.25 inches apart on the map?

a. $\frac{0.5}{15} = \frac{5.25}{d}$

b. $\frac{15}{0.5} = \frac{5.25}{d}$

c. $\frac{0.5}{d} = \frac{15}{5.25}$

d. $\frac{d}{2.5} = \frac{0.5}{15}$

11. The Cougars played three basketball games last week. Monday's game lasted 113.9 minutes, Wednesday's game lasted 106.7 minutes, and Friday's game lasted 122 minutes. What is the average time, in minutes, for the three games?

a. 77.6 minutes

b. 103.2 minutes

c. 114.2 minutes

d. 115.6 minutes

12. A helicopter flies over a river at 6:02 A.M. and arrives at a heliport 20 miles away at 6:17 A.M. How many miles per hour was the helicopter traveling?

a. 120 miles per hour

b. 300 miles per hour

c. 30 miles per hour

d. 80 miles per hour

13. How many minutes are there in 12 hours?

a. 24 minutes

b. 1,440 minutes

c. 720 minutes

d. 1,200 minutes

14. Five people in Sonja's office are planning a party. Sonja will buy a loaf of French bread ($3 per loaf) and a platter of cold cuts ($23). Barbara will buy the soda ($1 per person) and two boxes of crackers ($2 per box). Mario and Rick will split the cost of two packages of Cheese Doodles ($1 per package). Danica will supply a package of five paper plates ($4 per package). How much more will Sonja spend than the rest of the office put together?

a. $14

b. $13

c. $12

d. $11

15. Kathy charges $7.50 per hour to mow a lawn. Sharon charges 1.5 times as much to do the same job. How much does Sharon charge to mow a lawn?

a. $5 per hour

b. $11.25 per hour

c. $10 per hour

d. $9 per hour

16. The height of the Eiffel Tower is 986 feet. A replica of the tower made to scale is 4 inches tall. What is the scale of the replica to the real tower?

a. 1 to 246.5

b. 1 to 3,944

c. 246.5 to 1

d. 1 to 2,958

17. On Sundays, Mike gives half-hour drum lessons from 10:30 A.M. to 5:30 P.M. He takes a half-hour lunch break at noon. If Mike is paid $20 for each lesson, what is the total amount he makes on Sunday?

a. $260

b. $190

c. $170

d. $140

18. Driving 60 miles per hour, it takes one-half hour to drive to work. How much *additional* time will it take to drive to work if the speed is now 40 miles per hour?
a. 1 hour
b. 2 hours
c. 15 minutes
d. 30 minutes

19. An 8″ × 10″ photograph is blown up to a billboard size that is in proportion to the original photograph. If 8″ is considered the height of the photo, what would be the length of the billboard if its height is 5.6 feet?
a. 7 feet
b. 400 feet
c. 56 feet
d. 9 feet

20. Membership dues at Arnold's Gym are $53 per month this year, but were $50 per month last year. What was the percentage increase in the gym's prices?
a. 5.5%
b. 6.0%
c. 6.5%
d. 7.0%

21. Which of the following best represents the following statement? Patricia (P) has four times the number of marbles Sean (S) has.
a. $P = S + 4$
b. $S = P - 4$
c. $P = 4S$
d. $S = 4P$

22. A piggy bank contains $8.20 in coins. If there are an equal number of quarters, nickels, dimes, and pennies, how many of each denomination are there?
a. 10
b. 20
c. 30
d. 40

23. Two saline solutions are mixed. Twelve liters of 5% solution are mixed with four liters of 4% solution. What percent saline is the final solution?
a. 4.25%
b. 4.5%
c. 4.75%
d. 5%

24. A neighbor has three dogs. Fluffy is half the age of Muffy, who is one-third as old as Spot, who is half the neighbor's age, which is 24. How old is Fluffy?
a. 2
b. 4
c. 6
d. 12

25. Mario has finished 35 out of 45 of his test questions. Which of the following fractions of the test does he have left?
a. $\frac{2}{9}$
b. $\frac{7}{9}$
c. $\frac{4}{5}$
d. $\frac{3}{5}$

26. D'Andre rides the first half of a bike race in 2 hours. If his partner, Adam, rides the return trip 5 miles per hour less, and it takes him 3 hours, how fast was D'Andre traveling?
- **a.** 10 miles per hour
- **b.** 15 miles per hour
- **c.** 20 miles per hour
- **d.** 25 miles per hour

27. Kate earns $26,000 a year. If she receives a 4.5% salary increase, how much will she earn?
- **a.** $26,450
- **b.** $27,170
- **c.** $27,260
- **d.** $29,200

28. Rudy forgot to replace his gas cap the last time he filled his car with gas. The gas is evaporating out of his 14-gallon tank at a constant rate of $\frac{1}{3}$ gallon per day. How much gas does Rudy lose in one week?
- **a.** 2 gallons
- **b.** $2\frac{1}{3}$ gallons
- **c.** $4\frac{2}{3}$ gallons
- **d.** 6 gallons

29. Veronica took a trip to the lake. If she drove steadily for 5 hours traveling 220 miles, what was her average speed for the trip?
- **a.** 44 miles per hour
- **b.** 55 miles per hour
- **c.** 60 miles per hour
- **d.** 66 miles per hour

30. A rectangular tract of land measures 860 feet by 560 feet. Approximately how many acres is this? (*Note:* one acre = 43,560 square feet.)
- **a.** 12.8 acres
- **b.** 11.06 acres
- **c.** 10.5 acres
- **d.** 8.06 acres

Subtest 3: Word Knowledge
Questions: 35
Time: 11 minutes

1. *Lucid* most nearly means
- **a.** confusing.
- **b.** quick.
- **c.** understandable.
- **d.** slippery.

2. *Mourning* most nearly means
- **a.** early.
- **b.** sorrowing.
- **c.** celebration.
- **d.** night.

3. *Resolute* most nearly means
- **a.** yielding.
- **b.** agreeable.
- **c.** cowardly.
- **d.** determined.

4. *Ambivalent* most nearly means
- **a.** left-handed.
- **b.** right-handed.
- **c.** uncertain.
- **d.** energetic.

5. *Dissent* most nearly means
- **a.** fall.
- **b.** disagreement.
- **c.** honest.
- **d.** stop.

6. *Grave* most nearly means
- **a.** dead.
- **b.** serious.
- **c.** angry.
- **d.** excited.

7. *Hapless* most nearly means
   a. unlucky.
   b. careless.
   c. joyful.
   d. fortunate.

8. *Dreary* most nearly means
   a. dull.
   b. sleepy.
   c. interesting.
   d. awake.

9. *Arid* most nearly means
   a. big.
   b. lost.
   c. busy.
   d. dry.

10. *Deter* most nearly means
   a. shortcut.
   b. choose.
   c. discourage.
   d. clean.

11. *Covert* most nearly means
   a. altered.
   b. secret.
   c. obvious.
   d. missed.

12. *Allusion* most nearly means
   a. reference.
   b. mirage.
   c. escape.
   d. rhyme.

13. *Desist* most nearly means
   a. help.
   b. stop.
   c. want.
   d. chose.

14. *Pariah* most nearly means
   a. sage.
   b. fish.
   c. outcast.
   d. leader.

15. *Precede* most nearly means
   a. lead.
   b. follow.
   c. continue.
   d. profit.

16. *Forgive* most nearly means
   a. commute.
   b. remember.
   c. pardon.
   d. skip.

17. *Potent* most nearly means
   a. ominous.
   b. uniform.
   c. secretive.
   d. powerful.

18. *Succinct* most nearly means
   a. heavy.
   b. tasteful.
   c. clever.
   d. concise.

19. *Console* most nearly means
   a. ask.
   b. comfort.
   c. associate.
   d. worry.

20. *Surmise* most nearly means
   a. complete.
   b. shock.
   c. guess.
   d. fill.

For questions 21 through 35, choose the answer that is closest in meaning to the italicized word.

21. Certain predators *mimic* a harmless species, allowing them to avoid detection by their prey.
   a. intimate
   b. intimidate
   c. imitate
   d. interpret

22. Sleeping during class is *tantamount* to being absent; you might as well not come at all.
   a. equal
   b. encouraged
   c. unlike
   d. preferable

23. Without a goal in mind, Greg wandered *aimlessly* through the woods.
   a. purposefully
   b. nervously
   c. quickly
   d. randomly

24. Surprisingly, the very *meticulous* writer made many typos on her latest manuscript.
   a. careless
   b. fast
   c. intelligent
   d. thorough

25. It is *imperative* that you finish the reports this morning; they are due at the end of the day!
   a. optional
   b. acceptable
   c. crucial
   d. encouraged

26. Because he got no sleep the night before, the boy was so *lethargic* that he did not get up from the couch all day.
   a. exhausted
   b. hurt
   c. awake
   d. frightened

27. The *overbearing* supervisor would not approve anyone's ideas except his own.
   a. friendly
   b. arrogant
   c. busy
   d. judicious

28. Do not *deviate* from the instructions; just one small error will ruin the project!
   a. follow
   b. stray
   c. undervalue
   d. read

29. Burnett was scared and *anxious* about meeting new people on her first day at school.
   a. confident
   b. relaxed
   c. nervous
   d. bored

30. The gopher was a *menace* on the golf course; it kept ruining the carefully mowed grass.
   a. asset
   b. nuisance
   c. pet
   d. rival

31. The speaker was so *riveting* that no one in the audience got up from his or her seat during the presentation.
   a. boring
   b. short
   c. long
   d. fascinating

32. The notes on the document were *incomprehensible*; no one could read them.
- **a.** illegible
- **b.** numerous
- **c.** sparse
- **d.** tiny

33. The *callow* intern made many mistakes at his first job.
- **a.** experienced
- **b.** inexperienced
- **c.** friendly
- **d.** intelligent

34. Don't bother me with small, *trivial* details; we have more important things to think about!
- **a.** essential
- **b.** specific
- **c.** petty
- **d.** general

35. After being pestered for weeks, the boy's parents finally *acceded* to his requests and bought him a puppy.
- **a.** disagreed
- **b.** agreed
- **c.** asked
- **d.** stopped

Subtest 4:
Paragraph Comprehension
Questions: 15
Time: 13 minutes

The taxpayers' association rose up in protest at the town meeting when it was announced that the school budget would be increased by 50% over the next year. "We will no longer tolerate wasting money on swimming pools and skating rinks," stated Bob Smith. "It is time for this council to be held accountable for proper use of the taxpayers' money."

Other members of the taxpayers' association stated that they intend to run for town council in the coming election in order to remove members of the board who have *persistently* raised taxes over the last three fiscal years.

1. Why was the taxpayers' association upset at the recent town meeting?
- **a.** They had not been allowed to speak.
- **b.** Taxes keep going up.
- **c.** The town council had not fulfilled the school budget.
- **d.** Students were learning to skate instead of studying.

2. As used in the passage, *persistently* most nearly means
- **a.** ongoing.
- **b.** increasingly.
- **c.** overused.
- **d.** ended.

3. Bob Smith complained about swimming pools and skating rinks because
- **a.** he is not athletic.
- **b.** he was concerned about the environment.
- **c.** he felt that such things are a waste of taxpayers' money.
- **d.** he was at the wrong meeting.

4. One of the solutions offered by the taxpayers' association was
- **a.** to drain the swimming pool.
- **b.** to close the local schools.
- **c.** to pass a bill lowering taxes.
- **d.** to run for town council and replace the existing members.

Recent flooding in the county has caused a shortage of sump pumps, vacuum cleaners, and other cleanup utilities. Recently, one hardware store resorted to handing out numbered tickets to customers, because they had a limited number of pumps on hand and wanted to ensure that each customer purchased only one on a first-come, first-served basis. This led to resentment on the part of those who had stood in the rain, waiting for an hour to get inside, only to discover that they had to take a numbered ticket and come back the next day when another shipment of pumps would arrive.

These hardships, however, were small compared to the suffering of many residents. Hundreds of houses were *deluged* with the rising waters, and residents were forced to flee their homes in boats. The anger of those who were forced to take numbered tickets seemed childish in the eyes of those people whose homes were destroyed.

5. Why did the hardware store hand out numbered tickets to people buying pumps?
  a. They were holding a raffle for free sump pumps.
  b. They did not have enough pumps to sell more than one to a customer.
  c. The customers were getting angry.
  d. Ownership of sump pumps is regulated by law.

6. As used in the passage, *deluge* most nearly means
  a. strong winds.
  b. a new law.
  c. a flood.
  d. cold weather.

7. What is the main idea of this passage?
  a. There is always someone who is suffering more than you are.
  b. The area should have been declared a national disaster zone.
  c. The hardware store owners were heartless people.
  d. Raffle tickets should be outlawed.

8. Why does the author describe the hardware store customers as childish?
  a. They were playing games while waiting to get inside.
  b. The hardware store owners were their parents.
  c. They were angry about a small problem.
  d. They were being irresponsible by not helping their neighbors.

Light pollution is a growing problem worldwide. Like other forms of pollution, light pollution degrades the quality of the environment. Where it was once possible to look up at the night sky and see thousands of twinkling stars in the inky blackness, one now sees little more than the yellow glare of urban sky. When we lose the ability to connect visually with the vastness of the universe by looking up at the night sky, we lose our connection with something profoundly important to the human spirit, our sense of wonder.

9. The passage implies that the most serious damage done by light pollution is to our
  a. artistic appreciation.
  b. sense of physical well-being.
  c. cultural advancement.
  d. spiritual selves.

10. According to the passage, which of the following is important to the human spirit?
   a. a clean environment
   b. our sense of wonder
   c. dark skies
   d. looking at the stars

George walked out of his boss's office in anger after being *reprimanded* for his *slovenly* appearance. "I dress as well as anyone else," he fumed. "I think the boss is just singling me out." Two days later, George resigned from his job and went to work at the competitor's company for a smaller salary.

11. Which of the following was probably the reason that George left his job?
   a. He was angry at his boss.
   b. The new job was closer to home.
   c. He was bored with his old job.
   d. The new job paid more than the old job.

12. As used in the passage, *reprimanded* most nearly means
   a. fired.
   b. demoted.
   c. scolded.
   d. given an award.

13. George got into trouble at work because
   a. he was a careless employee.
   b. he did not dress properly.
   c. he wanted more money.
   d. the boss did not like him.

14. As used in the passage, *slovenly* most nearly means
   a. lazy.
   b. tardy.
   c. heavenly.
   d. sloppy.

When writing business letters or memos, it is not practical to be personal. The first-person point of view may make the reader feel close to the writer, but it also implies a certain subjectivity. That is, the writer is expressing a personal view from a personal perspective.

15. This paragraph best supports the statement that
   a. writing a first-person business correspondence will prevent the writer from getting promoted.
   b. effective business writing is one of the most important skills to have in an office environment.
   c. using the first-person point of view in business correspondence is not a wise choice.
   d. the first-person point of view expresses a personal view and a personal perspective.

Subtest 5: Math Knowledge

Questions: 25
Time: 24 minutes

1. Which of the following has the greatest value?
   a. $\frac{7}{8}$
   b. $\frac{3}{4}$
   c. $\frac{2}{3}$
   d. $\frac{5}{6}$

2. Factor the expression completely: $x^2 - 25$.
   a. $x(x - 25)$
   b. $(x + 5)(x - 5)$
   c. $(x + 5)(x + 5)$
   d. $(x - 5)(x - 5)$

3. Solve the equation for b: $\sqrt{b-4} = 5$.
  a. 1
  b. 9
  c. 21
  d. 29

4. If one angle of a triangle measures 42° and the second measures 59°, what does the third angle measure?
  a. 101°
  b. 89°
  c. 90°
  d. 79°

5. What is the perimeter of the figure below?

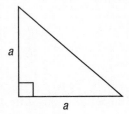

  a. $a^2 \div 2$
  b. $2a + 2a^2$
  c. $2a + \sqrt{2a^2}$
  d. $4a$

6. The area of a right triangle is 60 square centimeters. The height is 15 centimeters. How many centimeters is the base?
  a. 8 centimeters
  b. 4 centimeters
  c. 6 centimeters
  d. 12 centimeters

7. Which of the following number statements is true?
  a. 4 feet > 3 feet
  b. 7 feet < 6 feet
  c. 5 feet > 6 feet
  d. 3 feet < 2 feet

8. Choose the answer to the following problem:
$10^5 \div 10^2 =$
  a. 1^3
  b. 10^3
  c. 10^7
  d. 10^{10}

9. Which of the following is the equivalent of $\frac{18}{45}$?
  a. 0.45
  b. 0.5
  c. 0.42
  d. 0.4

10. One side of a rectangle measures 834 centimeters and another side measures 1,288 centimeters. What is the perimeter of the rectangle?
  a. 2,148,384 square feet
  b. 1,074,192 square feet
  c. 4,244 feet
  d. 2,122 feet

11. How many minutes are in $7\frac{1}{6}$ hours?
  a. 258 minutes
  b. 430 minutes
  c. 2,580 minutes
  d. 4,300 minutes

12. What is the area of a circle that has a diameter of 94 centimeters?
  a. 188π square centimeters
  b. 47π square centimeters
  c. 94π square centimeters
  d. 2,209π square centimeters

13. How does the area of a rectangle change if the base and the height of the original rectangle are tripled?
  a. The area is tripled.
  b. The area is 6 times as large.
  c. The area is 9 times as large.
  d. The area remains the same.

14. Plattville is 80 miles west and 60 miles north of Quincy. How long is a direct route from Plattville to Quincy?
a. 100 miles
b. 110 miles
c. 120 miles
d. 140 miles

15. Which of the following numbers is divisible by 6?
a. 232
b. 341
c. 546
d. 903

16. A triangle has two congruent sides, and the measure of one angle is 40°. Which of the following types of triangles is it?
a. isosceles
b. equilateral
c. right
d. scalene

17. Multiply the binomials: $(3x + 4)(x - 6)$.
a. $3x^2 - 22x - 24$
b. $3x^2 + 14x - 24$
c. $3x^2 - 14x - 24$
d. $3x^2 + 14x + 24$

18. An acute angle is
a. 180°.
b. greater than 90°.
c. 90°.
d. less than 90°.

19. Choose the answer to the following problem:
$| 4 - 15 | =$
a. −11
b. 11
c. −19
d. 19

20. Which of the following is equivalent to $2\sqrt{6}$?
a. $\sqrt{24}$
b. $6\sqrt{2}$
c. $12\sqrt{2}$
d. $\sqrt{12}$

21. Which of the following answer choices is equivalent to 10^4?
a. $10 \times 10 \times 10 \times 10$
b. 10×4
c. $(10 + 4) \times 10$
d. $10 + 4$

22. 56.73647 rounded to the nearest hundredth is equal to
a. 100
b. 57
c. 56.7
d. 56.74

23. In the following decimal, which digit is in the hundredths place: 0.2153
a. 2
b. 1
c. 5
d. 3

24. Solve for all values of x in the equation: $x^2 - 25 = 0$.
a. 5
b. 0, 5
c. −5
d. 5, −5

25. How many $5\frac{1}{4}$-ounce glasses can be completely filled from a $33\frac{1}{2}$-ounce container of juice?
a. 4
b. 5
c. 6
d. 7

Subtest 6: Electronics Information

Questions: 20
Time: 9 minutes

1. In which of the following is a quartz crystal most likely to be found?
   a. a transformer
   b. a capacitor
   c. a battery
   d. an oscillator

2. What type of voltage is available from a typical domestic wall outlet?
   a. DC
   b. AC
   c. static
   d. dynamic

3. Which of the following has the longest wavelength?
   a. ultraviolet waves
   b. radio waves
   c. x-rays
   d. microwaves

4. What is needed to convert 120 volts to 12 volts?
   a. a step-down transformer
   b. a step-up transformer
   c. a rectifier
   d. a diode reduction device

5. What does the following schematic symbol represent?

   a. a battery
   b. a circuit breaker
   c. a fuse
   d. a headphone

6. One coulomb per second is equal to one
   a. ampere.
   b. volt.
   c. watt.
   d. decibel.

7. Which of the following devices would be affected by a diode?
   a. amplifier
   b. capacitor
   c. filter
   d. rectifier

8. A photovoltaic cell produces
   a. direct current.
   b. alternating current.
   c. square wave current.
   d. All of the above.

9. Which symbol represents a wattmeter?
   a.

   b.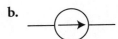

   c.

   d.

10. *Low potential*, for electricians, most closely means
    a. 600 watts or lower.
    b. circuits that have low chance of overload.
    c. a low risk of fire.
    d. a low cost of wiring.

11. The frequency of a signal is *inversely* proportional to which of the following?
- **a.** power
- **b.** phase
- **c.** amplitude
- **d.** period

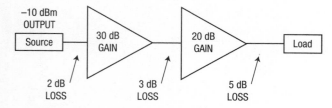

12. What would the expected power level be at the input to the receiver?
- **a.** 20 dBm
- **b.** 30 dBm
- **c.** 40 dBm
- **d.** 50 dBm

13. A capacitor's storage potential, or capacitance, is measured in
- **a.** coulombs.
- **b.** decibels.
- **c.** Fahrenheit.
- **d.** farads.

14. What is true of a random access memory (RAM) electronic chip?
- **a.** Its contents are erased when power is turned off.
- **b.** Its contents are saved when power is turned off.
- **c.** It is no different from a read-only-memory (ROM) chip.
- **d.** All the above.

15. Electrons have a _____ charge while protons have a _____ charge.
- **a.** neutral, positive
- **b.** negative, neutral
- **c.** positive, negative
- **d.** negative, positive

16. If you have a 10-ohm resistor and a 55-ohm resistor in series, what is the total resistance?
- **a.** 15 ohms
- **b.** 35 ohms
- **c.** 65 ohms
- **d.** 110 ohms

17. Amplification factor is typically stated in
- **a.** volts.
- **b.** watts.
- **c.** hertz.
- **d.** decibels.

18. An ammeter reads 287 microamps. Which of the following is equivalent to the meter reading?
- **a.** 0.00287 A
- **b.** 0.287 A
- **c.** 0.0287 A
- **d.** 0.000287 A

19. What is the minimum gauge of wire that must be used for a piece of equipment that draws 55 amps?
- **a.** #14
- **b.** #10
- **c.** #8
- **d.** #4

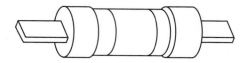

20. What would be the rated amps for the fuse shown here?
- **a.** 20
- **b.** 40
- **c.** 60
- **d.** unknown

Subtest 7: Auto and Shop Information

Questions: 25
Time: 11 minutes

1. Using only water in an automobile's cooling system can result in
   a. engine parts rusting.
   b. the water boiling away.
   c. the water freezing during winter.
   d. All of the above.

2. Which of the following systems connects directly to the internal combustion engine in an automobile?
   a. the suspension system
   b. the braking system
   c. the oil system
   d. the electrical system

3. Of which automotive system does the driver have the most direct control while driving?
   a. the emissions system
   b. the steering system
   c. the fuel system
   d. the drive train

4. A knock or ping sound when accelerating typically indicates
   a. the suspension needs adjusting.
   b. the tires need rotating.
   c. the fuel-air mixture is igniting too soon inside the engine cylinders.
   d. the ignition timing sequence needs adjusting.

5. Solving the knock or ping sound heard when accelerating usually entails
   a. using a higher octane gasoline.
   b. changing the spark plugs.
   c. changing the timing sequence.
   d. All of the above.

6. If you press down on your brake pedal and the reaction feels spongy, what could be the problem?
   a. misaligned brake pads
   b. an overfilled master cylinder
   c. air in the hydraulic system
   d. water in the hydraulic system

7. Engine oil SAE numbers measure
   a. flash point of the oil.
   b. oil viscosity.
   c. chemical composition.
   d. None of the above.

8. Tires on a typical car will generally last how long?
   a. 10,000 to 30,000 miles
   b. 15,000 to 25,000 miles
   c. 30,000 to 80,000 miles
   d. 100,000 miles and up

9. Looking at what on a tire will give you an indication of when it should be replaced?
   a. the valve stem
   b. the sidewalls
   c. the steel-belted radials
   d. the wear bars

10. A squealing noise from your engine as you accelerate usually indicates
    a. problems with the steering gearbox.
    b. worn tires.
    c. a worn or loose fan belt.
    d. All of the above.

11. A spark plug that is not firing will usually result in
    a. the environmental control system not operating properly.
    b. a higher rate of gasoline consumption.
    c. an engine not starting.
    d. an engine running rough.

12. Before an oil change, the engine should be
   a. off for at least one hour to let the oil settle.
   b. at minimum rpm.
   c. running at idle.
   d. run for at least 10 minutes to warm the oil up, increasing viscosity.

13. When making a circular cut in a piece of metal, the best chisel to use is a
   a. butt chisel.
   b. round chisel.
   c. framing chisel.
   d. socket chisel.

14. If you want to thin paint, which of the following should be used?
   a. varnish
   b. turpentine
   c. mineral spirits
   d. benzene

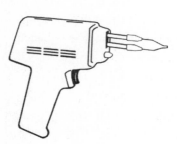

15. The tool shown here is used to
   a. drive screws.
   b. drill holes.
   c. melt solder.
   d. melt glue.

16. What would be the strongest material to use when building a permanent building foundation?
   a. wood timbers
   b. concrete
   c. cinder blocks
   d. brick and mortar

17. A Forstner bit is characterized by
   a. its quick release mechanism.
   b. its wide circular cutting edge with a spur in the middle of the drill.
   c. its extended length to drill through multiple pieces of lumber.
   d. None of the above.

18. Which of the following is the small thin nail with a small head often used in picture frames and light assembly?
   a. the spiral
   b. the tack
   c. the brad
   d. the sinker

19. A torque wrench is used to
   a. maximize the leverage needed to overcome resistance.
   b. tighten bolts to a specific tightness.
   c. apply the maximum amount of torque allowed to a bolt.
   d. None of the above.

20. Which of the following is not considered a carpenter's hand tool?
   a. a hammer
   b. a coping saw
   c. a table saw
   d. a wood chisel

21. The best tool to use to dig a small, circular hole a foot or two deep would be a
   a. posthole digger.
   b. shovel.
   c. backhoe.
   d. garden trowel.

22. The word *kerf* describes
   a. the length of a saw cut.
   b. the depth of a saw cut.
   c. the width of the saw cut.
   d. None of the above.

23. Which of the following tools are most likely to be used together?

   a. a lathe and a claw hammer

   b. an electric winch and a center punch

   c. a ball-peen hammer and a Phillips-head screwdriver

   d. a table saw and a fence guide

24. What is the tool shown here?

   a. an open-end wrench

   b. a rivet tool.

   c. a pair of pliers

   d. a bolt cutter

25. What is the abrasive material used on most sandpapers?

   a. pumice

   b. aluminum oxide

   c. emery

   d. None of the above.

Subtest 8:
Mechanical Comprehension
Questions: 25
Time: 19 minutes

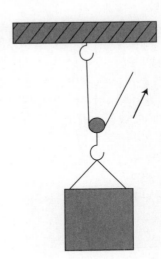

1. A 250-pound weight is being lifted using the pulley system shown here. How much force is necessary to lift the weight?

   a. 50 pounds

   b. 100 pounds

   c. 125 pounds

   d. 250 pounds

2. When a mercury thermometer is placed in hot liquid, mercury will travel up the thermometer to provide an accurate temperature reading. Why does mercury rise in a thermometer when it is exposed to heat?

   a. Heat causes mercury to expand.

   b. Mercury is repelled by heat.

   c. Heat causes mercury to contract.

   d. Air bubbles push mercury up the thermometer.

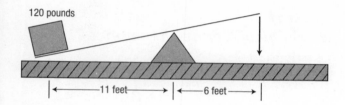

3. In this diagram, Holly wants to lift a 120-pound block using a lever. If the block is 11 feet from the pivot point and Holly is 6 feet from the pivot point, how much force must she apply to lift the block?
- **a.** 220 pounds
- **b.** 66 pounds
- **c.** 120 pounds
- **d.** 720 pounds

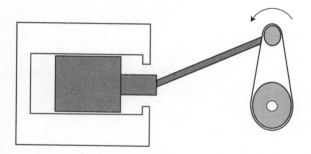

4. The vertical motion of a piston is transferred to rotational motion at the crank. Based on this figure, what description best describes the position and direction of the piston when the crank arm is pointing downward?
- **a.** far left and stationary
- **b.** in the center and moving to the left
- **c.** in the center and moving to the right
- **d.** far right and stationary

5. Ian goes on a trail run and covers 12 miles in 1.5 hours. How fast was Ian running?
- **a.** 6 mph
- **b.** 8 mph
- **c.** 10 mph
- **d.** 18 mph

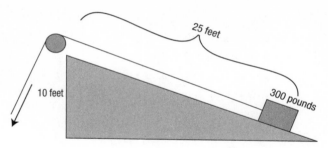

6. A 300-pound block is being pulled up an incline by a pulley. The incline is 25 feet long and rises 10 feet. Neglecting friction, how much force is necessary to move the block up the incline shown here?
- **a.** 120 pounds
- **b.** 250 pounds
- **c.** 300 pounds
- **d.** 35 pounds

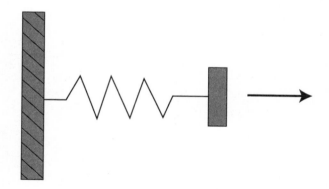

7. A force of 10 pounds is required to move a spring 8 inches. How far will the spring shown here stretch under 15 pounds of force?
- **a.** 12 inches
- **b.** 14 inches
- **c.** 16 inches
- **d.** 18 inches

8. If 18 full turns are required to move a nut 1.2 inches, how many threads per inch does the screw have?
- **a.** 10
- **b.** 12
- **c.** 15
- **d.** 20

9. Using a lever, a man is able to lift a 120-pound load with only 40 pounds of force. What is the mechanical advantage of the lever?
   a. $\frac{1}{3}$
   b. 3
   c. 20
   d. 80

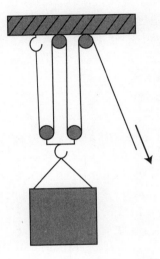

10. How much force is required to lift a 300-pound weight using the pulley system shown here?
   a. 75 pounds
   b. 100 pounds
   c. 150 pounds
   d. 900 pounds

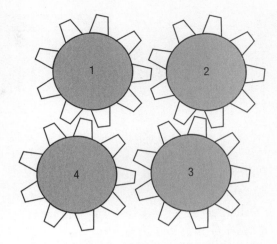

11. If gear 1 turns clockwise, which other gears, if any, will also turn clockwise?
   a. 2 only
   b. 3 only
   c. 2 and 4
   d. None

12. When a submarine dives, it fills its ballast tanks with water, causing all the following *except*
   a. the density of the submarine to increase.
   b. the buoyancy of the submarine to decrease.
   c. the weight of the submarine to increase.
   d. the volume of the submarine to increase.

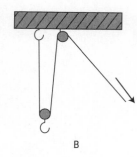

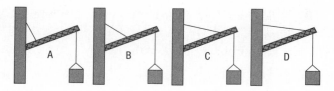

13. Pulley system A offers no mechanical advantage, whereas pulley system B has a mechanical advantage of 2. In pulley system A, if the rope is pulled 10 feet, the hook will rise 10 feet. How many feet of rope must be pulled to raise the hook in pulley system B by 10 feet?
a. 5 feet
b. 10 feet
c. 15 feet
d. 20 feet

15. The cable supporting the arm of this crane is shown attached to the arm in four different positions. In which position is the cable strained the most?
a. cable A
b. cable B
c. cable C
d. cable D

16. A steel block has a density of 0.3 pounds per cubic inch. Its dimensions are $2'' \times 2'' \times 5''$. What is the weight of the block?
a. 6 pounds
b. 10 pounds
c. 20 pounds
d. 27 pounds

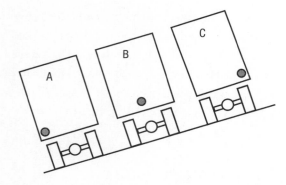

14. Three trucks are parked on an incline. Their centers of gravity are marked by dots. Which of these trucks is most likely to tip over?
a. truck A
b. truck B
c. truck C
d. All trucks are stable.

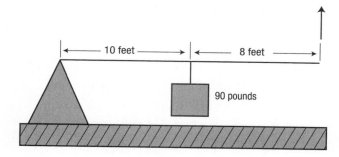

17. In this diagram, Talia wants to lift a 90-pound block using a lever. If the block is 10 feet from the pivot point and Talia is 8 feet beyond that, how much force must she apply to lift the block?
a. 45 pounds
b. 80 pounds
c. 90 pounds
d. 50 pounds

18. Which material is best suited for building a raft?

   a. metal

   b. wood

   c. glass

   d. concrete

19. A single-speed bicycle has a front chain ring with 48 teeth and a back gear with 12 teeth. If the bicycle is pedaled at 90 rpm, how fast will the rear wheel turn?

   a. 15 rpm

   b. 90 rpm

   c. 180 rpm

   d. 360 rpm

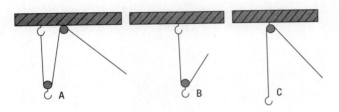

20. Which of the following pulley systems offers the least mechanical advantage?

   a. A

   b. B

   c. C

   d. They all offer the same advantage.

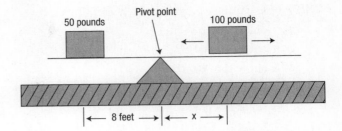

21. In this diagram, two blocks are balanced on either side of a lever. One block weighs 50 pounds and the other weighs 100 pounds. If the 50-pound block is 8 feet to the left of the pivot point, how far to the right of the pivot point is the 100 pound block?

   a. 2 feet

   b. 4 feet

   c. 8 feet

   d. 16 feet

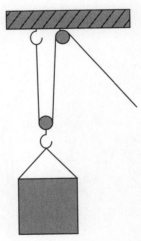

22. What is the mechanical advantage of the pulley system shown here?

   a. 1

   b. 2

   c. 3

   d. 4

23. Which of the following is heaviest?
  a. 1 cubic foot of water
  b. 1 cubic foot of lead
  c. 1 cubic foot of wood
  d. 1 cubic foot of ice

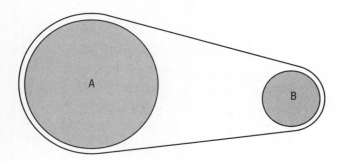

24. Pulley A has 2.5 times the circumference of pulley B. If pulley A rotates at 50 revolutions per minute (rpm), how fast must pulley B rotate?
  a. 20 rpm
  b. 50 rpm
  c. 125 rpm
  d. 250 rpm

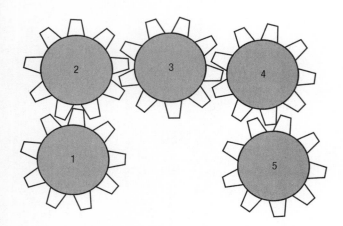

25. If gear 3 turns counterclockwise, which other gear(s), if any, will turn clockwise?
  a. 1 and 5
  b. 2 and 4
  c. All will turn clockwise.
  d. None will turn clockwise.

Subtest 9: Assembling Objects

Directions: Each question is composed of five separate drawings. The problem is presented in the first drawing, and the remaining four drawings are possible solutions. Determine which of the four choices contains all of the pieces assembled properly that are shown in the first picture. Note: images are not drawn to scale.

Questions: 25
Time: 15 minutes

1.

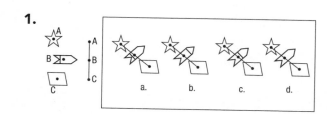

2.

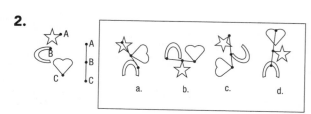

3.

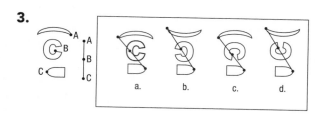

4.

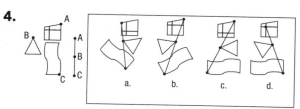

5.

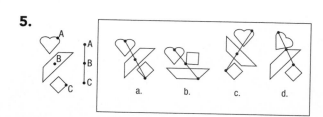

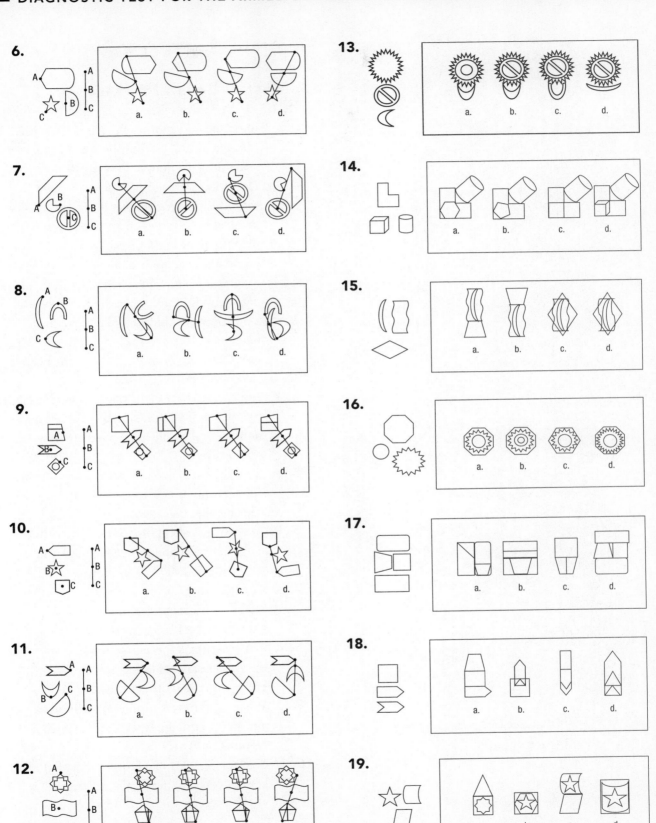

20.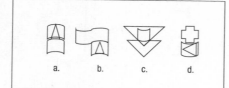

21.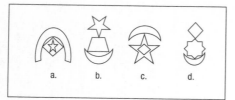

22.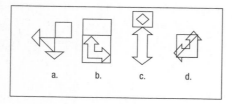

23.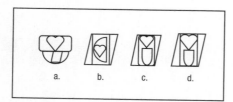

24.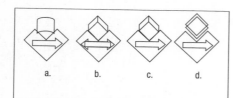

25.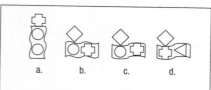

Answer Key

Subtest 1: General Science

1. b. About a third of the world's land is unusable and another third is already used for agriculture, leaving about a third remaining for human development.

2. b. Flowering plants (angiosperms) might reproduce faster because their reproduction involves flowers, which attract insects to help pollinate and other animals to spread seeds. Also, the seeds of angiosperms have a tough skin, which may help them tolerate harsh conditions.

3. a. Veins transport blood to the heart and *pulmonary* refers to the lungs. Therefore, the blood coming from the lungs to the heart is full of oxygen.

4. d. Noble gases have eight valence electrons and full orbital shells, making them stable and nonreactive. Noble gases have very low boiling points.

5. c. Materials such as water are used to slow the acceleration of neutrons, which prevents the uncontrolled release of energy.

6. b. A mixture is a combination of two or more components that do not change chemically. Choices **a** and **c** are compounds.

7. a. The renal system, also called the excretory system, consists of the kidneys and excretory accessory organs.

8. c. The placenta is specialized tissue that provides nutrients to the developing embryo in the mother's uterus.

9. d. When light moves from one medium to another it undergoes refraction, which is the bending of light.

10. b. Nucleotides are linked together according to genetic code and form nucleic acids.

11. b. Iridium is a rare element that occurs at high concentrations in meteorites. There is evidence of a huge impact on Earth 65 million years ago, which left high concentrations of iridium.

12. b. Generally, atomic radii increase when moving from left to right in the periodic table. Anions are much larger than their corresponding atoms and cations are much smaller than their corresponding atoms. In the case of Br^-, it accepts another electron, but does not change its number of protons. As a result, Br^- has a lesser pull on the electrons than Kr does, which has 8 protons and 8 electrons.

13. d. Nerves are composed of nervous tissue, which would exclude it from the category of connective tissue.

14. c. The molecular mass of carbon (C) is 12 g and the molecular mass of oxygen (O) is 8 g. Therefore, the molecular mass of carbon dioxide (CO_2) is 28 g. With 7 g of CO_2 there is $\frac{1}{4}$ mole, equivalent to 3.0 g carbon. $\frac{1}{4}$ mole $CO_2 \times \frac{mol\ C}{mol\ CO_2} \times \frac{12\ g}{mol\ C} = 3.0$ g.

15. b. Metamorphic rock is formed from other rock types at extreme temperature and pressure.

16. b. With an excessive food supply, animals would not have to compete with other animals, and their population would probably continue growing. All the other choices would limit the growth rate of a population.

17. c. The ants seem to have driven away the termites that would have eventually killed the tree. The ants that now have found a home in the tunnels protect the tree from intruders, allowing it to grow and remain healthy. This is an example of mutualism, because both species (tree and ant) benefit each other.

18. d. Endothermic reactions require an intake of energy or heat for the reactions to progress forward. Sublimation is the change of state from solid to gas, which requires energy. The other choices give off heat or energy, which is exothermic.

19. a. Because this is a recessive trait, to present the disorder an individual must be homozygous recessive for the disease. Even with a shortened life expectancy, the gene is not expected to leave the gene pool, eliminating choice **b**. Choice **c** is not true, because a parent carrying one recessive gene will not show symptoms. Choice **d** is not true, because carriers are resistant to malaria, which is extremely useful in parts of the world where malaria is a risk.

20. a. Structural isomers are molecules with the same molecular formula but different structures. The different structures result in different properties for the compounds. Isomers are very common in organic molecules.

21. d. Transfer RNA (tRNA) is responsible for delivering amino acids to the ribosome according to the sequence on mRNA. If the mutation affects tRNA, its anticodons may not be able to read the sequence of codons or it may not be able to attach to the appropriate amino acid.

22. b. Enough sugar needs to be added to 500 mL so that the ratio of the weight to volume is 5%, $5\% = \frac{1}{20} = \frac{?\ g\ sugar}{500\ mL} = 25$ g.

23. d. Comets are loose collections of ice, dust, and small rock particles that regularly orbit the solar system. They are seen from Earth as patches of light with long tails.

24. a. Angiosperms use flowers for reproduction.

25. d. According to the ideal gas law, temperature is directly proportional to pressure and volume. Because the piston is sealed, the moles of the gas cannot change. Therefore, the only possibility is for volume to increase.

Subtest 2: Arithmetic Reasoning

1. d. You are looking for n, and $\frac{n}{200,000} = \frac{2}{5}$ or $n = \frac{2}{5} \times 200,000$. $\frac{2}{5}$ of the 200,000 sample population bicycle to work. $\frac{2}{5} \times 200,000 = 80,000$.

2. c. Each job will pay $21,200 after 4 years. You can see this by making a chart:

	1	2	3	4
Books R Us	$18,800	$19,600	$20,400	$21,200
Readers Galore	$17,600	$18,800	$20,000	$21,200

3. a. Ricardo spends 11% for his car, half of the 22% he saves. (You can use % for the pie chart values without doing any additional math, since the values are already out of 100.)

4. a. Savings and housing together make up 50% of Ricardo's budget: 22% + 28%.

5. c. Ricardo spent 6 cents more per dollar on housing than on food: 28 − 22 = 6. Six cents is 6% of each budgeted dollar. $46,500 × 0.06 = $2,790, which is about $2,800.

6. a. The unreduced ratio is 8,000:5,000,000; reduced, the ratio is 8:5,000. Now divide: 5,000 ÷ 8 = 625, for a ratio of 1:625.

7. d. It takes 9 square feet to make a square yard. To find out how many square yards are in 182 square feet, divide: $182 \text{ ft.}^2 \div 9 \frac{\text{ft.}^2}{\text{yd.}^2} = 20.22$ square yards. Since Donna cannot purchase part of a square yard, she has to round up. She must purchase 21 square yards to have enough to carpet the room.

8. b. Jack is likely to make $\frac{2}{5} \times 25 = 10$ of his next 25 free-throw attempts.

9. b. Let x equal the number of people remaining in the room. You have: $x = 12 - (\frac{2}{3}(12) + 3)$ or $x = 12 - (8 + 3) = 12 - 11$. Thus, $x = 1$ person.

10. a. $\frac{0.5}{15} = \frac{5.25}{d}$, or map distance in inches/actual distance in miles.

11. c. This is a two-step problem involving both addition and division. First, arrange the three numbers in a column, keeping the decimal points aligned. Add: 113.9 + 106.7 + 122 = 342.6. Next, divide your answer by 3: 342.6 ÷ 3 = 114.2.

12. d. You want to know R = helicopter's speed in miles per hour. To solve this problem, recall that $rate \times time = distance$. It is given that $T = 6{:}17 - 6{:}02 = 15$ minutes = 0.25 hour and $D = 20$ miles. Substitute: $r \times 0.25 = 20$. Simplify: $r = 20 \div 0.25$. Thus, $r = 80$ miles per hour.

13. c. Multiply the number of minutes in an hour by the given number of hours. There are 60 minutes in each hour. Therefore, there are 720 minutes in 12 hours: 12 hours × 60 minutes = 720 minutes.

14. d. Figure the amounts by setting up the following equations: First, S = $3 + $23 = $26. Now, B = ($1 × 5) + ($2 × 2) or $5 + $4 = $9. MR = $1 × 2 = $2; and D = $4 × 1 = $4. Now, add: $9 + $2 + $4 = $15. Now subtract: $26 − $15 = $11.

15. b. You want to find S, the rate Sharon charges to mow a lawn in dollars per hour. You are given Kathy's rate, which is K = 7.50, and you are told that S = 1.5K. Substitute: S = 1.5(7.50). Thus, S = $11.25 per hour.

16. d. A scale is a ratio of model to real, keeping the units consistent. The tower is 986 feet tall, and the replica is 4 inches; 986 feet must be converted to inches, by multiplying by 12: 986 times 12 is 11,832 inches. Set up the ratio of replica to real and simplify: $\frac{4}{11,832} \div \frac{4}{4} = \frac{1}{2,958}$.

17. a. 10:30 A.M. to 5:30 P.M. is a seven-hour period. Mike can give 13 lessons, each lasting 30 minutes, if he takes 30 minutes for lunch. $20 × 13 = $260.

18. c. First, determine the distance to drive to work, using the formula $D = R × T$. Substitute known values and then multiply: $D = 60 × \frac{1}{2}$, so $D = 30$. The distance to work is 30 miles. Now, determine the time to drive to work at a rate of 40 miles per hour, again using the formula $D = R × T$. Substitute known values and then divide by 40: $30 = 40 × T$, so $0.75 = T$. The new time is 0.75 hour, or three-quarters of an hour. The problem asks how much *extra* time it will take to drive. This is the difference between one-half hour and three-quarters of an hour. Subtract the fractions, after changing one-half to two-quarters: $\frac{3}{4} - \frac{2}{4} = \frac{1}{4}$. One-quarter of an hour is 15 minutes.

19. a. Set up a ratio of length to height. The proportion is $\frac{10}{8} = \frac{l}{5.6}$. Cross-multiply to get $8 × l = 10 × 5.6$. Multiply 10 times 5.6 to get $8 × l = 56$. Divide 56 by 8 to get 7 feet long.

20. b. There has been an increase in price of $3; $3 ÷ $50 = 0.06. This is an increase of 0.06, or 6%.

21. c. Take the words in order and substitute the letters and numbers. Patricia has (P =), four times (4 ×) the number of marbles Sean has (S). The statement becomes P = 4 × S, which is equal to P = 4S.

22. b. Let x equal the unknown quantity of each denomination. You know that all the coins total $8.20 and that each denomination is multiplied by the same number, x. Therefore, $0.25x + 0.10x + 0.05x + 0.01x = 8.20$. This reduces to $(0.25 + 0.10 + 0.05 + 0.01)x = 8.20$, or $0.41x = 8.20$. Thus, $x = 20$ coins in each denomination.

23. c. $12 × 5\% + 4 × 4\% = x$ times 16; $x = 4.75\%$.

24. a. You are asked to find F, Fluffy's age. Begin the solution by breaking the problem into parts: Fluffy is half the age of Muffy becomes $F = (\frac{1}{2})(M)$, Muffy is one-third as old as Spot becomes $M = (\frac{1}{3})(S)$, and Spot is half the neighbor's age becomes $S = (\frac{1}{2})(N)$. You know the neighbor's age is 24 or N = 24. Substitute and work backward through the problem: $S = \frac{1}{2}(24) = 12$, $M = \frac{1}{3}(12) = 4$, $F = \frac{1}{2}(4)$. Thus, Fluffy is 2 years old.

25. a. Mario has finished $\frac{35}{45}$ of his test, which reduces to $\frac{7}{9}$, so he has $\frac{2}{9}$ of the test to go.

26. b. Let x equal D'Andre's rate. D'Andre's rate multiplied by his travel time equals the distance he travels; this equals Adam's rate multiplied by his travel time: $2x = D = 3(x - 5)$. Therefore, $2x = 3x - 15$, or $x = 15$ miles per hour.

27. b. There are three steps involved in solving this problem. First, convert 4.5% to a decimal: 0.045. Multiply that by $26,000 to find out how much the salary increases. Finally, add the result ($1,170) to the original salary of $26,000 to find out the new salary, $27,170.

28. b. Let L equal the number of gallons of gas lost, which is equal to the rate of loss times the time over which it occurs, or L = RT. Substitute: $L = (7)(\frac{1}{3}) = 2(\frac{1}{3})$ gallons. Notice that the 14-gallon tank size is irrelevant information in this problem.

29. a. Let R equal Veronica's average speed. Recall that for uniform motion, *distance = rate × time* or $D = RT$. Substitute: $220 = R(5)$ or $R = \frac{220}{5}$. Thus, $R = 44$ miles per hour.

30. b. 860 feet × 560 feet ÷ 43,560 square feet per acre = 11.06 acres.

Subtest 3: Word Knowledge

1. c. Something that is *lucid* is clear, comprehensible, or *understandable*.

2. b. *Mourning*, not to be confused with morning, is the act of expressing grief or sadness, or *sorrowing*.

3. d. Someone who is *resolute* is steadfast, resolved, or *determined*.

4. c. *Ambivalent* means conflicted, fluctuating, or *uncertain*. If you chose choice **a** or **b**, you were probably thinking of ambidextrous, which means able to use both hands equally well.

5. b. *Dissent* and *disagreement* occur when there is a difference of opinion. You were probably thinking of descent if you chose choice **a**. Choice **c** would be a good answer for *decent*.

6. b. As an adjective, *grave* means somber, solemn, or *serious*.

7. a. *Hapless* means unfortunate or *unlucky*.

8. a. *Dreary* means *dull* or boring. Something dreary can cause sleepiness, but does not itself mean sleepy.

9. d. *Arid* means *dry*, parched, or barren due to a lack of rainfall.

10. c. To *deter* means to dissuade, prevent, or *discourage*. If you chose choice **a**, you may have been thinking of detour.

11. b. *Covert* means disguised, concealed, or *secret*.

12. a. An *allusion* is a direct or implied *reference* to something. Choice **b** is a synonym for illusion. If you chose choice **c**, you were probably thinking of elude, which means to avoid.

13. b. Both *desist* and *stop* mean to cease.

14. c. A *pariah* is a person who has been shunned from the community, or an *outcast*. A piranha is a fish (choice **b**).

15. a. To *precede* means to come before, or *lead*. If you chose choice **b** or **c**, you probably mistook precede for proceed, and if you chose choice **d**, you may have been thinking of proceeds.

16. c. To *forgive* means to excuse, allow, or *pardon*. If you chose choice **d**, you may have been thinking of forgo.

17. d. *Potent* means strong, influential, or *powerful*.

18. d. Something *succinct* is brief or *concise*.

19. b. To *console* means to provide *comfort*. If you chose choice **a**, you may have been thinking of consult.

20. c. To *surmise* or *guess* means to come to a conclusion without evidence.

21. c. *Mimic* means to copy or *imitate* the behavior or qualities of something. The key phrase *to avoid detection* suggests that the predators somehow blend in; the only answer choice that would make this possible is choice **c**.

22. a. *Tantamount* means *equal to*. You know it is not choice **d**, because the second part of the sentence tells you they are comparable actions.

23. d. *Aimlessly* means without aim or objective. The key phrase is *Without a goal in mind*, which suggests he is walking without direction, or *randomly*. The sentence does not mention anything about Greg's mood or his speed, so choices **b** and **c** are incorrect even though they might appear logical.

24. d. In order to find the answer, ask yourself what kind of a writer would be unlikely to make many typos. That should eliminate choices **a** and **b**. Choice **c** might make sense, but a very intelligent writer who is not thorough could still make many typos.

25. c. Any of these choices could fit, but the second part of the sentence conveys a sense of urgency that only choice **c** makes clear.

26. a. You might narrow this question down to choices **a** and **b** because they both provide logical reasons why the boy would be on the couch all day. Because the sentence tells you that the boy got no sleep, however, choice **a** makes the most sense.

27. b. Someone who approves only his own ideas can be described as *arrogant*.

28. b. The second part of the sentence clarifies the importance of not making mistakes, which might occur if you do not follow or if you *stray* from the instructions.

29. c. Choice **c** is the only logical choice to describe someone who is also scared.

30. b. The gopher's behavior, ruining the grass, suggests it is troublesome. The only answer that conveys this idea is choice **b**.

31. d. *Riveting* means extremely interesting. The only choice here that logically fits is choice **d**.

32. a. Only choices **a** and **b** fit logically in this sentence. Choice **a** is best because there is no indication why the writing is unreadable; it could be too tiny, too sloppy, or in an unfamiliar language.

33. b. Consider the context of the sentence. Someone who makes many mistakes and who is just starting a career is likely *inexperienced*.

34. c. The second part of the sentence implies that trivial details are unimportant. Choice **c** is the only choice that fits this definition.

35. b. The sentence implies that the parents originally did not want to buy the boy a puppy but eventually changed their minds. Choice **b** reflects this change of opinion.

Subtest 4: Paragraph Comprehension

1. b. The taxpayers' association pointed to the school budget as an example of their complaint, but their overall concern was with rising taxes.

2. a. Something that is *persistent* is *ongoing*, continuing over a period of time. A persistent person keeps trying despite repeated failure, and a persistent problem continually reappears.

3. c. Bob Smith mentioned the school budget because it was an example of waste of taxpayers' money, not because he was anti-education or unathletic.

4. d. The passage states in the last paragraph that some members of the taxpayers' association would run for town council to replace members who kept raising taxes.

5. b. The passage states that the hardware store wanted to ensure that each customer was able to buy a pump, so they used tickets to enforce that.

6. c. The word *deluge* means *a flood*, an overwhelming rush of water.

7. a. The central idea in this passage is that one should not complain, because there is always someone else whose suffering is worse. The hardware store owners were not heartless, because they were trying to help as many people as possible.

8. c. The author refers to the complaining customers as childish because their problems were not as severe as their neighbors' problems, yet they were very angry at a small inconvenience.

9. d. See the final sentence of the passage.

10. b. The final sentence states that a sense of wonder is important to the human spirit. Choice **d** does mention looking at the stars, but it is the sense of wonder that is important; the stars merely excite one's wonder. Dark skies and clean environment (choices **a** and **c**) might be important, but the author addresses wonder as specifically important to one's spirit.

11. a. George's reaction to his boss's words was anger. We can infer that he left his job because of that anger, since he took a new job earning less money.

12. c. The word *reprimand* means to scold or rebuke. George was *scolded* for his appearance at work.

13. b. George's boss was angry because George did not dress properly, and his appearance was unprofessional.

14. d. The word *slovenly* means untidy or messy. George's appearance looked *sloppy* in the office.

15. c. The first sentence points out that it is not practical to use the first-person point of view in business correspondence. Choices **a** and **b** are not in the paragraph. Although choice **d** is in the paragraph and it does tell us something about the first-person point of view, it is too narrow to represent the main idea, which has to do with the first-person point of view as it is related to writing in a business environment.

Subtest 5: Math Knowledge

1. a. To solve this problem, you must first convert all the fractions to the lowest common denominator, which is 24; $\frac{7}{8} = \frac{21}{24}$; $\frac{3}{4} = \frac{18}{24}$, $\frac{2}{3} = \frac{16}{24}$, $\frac{5}{6} = \frac{20}{24}$. The fraction with the largest numerator, $\frac{21}{24}$, has the greatest value.

2. b. This is a special expression called a *perfect square*. The x terms cancel each other out, leaving just two terms in the expression; therefore, $(x + 5)(x - 5)$ is the correct factoring of the expression.

3. d. Square each side of the equal sign to eliminate the radical: $(\sqrt{b-4})^2 = 5^2$ becomes $b - 4 = 25$. Add 4 to both sides of the equation: $b = 29$.

4. d. The three angles of a triangle add up to 180°. When you subtract 42 and 59 from 180, the result is 79°.

5. c. The perimeter is the sum of the triangle's two legs plus the hypotenuse. Knowing two of the sides, you can find the third side, or hypotenuse (h), using the Pythagorean theorem: $a^2 + a^2 = h^2$, which simplifies to $2a^2 = h^2$. So $h = \sqrt{2a^2}$. This means the perimeter is $2a + \sqrt{2a^2}$.

6. a. The formula for finding the area of a triangle is $\frac{1}{2} \times$ the base $\times$ the height; therefore, dividing the given area, 60, by the height, 15, will give half the base, 4. The base is 8 centimeters.

7. a. The symbol $>$ means *greater than*, and the symbol $<$ means *less than*. The only correct choice is **a**: four feet is greater than three feet. The other choices are untrue.

8. b. To solve this division problem, subtract the exponents only: $5 - 2 = 3$, so the answer is 10^3.

9. d. Divide the numerator by the denominator to get the correct answer of 0.4.

10. c. To find the perimeter, you can double each of the sides and add the sums: $2(834) + 2(1,288) = 1,668 + 2,576 = 4,244$ feet.

11. b. There are 60 minutes in one hour. Multiply $60 \times 7\frac{1}{6}$ by multiplying $60 \times 7 = 420$ and $60 \times \frac{1}{6} = 10$. Then add $420 + 10$ to get 430 minutes.

12. d. First, the radius needs to be found, which is $\frac{1}{2}$ of the diameter: $r = 47$ centimeters; then, to find the area, square the radius and multiply by π. The correct answer is $2,209\pi$.

13. c. Since both dimensions are tripled, there are two additional factors of 3. Therefore, the new area is $3 \times 3 = 9$ times as large as the original.

14. a. The distance between Plattville and Quincy is the hypotenuse of a right triangle with sides of length 80 and 60. The length of the hypotenuse equals $\sqrt{80^2 + 60^2}$, which equals $\sqrt{6,400 + 3,600}$, which equals $\sqrt{10,000}$, which equals 100 miles.

15. c. In order for a number to be divisible by 6, it must be able to be divided by 6 without a remainder. A shortcut to check divisibility by 6 is to see if the number is divisible by both 2 and 3. Since 546 is even (ends in 6), the number is divisible by 2. Since the sum of the digits is $5 + 4 + 6 = 15$ and 15 is divisible by 3, 546 is also divisible by three. Since 546 is divisible by both 2 and 3, it is also divisible by 6.

16. a. A triangle with two congruent sides could be either isosceles or equilateral. However, because one angle is 40°, it cannot be equilateral (the angles would be 60°).

17. c. Use the FOIL method to find the answer. This stands for the order by which the terms are multiplied: First + Outside + Inside + Last: $(3x \times x) + (3x \times -6) + (4x) + (4 \times -6)$; $3x^2 - 18x + 4x - 24$. The correct answer is $3x^2 - 14x - 24$.

18. d. An acute angle is less than 90°.

19. b. The vertical bars on either side of the expression tell you to find the *absolute value* of $4 - 15$. To complete the question, find $4 - 15$ to get -11. Then find the absolute value (the distance the number is away from zero on a number line) of -11, which is 11.

20. a. Since 4 and 6 are factors of 24, and 4 is a perfect square, $\sqrt{24} = \sqrt{4} \times \sqrt{6} = 2 \times \sqrt{6}$ or $2\sqrt{6}$.

21. a. In this question, 10 is the base and 4 is the exponent; 10^4 means 10 is used as a factor four times, or $10 \times 10 \times 10 \times 10$.

22. d. The hundredth is the second digit to the right of the decimal point. Because the third decimal is 6, the second is rounded up to 4.

23. b. The correct answer is 1.

24. d. Factor the left side of the equation and set each factor equal to zero: $x^2 - 25 = (x - 5)(x + 5)$; $x - 5 = 0$ or $x + 5 = 0$. Therefore, $x = 5$ or -5.

25. c. This is a division problem with mixed numbers. First, convert the mixed numbers to fractions: $33\frac{1}{2} = \frac{67}{2}$ and $5\frac{1}{4} = \frac{21}{4}$. Next, invert the second fraction and multiply: $\frac{67}{2} \times \frac{4}{21} = \frac{134}{21}$. Reduce to a mixed number: $\frac{134}{21} = 6\frac{8}{21}$. With this result, you know that only six glasses can be completely filled.

Subtest 6: Electronics Information

1. d. A quartz crystal is typically found in an oscillator and uses the piezoelectric effect to create an electrical signal. This capability is commonly used to keep track of time (as in quartz wristwatches).

2. b. A typical residential wall outlet in North America uses alternating current (AC) voltage.

3. b. Radio waves have the longest wavelengths of the answers given.

4. a. A step-down transformer would be required to reduce the voltage.

5. b. This is the schematic symbol for a circuit breaker.

6. a. One coulomb is the amount of electric charge transported in one second by a steady current of one ampere.

7. d. A diode allows electrical current to flow through it in one direction. This unidirectional behavior is called *rectification*, thus, one of the devices affected by a diode is a rectifier.

8. a. A photovoltaic cell, or solar cell, takes the energy from solar radiation and produces direct current.

9. d. Choice **a** represents a polarized two-plug wire, choice **b** represents the source of a constant current, and **c** represents a speaker.

10. a. *Low potential*, for electricians, most closely means 600 watts or lower.

11. d. As the frequency of a signal goes higher, the period becomes shorter: 10,000 Hz has a period of 0.0001 seconds ($\frac{1}{10,000}$ of a second). Therefore, frequency and period are inversely related. All the other answer choices have no bearing on frequency.

12. b. When values are in decibels, the gains and losses in power are simply added together to determine the expected power level: -10 dBm $- 2$ dB $+ 30$ dB $- 3$ dB $+ 20$ dB $- 5$ dB $= 30$ dBm.

13. d. A capacitor's storage potential, or capacitance, is measured in units called *farads*, named after the English physicist Michael Faraday.

14. a. Random access memory (RAM) chips are known as *volatile*, which means that the data contained is lost when power is turned off.

15. d. The charge polarity of electrons is negative; the charge polarity of protons is positive.

16. c. Remember that in a series circuit the sum of the individual resistors determines the total resistance: $10 + 55 = 65$.

17. d. The amplification factor (also called gain) is usually expressed in terms of power. The decibel (dB), a logarithmic unit, is the most common way of expressing the amplification factor.

18. d. The prefix "micro" indicates that you multiply by 10^{-6}, so 287 microamps equals 0.000287 A.

19. d. A minimum of #4 wire gauge is required. The amount of power that is transmitted through the electrical line dictates how large the gauge wire should be. In American wire gauge (AWG) standards, the larger the wire gauge, the lower the number.

20. c. Cartridge fuses with a rating of 60 amps or higher will have knife-blade terminals on either end, as illustrated.

Subtest 7: Auto and Shop Information

1. d. Using water alone can indeed help cool the system down. However, the absence of an additive to raise the boiling point or lower the freezing point could limit the operating environments the car could operate in. In addition, pure water can rust the internal mechanisms of the vehicle.

2. c. With the oil pump supplying oil to the entire engine for lubrication, the oil system can be said to connect directly to the internal combustion engine. The other systems mentioned are all automobile systems that are stand-alone (suspension, braking) or are tied solely to the automobile battery.

3. b. The driver has direct control of the steering system through the inputs to the steering mechanism. The other systems mentioned are all stand-alone systems where the driver has little or no input.

4. c. A knock or ping sound from your engine generally means the fuel-air mixture is igniting too soon inside the engine cylinders.

5. a. Using a higher octane gasoline will solve this problem. The octane rating of gasoline is related to its ability to resist the knock, or the ignition of the fuel-air mixture outside the envelope of the normal combustion region.

6. c. Since hydraulic fluid is not compressible, there should be no spongy feeling in the brakes. This sort of brake performance could mean there is air in the brake lines. Bleeding the air out of the system through bleeder valves should solve the problem.

7. b. The Society of Automotive Engineers (SAE) established a numerical code system for grading motor oils according to their viscosity characteristics. This SAE rating is used depending on what sort of driving environment the engine will be operating in.

8. c. Depending on driving conditions, tires will usually last 30,000 to 80,000 miles.

9. d. Specific structures called *wear bars* are built into the tire tread. When these wear bars have been worn down to where they are flush with the surrounding tread, the tire is in need of replacement.

10. c. A worn or loose fan belt will make a squealing noise as the rotating pulley spins around without moving the loose fan belt.

11. d. A spark plug that is not firing properly will result in an engine running rough since one of the cylinders is not firing in proper order and contributing its power cycle to the overall operation.

12. d. You should run the engine for at least 10 minutes to warm the oil up, increasing viscosity and making it easier to drain.

13. b. When making a circular cut in a piece of metal, the best chisel to use is a round chisel. The butt chisel and the framing chisel are both wood chisels. A socket chisel is a type of framing chisel.

14. b. Paint should always be thinned with turpentine. Any of the other compounds will change the chemical makeup of the paint.

15. c. The tool shown is an electric soldering gun.

16. b. Wood, cinder blocks, and brick and mortar are all materials that could be used to build a permanent foundation, but concrete would be the strongest.

17. b. A Forstner bit has a wide circular cutting edge with a spur in the middle for precise placement.

18. c. A brad is often used in picture frames and light assembly.

19. b. A torque wrench is used to apply a specific amount of tightness to nuts or bolts. It is used where exact tolerances are needed and large amounts of stress or pressure could be expected on the nuts or bolts.

20. c. A table saw is not considered a carpenter's hand tool.

21. a. A posthole digger would be the best tool to dig a small, circular hole a foot or two deep, such as for a mailbox post or a fence post. The other tools listed could be used to dig such a hole, but would require more effort and work.

22. c. The width of the saw cut is called the *kerf* of a saw. On most saws, the kerf is wider than the saw blade because the teeth are flared out sideways.

23. d. A fence guide would be used to help guide a piece of wood through a table saw. The other combinations of tools are not usually used together.

24. d. A bolt cutter is used to cut chains, padlocks, bolts, and other hard, thin metals.

25. b. Aluminum oxide is the material used on most sandpapers. Pumice and emery are also used as abrasives but not on standard sandpaper.

Subtest 8:
Mechanical Comprehension

1. c. A pulley system of this type has a mechanical advantage of 2. So, a 250-pound weight can be lifted with 250 pounds ÷ 2 = 125 pounds.

2. a. The density of mercury is strongly temperature dependent. When placed in hot liquid, mercury expands by a known amount, forcing small amounts of liquid mercury up the thermometer.

3. a. Use the equation $w_1 \times d_1 = w_2 \times d_2$. 120 pounds $\times$ 11 feet $= w_2 \times$ 6 feet. Solving for w_2 gives 220 pounds.

4. c. The crank is moving counterclockwise, meaning that when it is pointing downward it is moving away from the piston (to the right). So, the piston will be in a central position. Since the crank is moving to the right, the piston will also be moving to the right.

5. b. 12 miles ÷ 1.5 hours = 8 miles per hour.

6. a. The mechanical advantage (MA) of a ramp is determined by the length of the ramp, l, divided by the height gained, h. In this case, MA $= \frac{l}{h} =$ 25 feet ÷ 10 feet = 2.5. The force required to pull a 300-pound block up a ramp is 300 pounds ÷ 2.5 = 120 pounds.

7. a. The force constant of the spring is 10 pounds ÷ 8 inches = 1.25 pounds per inch. Using the equation, $F = kx$, we have 15 pounds = 1.25 pounds per inch $\times x$. Solving for x gives 12 inches.

8. c. If 18 turns move the nut 1.2 inches, there are 18 turns ÷ 1.2 inches = 15 threads per inch.

9. b. Mechanical advantage = output force ÷ input force. Here, 40 pounds of force is input to lift a 120-pound load. The mechanical advantage is 120 ÷ 40 = 3.

10. a. The mechanical advantage of this pulley system is 4. The force required to lift the 300-pound load is 300 pounds ÷ 4 = 75 pounds.

11. b. Gear 1 turning clockwise will cause gears 2 and 4 to turn counterclockwise. Gear 3 will be the only other gear that turns clockwise.

12. d. When a submarine fills its tanks with water it becomes heavier, which decreases its buoyancy and increases its density. The volume of the submarine remains unchanged through the entire process.

13. d. Because pulley system B has a mechanical advantage of 2, the rope must be pulled twice as far as pulley system A to do the same amount of work: 2 × 10 feet = 20 feet.

14. a. If a vertical line is drawn straight down from the center of gravity, only the line for truck A reaches the ground outside of the truck's tires. This makes the truck unstable.

15. a. Cable A is attached to the arm closest to the crane. Therefore, it has the weakest mechanical advantage and so will be under the most strain to support the weight of the arm.

16. a. The total volume of the block is 2 inches × 2 inches × 5 inches = 20 inches^3. Its density is 0.3 pounds per cubic inch, so its total weight must be 20 inches^3 × 0.3 pounds per inch^3 = 6 pounds.

17. d. $w_1 \times d_1 = w_2 \times d_2$. Talia is 18 feet away from the pivot point. 90 pounds × 8 feet = 10 feet × w_2. Solving for w_2 gives 50 pounds.

18. b. Wood is the best choice. All other objects are very dense and will quickly sink. Wood offers a lower density while still remaining strong enough to function as a raft.

19. d. Each full turn of the pedals will turn the rear wheel 48 ÷ 12 = 4 revolutions. If the pedals are turning at 90 rpm, the rear wheel will move at 4 × 90 rpm = 360 rpm.

20. c. Pulley systems A and B offer a mechanical advantage of 2, whereas pulley system C offers a mechanical advantage of 1. In A and B, the rope used to raise the weight moves 2 feet for every 1 foot the pulley is raised, whereas in C the rope used to raise the weight moves 1 foot for every foot the weight is raised.

21. b. $w_1 \times d_1 = w_2 \times d_2$. 50 pounds × 8 feet = 100 pounds × d_2. Solving for d_2 gives 4 feet.

22. b. In this pulley system, the weight of the load is shared over 2 cables and so the mechanical advantage is 2.

23. b. Since all materials occupy the same volume, the material with the greatest density will be the heaviest. Lead is an extremely dense material and is much denser than all other options.

24. c. Since pulley A is 2.5 times greater in diameter than pulley B, each revolution of A will lead to 2.5 revolutions of B. If A rotates at 50 rpm, then B will rotate at 50 rpm × 2.5 = 125 rpm.

25. b. If gear 3 turns counterclockwise, it will cause its neighboring gears (2 and 4) to turn clockwise.

Subtest 9: Assembling Objects

1. a.
2. c.
3. b.
4. b.
5. c.

6. c.
7. d.
8. a.
9. b.
10. c.
11. d.
12. a.
13. b.
14. d.
15. c.
16. a.
17. d.
18. b.
19. c.
20. b.
21. c.
22. d.
23. c.
24. c.
25. b.

Scoring of the official ASVAB is discussed in Chapter 3.

SAMPLE OFFICER CANDIDATE TEST QUESTIONS

CHAPTER SUMMARY

The sample test in this chapter consists of 19 different sections found in at least one if not all three of the officer candidate tests. For these sample questions, do not worry about time limits. Just work at a steady, relaxed pace. The answers and rationale are provided in Chapter 9.

Subtest 1: Verbal Analogies

1. ⓐ ⓑ ⓒ ⓓ ⓔ
2. ⓐ ⓑ ⓒ ⓓ ⓔ
3. ⓐ ⓑ ⓒ ⓓ ⓔ
4. ⓐ ⓑ ⓒ ⓓ ⓔ

5. ⓐ ⓑ ⓒ ⓓ ⓔ
6. ⓐ ⓑ ⓒ ⓓ ⓔ
7. ⓐ ⓑ ⓒ ⓓ ⓔ
8. ⓐ ⓑ ⓒ ⓓ ⓔ

9. ⓐ ⓑ ⓒ ⓓ ⓔ
10. ⓐ ⓑ ⓒ ⓓ ⓔ

Subtest 2: Arithmetic Reasoning

1. ⓐ ⓑ ⓒ ⓓ ⓔ
2. ⓐ ⓑ ⓒ ⓓ ⓔ
3. ⓐ ⓑ ⓒ ⓓ ⓔ
4. ⓐ ⓑ ⓒ ⓓ ⓔ

5. ⓐ ⓑ ⓒ ⓓ ⓔ
6. ⓐ ⓑ ⓒ ⓓ ⓔ
7. ⓐ ⓑ ⓒ ⓓ ⓔ
8. ⓐ ⓑ ⓒ ⓓ ⓔ

9. ⓐ ⓑ ⓒ ⓓ ⓔ
10. ⓐ ⓑ ⓒ ⓓ ⓔ

Subtest 3: Reading Skills

1. ⓐ ⓑ ⓒ ⓓ ⓔ
2. ⓐ ⓑ ⓒ ⓓ ⓔ
3. ⓐ ⓑ ⓒ ⓓ ⓔ
4. ⓐ ⓑ ⓒ ⓓ ⓔ

5. ⓐ ⓑ ⓒ ⓓ ⓔ
6. ⓐ ⓑ ⓒ ⓓ ⓔ
7. ⓐ ⓑ ⓒ ⓓ ⓔ
8. ⓐ ⓑ ⓒ ⓓ ⓔ

9. ⓐ ⓑ ⓒ ⓓ ⓔ
10. ⓐ ⓑ ⓒ ⓓ ⓔ

Subtest 4: Word Knowledge

1. ⓐ ⓑ ⓒ ⓓ ⓔ
2. ⓐ ⓑ ⓒ ⓓ ⓔ
3. ⓐ ⓑ ⓒ ⓓ ⓔ
4. ⓐ ⓑ ⓒ ⓓ ⓔ

5. ⓐ ⓑ ⓒ ⓓ ⓔ
6. ⓐ ⓑ ⓒ ⓓ ⓔ
7. ⓐ ⓑ ⓒ ⓓ ⓔ
8. ⓐ ⓑ ⓒ ⓓ ⓔ

9. ⓐ ⓑ ⓒ ⓓ ⓔ
10. ⓐ ⓑ ⓒ ⓓ ⓔ

Subtest 5: Math Knowledge

1. ⓐ ⓑ ⓒ ⓓ ⓔ
2. ⓐ ⓑ ⓒ ⓓ ⓔ
3. ⓐ ⓑ ⓒ ⓓ ⓔ
4. ⓐ ⓑ ⓒ ⓓ ⓔ

5. ⓐ ⓑ ⓒ ⓓ ⓔ
6. ⓐ ⓑ ⓒ ⓓ ⓔ
7. ⓐ ⓑ ⓒ ⓓ ⓔ
8. ⓐ ⓑ ⓒ ⓓ ⓔ

9. ⓐ ⓑ ⓒ ⓓ ⓔ
10. ⓐ ⓑ ⓒ ⓓ ⓔ

Subtest 6: Mechanical Comprehension

1. (a) (b) (c) (d) (e)
2. (a) (b) (c) (d) (e)
3. (a) (b) (c) (d) (e)
4. (a) (b) (c) (d) (e)

5. (a) (b) (c) (d) (e)
6. (a) (b) (c) (d) (e)
7. (a) (b) (c) (d) (e)
8. (a) (b) (c) (d) (e)

9. (a) (b) (c) (d) (e)
10. (a) (b) (c) (d) (e)

Subtest 7: Instrument Comprehension

1. (a) (b) (c) (d)
2. (a) (b) (c) (d)
3. (a) (b) (c) (d)
4. (a) (b) (c) (d)

5. (a) (b) (c) (d)
6. (a) (b) (c) (d)
7. (a) (b) (c) (d)
8. (a) (b) (c) (d)

9. (a) (b) (c) (d)
10. (a) (b) (c) (d)

Subtest 8: Block Counting

1. (a) (b) (c) (d) (e)
2. (a) (b) (c) (d) (e)
3. (a) (b) (c) (d) (e)
4. (a) (b) (c) (d) (e)

5. (a) (b) (c) (d) (e)
6. (a) (b) (c) (d) (e)
7. (a) (b) (c) (d) (e)
8. (a) (b) (c) (d) (e)

9. (a) (b) (c) (d) (e)
10. (a) (b) (c) (d) (e)

Subtest 9: Table Reading

1. (a) (b) (c) (d) (e)
2. (a) (b) (c) (d) (e)
3. (a) (b) (c) (d) (e)
4. (a) (b) (c) (d) (e)

5. (a) (b) (c) (d) (e)
6. (a) (b) (c) (d) (e)
7. (a) (b) (c) (d) (e)
8. (a) (b) (c) (d) (e)

9. (a) (b) (c) (d) (e)
10. (a) (b) (c) (d) (e)

Subtest 10: Aviation Information

1. (a) (b) (c) (d)
2. (a) (b) (c) (d)
3. (a) (b) (c) (d)
4. (a) (b) (c) (d)

5. (a) (b) (c) (d)
6. (a) (b) (c) (d)
7. (a) (b) (c) (d)
8. (a) (b) (c) (d)

9. (a) (b) (c) (d)
10. (a) (b) (c) (d)

Subtest 11: Rotated Blocks

1. (a) (b) (c) (d) (e)   5. (a) (b) (c) (d) (e)   9. (a) (b) (c) (d) (e)
2. (a) (b) (c) (d) (e)   6. (a) (b) (c) (d) (e)   10. (a) (b) (c) (d) (e)
3. (a) (b) (c) (d) (e)   7. (a) (b) (c) (d) (e)
4. (a) (b) (c) (d) (e)   8. (a) (b) (c) (d) (e)

Subtest 12: General Science

1. (a) (b) (c) (d) (e)   5. (a) (b) (c) (d) (e)   9. (a) (b) (c) (d) (e)
2. (a) (b) (c) (d) (e)   6. (a) (b) (c) (d) (e)   10. (a) (b) (c) (d) (e)
3. (a) (b) (c) (d) (e)   7. (a) (b) (c) (d) (e)
4. (a) (b) (c) (d) (e)   8. (a) (b) (c) (d) (e)

Subtest 13: Hidden Figures

1. (a) (b) (c) (d) (e)   5. (a) (b) (c) (d) (e)   9. (a) (b) (c) (d) (e)
2. (a) (b) (c) (d) (e)   6. (a) (b) (c) (d) (e)   10. (a) (b) (c) (d) (e)
3. (a) (b) (c) (d) (e)   7. (a) (b) (c) (d) (e)
4. (a) (b) (c) (d) (e)   8. (a) (b) (c) (d) (e)

Subtest 14: Spatial Apperception

1. (a) (b) (c) (d) (e)   5. (a) (b) (c) (d) (e)   9. (a) (b) (c) (d) (e)
2. (a) (b) (c) (d) (e)   6. (a) (b) (c) (d) (e)   10. (a) (b) (c) (d) (e)
3. (a) (b) (c) (d) (e)   7. (a) (b) (c) (d) (e)
4. (a) (b) (c) (d) (e)   8. (a) (b) (c) (d) (e)

Subtest 15: Electronics Information

1. (a) (b) (c) (d) (e)   5. (a) (b) (c) (d) (e)   9. (a) (b) (c) (d) (e)
2. (a) (b) (c) (d) (e)   6. (a) (b) (c) (d) (e)   10. (a) (b) (c) (d) (e)
3. (a) (b) (c) (d) (e)   7. (a) (b) (c) (d) (e)
4. (a) (b) (c) (d) (e)   8. (a) (b) (c) (d) (e)

Subtest 16: Auto and Shop Information

1. ⓐ ⓑ ⓒ ⓓ ⓔ
2. ⓐ ⓑ ⓒ ⓓ ⓔ
3. ⓐ ⓑ ⓒ ⓓ ⓔ
4. ⓐ ⓑ ⓒ ⓓ ⓔ

5. ⓐ ⓑ ⓒ ⓓ ⓔ
6. ⓐ ⓑ ⓒ ⓓ ⓔ
7. ⓐ ⓑ ⓒ ⓓ ⓔ
8. ⓐ ⓑ ⓒ ⓓ ⓔ

9. ⓐ ⓑ ⓒ ⓓ ⓔ
10. ⓐ ⓑ ⓒ ⓓ ⓔ

Subtest 17: Mechanical Comprehension

1. ⓐ ⓑ ⓒ ⓓ ⓔ
2. ⓐ ⓑ ⓒ ⓓ ⓔ
3. ⓐ ⓑ ⓒ ⓓ ⓔ
4. ⓐ ⓑ ⓒ ⓓ ⓔ

5. ⓐ ⓑ ⓒ ⓓ ⓔ
6. ⓐ ⓑ ⓒ ⓓ ⓔ
7. ⓐ ⓑ ⓒ ⓓ ⓔ
8. ⓐ ⓑ ⓒ ⓓ ⓔ

9. ⓐ ⓑ ⓒ ⓓ ⓔ
10. ⓐ ⓑ ⓒ ⓓ ⓔ

Subtest 18: Assembling Objects

1. ⓐ ⓑ ⓒ ⓓ ⓔ
2. ⓐ ⓑ ⓒ ⓓ ⓔ
3. ⓐ ⓑ ⓒ ⓓ ⓔ
4. ⓐ ⓑ ⓒ ⓓ ⓔ

5. ⓐ ⓑ ⓒ ⓓ ⓔ
6. ⓐ ⓑ ⓒ ⓓ ⓔ
7. ⓐ ⓑ ⓒ ⓓ ⓔ
8. ⓐ ⓑ ⓒ ⓓ ⓔ

9. ⓐ ⓑ ⓒ ⓓ ⓔ
10. ⓐ ⓑ ⓒ ⓓ ⓔ

Subtest 1: Verbal Analogies

Directions: The Verbal Analogies subtest measures your ability to reason and to see relationships between words. Choose the answer that best completes the analogy developed at the beginning of each question. The best way to approach this type of test is to look for patterns or comparisons between the first phrase and the choices available to you.

Questions: 10

1. *Flight station* is to *airplane* as *bridge* is to
   a. tunnel
   b. road
   c. ship
   d. mountain
   e. highway

2. *Racquet* is to *court* as
   a. tractor is to field
   b. blossom is to bloom
   c. stalk is to prey
   d. plan is to strategy
   e. moon is to planet

3. *Sweater* is to *clothing* as
   a. bottle is to cork
   b. hand is to finger
   c. shoe is to foot
   d. rose is to flowers
   e. dog is to cat

4. *Row* is to *boat* as *sail* is to
   a. ocean
   b. navigate
   c. rudder
   d. ship
   e. travel

5. *Fly* is to *airplane* as
   a. drive is to stake
   b. skate is to slide
   c. push is to fall
   d. swim is to float
   e. rod is to hook

6. *Garage* is to *truck* as *hangar* is to
   a. street
   b. overpass
   c. runway
   d. airplane
   e. cockpit

7. *Bend* is to *knee* as
   a. elbow is to arm
   b. twist is to move
   c. speak is to tongue
   d. look is to see
   e. turn is to neck

8. *Spatula* is to *kitchen* as
   a. scalpel is to operating room
   b. cupcake is to bakery
   c. ravioli is to pasta
   d. sparkplug is to engine
   e. tooth is to mouth

9. *Ride* is to *motorcycle* as
   a. navigate is to map
   b. wash is to car
   c. fly is to helicopter
   d. foot is to hand
   e. jump is to hurdle

10. *Violet* is to *shade* as
    a. white is to black
    b. flower is to daisy
    c. lamp is to bulb
    d. circle is to shape
    e. sofa is to couch

Subtest 2: Arithmetic Reasoning

Directions: The Arithmetic Reasoning subtest measures mathematical reasoning and problem solving. Each problem is followed by five possible answers. Decide which one of the five answers is correct. A method for attacking each of these questions is given in the answer block in Chapter 5.

Questions: 10

1. A field with an area of 420 square yards is twice as large in area as a second field. If the second field is 15 yards long, how wide is it?
   a. 7 yards
   b. 14 yards
   c. 28 yards
   d. 56 yards
   e. 9 yards

2. A passenger plane can carry two tons of cargo. A freight plane can carry five tons of cargo. If an equal number of both kinds of planes are used to ship 105 tons of cargo, and each plane carries its maximum cargo load, how many tons of cargo are shipped on the passenger planes?
   a. 15 tons
   b. 30 tons
   c. 42 tons
   d. 52.5 tons
   e. 75 tons

3. A fighter jet was scheduled to fly four sorties. The average duration of the sorties flown was 93 minutes. If sortie one was canceled and sorties two and three were 42 minutes each, what was the duration of sortie four?
   a. 288 minutes
   b. 93 minutes
   c. 168 minutes
   d. 195 minutes
   e. 126 minutes

4. A recruiting station enlisted 450 people. Of these, 40% were under 22 years old. How many of the recruits were over 22 years old?
   a. 130
   b. 140
   c. 175
   d. 180
   e. 270

5. If an aircraft travels at 330 miles per hour, how far did the aircraft fly in 1,800 seconds?
   a. 11 miles
   b. 300 miles
   c. 30 miles
   d. 165 miles
   e. 660 miles

6. What is the estimated product when 157 and 817 are rounded to the nearest hundred and multiplied?
   a. 16,000
   b. 80,000
   c. 160,000
   d. 180,000
   e. 200,000

7. A large coffee pot holds 120 cups. It is about two-thirds full. About how many cups are in the pot?
   a. 20 cups
   b. 40 cups
   c. 60 cups
   d. 80 cups
   e. 90 cups

8. To find the volume of a pyramid that has a rectangular base of 10 inches by 12 inches and a height of 10 inches, use ($V = \frac{1}{3}lwh$).
   a. 40 cubic inches
   b. 320 cubic inches
   c. 400 cubic inches
   d. 1,200 cubic inches
   e. 1,400 cubic inches

9. Jason is six times as old as Kate. In two years, Jason will be twice as old as Kate is then. How old is Jason now?

   a. 3 years old

   b. 6 years old

   c. 9 years old

   d. 12 years old

   e. 14 years old

10. A Boeing 747 airplane burns approximately 1 gallon of fuel for every second flown. If the flight from New York to Beijing is 13.5 hours, approximately how many gallons of fuel will be used during this trip?

   a. 10,084 gallons

   b. 810 gallons

   c. 48,600 gallons

   d. 68,400 gallons

   e. cannot be determined with the information given

Subtest 3: Reading Skills

Directions: The Reading Skills subtest measures your ability to read and understand paragraphs. For each question, choose the answer that best completes the meaning of the paragraph. Pay close attention as you read, and try to find the point that the author is trying to make. Once you have read the paragraph all the way through, you will find that one or two of the possible answers can be quickly eliminated based on the context.

Questions: 10

1. If they are to function effectively, organizations, like other systems, must achieve a natural harmony, or coherence, among their component parts. The structural and situational elements of an effective organization form themselves into a tightly knit, highly cohesive package. An organization whose parts are mismatched, however, cannot carry out its missions. If managers are to design effective organizations, they need to

   a. simplify organizational structures.

   b. encourage greater specialization of labor.

   c. emphasize the fit of organizational parts.

   d. introduce more technological innovations.

   e. reduce the span of control in the organization.

2. For botulism to develop, first *Clostridium botulinum*, the bacterium that produces the poison, must be present. These bacteria are widespread in the environment and are considered by some to be everywhere. Second, the bacterium that produces the deadly toxin must be treated to an atmosphere that is free of oxygen and to temperatures that are just warm enough, but not too warm. These conditions have to be held long enough for the toxin to develop. Acid will prevent the growth of the organism and the production of the toxin. The following condition is necessary for botulism to develop.

   a. the presence of oxygen

   b. a brief period of time

   c. the presence of acid

   d. warm temperatures

   e. exposure to rare bacteria

3. Because of our short lifespan of 70-odd years, it is easy for human beings to think of the earth as a planet that never changes. Yet we live on a dynamic planet with many factors contributing to change. We know that wind and rain erode and shape our planet. Many other forces are also at work, such as volcanic activity, temperature fluctuations, and even extraterrestrial interaction such as meteors and gravitational forces. The earth, in actuality, is a large rock

   a. in a state of inertia.

   b. that is quickly eroding.

   c. that is evolving.

   d. that is subject to temperature fluctuations caused by interplanetary interaction.

   e. that is subject to winds caused by meteor activity.

4. *Mustela nigripes*, the rarely seen black-footed ferret, is often confused with *Mustela putorius*, the common European polecat. It is true that these two mammals resemble each other in some ways. However, they are two distinct and separate species, with differences in color, body form, and other attributes. Who knows how many sightings of the black-footed ferret

   a. were the result of seeing the European polecat running loose?

   b. were of species other than the common European polecat?

   c. were made of a related species of the same form and color?

   d. were instead sightings of *Mustela nigripes*?

   e. were due to the European polecat destroying their habitat?

5. One theory that explains the similarities between Mayan art and ancient Chinese art is called diffusion. This theory evolves from the belief that invention is so unique that it happens only once, and then it is diffused to other cultures through travel, trade, and war. This theory might explain why

   a. the airplane and birds both have wings.

   b. certain artifacts in Central America resemble those found in Southeast Asia.

   c. most great art comes from Europe, where there is much travel between countries.

   d. rivers in South America and Africa have similar features.

   e. England, being so remote in the Middle Ages, is the only country to have castles.

6. Voting is the privilege for which wars have been fought, protests have been organized, and editorials have been written. Women struggled for suffrage, as did all minorities. Eighteen-year-olds clamored for the right to vote, saying that if they were old enough to go to war, they should be allowed to vote. Yet there are individuals who state that they have never voted. Often, they claim that their individual vote does not matter. Some people blame their absence from the voting booth on the fact that they do not know enough about the issues. In essence, Americans should take greater

   a. pleasure in their ability to make radical changes in their country.

   b. pains to win suffrage.

   c. advantage of the rights for which they fought so hard.

   d. interest in the plight of others.

   e. measures to ensure that people all over the world earn the right to vote.

7. A recent *New York Times* "House and Home" article featured the story of a man who lives in a glass house. Every wall in his home is transparent; he has no walls to hide behind, not even in the bathroom. Of course, he lives in an isolated area, so he does not exactly have neighbors peering in and watching his every move. But he has chosen to live without any physical privacy in a home that allows every action to be seen. He has created his own panopticon of sorts, a place in which

   a. a man can achieve fame for doing little.

   b. comfort goes hand in hand with style.

   c. beauty is in the eye of the beholder.

   d. secrets are kept well hidden from the public eye.

   e. everything is in full view of others.

8. Ecosystems include physical and chemical components, such as soils, water, and nutrients that support the organisms living there. These organisms may range from large animals to microscopic bacteria. Ecosystems also can be thought of as the interactions among all organisms in a given habitat; for instance, one species may serve as food for another. Human activities can harm or destroy local ecosystems unless such actions as land development for housing or businesses are carefully planned to

   a. conserve and sustain the ecology of the area.

   b. be identical to the organisms in the surrounding area.

   c. help form new habitats.

   d. create new jobs for the unemployed.

   e. prove that humans care about the environment.

9. Benjamin Franklin first conceived the idea of daylight saving during his tenure as an American delegate in Paris in 1784 and wrote about it extensively in his essay, "An Economical Project." It is said that Franklin awoke early one morning and was surprised to see the sunlight at such an hour. Always the economist, Franklin believed the practice of moving the time could save on the use of candlelight,

   a. and thus introduced the idea of daylight saving time.

   b. which also saved on the use of candlelight.

   c. coming to that conclusion during a stay in Paris.

   d. as candles were expensive at the time.

   e. so he wrote an essay called "An Economical Project."

10. Everglades National Park is the largest remaining subtropical wilderness in the continental United States. It is home to abundant wildlife, including alligators, crocodiles, manatees, and Florida panthers. The climate of the Everglades is mild and pleasant from December through April, though rare cold fronts may create near-freezing conditions. Summers are hot and humid. In summer, the temperatures often soar to around 90° and the humidity climbs to over 90%. Afternoon thunderstorms are common, and mosquitoes are abundant. If you visit the Everglades, wear comfortable sportswear in winter. Lightweight, loose-fitting, long-sleeved shirts and pants, and insect repellent

   a. are also necessary during winters.

   b. make any trip to the Everglades lots of fun!

   c. will not help fend off those mosquitoes.

   d. are recommended in the summer.

   e. are attractive and inexpensive.

Subtest 4: Word Knowledge

Directions: The Word Knowledge subtest measures your vocabulary. For each question, choose the answer that most closely means the same as the italicized word. If you are somewhat familiar with the italicized word, you can quickly eliminate the options that you know are incorrect.

Questions: 10

1. *Crimson*
   a. crisp
   b. neatly dressed
   c. reddish
   d. colorful
   e. lively

2. *Cease*
   a. start
   b. change
   c. continue
   d. stop
   e. fold

3. *Benign*
   a. harmless
   b. active
   c. dangerous
   d. unfavorable
   e. explosion

4. *Sullen*
   a. grayish yellow
   b. soaking wet
   c. very dirty
   d. angrily silent
   e. mildly nauseated

5. *Terse*
   a. pointed
   b. trivial
   c. oral
   d. lengthy
   e. raggedy

6. *Meander*
   a. mean
   b. ended
   c. trot
   d. engage
   e. wander

7. *Recuperate*
   a. reverse
   b. disturb
   c. improve
   d. fail
   e. convince

8. *Kindle*
   a. ignite
   b. friendly
   c. well-read
   d. aware
   e. instruct

9. *Embargo*
   a. agreement
   b. ban
   c. assignment
   d. discovery
   e. embarrass

10. *Proficient*
   a. athletic
   b. weary
   c. significant
   d. capable
   e. tight

Subtest 5: Math Knowledge

Directions: The Math Knowledge subtest measures your ability to use learned mathematical relationships. Each problem is followed by five possible answers. You must decide which one of the five answers is correct. The best method for attacking each of these questions is given in the answer block in Chapter 5. When you take the actual test, scratch paper will be provided for working out the problems.

Questions: 10

1. The first digit of the square root of 59,043 is
   a. 1
   b. 2
   c. 3
   d. 4
   e. 5

2. The distance in miles around a circular course with a radius of 35 miles is (use $\pi = \frac{22}{7}$)
   a. 110 miles.
   b. 156 miles.
   c. 220 miles.
   d. 440 miles.
   e. 880 miles.

3. The expression *4 factorial* equals
   a. $\frac{1}{4}$
   b. $\frac{1}{16}$
   c. 12
   d. $\frac{1}{24}$
   e. 24

4. Solve for x: $\frac{2x}{7} = 2x^2$
   a. $\frac{1}{7}$
   b. $\frac{2}{7}$
   c. 2
   d. 7
   e. 14

5. The reciprocal of 5 is
   a. 0.1
   b. 0.2
   c. 0.5
   d. 1.0
   e. 2.0

6. $\frac{4}{5}$ is equal to
   a. 0.45
   b. 0.50
   c. 0.60
   d. 0.80
   e. 0.90

7. Choose the answer to the following problem: $x(3x^2 + y) =$
   a. $4x^2 + xy$
   b. $4x^2 + x + y$
   c. $3x^3 + 2xy$
   d. $3x^3 + xy$
   e. $3xy^3$

8. 35% of what number is equal to 14?
   a. 4
   b. 40
   c. 49
   d. 400
   e. 440

9. $\frac{1}{4}$ is equal to
   a. 0.14
   b. 0.15
   c. 0.25
   d. 0.20
   e. 0.75

10. If $6x + 30 = 90$, then x is
    a. 5
    b. 10
    c. 15
    d. 20
    e. 60

Subtest 6:
Mechanical Comprehension

Directions: The Mechanical Comprehension subtest measures your ability to understand and reason with mechanical terms. Included in this part of the test are diagrams showing various mechanical devices. Following each diagram are several questions or incomplete statements. Study each diagram carefully, as details do make a difference in how each device operates, and then select the choice that best answers the question or completes the statement.

Questions: 10

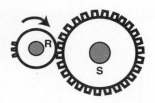

1. If gear R is the driver, at the moment shown, gear S is
a. not moving.
b. jammed.
c. moving at a high speed.
d. moving in the same direction as R.
e. moving in the opposite direction as gear R.

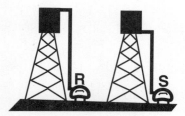

2. Which water wheel will turn for the longer time?
a. R
b. S
c. Both wheels will turn an equal amount of time.
d. Neither wheel will turn at all.
e. This cannot be determined from the figure.

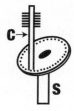

3. As shaft S makes one complete turn from the position shown, C moves
a. left, then right.
b. right, then left.
c. up only.
d. down only.
e. up and down.

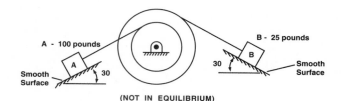

(NOT IN EQUILIBRIUM)

4. If weight B is to slide to the right, what change must be made in the diagram?
a. The slope of the inclined plane under A must be increased.
b. The slope of the inclined plane under B must be increased.
c. The radius of the inner pulley must be decreased.
d. The radius of the inner pulley must be increased to a size nearer to that of the outer pulley.
e. The radius of the outer pulley must be twice that of the inner pulley.

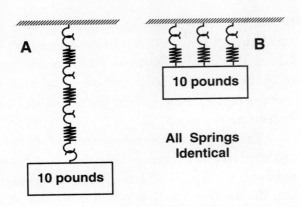

All Springs Identical

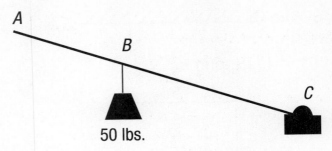

50 lbs.

5. Ten-pound weights are each suspended from a ceiling by three identical springs. In drawing A, the extension of each spring is

a. nine times greater than in B.

b. three times greater than B.

c. the same as in B.

d. $\frac{1}{3}$ less than in B.

e. $\frac{1}{9}$ less than in B.

7. The distance from A to B is three feet, and the distance from B to C is 7 feet. How much force must be applied at A to lift the 50 lbs. at point B?

a. 25 lbs

b. 35 lbs

c. 45 lbs

d. 55 lbs

e. 65 lbs

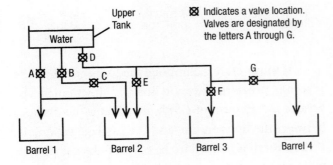

6. In the figure, all valves are initially closed. Gravity will cause water to drain down into the barrels when valves are opened. Which barrels will be filled if valves B, D, and F are opened and valves A, C, E, and G are left closed?

a. barrels 3 and 4

b. barrels 1 and 2

c. barrel 1

d. barrel 3

e. barrels 1, 2, 3, and 4

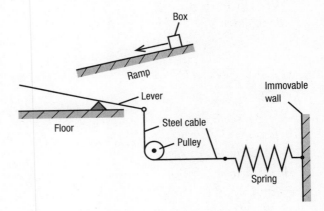

8. If the box slides down the ramp and drops onto the left side of the lever, what will happen to the spring?

a. It will touch the box.

b. It will remain as it is.

c. It will be compressed, or shortened.

d. It will be stretched, or lengthened.

e. None of the above.

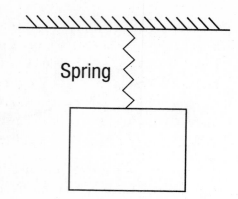

Spring

9. The spring in the figure shown has a stiffness of 20 lbs/in. How much is the spring stretched if the weight of the block is 400 lbs.?

   a. 2 inches

   b. 4 inches

   c. 10 inches

   d. 20 inches

   e. 0.5 inch

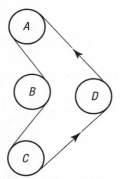

10. Which gears are turning counterclockwise?

   a. B

   b. B and D

   c. D

   d. A, B, C, and D

   e. A, C, and D

Subtest 7:
Instrument Comprehension

Directions: The Instrument Comprehension subtest measures your ability to determine the position of an aircraft in flight by reading instruments showing its compass heading, its amount of climb or dive, and its degree of bank to right or left. In each test item,

the left-hand dial is labeled *artificial horizon*. The small aircraft silhouette remains stationary on the face of this dial, while the positions of the heavy black line and the black pointer vary with the changes in the position of the aircraft in which the instrument is located.

The heavy black line represents the *horizon line*, and the black pointer shows the degree of *bank* to right or left. If the aircraft is neither climbing nor diving, the horizon line is directly on the silhouette's fuselage. If the aircraft has no bank, the black pointer will point to zero (Dial 1).

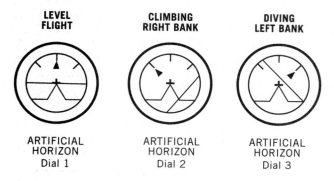

If the aircraft is climbing, the fuselage silhouette is seen between the horizon line and the pointer. The greater the amount of climb, the greater the distance between the horizon line and the fuselage silhouette. If the aircraft is banked to the pilot's right, the pointer will point to the left of zero (Dial 2).

If the aircraft is diving, the horizon line is between the fuselage silhouette and the pointer. The greater the amount of dive, the greater the distance between the horizon line and the fuselage silhouette. If the aircraft is banked to the pilot's left, the pointer will point to the right of zero (Dial 3).

The *horizon line* tilts as the aircraft is banked. It is always at a right angle to the pointer.

In each test item, the right-hand dial is the *compass*. This dial shows the direction in which the aircraft is headed. Dial 4 shows north, Dial 5 is west, and Dial 6 is northwest.

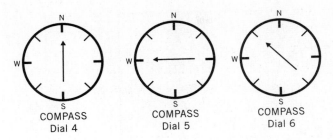

COMPASS
Dial 4

COMPASS
Dial 5

COMPASS
Dial 6

Each item in this test consists of two dials and four silhouettes of aircraft in flight. Your task is to de-

termine which of the four aircraft is closest to the position indicated by the two dials. Remember, you are always looking *north* at the same altitude as each plane. East is always to the *right* as you look at the page.

In the following example, the *artificial horizon* shows no bank and the *compass* shows southwest. Box C is the silhouette that meets the specifications. (*Note:* B is the rear view of the aircraft, and D is the front view. A is banked right, and B is banked left.)

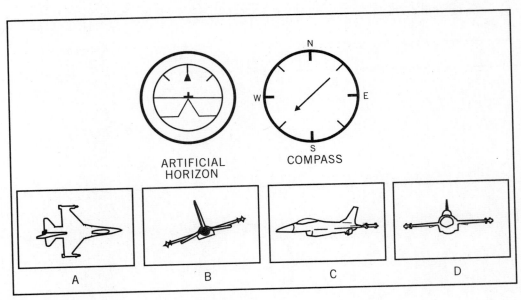

ARTIFICIAL HORIZON

COMPASS

A   B   C   D

Questions: 10

1.

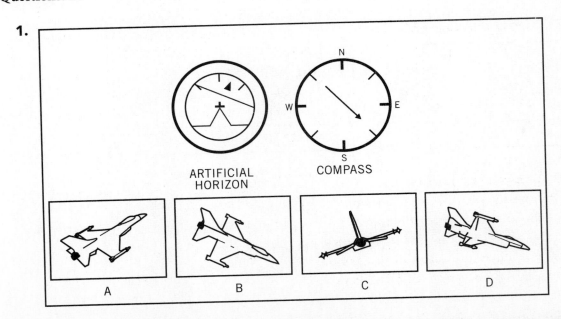

ARTIFICIAL HORIZON

COMPASS

A   B   C   D

2.

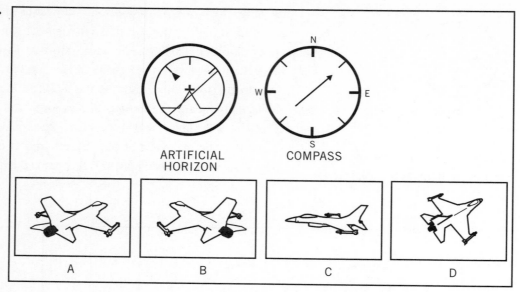

3.

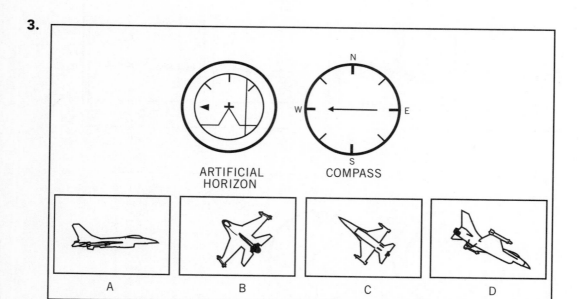

4.

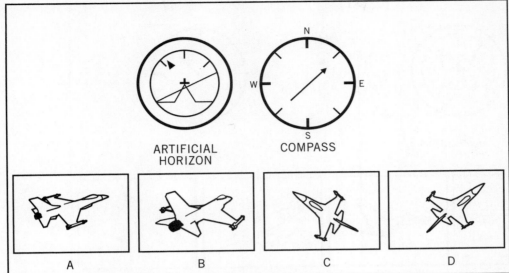

ARTIFICIAL HORIZON   COMPASS

A   B   C   D

5.

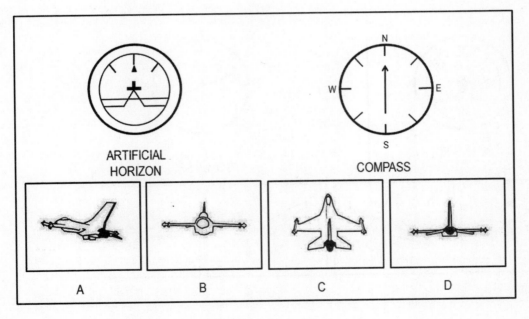

ARTIFICIAL HORIZON   COMPASS

A   B   C   D

6.

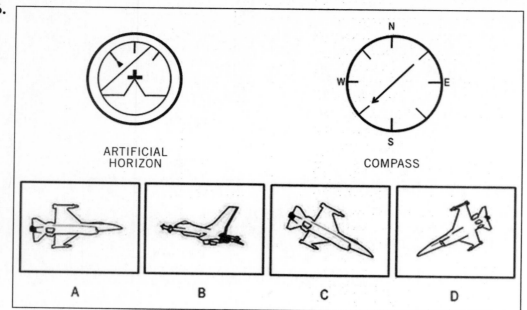

7.

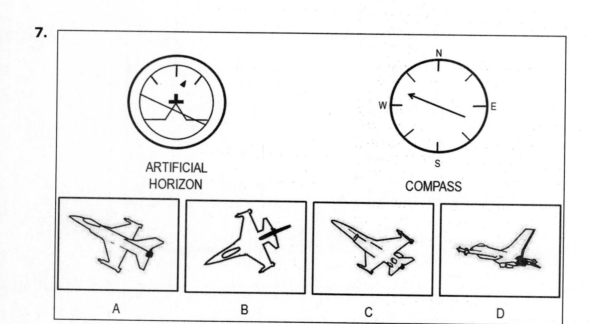

8.

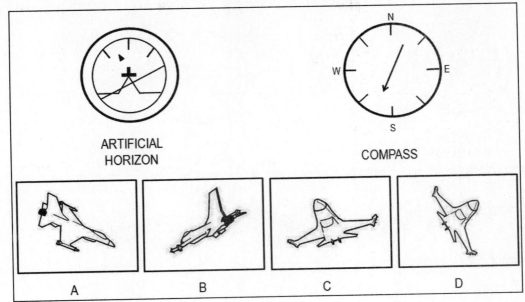

ARTIFICIAL HORIZON

COMPASS

A   B   C   D

9.

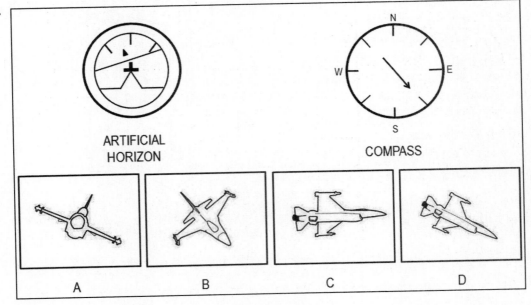

ARTIFICIAL HORIZON

COMPASS

A   B   C   D

10.

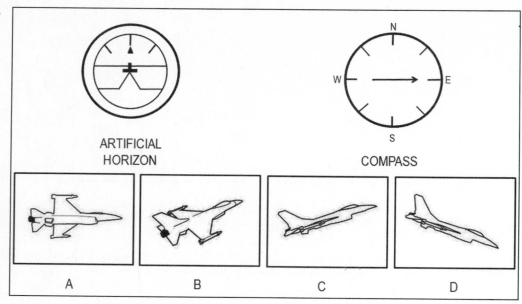

ARTIFICIAL HORIZON

COMPASS

A   B   C   D

Subtest 8: Block Counting

Directions: The Block Counting subtest measures your ability to see into a three-dimensional stack of blocks to determine how many pieces are touched by the numbered blocks. It is also a test of your abilities to observe and deduce what you cannot specifically see. Closely study the way in which the blocks are stacked. You may find it helpful to remember that all of the blocks in the pile are the same size and shape. While there will be several stacks of blocks on the actual test, for this practice example there is only one.

Questions: 10

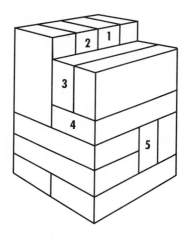

1. Block 1 is touched by _____ other blocks.
   a. 2
   b. 3
   c. 4
   d. 5
   e. 6

2. Block 2 is touched by _____ other blocks.

   a. 2

   b. 3

   c. 4

   d. 5

   e. 6

3. Block 3 is touched by _____ other blocks.

   a. 3

   b. 4

   c. 5

   d. 6

   e. 7

4. Block 4 is touched by _____ other blocks.

   a. 5

   b. 6

   c. 7

   d. 8

   e. 9

5. Block 5 is touched by _____ other blocks.

   a. 4

   b. 5

   c. 6

   d. 7

   e. 8

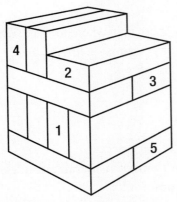

6. Block 1 is touched by _____ other blocks.

   a. 4

   b. 5

   c. 6

   d. 7

   e. 8

7. Block 2 is touched by _____ other blocks.

   a. 2

   b. 3

   c. 4

   d. 5

   e. 6

8. Block 3 is touched by _____ other blocks.

   a. 4

   b. 5

   c. 6

   d. 7

   e. 8

9. Block 4 is touched by _____ other blocks.

   a. 2

   b. 3

   c. 4

   d. 5

   e. 6

10. Block 5 is touched by _____ other blocks.

   a. 2

   b. 3

   c. 4

   d. 5

   e. 6

Subtest 9: Table Reading

Directions: The Table Reading subtest measures your ability to read tables quickly and accurately. Look at the following table. Notice that the X values are shown at the top of the table and the Y values are shown at the left of the table. In this test, you are to find the entry that occurs at the intersection of the row and the column corresponding to the values given. On your answer sheet, fill in the letter that corresponds with the number at the intersection of the X and Y values. Accuracy is important.

Questions: 10

X VALUE

Y VALUE	-3	-2	-1	0	+1	+2	+3
+3	22	23	25	27	28	29	30
+2	23	25	27	29	30	31	32
+1	24	26	28	30	32	33	34
0	26	27	29	31	33	34	35
-1	27	29	30	32	34	35	37
-2	28	30	31	33	35	36	38
-3	29	31	32	34	36	37	39

	X	Y		a.	b.	c.	d.	e.
1.	0	0		29	31	32	35	34
2.	-3	+3		22	29	30	39	35
3.	+2	-2		25	31	36	30	27
4.	0	+2		33	34	35	27	29
5.	-2	+3		31	38	32	23	22

X VALUE

Y VALUE	-3	-2	-1	0	+1	+2	+3
-3	41	42	44	45	46	47	48
-2	49	50	51	52	53	54	56
-1	58	59	60	61	62	63	64
0	65	66	67	68	41	42	43
+1	44	45	46	47	48	49	50
+2	51	52	53	54	55	56	57
+3	59	60	61	62	63	64	65

	X	Y		a.	b.	c.	d.	e.
6.	-3	-2		49	44	54	48	65
7.	+1	0		62	55	41	42	60
8.	-3	+2		59	40	63	44	51
9.	-1	0		61	67	45	53	55
10.	-1	+1		44	46	64	54	52

Subtest 10: Aviation Information

Directions: The Aviation Information subtest measures your knowledge of aviation. This portion is common to all three services' selection tests, although the number of questions varies from one service to another. Each of the questions or incomplete statements is followed by several choices. You must decide which one of the choices best completes the statement or answers the question. Eliminating any obviously incorrect choices first will increase your chances of selecting the right answer.

Questions: 10

1. At 0° angle of attack, a symmetrical airfoil will produce
   a. lift, but less than a positively cambered airfoil.
   b. no form drag.
   c. no induced drag.
   d. no net aerodynamic force.

2. Airport runways are numbered according to
   a. length and width.
   b. wind direction.
   c. the first two digits of compass direction.
   d. order of construction.

3. Which of the following, when doubled, will cause the greatest change in lift?
   a. coefficient of lift
   b. velocity
   c. density
   d. area

4. All motion or changes in aircraft attitude occur about which position?
   a. aerodynamic center (AC)
   b. center of pressure (CP)
   c. center of gravity (CG)
   d. the cockpit

5. What are the colors of the port and starboard running lights?
   a. white/white
   b. red/green
   c. green/red
   d. red/white

6. A pilot is flying under standard day conditions at sea level. His true airspeed will
   a. equal indicated airspeed.
   b. be greater than indicated airspeed.
   c. be less than indicated airspeed.

7. The transponder codes for loss of communication and for emergency are
   a. 7600 and 7500.
   b. 7700 and 7600.
   c. 7600 and 7700.
   d. 7500 and 7700.

8. What are the five major components of an airplane?
   a. wings, fuselage, empennage, landing gear, and engine
   b. wings, cockpit, empennage, flaps, and engine
   c. fuselage, rudder, empennage, ailerons, and engine
   d. fuselage, empennage, engine/transmission assembly, vertical stabilizer, and tail rudder

9. *Yaw* is defined as the motion of the longitudinal axis about which axis?
   a. the lateral axis
   b. the longitudinal axis
   c. the vertical axis
   d. the horizon

10. *Vertigo* can be described as
   a. the sensation of spinning while stationary.
   b. too little oxygen in the bloodstream.
   c. the sensation of feeling no movement.
   d. a form of blackout.

Subtest 11: Rotated Blocks

Directions: The Rotated Blocks subtest measures your ability to visualize and manipulate objects in space. For each question in this test, you will be shown a picture of a block. You must find a second block that is identical to the first. To see how to approach this test, study the following two blocks. Although you see them from different points, you can see that the blocks are **exactly alike**.

Look at the next two blocks. They are not alike, and they can never be turned so they will be exactly alike.

Now look at the following sample item. Which of the five choices is identical to the first block?

SAMPLE

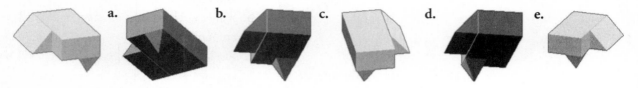

The correct choice in the sample is **a.**

Questions: 10

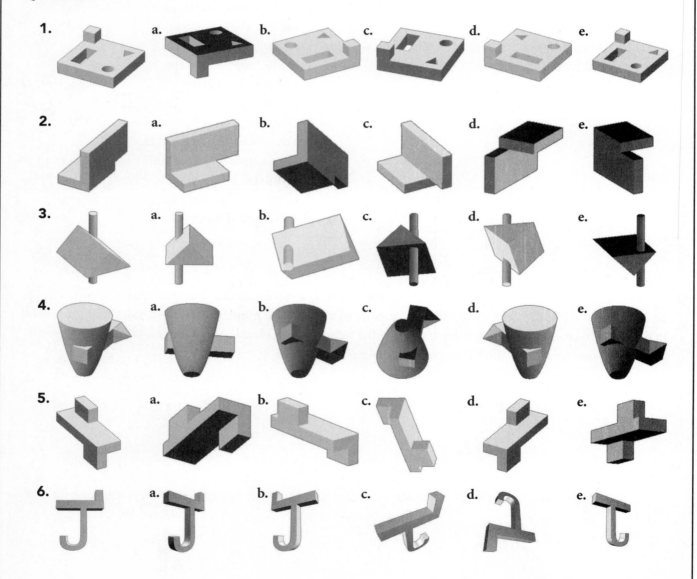

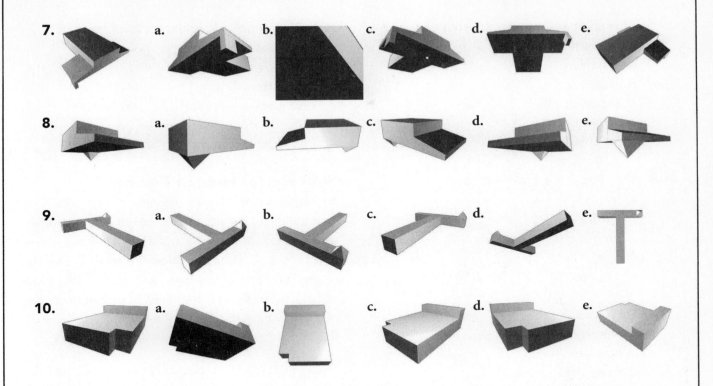

Subtest 12: General Science

Directions: The General Science subtest measures your knowledge in the area of science. Each of the questions or incomplete statements is followed by five choices. You must decide which one of the choices best answers the question or completes the statement. Again, if you are unsure of an answer, use the process of elimination. Remember, there are no penalties for guessing.

Questions: 10

1. An eclipse of the sun throws the shadow of the
   a. moon on the sun.
   b. earth on the sun.
   c. sun on the earth.
   d. earth on the moon.
   e. moon on the earth.

2. Substances that hasten a chemical reaction without themselves undergoing change are called
   a. buffers.
   b. catalysts.
   c. colloids.
   d. reducers.
   e. polymers.

3. Lack of iodine in the diet is often related to which of the following diseases?
   a. beriberi
   b. scurvy
   c. rickets
   d. goiter
   e. asthma

4. The chief nutrient in lean meat is
   a. starch.
   b. protein.
   c. fat.
   d. carbohydrates.
   e. Vitamin B.

5. After adding salt to water, the freezing point of the water is
   a. variable.
   b. inverted.
   c. the same.
   d. raised.
   e. lowered.

6. The fourth planet from the sun is
   a. Venus.
   b. Earth.
   c. Jupiter.
   d. Mars.
   e. Mercury.

7. Enzymes lower the _____ of a reaction.
   a. temperature
   b. activation energy
   c. free energy
   d. speed
   e. free radicals

8. Ornithology is the scientific study of
   a. mammals.
   b. birds.
   c. dinosaurs.
   d. horses.
   e. anger.

9. An angstrom is a measurement of
   a. a quantity of liquid.
   b. the length of light waves.
   c. the length of underwater communications cables.
   d. the speed of ships.
   e. the length of sound waves.

10. The ozone layer protects us from excessive amounts of
   a. ultraviolet radiation.
   b. carbon dioxide.
   c. gamma radiation.
   d. temperature variation.
   e. meteorite impact.

Subtest 13: Hidden Figures

Directions: The Hidden Figures subtest measures your ability to find a simple figure in a complex drawing. Above each group of questions are five figures, lettered A, B, C, D, and E. Below this set of figures are several numbered drawings. You are to determine which lettered figure is contained in each of the numbered drawings. In the following sample, the lettered figures are:

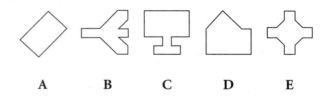

A B C D E

See if you can find one of the five figures in drawing X below.

Now look at drawing Y. It is exactly the same as X, but the outline of figure B has been darkened to show where it is located

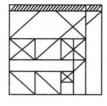 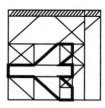

X   Y

As you work the following problems, remember that each numbered drawing contains only *one* of the lettered figures. The correct figure in each drawing will always be of the same size and in the same position as it appears in the set of figures. Look at each numbered drawing and decide which one of the five lettered figures is contained in it.

Questions: 10

A   B   C   D   E

1.

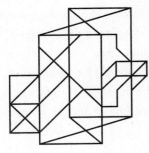

2.

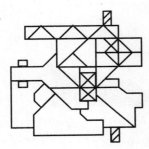

3.

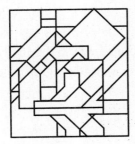

4.

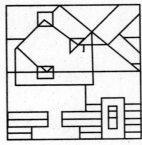

5.

A   B   C   D   E

6.

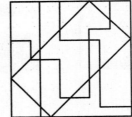

7.

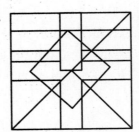

8.

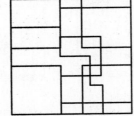

9.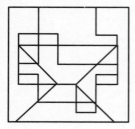

10.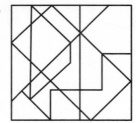

Subtest 14: Spatial Apperception

Directions: The Spatial Apperception subtest measures your ability to determine the position of an aircraft in flight in relation to a ship on the water. You are to determine whether it is climbing, diving, in level flight, banking to the right or left, flying straight toward the water (perpendicular to the coast), flying diagonally out toward the water, or any combination of these maneuvers. A sketch of the view seen directly out of the middle of the aircraft windscreen will be shown. You will be required to determine which aircraft below the sketch depicts the correct attitude and flight path shown in the windscreen view sketch. The position of the horizon will indicate whether the aircraft is climbing or diving. If the horizon is above the middle of the picture, the aircraft is diving (see the following examples).

Example 1: diving, banking left   Example 2: diving, no bank angle   Example 3: diving, banking right

Conversely, if the horizon is below the middle of the picture, the aircraft is climbing (see examples 4–6, following). The angle of the horizon will indicate the aircraft's bank angle. A horizon sloping down to the right indicates left bank (see examples 1, 4, and 7) and a horizon sloping down to the left indicates right bank (see examples 3, 6, and 9).

Example 4: climbing, left bank   Example 5: climbing, no bank   Example 6: climbing, right bank

Example 7: level flight, left bank   Example 8: level flight, no bank   Example 9: level flight, right bank

If the aircraft is in a bank, the position of the center of the horizon in the sketch will indicate whether the aircraft is also in a climb or a dive or in level flight. If the horizon is above the center, the aircraft is in a dive. The horizon is in the center for level flight and below center for a climb. Example 1 shows an aircraft in a dive and banking left.

The position of the coastline (left or right side of aircraft) will be important in questions when the sketch shows a view of the aircraft flying a course parallel to the coast. When the aircraft is flying a diagonal course out to sea, the coastline will slope up to one side, but the horizon will be level. This indicates a diagonal course with the coastline 45° off the aircraft's flight path and a direction straight out to sea 45° off the other side.

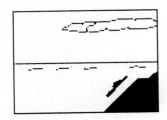

Example 10: level flight, no bank, diagonal heading, coastline on right

Remember that in all the sketches the aircraft is flying toward the ocean and not toward land. This should be your first check on all aircraft attitude pictures. Examples of the various aircraft attitudes follow.

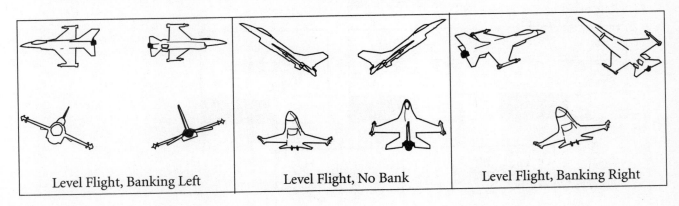

Level Flight, Banking Left   Level Flight, No Bank   Level Flight, Banking Right

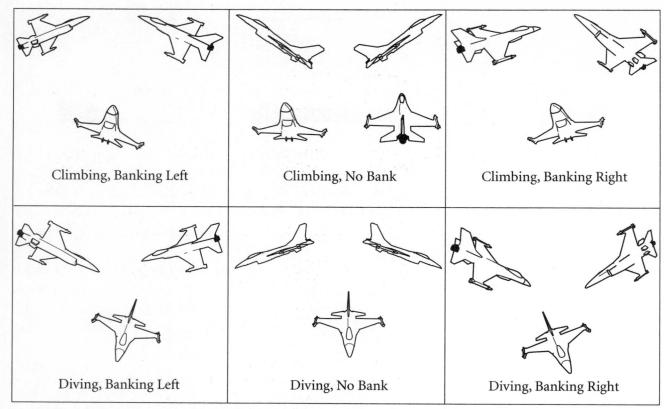

Climbing, Banking Left	Climbing, No Bank	Climbing, Banking Right
Diving, Banking Left	Diving, No Bank	Diving, Banking Right

For each of the following questions, select the choice that most nearly represents the aircraft's position in relation to the position of the ship.

Questions: 10

1.

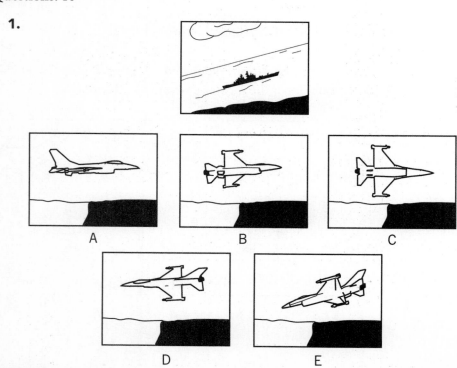

2.

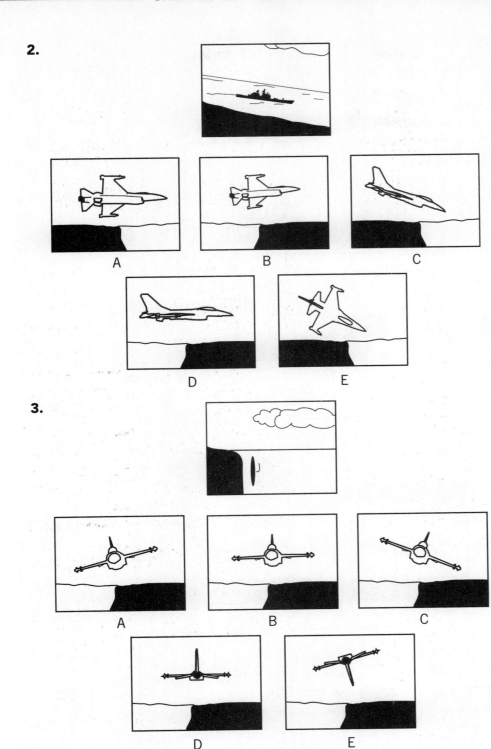

3.

4.

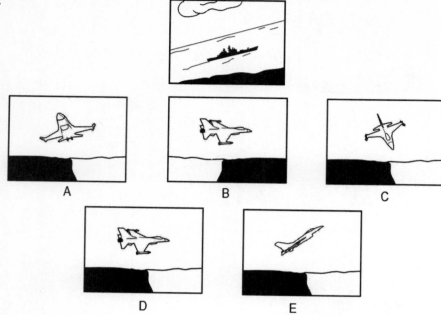

A B C

D E

5.

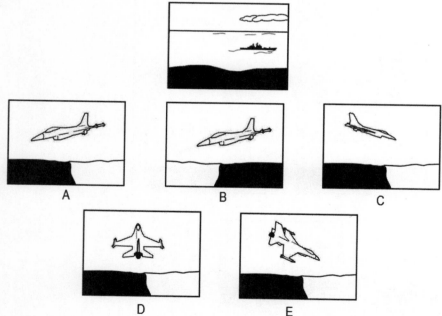

A B C

D E

6.

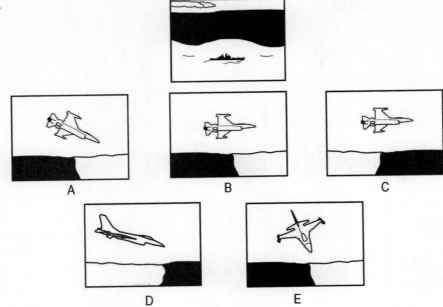

A B C

D E

7.

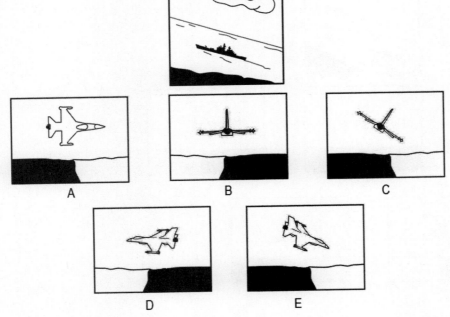

A B C

D E

8.

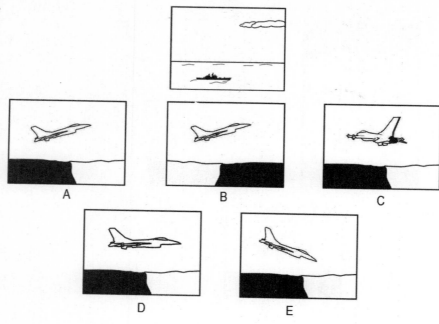

9.

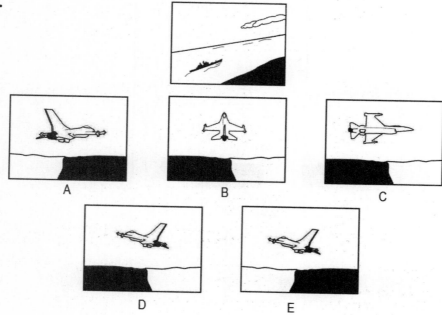

10.

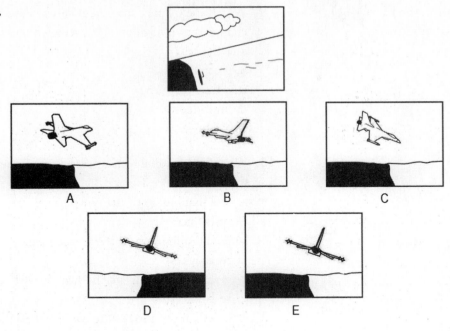

Subtest 15: Electronics Information

Directions: The Electronics Information subtest measures your basic knowledge of the principles of electrical and electronics systems: electrical tools, symbols, devices, and materials; electrical circuits; electricity and electronic systems; electrical current, voltage, conductivity, resistance, and grounding.

Questions: 10

1. Metals are very good conductors of electricity because they
   a. are high in resistance.
   b. have electrons that are able to move freely.
   c. are inexpensive.
   d. are easily formed into wires.
   e. are easily flammable.

2. A material with a very large resistance is classified as
   a. an insulator.
   b. a conductor.
   c. a semiconductor.
   d. a transformer.
   e. a generator.

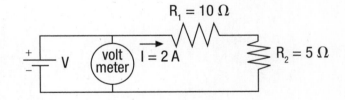

3. A voltmeter is connected to a circuit as shown. What will the meter read?
   a. 5 volts
   b. 10 volts
   c. 15 volts
   d. 30 volts
   e. 60 volts

4. Two light bulbs are connected to a parallel circuit. If another bulb is added in parallel, what will happen?
   a. The circuit resistance will increase.
   b. The current draw will increase.
   c. Choices **a** and **b** are correct.
   d. Nothing will happen.
   e. None of the above.

5. What is the total resistance when two 5-ohm light bulbs are connected in series?

a. $2.5\ \Omega$

b. $5.0\ \Omega$

c. $10.0\ \Omega$

d. $0.2\ \Omega$

e. $0.5\ \Omega$

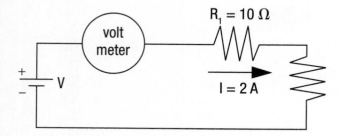

6. A voltmeter is connected to a circuit as shown. What will the meter read?

a. 0 volts

b. 10 volts

c. 20 volts

d. 30 volts

e. 200 volts

7. Two 8-ohm speakers are connected in series to an amplifier with a 24-volt output. What is the voltage across each speaker?

a. 3 volts

b. 6 volts

c. 12 volts

d. 24 volts

e. 32 volts

8. What does a semiconductor do?

a. It conducts electricity better than a conductor.

b. It inhibits the flow of electrons around the outer shell.

c. It insulates the electrical current from contact with other material.

d. It is useful for controlling the flow of electricity.

e. None of the above.

9. Which electronic component can be used to change the value of an alternating voltage?

a. a diode

b. a capacitor

c. a transformer

d. an inductor

e. a reducer

10. When two parallel resistances are combined, the equivalent resistance is

a. less than either of the two parallel resistances.

b. equal to the sum of the two parallel resistances.

c. greater than either of the two parallel resistances.

d. less than the sum of the two parallel resistances.

e. equal to the product of the two parallel resistances.

Subtest 16: Auto and Shop Information

Directions: The Auto and Shop Information subtest includes questions on automotive repair and building construction. General shop practices are also included. The questions measure your knowledge of automotive components, automotive systems, automotive tools, automotive troubleshooting and repair, shop tools, building materials, and building and construction procedures.

Questions: 10

1. What type of gauge would be read in units of mph (miles per hour)?

a. a speed gauge

b. a depth gauge

c. a pressure gauge

d. a temperature gauge

e. None of the above.

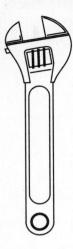

2. The tool shown here would most likely be used to
   a. drive nails.
   b. weld metal.
   c. tighten bolts.
   d. carve wood.
   e. pry.

3. Which of the following items is typically part of the suspension of a car?
   a. the carburetor
   b. the wheels
   c. the rods
   d. the pistons
   e. the alternator

4. *Stilson*, *strap*, *torque*, and *spanner* all denote types of
   a. saws.
   b. hammers.
   c. pliers.
   d. wrenches.
   e. screws.

5. The hand tool shown above is a(n)
   a. crowfoot wrench.
   b. offset wrench.
   c. box wrench.
   d. socket wrench.
   e. crescent wrench.

6. The subflooring of a typical residential house in the United States is normally made of which of the following materials?
   a. plastic
   b. wood
   c. fiberglass
   d. resin
   e. marble

7. Which of the following is a type of screwdriver?
   a. Phillips
   b. Allen
   c. socket
   d. veneer
   e. All of the above.

8. Which automotive system uses the following components: water pump, radiator, and thermostat?
   a. the interior heating system
   b. the engine cooling system
   c. the exhaust system
   d. the braking system
   e. the electrical system

9. Which of the following refers to a kind of chisel?
   a. diamond point
   b. dovetail
   c. coping
   d. duck bill
   e. ball-peen

10. If your car will not start because of a dead battery, which of the following measures should be taken to get the car started?
   a. install a new starter
   b. check the fuel level
   c. use jumper cables
   d. replace all of the fuses
   e. pump the gas pedal

Subtest 17:
Mechanical Comprehension

Directions: The Mechanical Comprehension subtest consists of problems—some of them illustrated—covering general mechanics, physical principles, and principles of simple machines such as gears, pulleys, levers, force, and fluid dynamics. Problems involving basic properties of materials are also included. The questions may test knowledge, application, and analysis of:

- **basic compound machines:** gears, cams, pistons, cranks, linkages, belts, and chains
- **simple machines:** levers, planes, pulleys, screws, wedges, wheels, and axles
- **mechanical motion:** friction, velocity, direction, acceleration, and centrifugal force

- **fluid dynamics:** hydraulic forces and compression
- **properties of materials:** weight, strength, expansion/contraction, absorption, and center of gravity
- **structural support**

Questions: 10

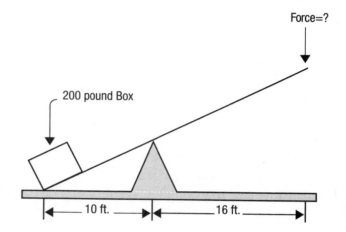

1. In this diagram, Frank must lift a 200-pound box using a lever. How many pounds of force must Frank apply to the right side of the lever to lift the box ($w \times d_1 = f \times d_2$)?
   a. 100 pounds
   b. 125 pounds
   c. 200 pounds
   d. 230 pounds
   e. 320 pounds

2. If there are five gears, with each gear turning the one next to it, and the first gear is turning clockwise at a constant speed of 10 rpm, what direction and speed would the last gear be turning?
   a. clockwise at 5 rpm
   b. counterclockwise at 10 rpm
   c. clockwise at 10 rpm
   d. counterclockwise at 20 rpm
   e. clockwise at 50 rpm

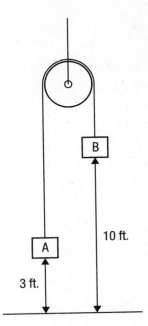

B

A

10 ft.

3 ft.

3. In this diagram, how much must block A be raised to allow block B to rest on the floor beneath it?
   a. 3 feet
   b. 7 feet
   c. 10 feet
   d. 13 feet
   e. 30 feet

4. A spring is most likely to be used on which of the following?
   a. a cabinet door
   b. a table
   c. an electric cord
   d. a pogo stick
   e. None of the above.

5. If there are two connected pulleys and one is smaller than the other, which one turns faster?
   a. The smaller one turns faster.
   b. The larger one turns faster.
   c. They turn at the same speed.
   d. It depends on the gears.
   e. Not enough information is provided to answer the question.

6. An elevator uses which of the following mechanical devices?
   a. a cable
   b. a pulley
   c. a motor
   d. All of the above.
   e. None of the above.

7. The Earth is a sphere that rotates about an axis that passes through the North Pole and the South Pole. If one person is standing at the North Pole, another at the South Pole, and a third at the equator of the Earth, which one will be traveling at a higher tangential velocity? (Tangential velocity means the speed parallel to the surface of the Earth.)
   a. The person at the South Pole will be traveling at a higher tangential velocity.
   b. The person at the North Pole will be traveling at a higher tangential velocity.
   c. The person at the equator will be traveling at a higher tangential velocity.
   d. All three will be traveling at the same tangential velocity.
   e. Not enough information is provided to answer the question.

8. What type of gauge is read in units of psi (pounds per square inch)?
   a. a pressure gauge
   b. a depth gauge
   c. a speed gauge
   d. an rpm gauge
   e. an altitude gauge

9. A block of wood rests on a level surface. What mechanical principle makes it more difficult to push this block sideways if the surface is made of sandpaper than if it is made of glass?

   a. centrifugal force

   b. gravity

   c. wind resistance

   d. friction

   e. lubrication

10. Water is flowing through a piping system. Eventually, due to friction losses and a rise in elevation of the piping, the flow rate of the water becomes very slow. What mechanical device can best be used to increase the flow of the water?

   a. a gear

   b. a winch

   c. a pump

   d. a compressor

   e. a pulley

Subtest 18: Assembling Objects

Directions: The Assembling Objects subtest consists of illustrated questions that test your ability to determine how an object should look when its parts are put together. These questions measure general mechanics and physical principles, aptitude for discerning spatial relations, and problem-solving abilities. Each question consists of five separate drawings. The problem is presented in the first drawing and the remaining four drawings are possible solutions. Determine which of the choices best solves the problem shown in the first picture. (*Note:* Images are not drawn to scale.)

Questions: 10

1.

2.

3.

4.

5.

6.

7.

8.

9.

10.

Subtest 19: Biographical Inventory

Directions: The Biographical Inventory subtest consists of 76 questions concerning your background, hobbies, and academic interests. Because this section is mostly biographical, there are no right or wrong answers. The purpose is to provide the military with some information about your personal strengths, education, and experience.

Background and personality questions may include:

Background

What was the highest level of education you completed?

What was the highest level of education your mother completed?

Is anyone in your immediate family a pilot?

What size community do you prefer to live in?

Do you consider yourself mechanically inclined?

What do your parents think of your joining the Army?

Personality

Have you ever planted a garden?

Have you ever skydived?

Do you prefer long or short hair?

On your day off, do you get up early or sleep until noon?

Do you like to take charge or to follow orders?

Answer Key

Subtest 1: Verbal Analogies

1. c. The *flight station* is where the *airplane* is controlled from, just as *bridge* is where a *ship* is controlled from.

2. a. A *tractor* is used on a *field*, as a *racquet* is used on a tennis *court*.

3. d. A *rose* is only one type of *flower*, just as a *sweater* is only one type of *clothing*.

4. d. A *sail* propels a *ship*, just as *rowing* propels a *boat*.

5. a. *Fly* and *drive* are both verbs, while *airplane* and *stake* are both nouns. The other phrase choices contain either both verbs or both nouns.

6. d. A *truck* is stored in a *garage* and an *airplane* is stored in a *hangar*. Choices **a** and **b** are incorrect because they are places where a truck might travel. Choice **c** is incorrect because it is a place where an airplane travels. Choice **e** is incorrect because it is a section of an airplane.

7. e. To *bend* is to move the *knee* and to *turn* is to move the *neck*. Choice **a** is incorrect because the elbow is situated on the arm. Choice **b** is incorrect because a twist is a kind of movement. Choice **c** refers to a function of the tongue, not to the way the tongue moves. Choice **d** contains synonyms.

8. a. A *spatula* is a tool used in the *kitchen* and a *scalpel* is a tool used in an *operating room*. Choice **b** is incorrect because a cupcake is made in a bakery. Choice **c** is incorrect because ravioli is a kind of pasta. Choices **d** and **e** are incorrect because they describe parts and the larger whole in which they are contained.

9. c. The operator of a *motorcycle* will *ride* it and the operator of a *helicopter* will *fly* it. Choices **a**, **b**, **d**, and **e** are wrong because none describe how a person operates a vehicle.

10. d. *Violet* is a kind of *shade* and a *circle* is a kind of *shape*. Choice **b** is incorrect because the order of the relationship is incorrect; a flower is not a kind of daisy. Choices **a**, **b**, and **e** are incorrect because they do not show the relationship between a category and an example of that category.

Subtest 2: Arithmetic Reasoning

1. b. The smaller field is one half the size of the larger field, making it 210 square yards. Since the area equals the length times the width, to get the width you must divide the area by the length. In this case, 210 divided by 15 equals 14 yards.

2. b. Since there are the same number of both types of plane, each pair of planes can carry a total of seven tons (two tons in the passenger plane and five tons in the cargo plane). Divide the total of 105 tons by seven tons per pair of aircraft to get 15 pairs. Two tons times the 15 passenger planes is a total of 30 tons.

3. d. The duration of sortie four is the total time flown, less the duration for each other sortie. One sortie was canceled, leaving only three sorties. First, solve for the total time flown: three sorties times the average of flight length of 93 minutes: $3 \times 93 = 279$ total minutes flown. Subtract 42 minutes each for sorties two and three: $279 - 42 - 42 = 195$ minutes.

4. e. If 40% were under 22 years of age, 60% would have been past their 22nd birthday. Multiply 450 by .6 (or 60%) to get 270 recruits.

5. d. To solve this distance problem, first convert to a common time base. Change seconds to minutes by dividing 1,800 seconds by 60 seconds per minute to get 30 minutes. Then, divide again by 60 minutes per hour to get .5 hours. To solve the distance, multiply 330 miles per hour by .5 hours to get 165 miles.

6. c. 157 is rounded to 200; 817 is rounded to 800; $(200)(800) = 160,000$.

7. d. Multiply 120 by $\frac{2}{3}$. Thus, $\frac{120}{1} \times \frac{2}{3} = \frac{240}{3} = 80$; 120 is written as a fraction with a denominator of 1. The fraction $\frac{240}{3}$ is simplified by dividing 240 by 3 to get 80 cups.

8. c. Using the formula, $V = \frac{1}{3}(10)(12)(10)$. $V = \frac{1}{3}(10)(12)(10) = \frac{1}{3}(1,200)$. One-third of 1,200 is 400.

9. a. $J = 6K$; $J + 2 = 2(K + 2)$, so $6K + 2 = 2K + 4$, which means K equals $\frac{1}{2}$. J equals 6K, or 3.

10. c. Change 13.5 hours into minutes by multiplying by 60: $13.5 \times 60 = 810$ minutes. Then change 810 minutes into seconds by multiplying by 60 again: $810 \times 60 = 48,600$ seconds. 48,600 seconds between the two cities means 48,600 gallons used.

Subtest 3: Reading Skills

1. c. The other options are concerned with technology, specialization, and managerial structure, but the topic of the paragraph is harmony and cooperation among the various components of an organization.

2. d. Choices **a** and **c** are wrong because both are factors that *prevent* the production of toxin. Choice **e** is wrong because *Clostridium botulinum* is not rare, and exposing it to another bacterium is not a factor for toxin production. Choice **b** contradicts the implication in the paragraph that it takes a relatively long time for the toxin to develop.

3. c. The paragraph has just stated that the earth is a dynamic planet, so choice **a** is wrong. Temperature fluctuations are not caused by planetary interaction, so choice **d** is wrong, and choices **b** and **e** are only two of the many factors involved in causing the changes on the earth.

4. a. Choices **b** and **c** are not correct because they refer to species other than the two discussed in the paragraph. Choice **d** is wrong because *Mustela nigripes* is the scientific name for the black-footed ferret, and choice **e** is wrong because destruction of habitat by the European polecat has nothing to do with confusion between it and the ferret.

5. b. This is the only choice that relates to the similarity of art between Central America and Southeast Asia, which is where the paragraph begins. The other choices all refer to other parts of the world, and choice **a** is not explained by this theory.

6. c. The paragraph begins by stating that Americans fought hard for the right to vote, then explains that they have not fully taken advantage of that right, as shown by the fact that so many Americans do not vote. Enjoying the change Americans made is not an issue discussed in the paragraph, so choice **a** is i... explains tha... suffrage, wh... paragraph i... and not peo... choices **d** a...

7. e. Although the man was the subject of an article just because he lives in an unusual house, there is a more specific and likely answer than choice **a**. Comfort, style, and beauty are not issues addressed in the paragraph, so choices **b** and **c** are incorrect. Choice **d** is wrong because the paragraph is about a house in which everything can be seen, so it would not be a good place to hide secrets.

8. a. Choice **b** does not make sense in the context of the final sentence in the paragraph. The paragraph never suggests that humans could aid existing ecosystems by creating new habitats, so choice **c** is incorrect. Employment is not a focus of the paragraph, so choice **d** is incorrect. Choice **e** is too vague and does not resolve the sentence well.

9. d. Choice **d** resolves the paragraph well by stating new information. Choices **a**, **b**, **c**, and **e** all repeat information already stated in the paragraph.

10. d. The second to last sentence of the paragraph already stated the kind of clothing that should be worn during the winter, so choice **a** is incorrect. Choice **b** would change the tone of the paragraph from formal to informal. Choice **c** is wrong because the final sentence of the paragraph explains measures that would help fend off mosquitoes. The look and price of the clothing and insect repellent described in the final sentence are not relevant to the topic being discussed, so choice **e** is wrong.

test 4: Word Knowledge

1. c. *Crimson* is a dark, *reddish* color.

2. d. To *cease* means to *stop*.

3. a. *Benign* means *harmless* or to no visible effect.

4. d. When someone is *sullen*, he or she is angry or annoyed and may demonstrate it by scowling rather than speaking.

5. a. People using *terse* speech are often sharp or *pointed* when they speak, making their point without many words.

6. e. To *meander* is to *wander* around aimlessly.

7. c. To *recuperate* means to *improve*, or get better, after an illness.

8. a. To *kindle* a fire is to *ignite* it.

9. b. An *embargo* is the same thing as a *ban*.

10. d. To be *proficient* at a task is to be *capable* of doing it well.

Subtest 5: Math Knowledge

1. b. When a number is marked off in groups of two digits each, starting at the decimal point, the square root of the largest square in the left-hand group, whether one or two digits, is the first digit of the square root of the number. In this case (5-90-43), 4 is the largest square in 5, and 2 is the square root of 4.

2. c. The circumference of a circle is two times the radius times π. So, in this case, the distance is two times 35, times 22, divided by seven, or 220 miles.

3. e. The factorial of a positive integer is that integer times each of the integers between it and 1. In this case, 4 times 3 times 2 equals 24.

4. a. Divide both sides of the equation by $2x$. The result is x equals $\frac{1}{7}$.

5. b. The reciprocal of a number is that number divided into one. In this case that is $\frac{1}{5}$, or 0.2.

6. d. Divide 4 by 5 in order to convert the fraction into a decimal. $4 \div 5 = 0.80$.

7. d. x times x^2 is x^3; x times y is xy.

8. b. Divide 14 by 35 and then multiply the answer by 100 to find the percent.

9. c. Divide 1 by 4 in order to convert the fraction into a decimal; $1 \div 4 = 0.25$.

10. b. The first step is to simplify the problem by subtracting 30 from each side, which results in $6x = 60$. Then divide both sides by 6, and $x = 10$.

Subtest 6: Mechanical Comprehension

1. a. As shown in the diagram, gears R and S are not meshing, so gear S is not moving.

2. b. Water wheel S will turn for a longer time than R because the source is near the bottom of the tank, while the source for R is near the top.

3. e. Shaft C is at the low point on the cam to start with, so it will move up for the first half turn of S, and then it will move back down.

4. c. For B to move to the right, the clockwise torque must be increased. Choices **a** and **d** can be eliminated because they would increase the counterclockwise torque. To increase the clockwise torque, the initial tension toward B would have to be increased, or the small pulley would have to be decreased with respect to the larger one. (The torque is the tension times the pulley's radius.) With 30° angles, the initial tension at A is 50 pounds, and the tension at B is 12.5 pounds. The tension at B could be increased to 25 pounds ($\frac{1}{2}$ the tension at A) if the angle were increased to 90°. That means the larger pulley would have to be more than twice the size of the small pulley for the system to turn clockwise. From the diagram, that does not appear to be the case, so choice **b** can be eliminated. To increase the clockwise torque by reducing the smaller pulley, the smaller pulley would have to be less than one-fourth the size of the larger pulley, because the tension at A is four times that at B. That eliminates choice **e**. Therefore, **c** is the answer.

5. b. In system A, all three springs have the same load. In system B, each spring carries of the load. Therefore, the tension of the springs in A is three times that of B.

6. d. Because valves D and F are opened, water will flow to barrel 3. With only valve B open, a closed valve C will prevent water from flowing to barrel 2.

7. b. The 50-lb weight at B creates a force about the fulcrum of 350 foot-lbs (50 lbs × 7 feet = 350 foot-lbs). If the distance from the fulcrum to the lifting point is 10 feet, then only 35 lbs of force must be used to lift the block (350 foot-lbs/10 feet = 35 lbs).

8. d. The box will force the left side of the lever down and the right side of the lever up, which will pull the cable up. The cable will pass across the pulley and apply a pulling force on the spring, so the spring will stretch.

9. d. If the block weighs 400 lbs and the stiffness of the spring is 20 lbs/in, then the spring will stretch $\frac{400 \text{ lbs}}{20 \text{ lbs/in}} = 20$ inches.

10. e. Gears A, C, and D are turning counterclockwise. B is turning clockwise. It helps to follow the direction of the chain, which is connected to all the gears.

Subtest 7: Instrument Comprehension

QUESTION	ANSWER	HEADING	PITCH	ROLL
1.	B	135° southeast	down	right
2.	D	045° northeast	up	right
3.	C	270° west	up	right
4.	A	045° northeast	up	right
5.	C	360° north	up	none
6.	D	225° southwest	down	right
7.	A	290° west-northwest	up	left
8.	C	195° south-southwest	up	right
9.	B	135° southeast	down	right
10.	D	090° east	down	none

Subtest 8: Block Counting

1. d. Block 1 touches five blocks. It is touching block 2, an unnamed block on the other side of block 1, block 3, and block 4 (in front of 1), and it is standing on block 5.

2. d. Block 2 touches five blocks. It is touching block 1, an unnamed block on the other side of block 2, block 3, and 4 (in front of 2), and it is standing on an unnumbered block.

3. d. Block 3 touches six blocks. It is touching blocks 1 and 2, and two unnumbered blocks (behind 3), and the unnumbered block (in front of 3), and it stands on block 4 (below block 3).

4. e. Block 4 touches nine blocks. It is touching blocks 1 and 2, the two unnumbered blocks behind block 4, block 3, an unnumbered block on top of block 4, block 5, and two unnumbered blocks below block 4.

5. d. Block 5 touches seven blocks. It is touching blocks 1 and 4 (above 5), three unnumbered blocks (on both sides of 5), and two unnumbered blocks (under block 5).

6. c. Block 1 touches six blocks. It is touching two unnamed blocks (on both sides of block 1), block 3, an unnamed block above block 1, block 5, and an unnamed block (below 1).

7. b. Block 2 touches three blocks. It is touching an unnamed block (on the side of block 2), block 3, and an unnamed block below block 3.

8. e. Block 3 touches eight blocks. It is touching an unnamed block on the side of block 3, block 2, block 4, an unnamed block above 1, block 1, and three unnamed blocks below block 3.

9. b. Block 4 touches three blocks. It is touching the unnamed block on the side of block 4, block 3, and the unnamed block below 4.

10. d. Block 5 touches five blocks. It is touching the unnamed block on the side of block 5, block 1, and three unnamed blocks above 5.

Subtest 9: Table Reading

1. b. The intersection of (X) 0 and (Y) 0 is 31.

2. a. The intersection of (X) −3 and (Y) +3 is 22.

3. c. The intersection of (X) +2 and (Y) −2 is 36.

4. e. The intersection of (X) 0 and (Y) +2 is 29.

5. d. The intersection of (X) −2 and (Y) +3 is 23.

6. a. The intersection of (X) −3 and (Y) −2 is 49.

7. c. The intersection of (X) +1 and (Y) 0 is 41.

8. e. The intersection of (X) −3 and (Y) +2 is 51.

9. b. The intersection of (X) −1 and (Y) 0 is 67.

10. b. The intersection of (X) −1 and (Y) +1 is 46.

Subtest 10: Aviation Information

1. a. At 0° angle of attack, a symmetrical airfoil will produce lift, but less than a positively cambered airfoil.

2. c. Airport runways are numbered according to the first two digits of compass heading, with the zero omitted for headings between 010 and 090.

3. b. Velocity will cause the greatest change in lift when doubled.

4. c. All changes in aircraft attitude occur about the center of gravity.

5. b. The port running lights are red; the starboard lights are green. Positional lights are white.

6. a. The pilot's true airspeed will equal indicated airspeed.

7. c. Transponder codes are as follows:

Loss of comms	7600
Emergency	7700
Hijacking	7500

8. a. The five major components of an aircraft are its wings, fuselage, empennage, landing gear, and engine.

9. c. *Yaw* is defined as the motion of the longitudinal axis about the vertical axis.

10. a. *Vertigo* is the sensation of spinning or whirling while the body remains stationary.

Subtest 11: Rotated Blocks

1. a.
2. b.
3. c.
4. b.
5. c.
6. a.
7. c.
8. b.
9. c.
10. e.

Subtest 12: General Science

1. e. It is the moon that appears to cover the sun, and the moon's shadow that darkens the earth.

2. b. Catalysts initiate chemical reactions without undergoing change themselves.

3. d. Lack of iodine in one's diet can cause goiter.

4. b. The chief nutrient in lean meat is protein.

5. e. Adding salt to water creates a solution that needs a lower temperature to freeze.

6. d. The fourth planet from the sun is Mars.

7. b. Enzymes lower the activation energy of a reaction, or the energy needed for a reaction to proceed.

8. b. Ornithology is the scientific study of birds.

9. b. An angstrom is a measurement of the length of light waves.

10. a. The ozone layer absorbs 97%–99% of the sun's high-frequency, ultraviolet radiation.

Subtest 13: Hidden Figures

1. a. This one is fairly obvious; the rectangle A is in the lower-left portion of the drawing.

2. a. This one is somewhat deceptive. At first glance you may see either figure B or D in this drawing, but neither of those figures is complete. The rectangle A is located in the upper-right portion of the drawing. Remember that only one correct figure will be found in each drawing.

3. e. Figure E seems to appear twice in this drawing, but two arms of the upper figure are longer than shown in the example. The one centered at the bottom is more accurate than the figure above it.

4. d. Another deceptive drawing. At first glance you may see figure C in the lower-left corner, but it is not complete, and its stem is off-center. Figure D is located directly above the incomplete figure C.

5. c. The correct figure C is vertically centered and located near the right border. This drawing also appears to contain figure A, overlapping figure C and touching the left border, but its lower right side is not complete.

6. b. At first glance this drawing appears to contain figure A, but the rectangle in figure A leans to the left and this one leans to the right. The correct figure starts in the upper left-hand corner.

7. e. This one is fairly obvious; the box in figure E is centered in this drawing.

8. c. Figure C is well hidden in this drawing, but it is there, taking up almost the entire right-hand side of the drawing.

9. d. Figure D touches the top of this drawing and is centered.

10. a. This is another fairly obvious one; figure A leans to the left and takes up the center of the drawing.

Section 14: Spatial Apperception

QUESTION	ANSWER	PITCH	ROLL	DIRECTION
1.	e.	diving	banking right	flying out to sea
2.	a.	level flight	banking left	flying out to sea
3.	b.	level flight	no bank angle	coastline on left
4.	d.	level flight	banking right	flying out to sea
5.	c.	diving	no bank	flying out to sea
6.	d.	diving	no bank	flying inland
7.	d.	level flight	banking left	flying out to sea
8.	a.	climbing	no bank	flying out to sea
9.	e.	level flight	banking slightly right	flying at an angle out to sea
10.	b.	level flight	banking slightly right	flying slightly inland, coast on left

Subtest 15: Electronics Information

1. b. A good conductor has electrons that are free to move, and metal is a good conductor. Metals are low in resistance and they can be expensive. They are easily formed into wires, but that is not why they are good conductors.

2. a. An insulator has very large resistance. A conductor (choice **b**) has a small resistance. A semiconductor (choice **c**) has a medium resistance. A transformer (choice **d**) is a coil of wire and has a small resistance.

3. d. The voltage across the meter will equal the sum of the voltages across the series resistors R_1 and R_2. So: $V = (I \times R_1) + (I \times R_2) = (2\,A \times 10\,\Omega) + (2\,A \times 5\,\Omega) = 20\,V + 10\,V = 30\,V$.

4. b. In a parallel circuit, the current will increase and the resistance will decrease.

5. c. The total resistance of series resistors is the sum of the resistance. So: $RT = R_1 + R_2 = 5\,\Omega + 5\,\Omega = 10\,\Omega$.

6. a. The meter will read zero because the meter is not connected across a resistance.

7. c. Because the resistances are equal, they will each have one-half of the applied voltage across them.

8. d. The semiconductor allows current to pass through but will add some resistance.

9. c. Transformers are used to scale the value of an AC voltage. The ratio of the number of coils determines the voltage.

10. a. The resistance that results from combining two parallel resistances is always less than either of the original resistances.

Subtest 16: Auto and Shop Information

1. a. A speed gauge is the correct answer. A depth gauge (choice **b**) would use units of length such as feet or meters. A pressure gauge (choice **c**) would use units of pressure such as psi (pounds per square inch) or bar. A temperature gauge (choice **d**) would use units of temperature such as degrees Celsius or degrees Fahrenheit.

2. d. This tool carves wood. Hammers are used to drive nails; welders or torches are used to weld metal; wrenches are used to tighten bolts; a crowbar could be used to pry.

3. b. The suspension of an automobile is typically composed of springs, shocks, wheels, and tires.

4. d. All these are names applied to various kinds of wrenches.

5. e. This hand tool is a crescent wrench.

6. b. The subflooring of a residential house consists of joists to support the structural load and decking for the surface. The joists are usually made of 2-inch by 10-inch lumber, and the decking is usually made of $\frac{3}{4}$-inch plywood.

7. a. A Phillips screwdriver is a very common type used on screws that have an indented cross on the head. You may find this type of screw on objects such as door hinges, television sets, and bicycles.

8. b. The internal combustion engine in an automobile generates heat and must be cooled. The typical cooling system is based on pumping water around the hot engine block. The heated water is then pumped into the radiator, where it is cooled and then recirculated back to the engine block. The thermostat is used to regulate the flow of water to keep the engine warm but not let it overheat.

9. a. *Diamond point* is a kind of chisel. *Dovetail* and *coping* describe kinds of saws. *Duck bill* describes a kind of plier; *ball-peen* is a type of hammer.

10. c. Jumper cables can be used to connect your dead battery to another live car battery to start the car. Installing a new starter will not help; the battery will still be dead. Adding fuel and changing fuses also will not recharge the battery.

Subtest 17: Mechanical Comprehension

1. b. (200 pounds)(10 feet) = f (16 feet). Solving for f gives 125 pounds.

2. c. All the gears would be turning at the same rate with every other one turning clockwise.

3. c. The blocks are tied together with a cable, which keeps the distance between the blocks constant. Therefore, if block B is to be lowered 10 feet to the floor, then block A must be raised the same amount.

4. d. Of all the items, only a pogo stick uses springs.

5. a. The smaller pulley has to go faster to keep up with the larger one.

6. d. All of the choices are correct. A motor is used to wind a cable around a pulley in order to raise and lower the elevator car.

7. c. The two people at the poles will just spin around the axis of rotation and have no tangential velocity. The person at the equator will travel much faster since he or she is rotating at the same rate as the people at the poles and is located far away—half the diameter of the Earth—from the axis of rotation.

8. a. A pressure gauge is measured in psi. The other gauges are read in the following units: A depth gauge uses a unit of length such as feet or meters; a speed gauge uses a unit of velocity such as miles per hour (mph) or kilometers per hour (kph); the rpm gauge measures revolutions per minute.

9. d. Friction is the force that must be overcome in order to slide one object across another.

10. c. Pumps are used to move liquids through piping systems.

Subtest 18: Assembling Objects

1. c.
2. d.
3. d.
4. b.
5. b.
6. d.
7. c.
8. d.
9. a.
10. d.

Subtest 19: Biographical Inventory

There are no "right" or "wrong" answers for this section.

PRACTICE TEST FOR THE AIR FORCE OFFICER QUALIFYING TEST

CHAPTER SUMMARY

This practice Air Force Officer Qualifying Test (AFOQT) tests you on the skills—verbal analogies, arithmetic reasoning, word knowledge, math knowledge, instrument comprehension, block counting, table reading, aviation information, general science, rotated blocks, and finding hidden figures—you will need in order to become a successful Air Force officer or aviator.

Subtest 1: Verbal Analogies

1.	ⓐ	ⓑ	ⓒ	ⓓ	ⓔ
2.	ⓐ	ⓑ	ⓒ	ⓓ	ⓔ
3.	ⓐ	ⓑ	ⓒ	ⓓ	ⓔ
4.	ⓐ	ⓑ	ⓒ	ⓓ	ⓔ
5.	ⓐ	ⓑ	ⓒ	ⓓ	ⓔ
6.	ⓐ	ⓑ	ⓒ	ⓓ	ⓔ
7.	ⓐ	ⓑ	ⓒ	ⓓ	ⓔ
8.	ⓐ	ⓑ	ⓒ	ⓓ	ⓔ
9.	ⓐ	ⓑ	ⓒ	ⓓ	ⓔ

10.	ⓐ	ⓑ	ⓒ	ⓓ	ⓔ
11.	ⓐ	ⓑ	ⓒ	ⓓ	ⓔ
12.	ⓐ	ⓑ	ⓒ	ⓓ	ⓔ
13.	ⓐ	ⓑ	ⓒ	ⓓ	ⓔ
14.	ⓐ	ⓑ	ⓒ	ⓓ	ⓔ
15.	ⓐ	ⓑ	ⓒ	ⓓ	ⓔ
16.	ⓐ	ⓑ	ⓒ	ⓓ	ⓔ
17.	ⓐ	ⓑ	ⓒ	ⓓ	ⓔ

18.	ⓐ	ⓑ	ⓒ	ⓓ	ⓔ
19.	ⓐ	ⓑ	ⓒ	ⓓ	ⓔ
20.	ⓐ	ⓑ	ⓒ	ⓓ	ⓔ
21.	ⓐ	ⓑ	ⓒ	ⓓ	ⓔ
22.	ⓐ	ⓑ	ⓒ	ⓓ	ⓔ
23.	ⓐ	ⓑ	ⓒ	ⓓ	ⓔ
24.	ⓐ	ⓑ	ⓒ	ⓓ	ⓔ
25.	ⓐ	ⓑ	ⓒ	ⓓ	ⓔ

Subtest 2: Arithmetic Reasoning

1.	ⓐ	ⓑ	ⓒ	ⓓ	ⓔ
2.	ⓐ	ⓑ	ⓒ	ⓓ	ⓔ
3.	ⓐ	ⓑ	ⓒ	ⓓ	ⓔ
4.	ⓐ	ⓑ	ⓒ	ⓓ	ⓔ
5.	ⓐ	ⓑ	ⓒ	ⓓ	ⓔ
6.	ⓐ	ⓑ	ⓒ	ⓓ	ⓔ
7.	ⓐ	ⓑ	ⓒ	ⓓ	ⓔ
8.	ⓐ	ⓑ	ⓒ	ⓓ	ⓔ
9.	ⓐ	ⓑ	ⓒ	ⓓ	ⓔ

10.	ⓐ	ⓑ	ⓒ	ⓓ	ⓔ
11.	ⓐ	ⓑ	ⓒ	ⓓ	ⓔ
12.	ⓐ	ⓑ	ⓒ	ⓓ	ⓔ
13.	ⓐ	ⓑ	ⓒ	ⓓ	ⓔ
14.	ⓐ	ⓑ	ⓒ	ⓓ	ⓔ
15.	ⓐ	ⓑ	ⓒ	ⓓ	ⓔ
16.	ⓐ	ⓑ	ⓒ	ⓓ	ⓔ
17.	ⓐ	ⓑ	ⓒ	ⓓ	ⓔ

18.	ⓐ	ⓑ	ⓒ	ⓓ	ⓔ
19.	ⓐ	ⓑ	ⓒ	ⓓ	ⓔ
20.	ⓐ	ⓑ	ⓒ	ⓓ	ⓔ
21.	ⓐ	ⓑ	ⓒ	ⓓ	ⓔ
22.	ⓐ	ⓑ	ⓒ	ⓓ	ⓔ
23.	ⓐ	ⓑ	ⓒ	ⓓ	ⓔ
24.	ⓐ	ⓑ	ⓒ	ⓓ	ⓔ
25.	ⓐ	ⓑ	ⓒ	ⓓ	ⓔ

Subtest 3: Word Knowledge

1.	ⓐ	ⓑ	ⓒ	ⓓ
2.	ⓐ	ⓑ	ⓒ	ⓓ
3.	ⓐ	ⓑ	ⓒ	ⓓ
4.	ⓐ	ⓑ	ⓒ	ⓓ
5.	ⓐ	ⓑ	ⓒ	ⓓ
6.	ⓐ	ⓑ	ⓒ	ⓓ
7.	ⓐ	ⓑ	ⓒ	ⓓ
8.	ⓐ	ⓑ	ⓒ	ⓓ
9.	ⓐ	ⓑ	ⓒ	ⓓ

10.	ⓐ	ⓑ	ⓒ	ⓓ
11.	ⓐ	ⓑ	ⓒ	ⓓ
12.	ⓐ	ⓑ	ⓒ	ⓓ
13.	ⓐ	ⓑ	ⓒ	ⓓ
14.	ⓐ	ⓑ	ⓒ	ⓓ
15.	ⓐ	ⓑ	ⓒ	ⓓ
16.	ⓐ	ⓑ	ⓒ	ⓓ
17.	ⓐ	ⓑ	ⓒ	ⓓ

18.	ⓐ	ⓑ	ⓒ	ⓓ
19.	ⓐ	ⓑ	ⓒ	ⓓ
20.	ⓐ	ⓑ	ⓒ	ⓓ
21.	ⓐ	ⓑ	ⓒ	ⓓ
22.	ⓐ	ⓑ	ⓒ	ⓓ
23.	ⓐ	ⓑ	ⓒ	ⓓ
24.	ⓐ	ⓑ	ⓒ	ⓓ
25.	ⓐ	ⓑ	ⓒ	ⓓ

Subtest 4: Math Knowledge

1. (a) (b) (c) (d) (e)
2. (a) (b) (c) (d) (e)
3. (a) (b) (c) (d) (e)
4. (a) (b) (c) (d) (e)
5. (a) (b) (c) (d) (e)
6. (a) (b) (c) (d) (e)
7. (a) (b) (c) (d) (e)
8. (a) (b) (c) (d) (e)
9. (a) (b) (c) (d) (e)

10. (a) (b) (c) (d) (e)
11. (a) (b) (c) (d) (e)
12. (a) (b) (c) (d) (e)
13. (a) (b) (c) (d) (e)
14. (a) (b) (c) (d) (e)
15. (a) (b) (c) (d) (e)
16. (a) (b) (c) (d) (e)
17. (a) (b) (c) (d) (e)

18. (a) (b) (c) (d) (e)
19. (a) (b) (c) (d) (e)
20. (a) (b) (c) (d) (e)
21. (a) (b) (c) (d) (e)
22. (a) (b) (c) (d) (e)
23. (a) (b) (c) (d) (e)
24. (a) (b) (c) (d) (e)
25. (a) (b) (c) (d) (e)

Subtest 5: Instrument Comprehension

1. (a) (b) (c) (d)
2. (a) (b) (c) (d)
3. (a) (b) (c) (d)
4. (a) (b) (c) (d)
5. (a) (b) (c) (d)
6. (a) (b) (c) (d)
7. (a) (b) (c) (d)

8. (a) (b) (c) (d)
9. (a) (b) (c) (d)
10. (a) (b) (c) (d)
11. (a) (b) (c) (d)
12. (a) (b) (c) (d)
13. (a) (b) (c) (d)
14. (a) (b) (c) (d)

15. (a) (b) (c) (d)
16. (a) (b) (c) (d)
17. (a) (b) (c) (d)
18. (a) (b) (c) (d)
19. (a) (b) (c) (d)
20. (a) (b) (c) (d)

Subtest 6: Block Counting

1. (a) (b) (c) (d) (e)
2. (a) (b) (c) (d) (e)
3. (a) (b) (c) (d) (e)
4. (a) (b) (c) (d) (e)
5. (a) (b) (c) (d) (e)
6. (a) (b) (c) (d) (e)
7. (a) (b) (c) (d) (e)

8. (a) (b) (c) (d) (e)
9. (a) (b) (c) (d) (e)
10. (a) (b) (c) (d) (e)
11. (a) (b) (c) (d) (e)
12. (a) (b) (c) (d) (e)
13. (a) (b) (c) (d) (e)
14. (a) (b) (c) (d) (e)

15. (a) (b) (c) (d) (e)
16. (a) (b) (c) (d) (e)
17. (a) (b) (c) (d) (e)
18. (a) (b) (c) (d) (e)
19. (a) (b) (c) (d) (e)
20. (a) (b) (c) (d) (e)

Subtest 7: Table Reading

1. (a) (b) (c) (d)
2. (a) (b) (c) (d)
3. (a) (b) (c) (d)
4. (a) (b) (c) (d)
5. (a) (b) (c) (d)
6. (a) (b) (c) (d)
7. (a) (b) (c) (d)
8. (a) (b) (c) (d)
9. (a) (b) (c) (d)
10. (a) (b) (c) (d)
11. (a) (b) (c) (d)
12. (a) (b) (c) (d)
13. (a) (b) (c) (d)
14. (a) (b) (c) (d)

15. (a) (b) (c) (d)
16. (a) (b) (c) (d)
17. (a) (b) (c) (d)
18. (a) (b) (c) (d)
19. (a) (b) (c) (d)
20. (a) (b) (c) (d)
21. (a) (b) (c) (d)
22. (a) (b) (c) (d)
23. (a) (b) (c) (d)
24. (a) (b) (c) (d)
25. (a) (b) (c) (d)
26. (a) (b) (c) (d)
27. (a) (b) (c) (d)
28. (a) (b) (c) (d)

29. (a) (b) (c) (d)
30. (a) (b) (c) (d)
31. (a) (b) (c) (d)
32. (a) (b) (c) (d)
33. (a) (b) (c) (d)
34. (a) (b) (c) (d)
35. (a) (b) (c) (d)
36. (a) (b) (c) (d)
37. (a) (b) (c) (d)
38. (a) (b) (c) (d)
39. (a) (b) (c) (d)
40. (a) (b) (c) (d)

Subtest 8: Aviation Information

1. (a) (b) (c) (d) (e)
2. (a) (b) (c) (d) (e)
3. (a) (b) (c) (d) (e)
4. (a) (b) (c) (d) (e)
5. (a) (b) (c) (d) (e)
6. (a) (b) (c) (d) (e)
7. (a) (b) (c) (d) (e)

8. (a) (b) (c) (d) (e)
9. (a) (b) (c) (d) (e)
10. (a) (b) (c) (d) (e)
11. (a) (b) (c) (d) (e)
12. (a) (b) (c) (d) (e)
13. (a) (b) (c) (d) (e)
14. (a) (b) (c) (d) (e)

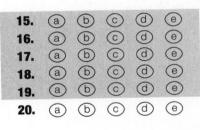

15. (a) (b) (c) (d) (e)
16. (a) (b) (c) (d) (e)
17. (a) (b) (c) (d) (e)
18. (a) (b) (c) (d) (e)
19. (a) (b) (c) (d) (e)
20. (a) (b) (c) (d) (e)

Subtest 9: General Science

1. (a) (b) (c) (d) (e)
2. (a) (b) (c) (d) (e)
3. (a) (b) (c) (d) (e)
4. (a) (b) (c) (d) (e)
5. (a) (b) (c) (d) (e)
6. (a) (b) (c) (d) (e)
7. (a) (b) (c) (d) (e)

8. (a) (b) (c) (d) (e)
9. (a) (b) (c) (d) (e)
10. (a) (b) (c) (d) (e)
11. (a) (b) (c) (d) (e)
12. (a) (b) (c) (d) (e)
13. (a) (b) (c) (d) (e)
14. (a) (b) (c) (d) (e)

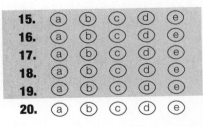

15. (a) (b) (c) (d) (e)
16. (a) (b) (c) (d) (e)
17. (a) (b) (c) (d) (e)
18. (a) (b) (c) (d) (e)
19. (a) (b) (c) (d) (e)
20. (a) (b) (c) (d) (e)

Subtest 10: Rotated Blocks

1.	ⓐ	ⓑ	ⓒ	ⓓ	ⓔ
2.	ⓐ	ⓑ	ⓒ	ⓓ	ⓔ
3.	ⓐ	ⓑ	ⓒ	ⓓ	ⓔ
4.	ⓐ	ⓑ	ⓒ	ⓓ	ⓔ
5.	ⓐ	ⓑ	ⓒ	ⓓ	ⓔ

6.	ⓐ	ⓑ	ⓒ	ⓓ	ⓔ
7.	ⓐ	ⓑ	ⓒ	ⓓ	ⓔ
8.	ⓐ	ⓑ	ⓒ	ⓓ	ⓔ
9.	ⓐ	ⓑ	ⓒ	ⓓ	ⓔ
10.	ⓐ	ⓑ	ⓒ	ⓓ	ⓔ

11.	ⓐ	ⓑ	ⓒ	ⓓ	ⓔ
12.	ⓐ	ⓑ	ⓒ	ⓓ	ⓔ
13.	ⓐ	ⓑ	ⓒ	ⓓ	ⓔ
14.	ⓐ	ⓑ	ⓒ	ⓓ	ⓔ
15.	ⓐ	ⓑ	ⓒ	ⓓ	ⓔ

Subtest 11: Hidden Figures

1.	ⓐ	ⓑ	ⓒ	ⓓ	ⓔ
2.	ⓐ	ⓑ	ⓒ	ⓓ	ⓔ
3.	ⓐ	ⓑ	ⓒ	ⓓ	ⓔ
4.	ⓐ	ⓑ	ⓒ	ⓓ	ⓔ
5.	ⓐ	ⓑ	ⓒ	ⓓ	ⓔ

6.	ⓐ	ⓑ	ⓒ	ⓓ	ⓔ
7.	ⓐ	ⓑ	ⓒ	ⓓ	ⓔ
8.	ⓐ	ⓑ	ⓒ	ⓓ	ⓔ
9.	ⓐ	ⓑ	ⓒ	ⓓ	ⓔ
10.	ⓐ	ⓑ	ⓒ	ⓓ	ⓔ

11.	ⓐ	ⓑ	ⓒ	ⓓ	ⓔ
12.	ⓐ	ⓑ	ⓒ	ⓓ	ⓔ
13.	ⓐ	ⓑ	ⓒ	ⓓ	ⓔ
14.	ⓐ	ⓑ	ⓒ	ⓓ	ⓔ
15.	ⓐ	ⓑ	ⓒ	ⓓ	ⓔ

Subtest 1: Verbal Analogies

Directions: This subtest measures your ability to reason and see relationships between words. You are to choose the answer that best completes the analogy developed at the beginning of each question. The best way to approach this type of test is to look for patterns or comparisons between the first phrase and the choices available to you. You have eight (8) minutes to complete this subtest.

Questions: 25
Time: 8 minutes

1. *Cup* is to *coffee* as *bowl* is to
   a. dish
   b. soup
   c. spoon
   d. food
   e. saucer

2. *Bicycle* is to *pedal* as *canoe* is to
   a. water
   b. kayak
   c. oar
   d. fleet
   e. lake

3. *Window* is to *pane* as *book* is to
   a. novel
   b. glass
   c. cover
   d. pages
   e. index

4. *Play* is to *actor* as *concert* is to
   a. symphony
   b. musician
   c. piano
   d. percussion
   e. violin

5. *Pride* is to *lion* as *school* is to
   a. teacher
   b. student
   c. self-respect
   d. learning
   e. fish

6. *Elated* is to *despondent* as *enlightened* is to
   a. aware
   b. ignorant
   c. miserable
   d. tolerant
   e. humble

7. *Embarrassed* is to *humiliated* as *frightened* is to
   a. terrified
   b. agitated
   c. courageous
   d. reckless
   e. timid

8. *Odometer* is to *mileage* as *compass* is to
   a. speed
   b. hiking
   c. needle
   d. direction
   e. humidity

9. *Fray* is to *ravel* as
   a. tremble is to roll
   b. hungry is to eat
   c. jolt is to shake
   d. stroll is to run
   e. stitch is to tear

10. *Elephant* is to *pachyderm* as
    a. mantis is to rodent
    b. poodle is to feline
    c. kangaroo is to marsupial
    d. zebra is to horse
    e. tuna is to mollusk

11. *Psychologist* is to *neurosis* as
   a. ophthalmologist is to cataract
   b. dermatologist is to fracture
   c. infant is to pediatrician
   d. rash is to orthopedist
   e. oncologist is to measles

12. *Cotton* is to *bale* as
   a. butter is to churn
   b. wine is to ferment
   c. grain is to shock
   d. curd is to cheese
   e. beef is to steak

13. *Division* is to *section* as
   a. layer is to tier
   b. tether is to bundle
   c. chapter is to verse
   d. riser is to stage
   e. dais is to speaker

14. *Mechanic* is to *garage* as
   a. teacher is to recess
   b. actor is to role
   c. jockey is to horse
   d. surgeon is to hospital
   e. author is to book

15. *Chickadee* is to *bird* as
   a. crocodile is to alligator
   b. giraffe is to reptile
   c. Siamese is to cat
   d. shepherd is to marsupial
   e. grasshopper is to ant

16. *Walk* is to *saunter* as
   a. trot is to race
   b. swim is to dive
   c. hop is to shuffle
   d. juggle is to bounce
   e. rain is to drizzle

17. *Tailor* is to *suit* as
   a. scheme is to agent
   b. edit is to manuscript
   c. revise is to writer
   d. mention is to opinion
   e. implode is to building

18. *Jaundice* is to *liver* as
   a. rash is to skin
   b. dialysis is to kidney
   c. smog is to lung
   d. valentine is to heart
   e. imagination is to brain

19. *Interest* is to *obsession* as
   a. mood is to feeling
   b. weeping is to sadness
   c. dream is to fantasy
   d. plan is to negation
   e. highlight is to indication

20. *Slapstick* is to *laughter* as
   a. fallacy is to dismay
   b. genre is to mystery
   c. satire is to anger
   d. mimicry is to tears
   e. horror is to fear

21. *Verve* is to *enthusiasm* as
   a. loyalty is to duplicity
   b. devotion is to reverence
   c. intensity is to color
   d. eminence is to anonymity
   e. generosity is to elation

22. *Conviction* is to *incarceration* as
   a. reduction is to diminution
   b. induction is to amelioration
   c. radicalization is to estimation
   d. marginalization is to intimidation
   e. proliferation is to alliteration

23. *Professor* is to *erudite* as
   a. aviator is to licensed
   b. inventor is to imaginative
   c. procrastinator is to conscientious
   d. overseer is to wealthy
   e. moderator is to vicious

24. *Dependable* is to *capricious* as
   a. fallible is to cantankerous
   b. erasable is to obtuse
   c. malleable is to limpid
   d. capable is to inept
   e. incorrigible is to guilty

25. *Dominance* is to *hegemony* as
   a. romance is to sympathy
   b. furtherance is to melancholy
   c. independence is to autonomy
   d. tolerance is to philanthropy
   e. recompense is to hilarity

Subtest 2: Arithmetic Reasoning

Directions: This subtest measures mathematical reasoning and problem solving. Each problem is followed by five possible answers. Decide which one of the five answers is most nearly correct. A method for attacking each of these questions is given in the answer block at the end of this chapter. You have twenty-nine (29) minutes to complete this subtest.

Questions: 25
Time: 29 minutes

   1. What is the estimated product when 157 and 817 are rounded to the nearest hundred and multiplied?
   a. 16,000
   b. 80,000
   c. 160,000
   d. 180,000
   e. 1,600,000

2. Mr. James Rossen is just beginning a computer consulting firm and has purchased the following equipment: 3 telephone sets, each costing $125; 2 computers, each costing $1,300; 2 computer monitors, each costing $950; 1 printer, costing $600; and 1 answering machine, costing $50. Mr. Rossen is reviewing his finances. What should he write as the total value of the equipment he has purchased so far?
   a. $3,025
   b. $4,025
   c. $5,400
   d. $5,525
   e. $6,525

3. One lap on a particular outdoor track measures a quarter of a mile around. To run a total of three-and-a-half miles, how many laps must a person complete?
   a. 7
   b. 9
   c. 10
   d. 13
   e. 14

4. $\frac{5}{8} \times \frac{4}{7} =$
   a. $\frac{5}{14}$
   b. $\frac{20}{8}$
   c. $\frac{25}{32}$
   d. $\frac{9}{16}$
   e. $\frac{10}{17}$

5. Newly hired nurses have to buy duty shoes at the full price of $84.50, but nurses who have served at least a year get a 15% discount. Nurses who have served at least three years get an additional 10% off the discounted price. How much does a nurse who has served at least three years have to pay for shoes?
   a. $63.78
   b. $64.65
   c. $67.49
   d. $71.83
   e. $72.05

6. The basal metabolic rate (BMR) is the rate at which our bodies use calories. The BMR for a man in his twenties is about 1,700 calories per day. If 204 of those calories should come from protein, about what percentage of this man's diet should be protein?
   a. 1.2%
   b. 8.3%
   c. 12%
   d. 16%
   e. 18%

7. How much water must be added to one liter of a 5% saline solution to get a 2% saline solution?
   a. .5 liter
   b. 1 liter
   c. 1.5 liters
   d. 2 liters
   e. 2.5 liters

8. All of the rooms in a building are rectangular, with 8-foot ceilings. One room is 9 feet wide by 11 feet long. What is the combined area of the four walls, including doors and windows?
   a. 90 square feet
   b. 160 square feet
   c. 180 square feet
   d. 280 square feet
   e. 320 square feet

9. A child has a temperature of 40° C. What is the child's temperature in degrees Fahrenheit?
$(F = \frac{9}{5}C + 32)$
   a. 100° F
   b. 101° F
   c. 102° F
   d. 103° F
   e. 104° F

10. A woman drives west at 45 miles per hour. After half an hour, a man starts to follow her. How fast must he drive to catch up to her three hours after he starts?
   a. 52.5 miles per hour
   b. 55 miles per hour
   c. 60 miles per hour
   d. 65 miles per hour
   e. 67.5 miles per hour

11. Jason is six times as old as Kate. In two years, Jason will be twice as old as Kate is then. How old is Jason now?
   a. 3 years old
   b. 6 years old
   c. 9 years old
   d. 12 years old
   e. 15 years old

12. A flash drive shows 827,036 bytes free. If you delete a file of size 542,159 bytes and create a new file of size 489,986 bytes, how many free bytes will the flash drive have?
   a. 489,986 free bytes
   b. 577,179 free bytes
   c. 681,525 free bytes
   d. 774,863 free bytes
   e. 879,209 free bytes

13. On the cardiac ward, there are 7 nursing assistants. NA Basil has 8 patients; NA Hobbes has 5 patients; NA McGuire has 9 patients; NA Hicks has 10 patients; NA Garcia has 10 patients; NA James has 14 patients; and NA Davis has 7 patients. What is the average number of patients per nursing assistant?

a. 6
b. 7
c. 8
d. 9
e. 10

14. A patient's hospice stay cost one-fourth as much as his visit to the emergency room. His home nursing cost twice as much as his hospice stay. If his total health care bill was $140,000, how much did his home nursing cost?

a. $10,000
b. $20,000
c. $40,000
d. $60,000
e. $80,000

15. At a certain school, half of all the students are female and one-twelfth of the students are from outside the state. Half of the out-of-state students are also female. What proportion of the students would you expect to be females from outside the state?

a. $\frac{1}{12}$
b. $\frac{1}{24}$
c. $\frac{1}{8}$
d. $\frac{1}{6}$
e. $\frac{1}{3}$

16. Based on the following information, estimate the weight of a person who is 5′5″ tall.

Height	Weight
5′	110 lbs.
6′	170 lbs.

a. 125
b. 130
c. 135
d. 140
e. 145

17. During exercise, a person's heart rate should be between 60% and 90% of the difference between 220 and the person's age. According to this guideline, what should a 30-year-old person's maximum heart rate be during exercise?

a. 114
b. 132
c. 156
d. 171
e. 198

18. A certain water pollutant is unsafe at a level of 20 ppm (parts per million). A city's water supply now contains 50 ppm of this pollutant. What percentage of improvement will make the water safe?

a. 20%
b. 30%
c. 40%
d. 50%
e. 60%

19. A study shows that 600,000 women die each year in pregnancy and childbirth, one-fifth more than scientists previously estimated. How many such deaths did the scientists previously estimate?
- **a.** 120,000
- **b.** 240,000
- **c.** 300,000
- **d.** 480,000
- **e.** 500,000

20. What is 250 milligrams in terms of grams?
- **a.** 0.0250 grams
- **b.** 0.250 grams
- **c.** 2.50 grams
- **d.** 25 grams
- **e.** 250,000 grams

21. An Army food supply truck can carry three tons. A breakfast ration weighs 12 ounces, and the other two daily meals weigh 18 ounces each. Assuming each soldier gets three meals per day, on a 10-day trip, how many soldiers can be supplied by one truck?
- **a.** 100 soldiers
- **b.** 150 soldiers
- **c.** 200 soldiers
- **d.** 320 soldiers
- **e.** 270 soldiers

	Aluminum	Cardboard	Glass	Plastic
Recycler X	6 cents/pound	3 cents/pound	8 cents/pound	2 cents/pound
Recycler Y	7 cents/pound	4 cents/pound	7 cents/pound	3 cents/pound

22. If you take recyclables to whichever recycler will pay the most, what is the greatest amount of money you could get for 2,200 pounds of aluminum, 1,400 pounds of cardboard, 3,100 pounds of glass, and 900 pounds of plastic?
- **a.** $440
- **b.** $447
- **c.** $454
- **d.** $469
- **e.** $485

23. A train must travel 3,450 miles in six days. How many miles must it travel each day?
- **a.** 525
- **b.** 550
- **c.** 600
- **d.** 575
- **e.** 625

24. A dormitory now houses 30 men and allows 42 square feet of space per man. If five more men are put into this dormitory, how much less space will each man have?
- **a.** 5 square feet
- **b.** 6 square feet
- **c.** 7 square feet
- **d.** 8 square feet
- **e.** 9 square feet

25. Ron is half as old as Sam, who is three times as old as Ted. The sum of their ages is 55. How old is Ron?

  a. 5 years old
  b. 10 years old
  c. 15 years old
  d. 20 years old
  e. 30 years old

Subtest 3: Word Knowledge

Directions: This subtest measures your vocabulary comprehension. For each question you are to choose the answer that most closely means the same as the italicized word. If you are somewhat familiar with the italicized word, you can quickly eliminate the options that you know are incorrect. You have five (5) minutes to complete this subtest.

Questions: 25
Time: 5 minutes

  1. *Gauche*
    a. awkward
    b. tactful
    c. graceful
    d. experienced
    e. expert

  2. *Enumerate*
    a. pronounce
    b. count
    c. explain
    d. plead
    e. exhaust

  3. *Triumphant*
    a. defeated
    b. vanquished
    c. victorious
    d. musical
    e. beaten

  4. *Magnanimous*
    a. enormous
    b. scholarly
    c. generous
    d. dignified
    e. wealthy

  5. *Aversion*
    a. harmony
    b. greed
    c. weariness
    d. dislike
    e. outrage

  6. *Poignant*
    a. varied
    b. exclusive
    c. singular
    d. distressing
    e. comprehensive

  7. *Antagonist*
    a. comrade
    b. leader
    c. master
    d. perfectionist
    e. opponent

  8. *Perseverance*
    a. unhappiness
    b. fame
    c. persistence
    d. humility
    e. efficiency

  9. *Homogeneous*
    a. alike
    b. plain
    c. native
    d. dissimilar
    e. ordinary

10. *Conspicuous*
   a. unknown
   b. excel
   c. obvious
   d. forgotten
   e. stellar

11. *Recluse*
   a. prophet
   b. fool
   c. intellectual
   d. hermit
   e. perfectionist

12. *Tote*
   a. acquire
   b. complete
   c. tremble
   d. abandon
   e. carry

13. *Preeminent*
   a. basic
   b. final
   c. observed
   d. responsible
   e. outstanding

14. *Grotesque*
   a. extreme
   b. frenzied
   c. bizarre
   d. typical
   e. majestic

15. *Outmoded*
   a. worthless
   b. unusable
   c. obsolete
   d. unnecessary
   e. pretentious

16. *Garbled*
   a. lucid
   b. unintelligible
   c. devoured
   d. outrageous
   e. invalid

17. *Frail*
   a. vivid
   b. delicate
   c. robust
   d. adaptable
   e. scarce

18. *Vindictive*
   a. disorderly
   b. outrageous
   c. insulting
   d. offensive
   e. spiteful

19. *Oration*
   a. nuisance
   b. independence
   c. address
   d. length
   e. elaboration

20. *Glib*
   a. angry
   b. superficial
   c. insulting
   d. dishonest
   e. descriptive

21. *Eccentric*
   a. normal
   b. frugal
   c. wild
   d. selective
   e. peculiar

22. *Panacea*
   a. cure
   b. result
   c. cause
   d. necessity
   e. problem

23. *Detrimental*
   a. harmful
   b. beneficial
   c. cumulative
   d. angered
   e. outstanding

24. *Ostentatious*
   a. hilarious
   b. pretentious
   c. outrageous
   d. obnoxious
   e. obsequious

25. *Negligible*
   a. insignificant
   b. delicate
   c. meaningful
   d. illegible
   e. nonchalant

Subtest 4: Math Knowledge

Directions: This subtest measures your ability to use learned mathematical relationships. Each problem is followed by five possible answers. You must decide which one of the five answers is correct. The best method for attacking each of these questions is given in the answer block at the end of this chapter. When you take the actual test, scratch paper will be provided for working out the problems. You have twenty-two (22) minutes to finish this subtest.

Questions: 25
Time: 22 minutes

1. The first digit of the square root of 112,092 is
   a. 1
   b. 2
   c. 3
   d. 4
   e. 5

2. Roberta draws two similar pentagons. The perimeter of the larger pentagon is 93 feet; one of its sides measures 24 feet. If the perimeter of the smaller pentagon equals 31 feet, then the corresponding side of the smaller pentagon measures
   a. $5s = 31$
   b. $93s = 24 \times 31$
   c. $93 \times 24 = 31s$
   d. $5 \times 31 = s$
   e. $31 \times 24 = s$

3. Which measurement uses the largest increment?
   a. perimeter
   b. area
   c. surface area
   d. volume
   e. They all use the same size increment.

4. What is the distance, in miles, around a circular course with a radius of 49 miles? (pi $= \frac{22}{7}$)
   a. 154 miles
   b. 308 miles
   c. 462 miles
   d. 539 miles
   e. 616 miles

5. Examine (A), (B), and (C) and choose the best answer.

(A) 0.5

(B) 5%

(C) $\frac{1}{5}$

a. (A) is greater than (B).

b. (B) is greater than (A).

c. (C) is greater than (A).

d. (A) and (B) are equal.

e. (B) times (A) is equal to (C).

6. Examine (A), (B), and (C) and choose the best answer.

(A) $n \times n$

(B) n^2

(C) $n(n)$

a. (A) plus (C) equals (B).

b. (B) is greater than (C) but less than (A).

c. (A) is less than (C).

d. (A), (B), and (C) are all equal.

e. (B) times (A) is equal to (C).

7. Find the circumference of a circle with a diameter of 10 centimeters.

a. 3.14 cm

b. 31.4 cm

c. 62.8 cm

d. 6.28 cm

e. none of the above

8. Which of the measures represents an obtuse angle?

a. 45°

b. 60°

c. 85°

d. 90°

e. 105°

9. $\frac{n^5}{n^2} =$

a. n^7

b. n^2

c. n^3

d. $2n^3$

e. $7n$

10. Simplify the following radical expression:

$\sqrt{3n^2}$

a. $n\sqrt{3}$

b. $9n$

c. $n\sqrt{9}$

d. $\sqrt{9}$

e. $3\sqrt{n}$

11. Look at this series: $\frac{1}{6}, \frac{1}{3}, \frac{1}{2}, \frac{2}{3}, \ldots$ What number should come next?

a. 1

b. $\frac{4}{6}$

c. $\frac{5}{6}$

d. $\frac{8}{9}$

e. $\frac{7}{12}$

12. Find the volume of a pyramid with four congruent base sides. The length of each base side and the prism's height measure 2.4 feet.

a. 46 cubic feet

b. 4.6 cubic feet

c. 4.8 cubic feet

d. 48 cubic feet

e. 1.2 cubic feet

13. What number is 42 less than $\frac{1}{5}$ of 820?

a. 98

b. 112

c. 122

d. 210

e. 222

14. Simplify the following radical expression:

$2\sqrt{7} - 3\sqrt{28}$

a. $-6\sqrt{7}$

b. $5\sqrt{196}$

c. $-5\sqrt{196}$

d. $\sqrt{7}$

e. $-4\sqrt{7}$

15. $\frac{8xy^2}{2xy} =$

a. $2xy$

b. $4x^2$

c. $16y$

d. $4y$

e. $4y^2$

16. What number is 6 less than $\frac{2}{5}$ of 25?

a. -4

b. 1

c. 4

d. 9

e. 12

17. What number is 3 times 4% of 20?

a. 2.4

b. 5.4

c. 24

d. 27

e. 32

18. Examine (A), (B), and (C) and choose the best answer.

(A) 7^2

(B) 4^3

(C) $3^2 + 6$

a. (A) and (B) are equal.

b. (A) is greater than (B).

c. (B) minus (A) is equal to (C).

d. (B) and (C) are equal to (A).

e. (B) times (A) is equal to (C).

19. The expression *5 factorial* equals

a. $\frac{1}{4}$

b. 16

c. 50

d. 120

e. 500

20. What number added to 15% of 30 equals 20?

a. -25

b. 4.5

c. 12

d. 15.5

e. 25.5

21. The reciprocal of 10 is

a. 0.1

b. 0.2

c. 0.5

d. 1.0

e. 2.0

22. What number plus 2 times the same number equals 99?

a. 16

b. 33

c. 66

d. 297

e. 365

23. Examine (A), (B), and (C) and choose the best answer.

(A) $\frac{2}{5}$ of 100

(B) $\frac{1}{2}$ of 80

(C) $\frac{1}{8}$ of 160

a. (A) is less than (B) or (C).

b. (A) and (B) are equal.

c. (B) and (C) are equal.

d. (B) is greater than (A) but less than (C).

e. (B) times (A) is equal to (C).

24. Isadora wants to know the perimeter of the face of a building; however, she does not have a ladder. She knows that the building's rectangular facade casts a 36-foot shadow at noon, while a nearby mailbox casts a 12-foot shadow at noon. The mailbox is 4.5-feet tall. If the length of the façade is 54 feet, what is the measure of the façade's perimeter?

a. $p = 13.5 \times 4$

b. $p = 54 \times 4$

c. $p = 4.5(2) + 12(2)$

d. $p = 13.5(2) + 54(2)$

e. $p = 13.5 + 4$

25. Find the circumference, in meters, of a circle with a radius of 25 centimeters.

a. 1.57 m

b. 157 m

c. 15.7 cm

d. 78.5 m

e. 7.85 m

Subtest 5:
Instrument Comprehension

Directions: This test measures your ability to determine the position of an aircraft in flight by reading instruments showing its compass heading, its amount of climb or dive, and its degree of bank to right or left. In each test item, the left-hand dial is labeled *artificial horizon*. The small aircraft silhouette remains stationary on the face of this dial, while the positions of the heavy black line and black pointer vary with the changes in the position of the aircraft in which the instrument is located.

The heavy black line represents the *horizon line*, and the black pointer shows the degree of *bank* to right or left. If the aircraft is neither climbing nor diving, the horizon line is directly on the silhouette's fuselage. If the aircraft has no bank, the black pointer will point to zero (Dial 1).

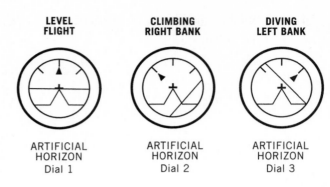

LEVEL FLIGHT	CLIMBING RIGHT BANK	DIVING LEFT BANK
ARTIFICIAL HORIZON Dial 1	ARTIFICIAL HORIZON Dial 2	ARTIFICIAL HORIZON Dial 3

If the aircraft is climbing, the fuselage silhouette is seen between the horizon line and the pointer. The greater the amount of climb, the greater the distance between the horizon line and the fuselage silhouette. If the aircraft is banked to the pilot's right, the pointer will point to the left of zero (Dial 2).

If the aircraft is diving, the horizon line is between the fuselage silhouette and the pointer. The greater the amount of dive, the greater the distance between the horizon line and the fuselage silhouette. If the aircraft is banked to the pilot's left, the pointer will point to the right of zero (Dial 3).

The *horizon line* tilts as the aircraft is banked. It is always at a right angles to the pointer.

In each test item, the right-hand dial is the *compass*. This dial shows the direction in which the aircraft is headed. Dial 4 shows north, Dial 5 is west, and Dial 6 is northwest.

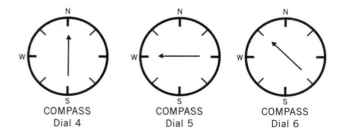

COMPASS Dial 4	COMPASS Dial 5	COMPASS Dial 6

Each item in this test consists of two dials and four silhouettes of aircraft in flight. Your task is to determine which of the four aircraft is closest to the position indicated by the two dials. Remember, you are always looking NORTH at the same altitude as each plane. East is always to the RIGHT as you look at the page. (*Note:* C in Question 3 is the rear view of the aircraft, and B is the front view.) You have nine (9) minutes to complete this subtest.

Questions: 20
Time: 9 minutes

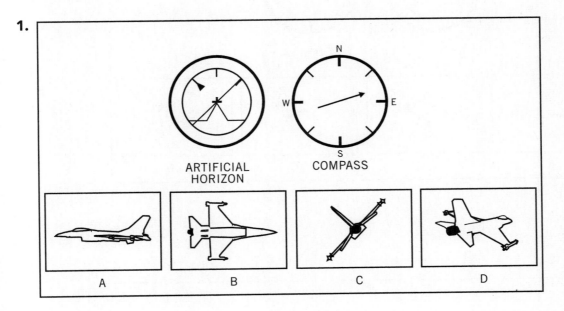

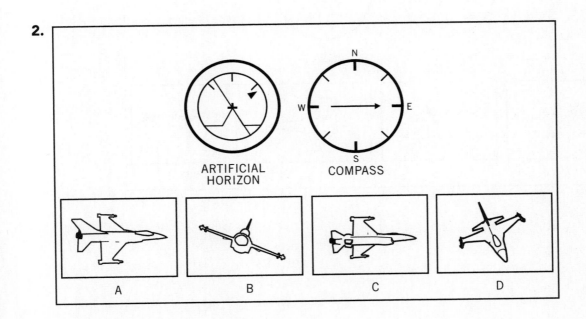

3.

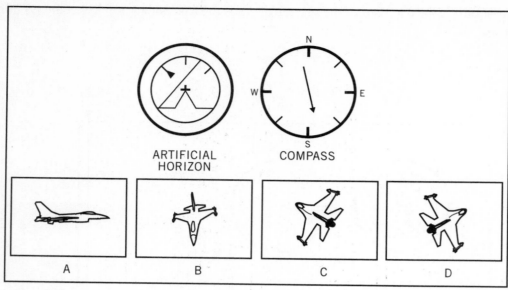

4.

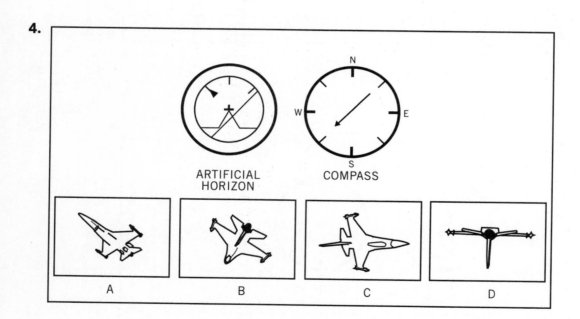

5.

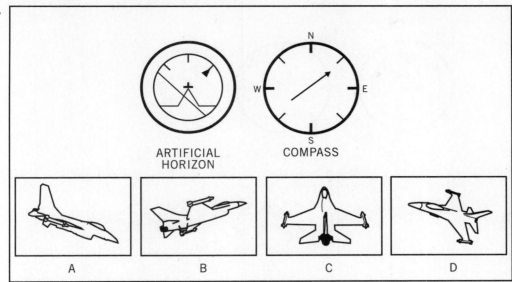

6.

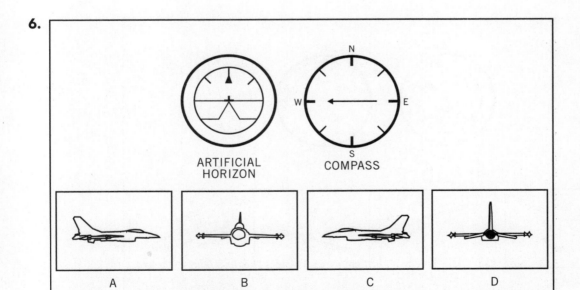

7.

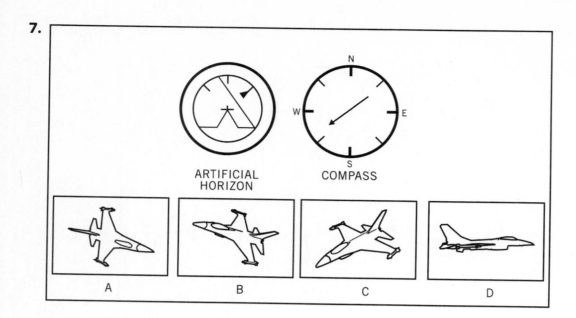

8.

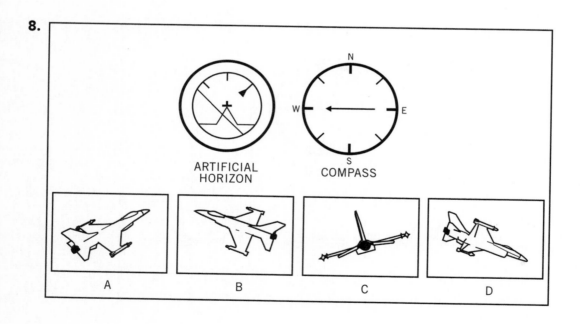

9.

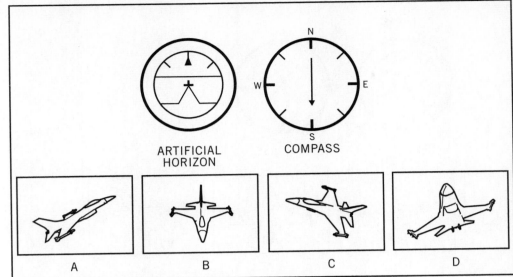

10.

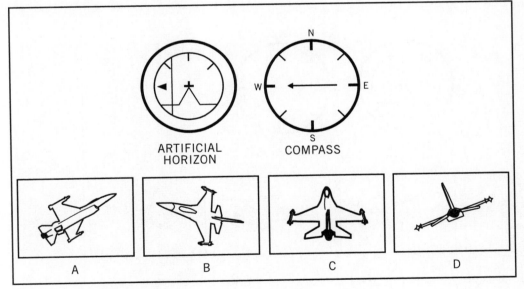

11.

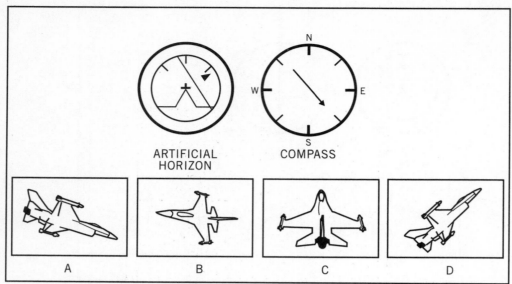

12.

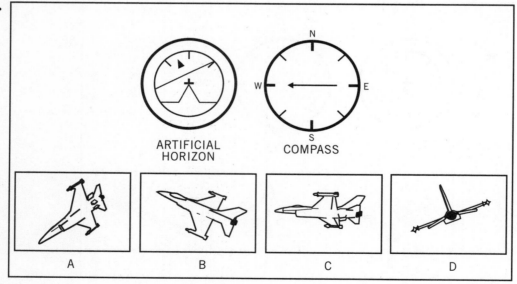

13.

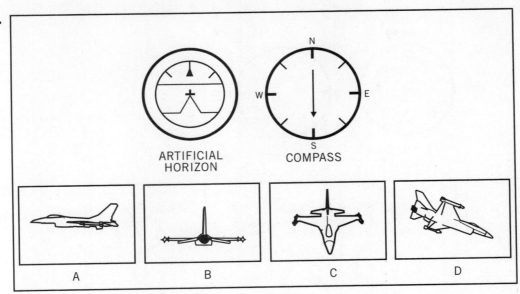

14.

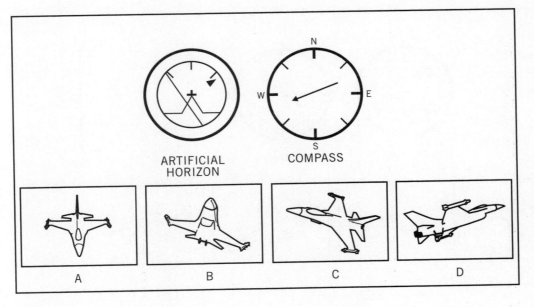

15.

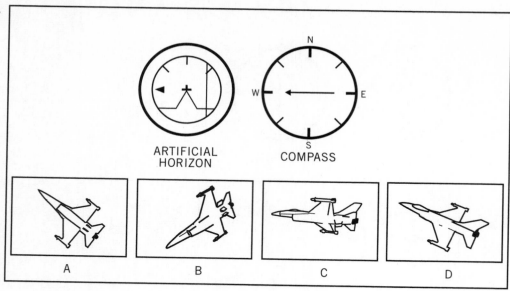

16.

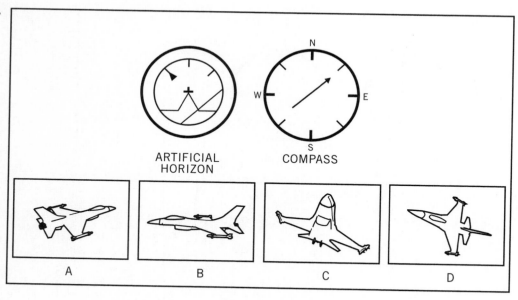

17.

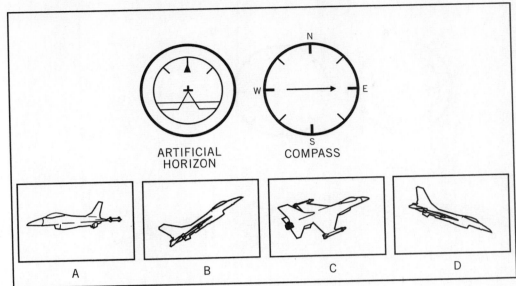

18.

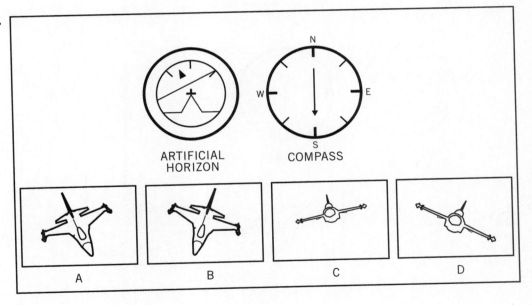

19.

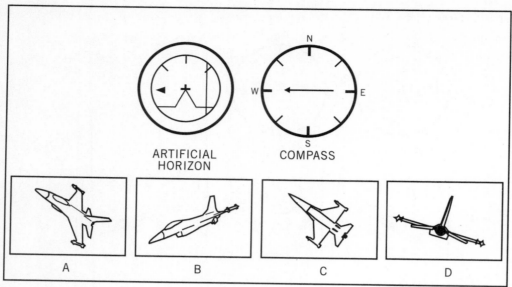

20.

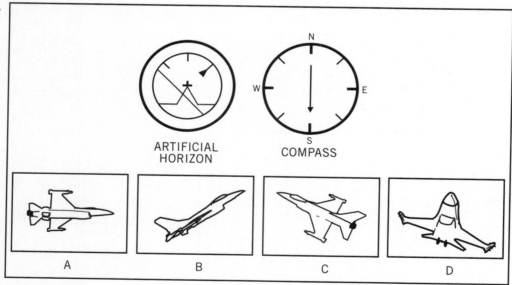

Subtest 6: Block Counting

Directions: This subtest measures your ability to see into a three-dimensional stack of blocks to determine how many pieces are touched by the numbered blocks. It is also a test of your abilities to observe and deduce what you cannot specifically see. Closely study the way in which the blocks are stacked. You may find it helpful to remember that all of the blocks in a pile are the same size and shape. Each stack of blocks is followed by five questions pertaining only to that stack. You have three (3) minutes to complete this subtest.

Questions: 20
Time: 3 minutes

Use the following figure to answer questions 1 through 5.

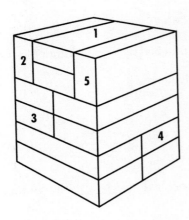

1. Block 1 is touched by _____ other blocks.
   a. 2
   b. 3
   c. 4
   d. 5
   e. 6

2. Block 2 is touched by _____ other blocks.
   a. 2
   b. 3
   c. 4
   d. 5
   e. 6

3. Block 3 is touched by _____ other blocks.
   a. 2
   b. 3
   c. 4
   d. 5
   e. 6

4. Block 4 is touched by _____ other blocks.
   a. 2
   b. 3
   c. 4
   d. 5
   e. 6

5. Block 5 is touched by _____ other blocks.
   a. 2
   b. 3
   c. 4
   d. 5
   e. 6

Use the following figure to answer questions 6 through 10.

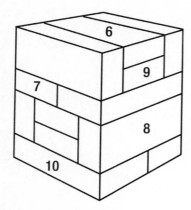

6. Block 6 is touched by _____ other blocks.
   a. 2
   b. 3
   c. 4
   d. 5
   e. 6

7. Block 7 is touched by _____ other blocks.
   a. 2
   b. 3
   c. 4
   d. 5
   e. 6

8. Block 8 is touched by _____ other blocks.
   a. 2
   b. 3
   c. 4
   d. 5
   e. 6

9. Block 9 is touched by _____ other blocks.
   a. 2
   b. 3
   c. 4
   d. 5
   e. 6

10. Block 10 is touched by _____ other blocks.
   a. 2
   b. 3
   c. 4
   d. 5
   e. 6

Use the following figure to answer questions 11 through 15.

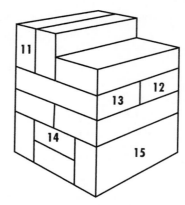

11. Block 11 is touched by _____ other blocks.
   a. 2
   b. 3
   c. 4
   d. 5
   e. 6

12. Block 12 is touched by _____ other blocks.
   a. 2
   b. 3
   c. 4
   d. 5
   e. 6

13. Block 13 is touched by _____ other blocks.
   a. 2
   b. 3
   c. 4
   d. 5
   e. 6

14. Block 14 is touched by _____ other blocks.
   a. 2
   b. 3
   c. 4
   d. 5
   e. 6

15. Block 15 is touched by _____ other blocks.
   a. 2
   b. 3
   c. 4
   d. 5
   e. 6

Use the following figure to answer questions 16 through 20.

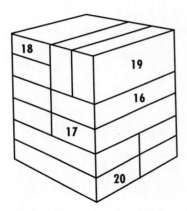

16. Block 16 is touched by _____ other blocks.
   a. 2
   b. 3
   c. 4
   d. 5
   e. 6

17. Block 17 is touched by _____ other blocks.
   a. 2
   b. 3
   c. 4
   d. 5
   e. 6

18. Block 18 is touched by _____ other blocks.
   a. 2
   b. 3
   c. 4
   d. 5
   e. 6

19. Block 19 is touched by _____ other blocks.
   a. 2
   b. 3
   c. 4
   d. 5
   e. 6

20. Block 20 is touched by _____ other blocks.
   a. 2
   b. 3
   c. 4
   d. 5
   e. 6

Subtest 7: Table Reading

Directions: This subtest assesses your ability to read tables quickly and accurately. Notice that the X values in each table are shown at the top of the table and the Y values are shown on the left of the table. In this subtest, you are to find the entry that occurs at the intersection of the row and the column corresponding to the values given. On your answer sheet, fill in the letter that corresponds with the number at the intersection of the X and Y values. Accuracy is important. You have seven (7) minutes to complete this subtest.

Questions: 40
Time: 7 minutes

Use the following table to determine the correct value for the X and Y values given in questions 1 through 5.

		X VALUE						
		−3	−2	−1	0	1	2	3
Y V A L U E	−3	45	23	77	93	52	54	92
	−2	82	12	71	55	25	48	30
	−1	13	65	33	14	50	38	19
	0	40	84	85	53	66	73	88
	1	55	43	22	70	20	99	32
	2	23	10	62	62	15	42	63
	3	32	44	55	72	83	11	60

1. −3,2
   a. 82
   b. 54
   c. 23
   d. 44
   e. 36

2. 2,−2
   a. 12
   b. 10
   c. 48
   d. 42
   e. 38

3. −2,3
   a. 44
   b. 82
   c. 30
   d. 23
   e. 32

4. 0,−1
   a. 85
   b. 33
   c. 53
   d. 70
   e. 14

5. 3,1
   a. 13
   b. 55
   c. 32
   d. 83
   e. 44

Use the following table to determine the correct value for the X and Y values given in questions 6 through 10.

		X VALUE						
		−3	−2	−1	0	1	2	3
Y V A L U E	−3	32	64	12	98	25	74	15
	−2	35	57	97	66	43	52	44
	−1	76	49	84	12	68	14	68
	0	45	29	79	61	37	82	11
	1	92	28	63	24	77	29	65
	2	74	26	99	54	55	16	62
	3	97	58	46	81	22	34	53

6. 2,−1
   a. 99
   b. 88
   c. 55
   d. 43
   e. 14

7. 0,0
  a. 11
  b. 45
  c. 0
  d. 61
  e. 76

8. −2,−1
  a. 25
  b. 33
  c. 39
  d. 45
  e. 49

9. −1,2
  a. 24
  b. 14
  c. 29
  d. 55
  e. 99

10. 3,3
  a. 32
  b. 53
  c. 61
  d. 82
  e. 62

Use the following table to determine the correct value for the X and Y values given in questions 11 through 15.

		X VALUE						
		−3	−2	−1	0	1	2	3
Y VALUE	−3	45	89	79	77	29	68	58
	−2	86	27	48	38	97	66	96
	−1	39	37	43	36	45	56	78
	0	18	17	55	98	44	87	34
	1	88	49	31	59	28	69	67
	2	37	76	47	22	16	45	33
	3	46	19	99	54	57	18	26

11. −1,−1
  a. 28
  b. 43
  c. 41
  d. 45
  e. 26

12. −2,1
  a. 49
  b. 56
  c. 86
  d. 93
  e. 99

13. −3,0
  a. 18
  b. 77
  c. 54
  d. 34
  e. 26

14. 1,3
    a. 29
    b. 34
    c. 41
    d. 52
    e. 57

15. −3,−2
    a. 96
    b. 86
    c. 33
    d. 18
    e. 89

Use the following table to determine the correct value for the X and Y values given in questions 16 through 20.

		X VALUE						
		−3	−2	−1	0	1	2	3
Y VALUE	−3	24	17	72	55	23	95	35
	−2	12	53	93	97	66	32	13
	−1	56	65	34	22	44	87	43
	0	75	52	43	48	92	45	85
	1	84	87	36	16	76	54	82
	2	46	15	86	64	83	14	26
	3	73	74	62	33	225	63	42

16. −3,−3
    a. 24
    b. 35
    c. 42
    d. 73
    e. 82

17. 2,2
    a. 14
    b. 53
    c. 34
    d. 23
    e. 13

18. −2,3
    a. 12
    b. 17
    c. 35
    d. 74
    e. 76

19. −1,0
    a. 22
    b. 48
    c. 34
    d. 52
    e. 43

20. 0,2
    a. 12
    b. 45
    c. 64
    d. 93
    e. 97

Use the following table to determine the correct value for the X and Y values given in questions 21 through 25.

		X VALUE						
		-3	-2	-1	0	1	2	3
Y V A L U E	-3	12	92	69	63	29	43	13
	-2	99	31	72	42	91	82	41
	-1	33	97	39	28	18	42	53
	0	49	52	23	21	51	32	23
	1	81	73	58	93	68	59	38
	2	78	89	61	79	98	22	19
	3	83	71	88	48	62	11	34

21. 2,−3
   a. 82
   b. 43
   c. 11
   d. 92
   e. 71

22. −1,3
   a. 69
   b. 88
   c. 29
   d. 62
   e. 53

21. 2,2
   a. 13
   b. 22
   c. 82
   d. 89
   e. 91

24. −3,1
   a. 53
   b. 69
   c. 81
   d. 88
   e. 93

25. 2,3
   a. 19
   b. 92
   c. 71
   d. 11
   e. 99

Use the following table to determine the correct value for the X and Y values given in questions 26 through 40.

		-9	-8	-7	-6	-5	-4	-3	-2	-1	0	1	2	3	4	5	6	7	8	9
	-9	48	57	52	13	86	91	54	82	52	87	46	68	92	47	53	38	52	45	78
	-8	78	58	26	90	54	77	50	41	24	18	12	32	54	16	39	28	59	83	57
	-7	54	43	77	23	49	54	45	81	64	21	54	87	56	10	15	50	35	68	99
	-6	52	56	21	42	25	62	70	88	28	55	15	48	56	15	85	52	87	74	62
	-5	19	23	58	98	38	58	47	56	74	21	99	84	28	48	24	56	65	11	56
	-4	25	82	54	12	33	76	25	43	93	53	31	10	20	34	76	92	28	33	52
	-3	43	65	21	45	21	58	86	96	35	71	70	80	45	85	43	23	51	52	14
Y	-2	58	87	26	65	52	55	43	76	55	26	29	96	54	19	14	87	74	55	92
V	-1	82	73	34	52	95	42	26	74	49	83	75	96	28	21	31	78	46	39	76
A	0	21	85	58	43	74	38	72	81	11	18	84	73	52	66	62	81	12	43	17
L	1	50	26	54	45	25	84	95	31	18	45	76	61	41	30	24	46	66	83	73
U	2	86	52	64	25	21	17	64	23	71	13	90	56	44	70	12	27	48	87	33
E	3	74	13	75	17	85	56	50	43	68	10	37	85	71	16	52	49	18	66	95
	4	32	69	78	68	73	54	15	61	42	78	91	28	93	85	34	70	59	46	35
	5	15	55	90	33	91	12	99	23	53	62	79	81	64	40	38	26	69	73	13
	6	64	38	62	54	18	22	36	28	93	38	61	98	14	30	49	63	88	12	41
	7	84	56	53	56	76	45	64	11	83	47	23	74	31	89	57	38	32	78	19
	8	56	84	21	86	21	18	29	31	12	25	59	40	72	98	53	22	45	88	74
	9	46	19	64	47	54	53	75	82	69	45	80	13	22	15	70	18	49	59	16

26. 9,-4
  a. 14
  b. 35
  c. 52
  d. 25
  e. 32

27. -5,9
  a. 54
  b. 90
  c. 32
  d. 53
  e. 56

28. −1,−4
   a. 14
   b. 93
   c. 28
   d. 91
   e. 42

29. −3,8
   a. 29
   b. 75
   c. 50
   d. 72
   e. 52

30. 5,−3
   a. 99
   b. 64
   c. 47
   d. 28
   e. 43

31. 0,−7
   a. 74
   b. 47
   c. 58
   d. 12
   e. 21

32. 4,−4
   a. 85
   b. 48
   c. 20
   d. 76
   e. 34

33. 7,−3
   a. 32
   b. 21
   c. 52
   d. 31
   e. 51

34. −9,3
   a. 43
   b. 74
   c. 54
   d. 92
   e. 47

35. 1,−8
   a. 34
   b. 74
   c. 24
   d. 12
   e. 73

36. 0,0
   a. 84
   b. 11
   c. 18
   d. 87
   e. 80

37. −5,0
   a. 62
   b. 74
   c. 21
   d. 26
   e. 58

38. −2,7
   a. 81
   b. 87
   c. 11
   d. 74
   e. 14

39. −8,5
   a. 55
   b. 23
   c. 39
   d. 54
   e. 83

40. −6,4
   a. 26
   b. 68
   c. 23
   d. 74
   e. 92

Subtest 8: Aviation Information

Directions: This subtest measures your knowledge of aviation. This portion is common to all three service selection tests, although the number of questions varies from one service to another. Each of the questions or incomplete statements is followed by several choices. You must decide which one of the choices best completes the statement or answers the question. Eliminating any obviously incorrect choices first will increase your chances of selecting the correct answer. You have eight (8) minutes to complete this subtest.

Questions: 20
Time: 8 minutes

1. If the rudder of an aircraft is deflected, the aircraft will move about the _____ axis.
   a. centroid
   b. pitch
   c. roll
   d. yaw
   e. none of the above

2. If the elevator is deflected, the aircraft will move about the _____ axis.
   a. centroid
   b. pitch
   c. roll
   d. yaw
   e. none of the above

3. If the aileron is deflected, the aircraft will move about the _____ axis.
   a. centroid
   b. pitch
   c. roll
   d. yaw
   e. none of the above

4. Pushing the right rudder pedal in causes the rudder to deflect to the right of center, causing which movement of the aircraft?
   a. Pushes the tail of the aircraft right, and the nose of the aircraft left.
   b. Pushes the tail of the aircraft left, and the nose of the aircraft right.
   c. Pushes the tail of the aircraft left, and the nose of the aircraft left.
   d. Pushes the tail of the aircraft right and the nose of the aircraft right.
   e. None of the above.

5. What is the angle of attack?
   a. the angle between airfoil chord and relative direction of motion
   b. the angle between blade center and angle of incidence
   c. the angle between airfoil chord and angle of incidence
   d. the angle between induced air flow and relative direction of motion
   e. none of the above

6. What do we call the force acting rearward on an aircraft caused by air friction and lift?
   a. lift
   b. thrust
   c. drag
   d. weight
   e. none of the above

7. The shape of a wing's cross-section, which causes lift, is described using what term?
   a. camber
   b. delta
   c. swept
   d. straight
   e. none of the above

8. Pulling back on the aircraft controls will deflect which control surface on the aircraft?
   a. rudder
   b. trim tabs
   c. ailerons
   d. flaps
   e. elevators

9. Increasing which parameter will eventually cause a stall of the aircraft?
   a. air density
   b. angle of attack
   c. airspeed
   d. pitch angle
   e. none of the above

10. Aviation speeds are generally measured in nautical miles per hour (knots). Which statement is true about knots?
    a. 100 knots is identical to 100 miles per hour (mph).
    b. 100 knots is faster than 100 mph.
    c. 100 knots is slower than 100 mph.
    d. 100 knots has no relationship to mph.
    e. None of the above.

11. The transponder codes for loss of communication and for emergency, respectively, are?
    a. 7600 and 7500
    b. 7700 and 7600
    c. 7600 and 7700
    d. 7500 and 7600
    e. 7500 and 7700

12. Used in aviation, *Zulu time* refers to what?
    a. Eastern Standard Time
    b. Eastern Daylight Saving Time
    c. Time at International Date Line
    d. Greenwich Mean Time
    e. Pacific Standard Time

13. What does the Pitot Static system in an aircraft measure?
    a. airspeed and altitude
    b. fuel quantity and fuel weight
    c. manifold pressure and air pressure
    d. cabin pressure and manifold pressure
    e. none of the above

14. Pitch angle is the angle between the fuselage of the aircraft and what?
    a. relative wind
    b. horizon
    c. runway threshold
    d. propeller
    e. none of the above

15. In general, which statement is true when an aircraft fully extends its flaps and does not change other parameters?
    a. Wing produces more lift and more drag.
    b. Wing produces more lift, but less drag.
    c. Wing produces same amount of lift, but more drag.
    d. Wing produces less lift and less drag.
    e. Wing produces less lift, but more drag.

16. In relation to the air flowing beneath the wing, how does the air flowing over the top of a wing, producing lift, move?
    a. same speed
    b. slower
    c. stops
    d. faster
    e. none of the above

17. Airport runways are numbered according to
   a. length and width.
   b. wind direction.
   c. the first two digits of compass direction.
   d. order of construction.
   e. aircraft type.

18. What causes wake turbulence?
   a. wind from thunderstorms blowing across runways
   b. microburst
   c. vortices off wings of aircraft caused by generating lift
   d. dust devils
   e. solar bursts

19. What are the colors of the port and starboard running lights?
   a. white/white
   b. red/green
   c. green/red
   d. red/white
   e. green/white

20. Mach 1 refers to what in aviation?
   a. speed of light
   b. speed of sound
   c. speed of heat
   d. speed of any jet
   e. none of the above

Subtest 9: General Science

Directions: This subtest measures your knowledge in the area of science. Each of the questions or incomplete statements is followed by five choices. You must decide which one of the choices best answers the question or completes the statement. Again, if you are unsure of an answer, use the process of elimination. Remember, there are no penalties for guessing. You have ten (10) minutes to complete this subtest.

Questions: 20
Time: 10 minutes

1. The element _____ is the most abundant component of air.
   a. helium
   b. hydrogen
   c. nitrogen
   d. oxygen
   e. carbon

2. According to Boyle's law, if the pressure of a fixed mass of gas is kept constant but the temperature is allowed to increase, the volume of gas will
   a. not increase.
   b. decrease in proportion to the change in temperature.
   c. increase in proportion to the change in temperature.
   d. increase at twice the rate of change in temperature.
   e. There is not enough information to complete the statement.

3. Ohm's law describes how, if voltage is kept constant, an increase in current results in
   a. an increase in resistance.
   b. a decrease in resistance.
   c. an increase or a decrease in resistance.
   d. no change in resistance.
   e. There is not enough information to complete the statement.

4. _____ wavelengths are longer than visible light and therefore have lower frequencies.
   a. Infrared
   b. Ultraviolet
   c. X-ray
   d. Gamma ray
   e. None of the above

5. If a substance has a pH of 1.0, it can be classified as a(n)
   a. acid.
   b. base.
   c. solvent.
   d. neutral compound.
   e. There is not enough information to complete the statement.

6. _____ in an atom's nucleus have a positive electrical charge.
   a. Electrons
   b. Neutrons
   c. Ions
   d. Photons
   e. Protons

7. A vector is defined by
   a. length.
   b. direction.
   c. neither length or direction.
   d. both length and direction.
   e. none of the above.

8. The organ that is responsible for the production of insulin is the
   a. spleen.
   b. kidney.
   c. pancreas.
   d. liver.
   e. intestine.

9. The four planets in the solar system that are considered the gas giants are
   a. Mercury, Venus, Jupiter, Saturn.
   b. Jupiter, Saturn, Uranus, Neptune.
   c. Venus, Saturn, Uranus, Neptune.
   d. Jupiter, Saturn, Neptune, Pluto.
   e. Saturn, Uranus, Neptune, Pluto.

10. Carbon dioxide is made up of
   a. carbon.
   b. oxygen.
   c. both carbon and oxygen.
   d. both carbon and nitrogen.
   e. none of the above.

11. What is a solution called when it can dissolve no more solutes?
   a. unsaturated
   b. supersaturated
   c. saturated
   d. volatile
   e. stable

12. What is the total number of atoms present in the molecule CH_3NH_2?
   a. 4
   b. 5
   c. 6
   d. 7
   e. 8

13. On the Celsius temperature scale, at what temperatures does water freeze and boil?
   a. It freezes at $-10°$ and boils at $100°$.
   b. It freezes at $32°$ and boils at $100°$.
   c. It freezes at $0°$ and boils at $212°$.
   d. It freezes at $32°$ and boils at $212°$.
   e. It freezes at $0°$ and boils at $100°$.

14. It is harder to stop a car moving at 60 miles per hour than a car moving at 15 miles per hour because the car moving at 60 miles per hour has more
   a. momentum.
   b. deceleration.
   c. mass.
   d. velocity.
   e. density.

15. What is the scientific notation for 617,000?
   a. 6.17×10^{-5}
   b. $.617 \times 10^{2}$
   c. $.617 \times 10^{3}$
   d. $.617 \times 10^{4}$
   e. 6.17×10^{5}

16. If you throw a baseball forward, it will accelerate downward because of
   a. orbital motion.
   b. terminal velocity.
   c. increase in resistance.
   d. Newton's third law of motion.
   e. gravity.

17. What type of rock is formed by the cooling of lava? (An example is granite.)
   a. metamorphic
   b. sedimentary
   c. igneous
   d. salt
   e. sandstone

18. One hundred centimeters equals how many kilometers?
   a. 0.001
   b. 0.01
   c. 0.1
   d. 1.0
   e. 10

19. Which of the following contains fiber?
   a. chicken breast
   b. raspberries
   c. steak
   d. butter
   e. yogurt

20. Which of the following ecosystems could be described as having a temperate climate and many leaf-shedding trees?
   a. a deciduous forest
   b. a tropical rain forest
   c. a tundra
   d. a taiga
   e. a prairie

Subtest 10: Rotated Blocks

Directions: This subtest measures your ability to visualize and manipulate objects in space. For each question in this test, you will be shown a picture of a block. You must find a second block that is identical to the first. You have thirteen (13) minutes to complete this subtest.

Questions: 15
Time: 13 minutes

1.

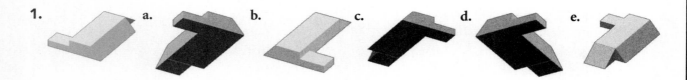

a.   b.   c.   d.   e.

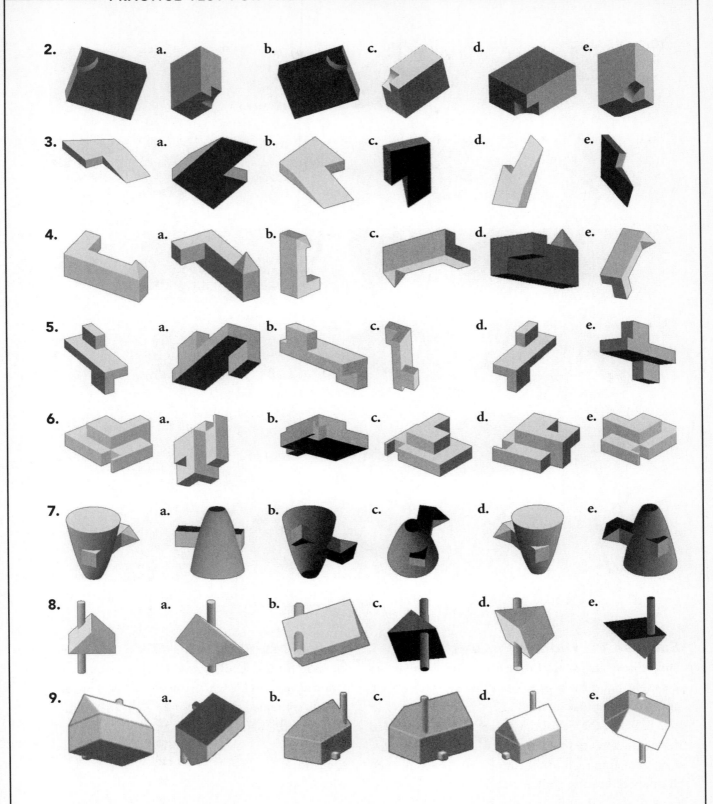

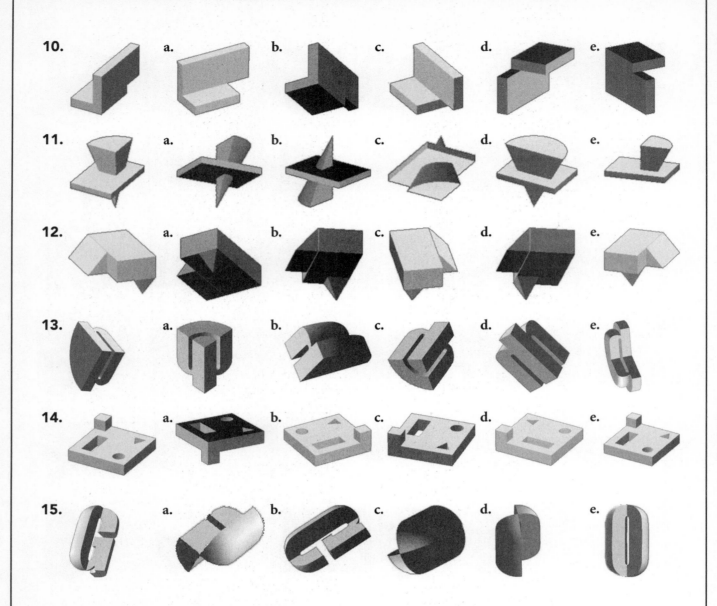

Subtest 11: Hidden Figures

Directions: This subtest measures your ability to see a simple figure in a complex drawing. Above each group of questions are five figures, lettered A, B, C, D, and E. Below this set of figures are several numbered drawings. You are to determine which lettered figure is contained in each of the numbered drawings. Each numbered drawing contains only *one* of the lettered figures. The correct figure in each drawing will always be of the same size and in the same position as it appears in the top set of figures. Look at each numbered drawing and decide which one of the five lettered figures is contained in it. You have eight (8) minutes to complete this subtest.

Questions: 15
Time: 8 minutes

Use the following figure to answer questions 1 through 5.

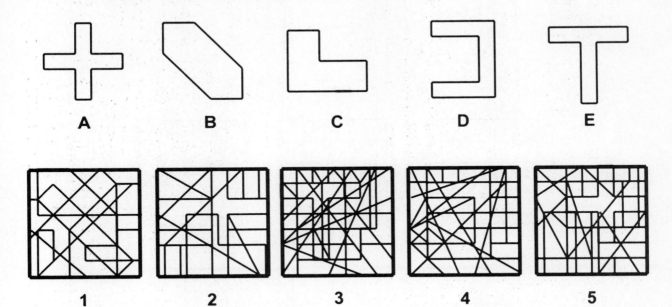

1. The hidden figure in block 1 is _____.
   a. A
   b. B
   c. C
   d. D
   e. E

2. The hidden figure in block 2 is _____.
   a. A
   b. B
   c. C
   d. D
   e. E

3. The hidden figure in block 3 is _____.
   a. A
   b. B
   c. C
   d. D
   e. E

4. The hidden figure in block 4 is _____.
   a. A
   b. B
   c. C
   d. D
   e. E

5. The hidden figure in block 5 is _____.
   a. A
   b. B
   c. C
   d. D
   e. E

Use the following figure to answer questions 6 through 10.

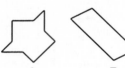

A   B   C   D   E

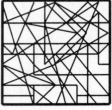 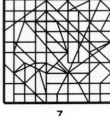 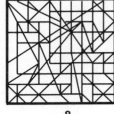

6   7   8

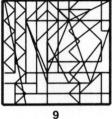 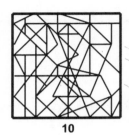

9   10

6. The hidden figure in block 6 is _____.
 a. A
 b. B
 c. C
 d. D
 e. E

7. The hidden figure in block 7 is _____.
 a. A
 b. B
 c. C
 d. D
 e. E

8. The hidden figure in block 8 is _____.
 a. A
 b. B
 c. C
 d. D
 e. E

9. The hidden figure in block 9 is _____.
 a. A
 b. B
 c. C
 d. D
 e. E

10. The hidden figure in block 10 is _____.
 a. A
 b. B
 c. C
 d. D
 e. E

Use the following figure to answer questions 11 through 15.

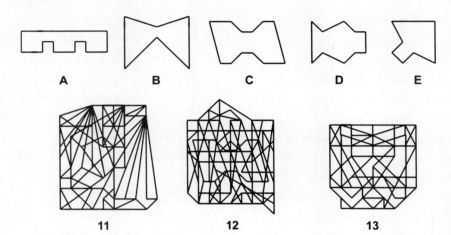

A   B   C   D   E

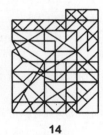

11   12   13

14   15

11. The hidden figure in block 11 is _____.
   a. A
   b. B
   c. C
   d. D
   e. E

12. The hidden figure in block 12 is _____.
   a. A
   b. B
   c. C
   d. D
   e. E

13. The hidden figure in block 13 is _____.
   a. A
   b. B
   c. C
   d. D
   e. E

14. The hidden figure in block 14 is _____.
   a. A
   b. B
   c. C
   d. D
   e. E

15. The hidden figure in block 15 is _____.
   a. A
   b. B
   c. C
   d. D
   e. E

Answer Key

Subtest 1: Verbal Analogies

1. b. *Coffee* goes into a *cup* and *soup* goes into a *bowl*. Choices **a**, **c**, and **e** are incorrect because they are other utensils. The answer is not choice **d** because the word *food* is too general.

2. c. A *bicycle* is put into motion by means of a *pedal*. A *canoe* is put into motion by means of an *oar*. The answer is not choice **a** or **e** because water does not necessarily put the canoe into motion. Kayak (choice **b**) is incorrect because it is a type of boat similar to a canoe. Choice **d** is incorrect because a fleet is a group of boats.

3. d. A *window* is made up of *panes*, and a *book* is made up of *pages*. The answer is not choice **a**, because a novel is a type of book. The answer is not choice **b**, because glass has no relationship to a book. Choices **c** and **e** are incorrect because a book is not made up of covers or indexes.

4. b. An *actor* performs in a *play*. A *musician* performs at a *concert*. Choices **a**, **c**, **d**, and **e** are incorrect because none include people who perform.

5. e. A group of *lions* is called a *pride*. A group of *fish* swim in a *school*. Teacher (choice **a**) and student (choice **b**) refer to another meaning of the word *school*. The answer is not choice **c** or **d** because self-respect and learning have no obvious relationship to this particular meaning of school.

6. b. *Elated* is the opposite of *despondent*; *enlightened* is the opposite of *ignorant*.

7. a. If someone has been *humiliated*, they have been greatly *embarrassed*. If someone is *terrified*, they are extremely *frightened*. Choice **e** may be related to a feeling of fright, but it is not an extreme emotion and therefore is not as good a match as choice **a**. The answer is not choice **b** because an agitated person is not necessarily frightened. Choices **c** and **d** are incorrect because neither word expresses a state of being frightened.

8. d. An *odometer* is an instrument used to measure *mileage*. A *compass* is an instrument used to determine *direction*. Choices **a**, **b**, **c**, and **e** are incorrect because none is an instrument.

9. c. *Fray* and *ravel* are synonyms, as are *jolt* and *shake*.

10. c. An *elephant* is a *pachyderm*; a *kangaroo* is a *marsupial*.

11. a. A *psychologist* treats a *neurosis*; an *ophthalmologist* treats a *cataract*.

12. c. Upon harvesting, *cotton* is gathered into *bales*; *grain* is gathered into *shocks*.

13. a. *Division* and *section* are synonyms; *layer* and *tier* are synonyms.

14. d. A *mechanic* works in a *garage*; a *surgeon* works in a *hospital*.

15. c. A *chickadee* is a type of *bird*; a *Siamese* is a type of *cat*.

16. e. To *saunter* is to *walk* slowly; to *drizzle* is to *rain* slowly.

17. b. To *tailor* a suit is to *alter* it; to *edit* a manuscript is to *alter* it.

18. a. *Jaundice* is an indication of a *liver* problem; *rash* is an indication of a *skin* problem.

19. c. *Obsession* is a greater degree of *interest*; *fantasy* is a greater degree of *dream*.

20. e. *Slapstick* results in *laughter*; *horror* results in *fear*.

21. b. *Verve* and *enthusiasm* are synonyms; *devotion* and *reverence* are synonyms.

22. a. A *conviction* results in *incarceration*; a *reduction* results in *diminution*.

23. b. Being *erudite* is a trait of a *professor*; being *imaginative* is a trait of an *inventor*.

24. d. *Dependable* and *capricious* are antonyms; *capable* and *inept* are antonyms.

25. c. *Hegemony* means *dominance*; *autonomy* means *independence*.

Subtest 2: Arithmetic Reasoning

1. c. Round 157 to 200 and round 817 to 800: $200 \times 800 = 160,000$.

2. d. It is important to remember to include all three telephone sets ($375 total), both computers ($2,600 total), and both monitors ($1,900 total) in the total value.

3. e. To solve this problem, you must convert $3\frac{1}{2}$ to $\frac{7}{2}$ and then divide $\frac{7}{2}$ by $\frac{1}{4}$. The answer, $\frac{28}{4}$, is then reduced to the number 14.

4. a. Cancel factors that are common to the numerator and denominator, then multiply: $\frac{5}{8} \times \frac{4}{7} = \frac{5}{(4)(2)} \times \frac{4}{7} = \frac{5}{14}$

5. b. You cannot simply take 25% off the original price, because the 10% discount after three years of service is taken off the price that has already been reduced by 15%. Figure the problem in two steps: After the 15% discount, the price is $71.83. Another 10% off that gives you $64.65.

6. c. The problem is solved by dividing 204 by 1,700. The answer, 0.12, is then converted to a percentage—12%.

7. c. Use the equation $.05(1) = .02(x)$, where x is the total amount of water in the resulting 2% solution. Solving for x, you get 2.5. Subtracting the 1 liter of water already present in the 5% solution, you will find that 1.5 liters need to be added.

8. e. Each 9-foot wall has an area of 9(8), or 72 square feet. There are two such walls, so those two walls combined have an area of 144 square feet. Each 11-foot wall has an area of 11(8), or 88 square feet, and again there are two such walls: 88(2) = 176. Finally, add 144 and 176 to get 320 square feet.

9. e. Substituting 40 for C in the equation yields $F = (\frac{9}{5})(40) + 32 = 72 + 32 = 104$.

10. a. The woman will have traveled 3.5 hours at 45 miles per hour for a distance of 157.5 miles. To reach her in 3 hours, the man must travel at 157.5 miles per 3 hours, or 52.5 mph.

11. a. J = 6K. J + 2 = 2(K + 2), so 6K + 2 = 2K + 4, which means K equals $\frac{1}{2}$. J equals 6K, or 3.

12. e. The 827,036 bytes free on the flash drive plus 542,159 bytes freed when the file was deleted equals 1,369,195 bytes: 1,369,195 bytes minus 489,986 bytes put into the new file leaves 879,209 bytes free.

13. d. First, add the number of patients to find the total: 63. Then, divide the number of patients by the number of nursing assistants: 63 divided by 7 is 9.

14. c. Let E = emergency room cost; H = hospice cost, which is $\frac{1}{4}E$; N = home nursing cost, which is $2H$, or $2(\frac{1}{4})E$. The total bill is $E + H + N$, which is $E + \frac{1}{4}E + \frac{2}{4}E = 140,000$. Add the left side of the equation to get $\frac{7}{4}E = 140,000$. To solve for E, multiply both sides of the equation by $\frac{4}{7}$. $E = 140,000(\frac{4}{7})$, or 80,000. $H = \frac{1}{4}E$, or 20,000, and $N = 2H$, or 40,000.

15. b. If half the students are female, then you would expect half of the out-of-state students to be female. One-half of $\frac{1}{12}$ is $\frac{1}{24}$.

16. c. A foot in height makes a difference of 60 pounds, or 5 pounds per inch of height over 5′. A person who is 5′5″ is (5)(5 pounds), or 25 pounds, heavier than the person who is 5′, so add 25 pounds to 110 pounds to get 135 pounds.

17. d. The difference between 220 and this person's age is 190. The maximum heart rate is 90% of this: $(0.9)(190) = 171$.

18. e. An amount equaling 30 ppm of the pollutant would have to be removed to bring the 50 ppm down to 20 ppm (30 ppm is 60% of 50 ppm).

19. e. Let E = the estimate. One-fifth more than the estimate would be $\frac{6}{5}$, or 120%, of E, so $600,000 = (1.20)(E)$. Dividing both sides by 1.2 leaves $E = 500,000$.

20. b. In terms of grams, 250 milligrams is $\frac{250}{1000}$ gram, or 0.250 grams.

21. c. Three tons = 6,000 pounds. At 16 ounces per pound, 6,000 pounds = 96,000 ounces that can be carried by the truck. The total weight of each daily ration is 12 ounces + 18 ounces + 18 ounces = 48 ounces per soldier per day, and $\frac{96,000}{48} = 2,000$. So $\frac{2,000}{10 \text{ days}}$ = 200 soldiers supplied.

22. e. Multiply the weight of each recyclable by the best price it will bring and add the amount together: $2,200(0.07) = \$154$; $\$154 + 1,400(0.04) = \$210$; $\$210 + 3,100(0.08) = \$458$; $\$458 + \$900(0.03) = \$485$.

23. d. The total number of miles, 3,450, divided by 6 days is 575 miles.

24. b. The present number of men, 30, multiplied by 42 square feet of space is 1,260 square feet of space; 1,260 square feet divided by 35 men is 36 square feet, so each man will have 6 square feet of space less.

25. c. Let T = Ted's age; S = Sam's age = $3T$; R = Ron's age = $\frac{S}{2}$, or $\frac{3T}{2}$. The sum of the ages is 55, which means $T + 3T + \frac{3T}{2} = 55$. To find the common denominator (2), you can add to the left side of the equation: $T = 10$. If Ted is 10, then Sam is 30, and Ron is $\frac{3T}{2}$, which is 15 years old.

Subtest 3: Word Knowledge

1. a. To be gauche is to lack social experience, grace, or aplomb; not tactful.

2. b. To enumerate is to ascertain the number of; to count.

3. c. To be triumphant is to rejoice in celebration of victory.

4. c. To be magnanimous is to be noble of mind or generous.

5. d. To have an aversion to something is to have a feeling of repugnance for it or to dislike it.

6. d. To be poignant means to be keenly distressing.

7. e. An antagonist is an opponent.

8. c. Perseverance means steadfast in one's course, or persistent.

9. a. Homogeneous means of the same or a similar kind; alike.

10. c. To be conspicuous is to be obvious to the eye or the mind.

11. d. A recluse is a person who lives withdrawn from the world; a hermit.

12. e. To tote something is to haul or carry it.

13. e. To be preeminent is to be outstanding or have supreme rank.

14. c. Something that is grotesque is distorted, misshapen, or bizarre.

15. c. To be outmoded is to be out-of-date or obsolete.

16. b. A statement that is garbled is scrambled and confusing, or unintelligible.

17. b. If something is frail, it is easily broken or delicate.

18. e. To be vindictive is to be vengeful or spiteful.

19. c. An oration is a formal speech or an address.

20. b. A glib remark is quick and insincere, or superficial.

21. e. To be eccentric is to be unconventional or peculiar.

22. a. A panacea is a remedy for all ills; a cure-all.

23. a. To be detrimental is to be obviously damaging and harmful.

24. b. To be ostentatious is to be showy or pretentious.

25. a. To be negligible is to be unimportant or insignificant.

Subtest 4: Math Knowledge

1. c. When a number is marked off in groups of two digits each, starting at the decimal point, the square root of the largest square in the left hand group, whether one or two digits, is the first digit of the square root of the number. In this case (11-20-92), 9 is the largest square in 11, and 3 is the square root of 9.

2. b. A proportion can find an unknown side of a figure using known sides of a similar figure; a proportion can also find an unknown side using known perimeters. $\frac{93}{24} = \frac{31}{s}$. Cross-multiply: $93s = (31)(24)$.

3. d. Perimeter uses a single measurement such as an inch to describe the outline of a figure. Area and surface area use square measurements, an inch times an inch, to describe two-dimensional space. Volume uses the largest measurement; it uses the cubic measurement, an inch times an inch times an inch. Volume is three-dimensional; its measurement must account for each dimension.

4. b. The circumference of a circle is two times the radius times pi. So, in this case, the distance is 2 times 49, times 22, divided by 7, or 308 miles.

5. a. First, change (B) and (C) to decimals: $5\% = 0.05$; $\frac{1}{5} = 0.2$. Then, find out which choice is true.

6. d. (B) and (C) are both equal to $n \times n$.

7. b. You are given the diameter, so use $C = \pi d$. Plug in the diameter and pi and multiply: $(3.14)(10) = 31.4$.

8. e. Obtuse angles are greater than 90°. Only one answer choice, **e**, is greater than 90°.

9. c. When dividing variables with exponents, if the variables are the same, you subtract the exponents to arrive at your answer: $\frac{n^5}{n^2} = \frac{n \cdot n \cdot n \cdot n \cdot n}{n \cdot n} = n^{5-2} = n^3$.

10. a. First, factor the radicand: $\sqrt{3n^2} = \sqrt{3 \cdot n \cdot n}$
Now take out the square root of the perfect square: $\sqrt{3 \cdot n \cdot n} = n\sqrt{3}$
You arrive at $n\sqrt{3}$, choice **a**.

11. c. This is a simple addition series. Each number increases by $\frac{1}{6}$.

12. b. *Volume* = 4.6 cubic feet. This is a square-based pyramid; its volume is a third of a cube's volume with the same base measurements, or $\frac{1}{3}bh$. Plug its measurements into the formula: $\frac{1}{3}(2.4 \text{ ft.})2.4 \text{ ft.}$
Volume of square pyramid $= \frac{1}{3}(5.76 \text{ sq. ft.})$ 2.4 ft. $= \frac{1}{3}(13.824 \text{ cubic ft.}) = 4.608$ cubic ft.

13. c. In this question, $\frac{1}{5}$ of 820 = 164; $164 - 42 = 122$.

14. e. Simplify the second term of the expression by factoring the radicand:
$2\sqrt{7} - 3\sqrt{28} = 2\sqrt{7} - 3\sqrt{4 \cdot 7}$
Now simplify the radicand:
$\sqrt{7} - 3\sqrt{4 \cdot 7} = 2\sqrt{7} - 3 \cdot 2\sqrt{7}$
Finally, combine like terms:
$2\sqrt{7} - 6\sqrt{7} = -4\sqrt{7}$, choice **e**.

15. d. Divide numerical terms: $\frac{8xy^2}{2xy} = \frac{4xy^2}{xy}$.
When similar factors, or bases, are being divided, subtract the exponent in the denominator from the exponent in the numerator. $\frac{4xy^2}{xy} = 4x^{1-1}y^{2-1}$.
Simplify: $4x^0y^1 = 4(1)y = 4y$.
The answer is $4y$, choice **d**.

16. c. In this question, $\frac{2}{5}$ of 25 = 10; $10 - 6 = 4$.

17. a. In this question, 4% of 20 = 0.8; $3 \times 0.8 = 2.4$.

18. c. First, solve for (A), (B), and (C): (A) = 49, (B) = 64, (C) = 15. Then, find out which choice is true.

19. d. The factorial of a positive integer is that integer times each of the integers between it and 1. In this case, 5 times 4 times 3 times 2 equals 120.

20. d. In this question, 15% of 30 = 4.5; 20 − 4.5 = 15.5, choice **d.**

21. a. The reciprocal of a number is that number divided into one. In this case, that is $\frac{1}{10}$, or 0.1.

22. b. First, set up the equation: $n + 2n = 99$. Then, solve: $3n = 99$; $n = 33$.

23. b. First, solve for (A), (B), and (C): (A) = 40, (B) = 40, (C) = 20. Then, find out which choice is true.

24. d. Using a proportion, find x: $\frac{12}{36} = \frac{4.5}{x}$. Cross-multiply: $12x = 36(4.5)$; $x = 13.5$. Polygon *CRXZ* is a rectangle whose sides measure 13.5, 54, 13.5, and 54. To find the perimeter of rectangle *CRXZ*, add the measures of its sides together.

25. a. You are given the radius, so use $C = 2\pi r$. Plug in the radius and pi and multiply: $(2)(3.14)(22) = 157$. So your answer is 157 cm, or 1.57 m, choice **a.**

Subtest 5: Instrument Comprehension

QUESTION	ANSWER	HEADING	PITCH	ROLL
1.	D	068° east-northeast	none	right
2.	C	090° east	none	left
3.	B	170° south	down	right
4.	A	235° southwest	up	right
5.	B	045° northeast	up	left
6.	C	270° west	none	none
7.	C	225° southwest	down	left
8.	B	270° west	up	left
9.	B	180° south	down	none
10.	B	270° west	up	left
11.	A	135° southeast	down	left
12.	A	270° west	down	right
13.	C	180° south	down	none
14.	C	255° west-southwest	up	left
15.	A	270° west	up	right
16.	A	045° northeast	up	right

17.	B	090° east	up	none
18.	A	180° south	down	right
19.	C	270° west	up	right
20.	D	180° south	up	left

Subtest 6: Block Counting

1. b. Block 1 touches three blocks: one block to the left, one block below, and one block to the right.

2. b. Block 2 touches three blocks: two blocks to the right and one block below.

3. c. Block 3 touches four blocks: one block above, one block below, and two blocks to the right.

4. c. Block 4 touches four blocks: one block above, one block to the left, and two blocks below.

5. b. Block 5 touches three blocks: two blocks to the left and one block below.

6. b. Block 6 touches three blocks: one block to the left, one block to the right, and one block below.

7. e. Block 7 touches four blocks: two blocks below, one block to the right, and one block above.

8. d. Block 8 touches five blocks: one block below, two blocks to the left, and one block above.

9. c. Block 9 touches four blocks: one block below, one block to the left, one block to the right, and one block above.

10. d. Block 10 touches five blocks: four blocks above and one block to the right.

11. b. Block 11 touches three blocks: one block below and two blocks to the right.

12. e. Block 12 touches six blocks: three blocks above, one block to the left, and two blocks below.

13. e. Block 13 touches six blocks: three blocks above, one block to the right, and two blocks below.

14. d. Block 14 touches five blocks: two blocks above, one block below, one block to the right, and one block to the left.

15. b. Block 15 touches three blocks: one block above and two blocks to the left.

16. c. Block 16 touches four blocks: two blocks above, one block to the left, and one block below.

17. c. Block 17 touches four blocks: one block above, one block to the left, and two blocks below.

18. a. Block 18 touches two blocks: one block to the right and one block below.

19. a. Block 19 touches two blocks: one block to the left and one block below.

20. a. Block 20 touches two blocks: one block above and one block to the right.

Subtest 7: Table Reading

1. c. The intersection of the −3 column with the 2 row yields an answer of 23.

2. c. The intersection of the 2 column with the −2 row yields an answer of 48.

3. a. The intersection of the −2 column with the 3 row yields an answer of 44.

4. e. The intersection of the 0 column with the −1 row yields an answer of 14.

5. c. The intersection of the 3 column with the 1 row yields an answer of 32.

6. e. The intersection of the 2 column with the −1 row yields an answer of 14.

7. d. The intersection of the 0 column with the 0 row yields an answer of 61.

8. e. The intersection of the −2 column with the −1 row yields an answer of 49.

9. e. The intersection of the −1 column with the 2 row yields an answer of 99.

10. b. The intersection of the 3 column with the 3 row yields an answer of 53.

11. b. The intersection of the −1 column with the −1 row yields an answer of 43.

12. a. The intersection of the −2 column with the 1 row yields an answer of 49.

13. a. The intersection of the −3 column with the 0 row yields an answer of 18.

14. e. The intersection of the 1 column with the 3 row yields an answer of 57.

15. b. The intersection of the −3 column with the −2 row yields an answer of 86.

16. a. The intersection of the −3 column with the −3 row yields an answer of 24.

17. a. The intersection of the 2 column with the 2 row yields an answer of 14.

18. d. The intersection of the −2 column with the 3 row yields an answer of 74.

19. e. The intersection of the −1 column with the 0 row yields an answer of 43.

20. c. The intersection of the 0 column with the 2 row yields an answer of 64.

21. b. The intersection of the 2 column with the −3 row yields an answer of 43.

22. b. The intersection of the −1 column with the 3 row yields an answer of 88.

23. b. The intersection of the 2 column with the 2 row yields an answer of 22.

24. c. The intersection of the −3 column with the 1 row yields an answer of 81.

25. d. The intersection of the 2 column with the 3 row yields an answer of 11.

26. c. The intersection of the 9 column with the −4 row yields an answer of 52.

27. a. The intersection of the −5 column with the 9 row yields an answer of 54.

28. b. The intersection of the −1 column with the −4 row yields an answer of 93.

29. a. The intersection of the −3 column with the 8 row yields an answer of 29.

30. e. The intersection of the 5 column with the −3 row yields an answer of 43.

31. e. The intersection of the 0 column with the 7 row yields an answer of 21.

32. e. The intersection of the 4 column with the −4 row yields an answer of 34.

33. e. The intersection of the 7 column with the −3 row yields an answer of 51.

34. b. The intersection of the −9 column with the 3 row yields an answer of 74.

35. d. The intersection of the 1 column with the −8 row yields an answer of 12.

36. c. The intersection of the 0 column with the 0 row yields an answer of 18.

37. b. The intersection of the −5 column with the 0 row yields an answer of 74.

38. c. The intersection of the −2 column with the 7 row yields an answer of 11.

39. a. The intersection of the −8 column with the 5 row yields an answer of 55.

40. b. The intersection of the −6 column with the 4 row yields an answer of 68.

Subtest 8: Aviation Information

1. d. The rudder is the control surface on the vertical stabilizer or tail. Any deflection of the rudder makes the aircraft move about the yaw, or vertical axis.

2. b. The elevator is the control surface on the horizontal stabilizer. Any deflection of the elevator makes the aircraft move about the pitch axis. The pitch axis runs from one wingtip to the other, passing through the aircraft's center of gravity.

3. c. The aileron is the control surface on the trailing edge of the wings. Any deflection of the aileron makes the aircraft move about the roll axis. The roll axis runs the length of the aircraft from nose to tail, passing through the center of gravity.

4. b. Pushing the right rudder pedal in causes the rudder control surface to move into the windstream to the right, which pushes the tail of the airplane left, and the nose of the airplane right.

5. a. *Angle of attack* is defined as the angle between the airfoil chord and the relative direction of motion.

6. c. *Drag* refers to the rearward force on an aircraft caused by air friction and lift. More specifically, *parasite drag* refers to the component of drag associated with friction, and *induced drag* refers to the component associated with lift.

7. a. *Camber* refers to the side (cross-section) view of a wing's shape. This shape causes the air to travel faster over the top portion of the wing and therefore causes lift.

8. e. Pulling back on the aircraft controls causes the elevators to be deflected up into the airstream, which pushes the tail of the aircraft down and the nose of the aircraft up.

9. b. Increasing the angle of attack of an aircraft will eventually cause a stall as the airflow over the wing detaches from the wing's surface.

10. b. One knot (nautical mile per hour) is equal to approximately $\frac{8}{7}$ of a mph (mile per hour). A nautical mile is approximately 6,080 feet, but a statute mile is approximately 5,280 feet. The ratio of these distances can be approximated with the ratio of 8:7. Therefore 100 knots is a faster speed than 100 mph.

11. c. Transponder codes are as follows:

Hijacking	7500
Loss of comms	7600
Emergency	7700

12. d. *Zulu time* refers to the time in Greenwich England, commonly known as *Greenwich Mean Time*. Zulu time is commonly used for aviation, especially when several time zones will be crossed.

13. a. The Pitot system measures airspeed by measuring the impact pressure of the relative wind and comparing it to the static pressure. The static system measures static pressure, which indicates altitude.

14. b. Pitch angle of an aircraft refers to the angle between the extended fuselage of the aircraft and the horizon. For example, an aircraft flying straight up would have a pitch angle of 90°.

15. a. A wing with flaps fully extended will generally produce more lift and more drag. The flaps increase the wing's camber, which causes more lift and more induced drag.

16. d. The wind flowing over a wing, which is creating lift, moves faster than the wind flowing beneath the wing. This increased velocity causes a lower air pressure on the top of the wing compared with the air pressure below the wing. This difference in air pressure is lift.

17. c. Airport runways are numbered according to the first two digits of compass heading, with the zero omitted for headings between 010 and 090.

18. c. Wake turbulence is caused by the higher-pressure air under a wing escaping in an outward direction from the wingtip to the lower-pressure air flowing above the wing. This escaping air will swirl upward, causing vortices, known as wake turbulence.

19. b. The port running lights are red; the starboard lights are green. Positional lights are white.

20. b. Mach 1 is the speed of sound for a given air density.

Subtest 9: General Science

1. c. Air consists of 78% nitrogen, 21% oxygen, and the remainder is made up of noble gases and rare earth elements.

2. c. Boyle's law states that for a given pressure, temperature and volume are directly proportional.

3. b. Ohm's law states that current and resistance are inversely proportional. Therefore, any increase in one would result in a corresponding decrease in the other.

4. a. Ultraviolet, x-ray, and gamma ray wavelengths are all shorter than visible light. Infrared wavelengths are slightly longer than visible light on the electromagnetic spectrum.

5. a. The pH scale ranges from 0 to 14. If a substance has a pH of 7.0, it is considered neutral; pH values of less than 7 indicate acids, and values greater than 7 are bases.

6. e. Protons are subatomic particles located in the nucleus of an atom and have positive electrical charges.

7. d. Vectors are defined by both length and direction.

8. c. The pancreas is the organ responsible for insulin production.

9. b. The four planets in our solar system that are considered gas giants are Jupiter, Saturn, Uranus, and Neptune.

10. c. Carbon dioxide, or CO_2, is made up of both carbon and oxygen.

11. c. The dissolved solution is in equilibrium with the undissolved in saturated solutions.

12. d. The molecule CH_3NH_2 contains one atom of carbon, one atom of nitrogen, and five atoms of hydrogen, for a total of seven atoms.

13. e. The Celsius scale is part of the metric system. On the Celsius scale, the freezing point of water is 0°; the boiling point is 100°.

14. a. Momentum equals mass (amount of matter in an object) times velocity (speed in a given direction).

15. e. To express a number in scientific notation, you move the decimal as many places as necessary until there is only one digit to the left of the decimal. For 617,000, you move the decimal to the left by five decimal places. The fact that you had to move it to the left means that the 10 should be raised to a positive power, so the result is 6.17×10^5.

16. e. Gravity pulls the ball downward as it moves forward.

17. c. Igneous rocks make up a group of rocks formed from the crystallization of magma (lava).

18. a. One hundred centimeters equals 1 meter, and 1,000 meters equals 1 kilometer.

19. b. Fiber is found only in plants. Raw vegetables, fruit with seeds, whole cereals, and bread are possible sources of fiber.

20. a. Deciduous forests are characterized by having mild temperatures and many trees that periodically shed leaves.

Subtest 10: Rotated Blocks

1. a.

2. a.

3. e.

4. c.

5. c.

6. d.

7. b.

8. c.

9. a.
10. b.
11. b.
12. a.
13. b.
14. a.
15. c.

Subtest 11: Hidden Figures

1. b.
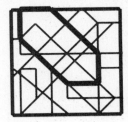

2. c.

3. e.
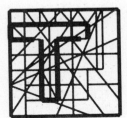

4. d.
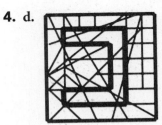

5. a.

6. d.
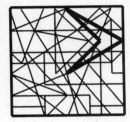

7. e.
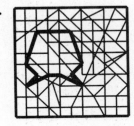

8. a.
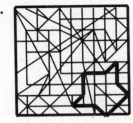

9. c.

10. b.
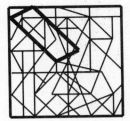

11. d.
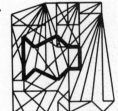

12. c.

13. b.

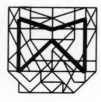

14. e.

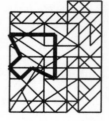

15. a.

For information on how the official AFOQT is scored, see Chapter 3.

10 ▶ PRACTICE TEST FOR THE AVIATION SELECTION TEST BATTERY

CHAPTER SUMMARY
In the official Aviation Selection Test Battery (ASTB), you will be tested on mathematical and verbal reasoning, mechanical comprehension, spatial apperception, and aviation and nautical knowledge.

Math Skills Test (MST)

1.	ⓐ	ⓑ	ⓒ	ⓓ	11.	ⓐ	ⓑ	ⓒ	ⓓ	21.	ⓐ	ⓑ	ⓒ	ⓓ
2.	ⓐ	ⓑ	ⓒ	ⓓ	12.	ⓐ	ⓑ	ⓒ	ⓓ	22.	ⓐ	ⓑ	ⓒ	ⓓ
3.	ⓐ	ⓑ	ⓒ	ⓓ	13.	ⓐ	ⓑ	ⓒ	ⓓ	23.	ⓐ	ⓑ	ⓒ	ⓓ
4.	ⓐ	ⓑ	ⓒ	ⓓ	14.	ⓐ	ⓑ	ⓒ	ⓓ	24.	ⓐ	ⓑ	ⓒ	ⓓ
5.	ⓐ	ⓑ	ⓒ	ⓓ	15.	ⓐ	ⓑ	ⓒ	ⓓ	25.	ⓐ	ⓑ	ⓒ	ⓓ
6.	ⓐ	ⓑ	ⓒ	ⓓ	16.	ⓐ	ⓑ	ⓒ	ⓓ	26.	ⓐ	ⓑ	ⓒ	ⓓ
7.	ⓐ	ⓑ	ⓒ	ⓓ	17.	ⓐ	ⓑ	ⓒ	ⓓ	27.	ⓐ	ⓑ	ⓒ	ⓓ
8.	ⓐ	ⓑ	ⓒ	ⓓ	18.	ⓐ	ⓑ	ⓒ	ⓓ	28.	ⓐ	ⓑ	ⓒ	ⓓ
9.	ⓐ	ⓑ	ⓒ	ⓓ	19.	ⓐ	ⓑ	ⓒ	ⓓ	29.	ⓐ	ⓑ	ⓒ	ⓓ
10.	ⓐ	ⓑ	ⓒ	ⓓ	20.	ⓐ	ⓑ	ⓒ	ⓓ	30.	ⓐ	ⓑ	ⓒ	ⓓ

Reading Skills Test (RST)

1.	ⓐ	ⓑ	ⓒ	ⓓ	11.	ⓐ	ⓑ	ⓒ	ⓓ	21.	ⓐ	ⓑ	ⓒ	ⓓ
2.	ⓐ	ⓑ	ⓒ	ⓓ	12.	ⓐ	ⓑ	ⓒ	ⓓ	22.	ⓐ	ⓑ	ⓒ	ⓓ
3.	ⓐ	ⓑ	ⓒ	ⓓ	13.	ⓐ	ⓑ	ⓒ	ⓓ	23.	ⓐ	ⓑ	ⓒ	ⓓ
4.	ⓐ	ⓑ	ⓒ	ⓓ	14.	ⓐ	ⓑ	ⓒ	ⓓ	24.	ⓐ	ⓑ	ⓒ	ⓓ
5.	ⓐ	ⓑ	ⓒ	ⓓ	15.	ⓐ	ⓑ	ⓒ	ⓓ	25.	ⓐ	ⓑ	ⓒ	ⓓ
6.	ⓐ	ⓑ	ⓒ	ⓓ	16.	ⓐ	ⓑ	ⓒ	ⓓ	26.	ⓐ	ⓑ	ⓒ	ⓓ
7.	ⓐ	ⓑ	ⓒ	ⓓ	17.	ⓐ	ⓑ	ⓒ	ⓓ	27.	ⓐ	ⓑ	ⓒ	ⓓ
8.	ⓐ	ⓑ	ⓒ	ⓓ	18.	ⓐ	ⓑ	ⓒ	ⓓ					
9.	ⓐ	ⓑ	ⓒ	ⓓ	19.	ⓐ	ⓑ	ⓒ	ⓓ					
10.	ⓐ	ⓑ	ⓒ	ⓓ	20.	ⓐ	ⓑ	ⓒ	ⓓ					

Mechanical Comprehension Test (MCT)

1.	ⓐ	ⓑ	ⓒ	ⓓ	ⓔ	11.	ⓐ	ⓑ	ⓒ	ⓓ	ⓔ	21.	ⓐ	ⓑ	ⓒ	ⓓ	ⓔ
2.	ⓐ	ⓑ	ⓒ	ⓓ	ⓔ	12.	ⓐ	ⓑ	ⓒ	ⓓ	ⓔ	22.	ⓐ	ⓑ	ⓒ	ⓓ	ⓔ
3.	ⓐ	ⓑ	ⓒ	ⓓ	ⓔ	13.	ⓐ	ⓑ	ⓒ	ⓓ	ⓔ	23.	ⓐ	ⓑ	ⓒ	ⓓ	ⓔ
4.	ⓐ	ⓑ	ⓒ	ⓓ	ⓔ	14.	ⓐ	ⓑ	ⓒ	ⓓ	ⓔ	24.	ⓐ	ⓑ	ⓒ	ⓓ	ⓔ
5.	ⓐ	ⓑ	ⓒ	ⓓ	ⓔ	15.	ⓐ	ⓑ	ⓒ	ⓓ	ⓔ	25.	ⓐ	ⓑ	ⓒ	ⓓ	ⓔ
6.	ⓐ	ⓑ	ⓒ	ⓓ	ⓔ	16.	ⓐ	ⓑ	ⓒ	ⓓ	ⓔ	26.	ⓐ	ⓑ	ⓒ	ⓓ	ⓔ
7.	ⓐ	ⓑ	ⓒ	ⓓ	ⓔ	17.	ⓐ	ⓑ	ⓒ	ⓓ	ⓔ	27.	ⓐ	ⓑ	ⓒ	ⓓ	ⓔ
8.	ⓐ	ⓑ	ⓒ	ⓓ	ⓔ	18.	ⓐ	ⓑ	ⓒ	ⓓ	ⓔ	28.	ⓐ	ⓑ	ⓒ	ⓓ	ⓔ
9.	ⓐ	ⓑ	ⓒ	ⓓ	ⓔ	19.	ⓐ	ⓑ	ⓒ	ⓓ	ⓔ	29.	ⓐ	ⓑ	ⓒ	ⓓ	ⓔ
10.	ⓐ	ⓑ	ⓒ	ⓓ	ⓔ	20.	ⓐ	ⓑ	ⓒ	ⓓ	ⓔ	30.	ⓐ	ⓑ	ⓒ	ⓓ	ⓔ

Spatial Apperception Test (SAT)

1.	ⓐ	ⓑ	ⓒ	ⓓ	ⓔ
2.	ⓐ	ⓑ	ⓒ	ⓓ	ⓔ
3.	ⓐ	ⓑ	ⓒ	ⓓ	ⓔ
4.	ⓐ	ⓑ	ⓒ	ⓓ	ⓔ
5.	ⓐ	ⓑ	ⓒ	ⓓ	ⓔ
6.	ⓐ	ⓑ	ⓒ	ⓓ	ⓔ
7.	ⓐ	ⓑ	ⓒ	ⓓ	ⓔ
8.	ⓐ	ⓑ	ⓒ	ⓓ	ⓔ
9.	ⓐ	ⓑ	ⓒ	ⓓ	ⓔ

10.	ⓐ	ⓑ	ⓒ	ⓓ	ⓔ
11.	ⓐ	ⓑ	ⓒ	ⓓ	ⓔ
12.	ⓐ	ⓑ	ⓒ	ⓓ	ⓔ
13.	ⓐ	ⓑ	ⓒ	ⓓ	ⓔ
14.	ⓐ	ⓑ	ⓒ	ⓓ	ⓔ
15.	ⓐ	ⓑ	ⓒ	ⓓ	ⓔ
16.	ⓐ	ⓑ	ⓒ	ⓓ	ⓔ
17.	ⓐ	ⓑ	ⓒ	ⓓ	ⓔ

18.	ⓐ	ⓑ	ⓒ	ⓓ	ⓔ
19.	ⓐ	ⓑ	ⓒ	ⓓ	ⓔ
20.	ⓐ	ⓑ	ⓒ	ⓓ	ⓔ
21.	ⓐ	ⓑ	ⓒ	ⓓ	ⓔ
22.	ⓐ	ⓑ	ⓒ	ⓓ	ⓔ
23.	ⓐ	ⓑ	ⓒ	ⓓ	ⓔ
24.	ⓐ	ⓑ	ⓒ	ⓓ	ⓔ
25.	ⓐ	ⓑ	ⓒ	ⓓ	ⓔ

Aviation and Nautical Information Test (ANIT)

1.	ⓐ	ⓑ	ⓒ	ⓓ	ⓔ
2.	ⓐ	ⓑ	ⓒ	ⓓ	ⓔ
3.	ⓐ	ⓑ	ⓒ	ⓓ	ⓔ
4.	ⓐ	ⓑ	ⓒ	ⓓ	ⓔ
5.	ⓐ	ⓑ	ⓒ	ⓓ	ⓔ
6.	ⓐ	ⓑ	ⓒ	ⓓ	ⓔ
7.	ⓐ	ⓑ	ⓒ	ⓓ	ⓔ
8.	ⓐ	ⓑ	ⓒ	ⓓ	ⓔ
9.	ⓐ	ⓑ	ⓒ	ⓓ	ⓔ
10.	ⓐ	ⓑ	ⓒ	ⓓ	ⓔ

11.	ⓐ	ⓑ	ⓒ	ⓓ	ⓔ
12.	ⓐ	ⓑ	ⓒ	ⓓ	ⓔ
13.	ⓐ	ⓑ	ⓒ	ⓓ	ⓔ
14.	ⓐ	ⓑ	ⓒ	ⓓ	ⓔ
15.	ⓐ	ⓑ	ⓒ	ⓓ	ⓔ
16.	ⓐ	ⓑ	ⓒ	ⓓ	ⓔ
17.	ⓐ	ⓑ	ⓒ	ⓓ	ⓔ
18.	ⓐ	ⓑ	ⓒ	ⓓ	ⓔ
19.	ⓐ	ⓑ	ⓒ	ⓓ	ⓔ
20.	ⓐ	ⓑ	ⓒ	ⓓ	ⓔ

21.	ⓐ	ⓑ	ⓒ	ⓓ	ⓔ
22.	ⓐ	ⓑ	ⓒ	ⓓ	ⓔ
23.	ⓐ	ⓑ	ⓒ	ⓓ	ⓔ
24.	ⓐ	ⓑ	ⓒ	ⓓ	ⓔ
25.	ⓐ	ⓑ	ⓒ	ⓓ	ⓔ
26.	ⓐ	ⓑ	ⓒ	ⓓ	ⓔ
27.	ⓐ	ⓑ	ⓒ	ⓓ	ⓔ
28.	ⓐ	ⓑ	ⓒ	ⓓ	ⓔ
29.	ⓐ	ⓑ	ⓒ	ⓓ	ⓔ
30.	ⓐ	ⓑ	ⓒ	ⓓ	ⓔ

Math Skills Test

Directions: The Math Skills test measures mathematical reasoning. It is concerned with your ability to arrive at solutions to problems. Each problem is followed by four possible answers. Decide which one of the answers is most nearly correct. A method for attacking each of these questions is given in the answer block at the end of this chapter. You have twenty-five (25) minutes to complete this portion of the test.

Questions: 30
Time: 25 minutes

1. What is the estimated product when 174 and 362 are rounded to the nearest hundred and multiplied?
   a. 160,000
   b. 180,000
   c. 16,000
   d. 80,000

2. Mr. Richard Tupper is purchasing gifts for his family. He stops to consider what else he has to buy. A quick mental inventory of his shopping bag so far reveals the following: 1 cashmere sweater, valued at $260; 3 diamond bracelets, each valued at $365; 1 computer game, valued at $78; and 1 cameo brooch, valued at $130. Later, having coffee in the food court, he suddenly remembers that he has purchased only two diamond bracelets, not three, and that the cashmere sweater was on sale for $245. What is the total value of the gifts Mr. Tupper has purchased so far?
   a. $833
   b. $1,183
   c. $1,198
   d. $1,563

3. One lap on a particular outdoor track measures a quarter of a mile around. To run a total of five-and-three-quarter miles, how many laps must a person complete?
   a. 7
   b. 10
   c. 23
   d. 35

4. Body mass index (BMI) is equal to weight in kilograms/(height in meters)^2. A man who weighs 64.8 kilograms has a BMI of 20. How tall is he?
   a. 1.8 meters
   b. 0.9 meters
   c. 2.16 meters
   d. 3.24 meters

5. A floor plan is drawn to scale so that $\frac{1}{4}$ inch represents two feet. If a hall on the plan is 4 inches long, how long will the actual hall be when it is built?
   a. 2 feet
   b. 8 feet
   c. 16 feet
   d. 32 feet

6. Newly hired referees have to buy uniforms at the full price of $116.75, but those who have worked at least a year get a 10% discount. Those who have worked at least three years get an additional 15% off the discounted price. How much does a referee who has worked at least three years have to pay for uniforms?
   a. $87.56
   b. $89.32
   c. $93.40
   d. $105.08

7. The condition known as Down syndrome occurs in about 1 in 1,500 children when the mothers are in their twenties. About what percentage of all children born to mothers in their twenties are likely to have Down syndrome?

   a. .0067%

   b. .67%

   c. 6.7%

   d. .067%

8. If a population of yeast cells grows from 10 to 320 in a period of five hours, what is the rate of growth?

   a. It doubles its numbers every hour.

   b. It triples its numbers every hour.

   c. It doubles its numbers every two hours.

   d. It triples its numbers every two hours.

9. How much water must be added to one liter of a 9% saline solution to get a 3% saline solution?

   a. 1 liter

   b. 1.5 liter

   c. 2 liters

   d. 2.5 liters

10. In the first week of his exercise program, John went on a 15-mile hike. The next week, he increased the length of his hike by 20%. How long was his hike in the second week?

   a. 17 miles

   b. 18 miles

   c. 30 miles

   d. 35 miles

11. All of the rooms in a building are rectangular, with 9-foot ceilings. One room is 10 feet wide by 14 feet long. What is the combined area of the four walls, including doors and windows?

   a. 99 square feet

   b. 160 square feet

   c. 320 square feet

   d. 432 square feet

12. A child has a temperature of 39.6°C. What is the child's temperature in degrees Fahrenheit? $(F = \frac{9}{5}C + 32)$

   a. 101.2°F

   b. 102°F

   c. 103.3°F

   d. 104.1°F

13. A dosage of a certain medication is 12 cc per 100 pounds. What is the dosage for a patient who weighs 175 pounds?

   a. 15 cc

   b. 18 cc

   c. 21 cc

   d. 24 cc

14. A hiker walks 40 miles on the first day of a five-day trip. On each day after that, he can walk only half as far as he did the day before. On average, how far does he walk each day?

   a. 10 miles

   b. 15.5 miles

   c. 20 miles

   d. 24 miles

15. A fugitive drives west at 50 miles per hour. After an hour, the police start to follow her. How fast must the police drive to catch up to her 4 hours after they start?

   a. 52.5 mph

   b. 55 mph

   c. 60 mph

   d. 62.5 mph

16. Jason is six times as old as Kate. In two years, Jason will be twice as old as Kate is then. How old is Jason now?

a. 3 years old

b. 6 years old

c. 9 years old

d. 12 years old

17. During her first three months at college, a student's long-distance phone bills are $103.30, $71.60, and $84.00. Her local phone bill is $18.00 each month. What is her average total monthly phone bill?

a. $86.30

b. $92.30

c. $98.30

d. $104.30

18. A car uses 16 gallons of gas to travel 448 miles. How many miles per gallon does the car get?

a. 22 miles per gallon

b. 24 miles per gallon

c. 26 miles per gallon

d. 28 miles per gallon

19. A hard drive has 962,342 bytes free. If you delete a file of 454,783 bytes and create a new file of 315,926 bytes, how many free bytes will the hard drive have?

a. 677,179 free bytes

b. 881,525 free bytes

c. 1,101,199 free bytes

d. 1,417,125 free bytes

20. Jackie is paid $822.40 twice a month. If she saves $150.00 per paycheck and pays $84.71 on her student loan each month, how much does she have left to spend each month?

a. $1,175.38

b. $1,260.09

c. $1,410.09

d. $1,310.29

21. $(.4)2 =$

a. .016

b. .8

c. .08

d. .16

22. A fuel additive requires that four parts be added per 12 gallons of fuel. How many parts need to be added for 51 gallons of fuel?

a. 4 parts

b. 5 parts

c. 17 parts

d. 48 parts

23. An aerial refueling tanker departs two hours prior to a fighter jet. If the tanker maintains a constant speed of 300 mph, how fast does the fighter jet have to fly to rendezvous with the tanker in two hours after the jet's takeoff?

a. 300 mph

b. 450 mph

c. 600 mph

d. 900 mph

24. A fighter jet burns 4,800 pounds of fuel per hour. The fuel has a specific density of 6 pounds per gallon. How much fuel will need to be requested for the aircraft to complete a three-hour flight and still have 3,000 pounds of fuel remaining upon landing?

a. 2,900 pounds

b. 2,400 gallons

c. 2,000 pounds

d. 2,900 gallons

25. An aerial tanker's refueling orbit is six miles in circumference. To fly 54 miles, how many orbits must the tanker complete?

a. 9 orbits

b. 10 orbits

c. 12 orbits

d. 14 orbits

26. A model plane is built scale so that .5 inch equals five feet. If the model plane is 10 inches long, how long is the actual airplane?

    a. 10 feet

    b. 20 feet

    c. 50 feet

    d. 100 feet

27. Bonnie has twice as many cousins as Robert. George has five cousins, which is 11 less than Bonnie has. How many cousins does Robert have?

    a. 17

    b. 21

    c. 4

    d. 8

28. Oscar sold two glasses of milk for every five sodas he sold. If he sold 10 glasses of milk, how many sodas did he sell?

    a. 45

    b. 20

    c. 25

    d. 10

29. Justin earned scores of 85, 92, and 95 on his science tests. What does he need to earn on his next science test to have an average (arithmetic mean) of 93%?

    a. 93

    b. 100

    c. 85

    d. 96

30. Which expression has an answer of 18?

    a. $2 \times 5 + 4$

    b. $2 \times (4 + 5)$

    c. $5 \times (2 + 4)$

    d. $4 \times 2 + 5$

Reading Skills Test

Directions: The Paragraph Comprehension subtest measures your ability to read and understand paragraphs. For each question, choose the answer that best completes the meaning of the paragraph. Pay close attention as you read, and try to find the point that the author was trying to make. Once you have read the paragraph all the way through, you will find that one or two of the possible answers can be quickly eliminated based on the context. You have twenty-five (25) minutes to complete this subtest.

Questions: 27

Time: 25 minutes

Anyone who lives in a large, modern city has heard the familiar sound of electronic security alarms. Although these mechanical alarms are fairly recent, the idea of a security system is not new. The oldest alarm system was probably a few strategically placed dogs that would discourage intruders with a loud warning cry.

1. This paragraph best supports the statement that

    a. dogs are more reliable than electronic alarms.

    b. city dwellers would be wise to use dogs for security.

    c. mechanical alarm systems break down, but dogs do not.

    d. a dog is an older alarm device than is a mechanical alarm.

In cities throughout the country, there is a new direction in local campaign coverage. Frequently, in local elections, journalists are not giving voters enough information to understand the issues and evaluate the candidates. The local news media devote too much time to scandal and not enough time to policy.

2. This paragraph best supports the statement that the local news media

   a. are not doing an adequate job when it comes to covering local campaigns.

   b. do not understand either campaign issues or politics.

   c. should learn how to cover politics by watching the national news media.

   d. have no interest in covering stories about local political events.

Many office professionals today have an interest in replacing the currently used keyboard, known as the QWERTY keyboard, with a keyboard that can keep up with technological changes and make offices more efficient. The best choice is the Dvorak keyboard. Studies have shown that people using the Dvorak keyboard can type 20 to 30% faster and cut their error rate in half. Dvorak puts vowels and other frequently used letters right under the fingers (on the home row), where typists make 70% of their keystrokes.

3. The paragraph best supports the statement that the Dvorak keyboard

   a. is more efficient than the QWERTY.

   b. has more keys right under the typists' fingers than the QWERTY.

   c. is favored by more typists than the QWERTY.

   d. is, on average, 70% faster than the QWERTY.

Every year, Americans use more than one billion sharp objects to administer health care in their homes. These sharp objects include lancets, needles, and syringes. If not disposed of in puncture-resistant containers, they can injure sanitation workers. Sharp objects should be disposed of in hard plastic or metal containers with secure lids. The containers should be clearly marked and be puncture resistant.

4. The paragraph best supports the idea that sanitation workers can be injured if they

   a. do not place sharp objects in puncture-resistant containers.

   b. come in contact with sharp objects that have not been placed in secure containers.

   c. are careless with sharp objects such as lancets, needles, and syringes in their homes.

   d. do not mark the containers they pick up with a warning that those containers contain sharp objects.

Close-up images of Mars by the *Mariner 9* probe indicated networks of valleys that looked like the streambeds on Earth. These images also implied that Mars once had an atmosphere that was thick enough to trap the sun's heat. If this is true, something must have happened to Mars billions of years ago that stripped away the planet's atmosphere.

5. This paragraph best supports the statement that

   a. Mars once had a thicker atmosphere than Earth does.

   b. the *Mariner 9* probe took the first pictures of Mars.

   c. Mars now has little or no atmosphere.

   d. Mars is closer to the sun than Earth is.

After a snow or ice fall, the city streets are treated with ordinary rock salt. In some areas, the salt is combined with calcium chloride, which is more effective in below-zero temperatures and which melts ice better. This combination of salt and calcium chloride is also less damaging to foliage along the roadways.

6. In deciding whether to use ordinary rock salt or the salt and calcium chloride mixture on a particular street, which of the following is NOT a consideration?
   a. the temperature at the time of treatment
   b. the plants and trees along the street
   c. whether there is ice on the street
   d. whether the street is a main or a secondary road

The city has distributed standardized recycling containers to all households with directions that read: "We would prefer that you use this new container as your primary recycling container, as this will expedite pickup of recyclables. Additional recycling containers may be purchased from the city."

7. According to the directions, each household
   a. may use only one recycling container.
   b. must use the new recycling container.
   c. should use the new recycling container.
   d. must buy a new recycling container.

It is well known that the world urgently needs adequate distribution of food so that everyone gets enough. Adequate distribution of medicine is just as urgent. Medical expertise and medical supplies need to be redistributed throughout the world so that people in emerging nations will have proper medical care.

8. This paragraph best supports the statement that
   a. the majority of the people in the world have no medical care.
   b. medical resources in emerging nations have diminished in the past few years.
   c. not enough doctors give time and money to those in need of medical care.
   d. many people who live in emerging nations are not receiving proper medical care.

In the past, suggesting a gas tax has usually been thought of as political poison. But that doesn't seem to be the case today. Several states are pushing bills in their state legislatures that would cut income or property taxes and make up the revenue with taxes on fossil fuel.

9. The paragraph best supports the statement that
   a. gas taxes produce more revenue than income taxes.
   b. states with low income tax rates are increasing their gas taxes.
   c. state legislators no longer fear increasing gas taxes.
   d. taxes on fossil fuels are more popular than property taxes.

Lawyer bashing is on the increase in the United States. Lawyers are accused of lacking principles, clogging the justice system, and increasing the cost of liability insurance. Lawyers have received undeserved criticism. A lawyer is more likely than not to try to dissuade a client from litigation by offering to arbitrate and settle conflict.

10. The main idea of the paragraph is best expressed in which of the following statements from the passage?
   a. Lawyer bashing is on the increase in the United States.
   b. Lawyers have received undeserved criticism.
   c. Lawyers are accused of lacking principles.
   d. A lawyer is more likely than not to try to dissuade a client from litigation by offering to arbitrate and settle conflict.

Generation Xers are those people born roughly between 1965 and 1981. As employees, Generation Xers tend to be more challenged when they can carry out tasks independently. This makes Generation Xers the most entrepreneurial generation in history.

11. This paragraph best supports the statement that Generation Xers
   a. work harder than people from other generations.
   b. have a tendency to be self-directed workers.
   c. tend to work in jobs that require risk-taking behavior.
   d. like to challenge their bosses' work attitudes.

Electronic mail (e-mail) has been in widespread use for more than a decade. E-mail simplifies the flow of ideas, connects people from distant offices, eliminates the need for meetings, and often boosts productivity. But e-mail should be carefully managed to avoid unclear and inappropriate communication. E-mail messages should be concise and limited to one topic. When complex issues need to be addressed, phone calls are still best.

12. The main idea of the paragraph is that e-mail
   a. is not always the easiest way to connect people from distant offices.
   b. has changed considerably since it first began a decade ago.
   c. causes people to be unproductive when it is used incorrectly.
   d. is effective for certain kinds of messages, but only if managed wisely.

Children start out in a world where fantasy and imagination are not substantially different from experience. But as they get older, they are shocked to discover that the world in which people reliably exist is the physical world. Computer games and virtual reality are two ways in which children can come to terms with this dilemma.

13. The main idea of the paragraph is that computer games and virtual reality
   a. can be important tools in children's lives.
   b. keep children from experiencing reality.
   c. help children to uncover shocking truths about the world.
   d. should take the place of children's fantasy worlds.

Native American art often incorporates a language of abstract visual symbols. The artist gives a poetic message to the viewer, communicating the beauty of an idea by using either religious symbols or a design from nature such as rain on leaves or sunshine on water. The idea communicated may even be purely whimsical, in which case the artist might start out with symbols developed from a bird's tracks or a child's toy.

14. The main idea of the passage is that Native American art
   a. is purely poetic and dreamlike.
   b. is usually abstract, although it can also be poetic and beautiful.
   c. communicates the beauty of ideas through the use of symbols.
   d. is sometimes purely whimsical.

The supervisors have received numerous complaints over the last several weeks about buses on several routes running hot. Drivers are reminded that each route has several checkpoints at which drivers should check the time. If the bus is ahead of schedule, drivers should delay at the checkpoint until it is the proper time to leave.

15. In the passage, saying a bus is *running hot* means
   a. the engine is overheating.
   b. the bus is running ahead of schedule.
   c. the air conditioning is not working.
   d. there is no more room for passengers.

Hazardous waste is defined as any waste designated by the U.S. Environmental Protection Agency as hazardous. If a worker is unclear whether a particular item is hazardous, he or she should not handle the item, but should instead notify the supervisor and ask for directions.

16. Hazardous waste is
   a. anything too dangerous for workers to handle.
   b. picked up by special trucks.
   c. defined by the United States Environmental Protection Agency.
   d. not allowed with regular residential garbage.

In the summer, the northern hemisphere is slanted toward the sun, making the days longer and warmer than in winter. The summer solstice is the first day of summer and the longest day of the year. However, June 21 marks the beginning of winter in the southern hemisphere, when that hemisphere is tilted away from the sun.

17. According to the passage, when it is summer in the northern hemisphere, in the southern hemisphere it is
   a. spring.
   b. summer.
   c. autumn.
   d. winter.

An ecosystem is a group of animals and plants living in a specific region and interacting with one another and with their physical environment. Ecosystems include physical and chemical components, such as soils, water, and nutrients that support the organisms living there. These organisms may range from large animals to microscopic bacteria. Ecosystems can also be thought of as the interactions among all organisms in a given habitat; for instance, one species may serve as food for another.

18. An ecosystem can most accurately be defined as a
   a. geographical area.
   b. community.
   c. habitat.
   d. protected environment.
   e. specific location.

The English-language premiere of Samuel Beckett's play *Waiting for Godot* took place in London in August 1955. *Godot* is an avant-garde play with only five characters (not counting Mr. Godot, who never arrives) and a minimal setting (one rock and one bare tree). The play has two acts. The second act repeats what little action occurs in the first with few changes; the tree, for instance, acquires one leaf. The play initially met with bafflement and derision. However, Harold Hobson, in his review in *The Sunday Times*, managed to recognize the play for what history has proven it to be: a revolutionary moment in theater.

19. Which of the following best describes the attitude of the author of the passage toward the play *Waiting for Godot*?
   a. It was a curiosity in theater history.
   b. It is the most important play of the twentieth century.
   c. It had no effect on theater.
   d. It represented a turning point in theater history.
   e. It was a mediocre play.

Everyone is sensitive to extreme weather conditions. But with age, the body may become less able to respond to long exposure to very hot or very cold temperatures. Some older people might develop hypothermia when exposed to cold weather. Hypothermia is a drop in internal body temperature, which can be fatal if not detected and treated.

20. This paragraph best supports the statement that
   a. cold weather is more dangerous for older people than warm weather.
   b. hypothermia is a condition that only affects older people.
   c. older people who live in warm climates are healthier than older people who live in cold climates.
   d. an older person is more susceptible to hypothermia than a younger person.
   e. young people prefer cold weather.

In the United States, the most frequently used nutritional standard for maintaining optimal health is known as the Recommended Dietary Allowance, or *RDA*. The RDA specifies the recommended amount of nutrients for people in many different age and gender groups. While the basic premise of an RDA is a good one, the current model has a number of shortcomings. First, it is based on the assumption that it is possible to define nutritional requirements accurately for a given group. However, individual nutritional requirements can vary widely within each group. The efficiency with which a person converts food intake into nutrients can also vary widely. Certain foods when eaten in combination actually prevent the absorption of nutrients. For example, spinach combined with milk reduces the amount of calcium available to the body from the milk. Also, the RDA approach specifies a different dietary requirement for each age and gender, and it is clearly unrealistic to prepare a different menu for each family member. Still, although we cannot rely solely upon the RDA to ensure our overall long-term health, it can be a useful guide so long as its limitations are recognized.

21. With which of the following would the author most likely agree?
    a. The RDA approach should be replaced by a more realistic nutritional guide.
    b. The RDA approach should be supplemented with more specific nutritional guides.
    c. In spite of its flaws, the RDA approach is definitely the best guide to good nutrition.
    d. The RDA approach is most suitable for a large family.
    e. The RDA approach is outdated.

The coast of Maine is one of the most irregular in the world. This irregularity is the result of what is called a *drowned coastline*. The term comes from the glacial activity of the Ice Age. During the Ice Age, the whole area that is now Maine was part of a mountain range that towered above the sea. As the glacier descended, however, it expended enormous force on those mountains, and they sank into the sea. As the mountains sank, ocean water charged over the lowest parts of the remaining land, forming a series of twisting inlets and lagoons. Once the glacier receded, the highest parts of the former mountain range that were nearest the shore remained as islands. Although the mountain ranges were never to return, the land rose somewhat over the centuries. On one of these islands, marine fossils have been found at 225 feet above today's sea level.

22. According to the passage, when the glacier moved over what is now the state of Maine, it helped to create all of the following *except*
    a. an irregular coastline.
    b. coastal islands.
    c. a mountain range.
    d. inlets.
    e. lagoons.

Light pollution is a growing problem world-wide. Like other forms of pollution, light pollution degrades the quality of the environment. Where once it was possible to look up at the night sky and see thousands of twinkling stars in the inky blackness, one now sees little more than the yellow glare of urban sky-glow. When we lose the ability to connect visually with the vastness of the universe by looking up at the night sky, we lose our connection with something profoundly important to the human spirit, our sense of wonder.

23. The passage implies that the most serious damage done by light pollution is to our
  a. artistic appreciation.
  b. sense of physical well-being.
  c. cultural advancement.
  d. aesthetic sensibilities.
  e. spiritual selves.

Law enforcement officers often do not like taking time from their regular duties to testify in court, but testimony is an important part of an officer's job. To be good witnesses, officers should keep complete notes detailing any potentially criminal or actionable incidents. When on the witness stand, officers may refer to those notes to refresh their memories about particular events. It is also very important for officers to listen carefully to the questions asked by the lawyers and to provide only the information requested. Officers should never volunteer opinions or any extra information that is beyond the scope of a question.

24. The paragraph best supports the statement that an unprepared police witness might
  a. rely on memory alone when testifying in court.
  b. hold an opinion about the guilt or innocence of a suspect before the trial is over.
  c. rely too much on notes and not enough on experience at the crime scene.
  d. be unduly influenced by prosecution lawyers when giving testimony.
  e. not offer extra information on the stand which would help the prosecution's case.

The Competitive Civil Service system is designed to give applicants fair and equal treatment and to ensure that federal applicants are hired based on objective criteria. Hiring has to be based solely on candidates' knowledge, skills, and abilities (which you will sometimes see abbreviated as *ksa*) and not on any external factors such as race, religion, sex, and so on. Whereas employers in the private sector can hire employees for subjective reasons, federal employers must be able to justify their decisions with objective evidence that the candidate is qualified.

25. The federal government's practice of hiring on the basis of *ksa* frequently results in the hiring of employees
  a. based on race, religion, sex, and so forth.
  b. who are unqualified for the job.
  c. who are qualified for the job.
  d. on the basis of subjective judgment.
  e. based on the unequal treatment of applicants.

On occasion, corrections officers may be involved in receiving a confession from an inmate under their care. Sometimes, one inmate may confess to another inmate, who may be motivated to pass the information on to correction officers. Often, however, these confessions are obtained by placing an undercover agent, posing as an inmate, in a cell with the prisoner. On the surface, this may appear to violate the principles of the constitutional Fifth Amendment privilege against self-incrimination. However, the courts have found that the Fifth Amendment is intended to protect suspects from coercive interrogation, which is present when a person is in custody and is subject to official questioning. In the case of an undercover officer posing as an inmate, the questioning does not appear to be official; therefore, confessions obtained in this manner are not considered coercive.

26. The privilege against self-incrimination can be found in
   a. a Supreme Court opinion.
   b. prison rules and regulations.
   c. state law governing prisons.
   d. the U.S. Constitution.
   e. Congressional legislature.

One of the most hazardous conditions a firefighter will ever encounter is a backdraft (also known as a smoke explosion). Firefighters should be aware of the conditions that indicate the possibility for a backdraft to occur. When there is a lack of oxygen during a fire, the smoke becomes filled with carbon dioxide or carbon monoxide and turns dense gray or black. Other warning signs of a potential backdraft are little or no visible flame, excessive heat, smoke leaving the building in puffs, muffled sounds, and smoke-stained windows.

27. Which of the following is NOT mentioned as a potential backdraft warning sign?
   a. windows stained with smoke
   b. flames shooting up from the building
   c. puffs of smoke leaving the building
   d. more intense heat than usual
   e. muffled sounds coming from the building

Mechanical Comprehension Test

Directions: This part of the ASTB measures your ability to learn and reason with mechanical terms. Included in this part of the test are diagrams showing various mechanical devices. Following each diagram are several questions or incomplete statements. Study each diagram carefully, as details do make a difference in how each device operates, and then select the choice that best answers the question or completes the statement. You have fifteen (15) minutes to complete this subtest.

Questions: 30
Time: 15 minutes

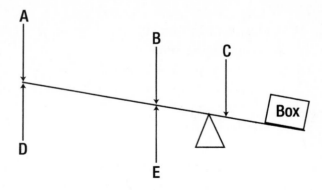

1. In this figure, you want to lift the box. At what point and in what direction would you get the maximum leverage to lift the box?
   a. point A
   b. point B
   c. point C
   d. point D
   e. point E

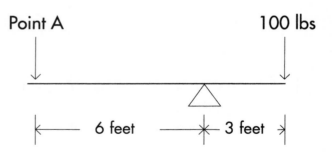

2. If you intend to keep the bar level, as depicted here, what force must you use at point A to counterbalance the 100 pounds at the other end?
   a. 10 pounds
   b. 50 pounds
   c. 100 pounds
   d. 150 pounds
   e. 200 pounds

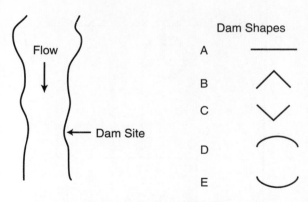

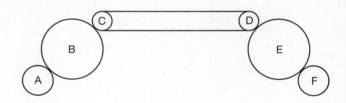

3. You have been instructed to build a dam on the river, as shown here. What shape should you make the dam for the given dam site?
   a. shape A
   b. shape B
   c. shape C
   d. shape D
   e. shape E

5. This figure shows a series of gears, A, B, and C, that are connected by a conveyor belt to gears D, E, and F. If gear A turns clockwise, what direction do gears E and F turn?
   a. clockwise, clockwise
   b. counterclockwise, counterclockwise
   c. clockwise, counterclockwise
   d. counterclockwise, clockwise
   e. not enough information

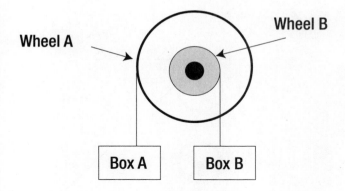

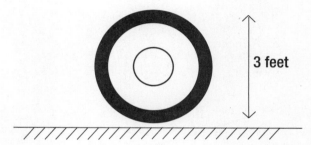

4. In this figure, box A weighs 75 pounds. The radius of wheel A is six feet and the radius of wheel B is two feet. If both wheels are balanced, what must box B weigh?
   a. 75 pounds
   b. 150 pounds
   c. 225 pounds
   d. 300 pounds
   e. 375 pounds

6. If the tire shown here is 3 feet in diameter and is turning at 500 revolutions per minute, what speed (in feet/minutes) is the tire traveling down the road?
   a. 500 feet/minute
   b. 1,500 feet/minute
   c. 1,860 feet/minute
   d. 2,355 feet/minute
   e. 4,710 feet/minute

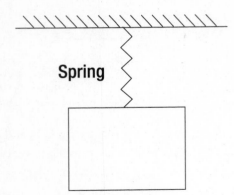

Spring

7. This spring has a stiffness of 16 lbs./in. How much is the spring stretched if the weight of the block is 98 pounds?

a. $4\frac{7}{8}$ inches

b. $5\frac{3}{4}$ inches

c. $6\frac{1}{8}$ inches

d. $7\frac{1}{4}$ inches

e. $7\frac{5}{8}$ inches

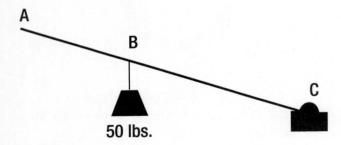

50 lbs.

8. In this figure, the distance from A to B is three feet, and the distance from B to C is seven feet. How much force must be applied at A to lift the 50 pounds at point B?

a. 25 pounds

b. 35 pounds

c. 45 pounds

d. 55 pounds

e. 65 pounds

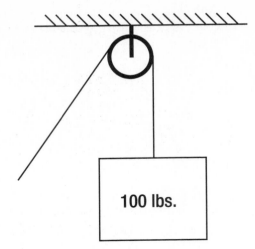

100 lbs.

9. How much effort must be used to raise the 100-lb. weight shown here?

a. 50 pounds

b. 100 pounds

c. 150 pounds

d. 200 pounds

e. 250 pounds

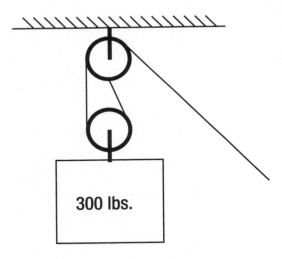

300 lbs.

10. How much effort must be used to raise the 300-pound weight shown?

a. 50 pounds

b. 90 pounds

c. 100 pounds

d. 120 pounds

e. 150 pounds

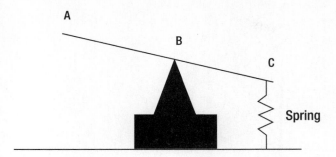

11. Given the lever shown, determine how much force you must push down on point A to stretch the spring 10 inches. (The distance from A to B is 6 feet and the distance from B to C is 4 feet. The spring has a stiffness of 20 lbs./in.)

  a. 110.0 pounds
  b. 120.5 pounds
  c. 133.3 pounds
  d. 142.5 pounds
  e. 155.5 pounds

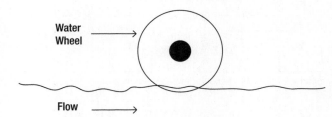

12. This water wheel has a diameter of nine feet. The flow of the river is 300 feet/minute. Approximately how many revolutions per minute is the water wheel turning and in what direction?

  a. 10 rpm, counterclockwise
  b. 10 rpm, clockwise
  c. 33 rpm, counterclockwise
  d. 33 rpm, clockwise
  e. 100 rpm, counterclockwise

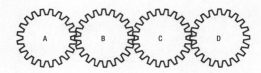

13. If gear C rotates five revolutions counterclockwise, what will gear D do?

  a. rotate one revolution clockwise
  b. rotate five revolutions clockwise
  c. rotate five revolutions counterclockwise
  d. rotate one revolution counterclockwise
  e. none of the above

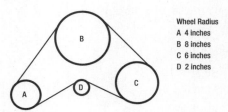

Wheel Radius
A 4 inches
B 8 inches
C 6 inches
D 2 inches

14. All four gears are connected by the same fan belt. What gear is turning at the highest revolution per minute (rpm)?

  a. gear A
  b. gear B
  c. gear C
  d. gear D
  e. They all turn at the same rpm.

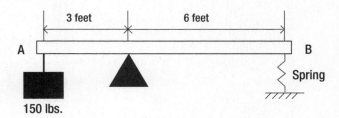

15. The 150-pound weight at point A is supported by a spring at point B. The spring has a stiffness of 25 lbs./inch. How many inches is the spring stretched?

  a. 1 inch
  b. 1.5 inches
  c. 2.0 inches
  d. 2.5 inches
  e. 3.0 inches

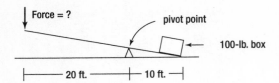

16. Using a lever, Joe must lift the 100-pound box shown here. How many pounds of force must he apply to the left side of the lever to lift the box? (The product of the weight of the box times the distance of the box from the pivot point must be equal to the product of the required force times the distance from the force to the pivot point: $w \times d_1 = f \times d_2$.)

   a. 100 pounds
   b. 200 pounds
   c. 50 pounds
   d. 33 pounds
   e. 15 pounds

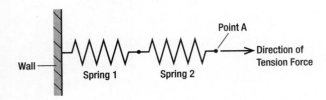

17. Two springs are arranged in series as shown. Spring 1 is very stiff and will become 1 inch longer when a tension force of 10 pounds is applied to it. Spring 2 is very soft and will become two inches longer when a tension force of five pounds is applied to it. What will be the change in length of the two springs when a force of 20 pounds is applied—that is, how far will point A move to the right?

   a. 10 inches
   b. 8 inches
   c. 6 inches
   d. 4 inches
   e. 3 inches

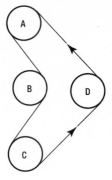

18. Which gears are turning clockwise?

   a. B
   b. B and D
   c. D
   d. A, B, C, and D
   e. A, C, and D

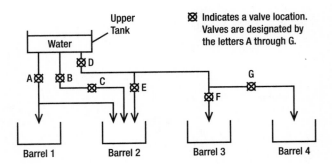

19. In this figure, all valves are initially closed. Gravity will cause the water to drain down into the barrels when the valves are opened. Which barrels will be filled if valves A, B, E, F, and G are opened and valves C and D are left closed?

   a. barrels 1 and 2
   b. barrels 3 and 4
   c. barrels 1, 2, 3, and 4
   d. barrels 1, 2, and 3
   e. barrels 1 and 4

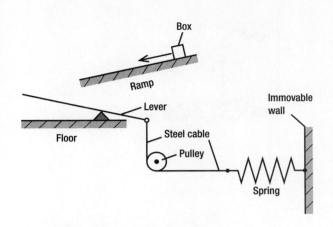

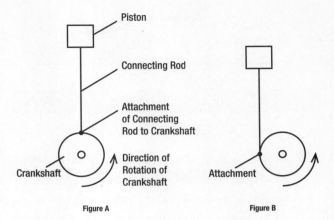

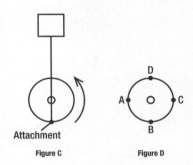

20. If the box slides down the ramp and drops onto the left side of the lever shown here, what will happen to the spring?
  a. It will touch the box.
  b. It will remain as it is.
  c. It will be compressed or shortened.
  d. It will be stretched or lengthened.
  e. none of the above

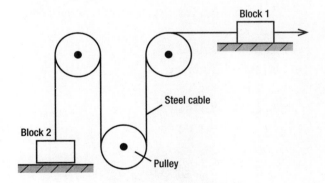

21. In this figure, if Block 1 is moved 10 feet to the right, how far upward is Block 2 lifted?
  a. 3 feet
  b. 5 feet
  c. 10 feet
  d. 15 feet
  e. 20 feet

22. Figure A shows the initial position of a piston that is connected to a crankshaft by a connecting rod; Figure B shows the relative positions after the crankshaft is rotated 90° (one quarter of a revolution) in the direction shown; and Figure C shows the relative positions after another 90° of rotation. In Figure D, what will be the position of the connecting rod attachment to the crankshaft after yet another 90° rotation?
  a. position A
  b. position B
  c. position C
  d. position D
  e. none of the above

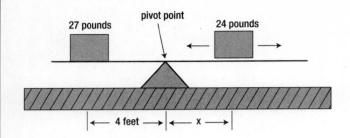

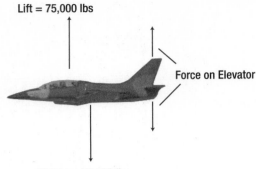

Lift = 75,000 lbs

Force on Elevator

Weight = 73,000 lbs

23. In the diagram, Kenneth wants to balance two blocks on either side of a lever. One block weighs 27 pounds and the other weighs 24 pounds. If the 27-pound block is 4 feet to the left of the pivot point, how far to the right of the pivot point should the 24-pound block be placed?

   a. 4.5 feet

   b. 7 feet

   c. 4 feet

   d. 8.5 feet

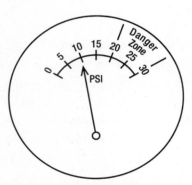

24. On the gauge in this figure, what is the maximum recommended operating pressure in psi (pounds per square inch) for the needle to remain in a safe zone?

   a. 10 psi

   b. 15 psi

   c. 20 psi

   d. 25 psi

   e. 30 psi

25. The aircraft shown is flying in a straight and level profile. The weight of the aircraft is 73,000 pounds, and the wings are generating 75,000 pounds of lift. The distance between the lift force and the weight force is 2.5 feet. Since the lift force and the weight force are not equal, the elevator must apply some force to maintain the straight and level profile. Determine what force is necessary from the elevator and if that force is in the up or the down direction. The distance from the elevator to the weight force is 23 feet.

   a. 217.4 lbs./up

   b. 217.4 lbs./down

   c. 2,174.3 lbs./up

   d. 2,174.3 lbs./down

   e. 4,348.6 lbs./down

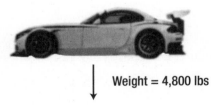

Weight = 4,800 lbs

26. This car weighs 4,800 pounds. How much weight does each tire support?

   a. 1,200 pounds

   b. 2,400 pounds

   c. 3,600 pounds

   d. 4,800 pounds

   e. 6,000 pounds

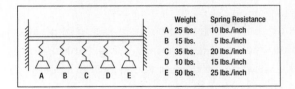

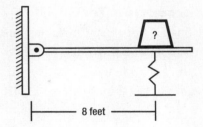

27. This figure depicts a series of weights suspended from a bar by means of springs. Using the given weights and spring resistances, determine which weight will stretch its respective spring the most.

a. weight A
b. weight B
c. weight C
d. weight D
e. weight E

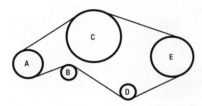

28. In this figure, wheel A turns clockwise. All the wheels are connected by the same fan belt. Determine the direction of rotation for all the other wheels.

a. clockwise: B, C; counterclockwise: D, E
b. clockwise: D, E; counterclockwise: B, C
c. clockwise: C, D, E; counterclockwise: B
d. clockwise: B; counterclockwise: C, D, E
e. clockwise: B, C, D; counterclockwise: E

29. In this figure, determine how much weight must be applied to compress the spring 10 inches. Neglect the weight of the bar and use 20 lbs./inch for the resistance of the spring. Assume that the weight is placed directly over the spring, eight feet from the hinge.

a. 25 pounds
b. 50 pounds
c. 100 pounds
d. 200 pounds
e. 400 pounds

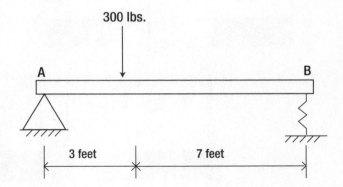

30. A 300-lb. force is applied to a bar supported at points A and B. The force is applied three feet from point A and seven feet from point B. The support at point B is a spring with a resistance of 15 lbs./inch. Determine how much the spring will be compressed in this configuration.

a. 2 inches
b. 3 inches
c. 4 inches
d. 5 inches
e. 6 inches

Spatial Apperception Test

Directions: The Spatial Apperception subtest measures your ability to determine the position of an aircraft in flight in relation to a ship on the water. You are to determine whether it is climbing, diving, banking to right or left, or in level flight. For each question, select the choice that most nearly represents the aircraft's position in relation to the position of the ship. You have ten (10) minutes to complete this subtest.

Questions: 25
Time: 10 minutes

1.

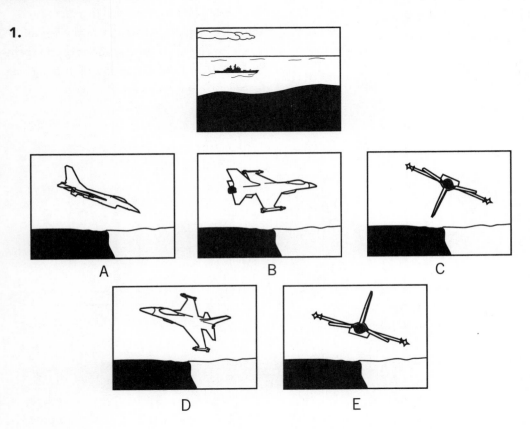

A   B   C

D   E

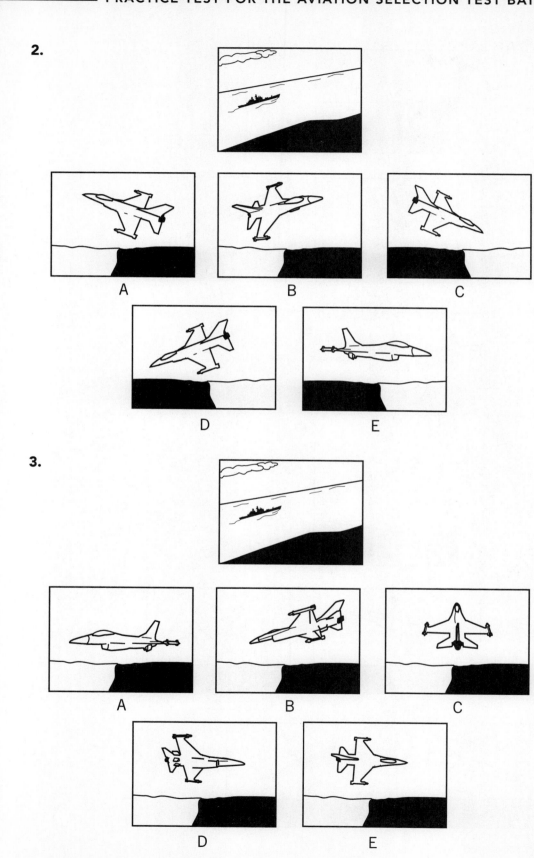

2.

A

B

C

D

E

3.

A

B

C

D

E

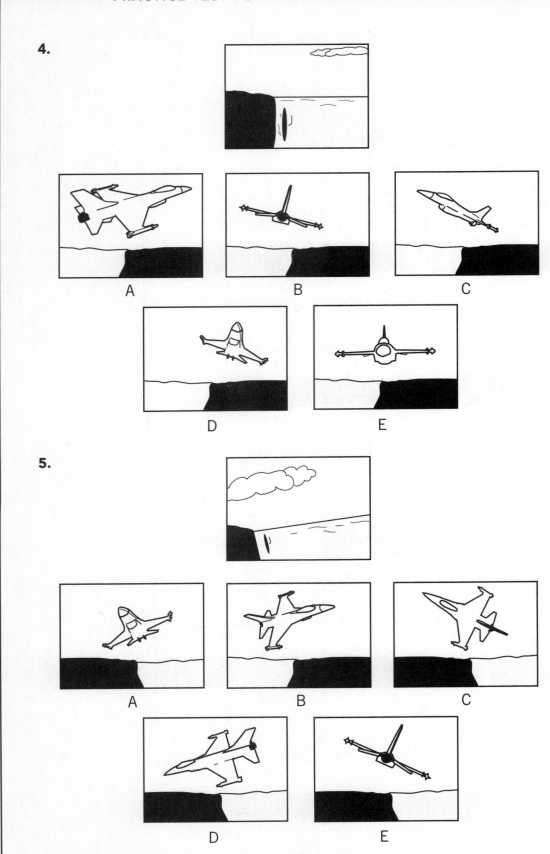

4.

A

B

C

D

E

5.

A

B

C

D

E

6.

A 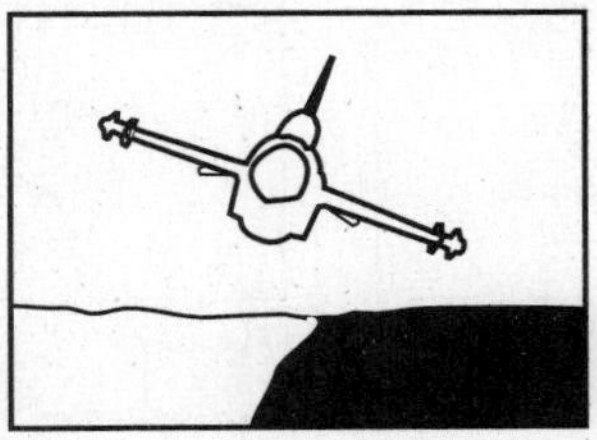   B    C

D    E

7.

A    B    C

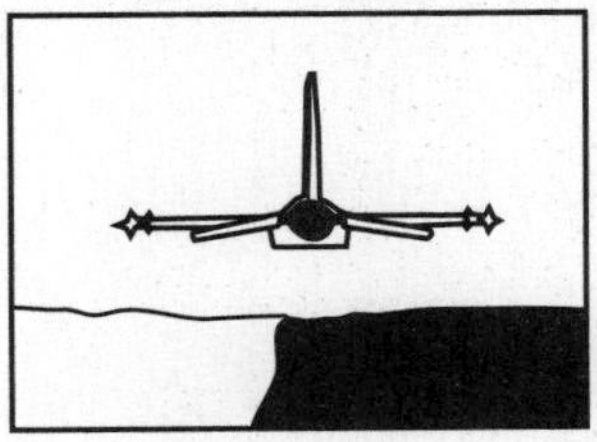

D    E

8.

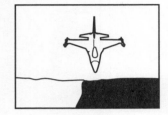

A B C

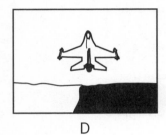
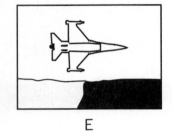

D E

9.

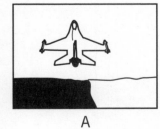
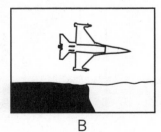

A B C

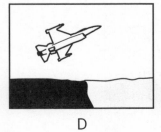

D E

10.

11.

12.

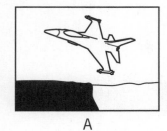
A

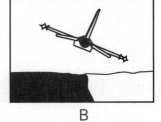
B

C

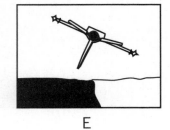
D   E

13.

A

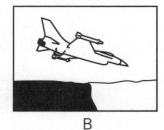
B

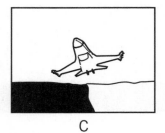
C

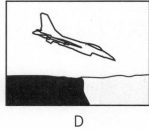
D

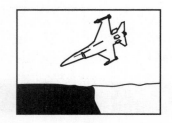
E

14.

A  B 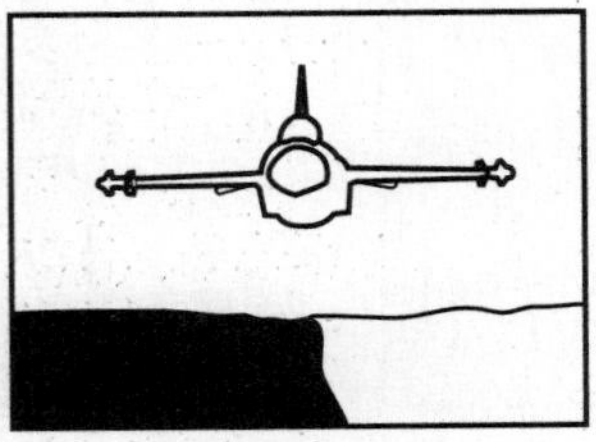 C

D  E

15.

A  B  C

D  E

16.

A

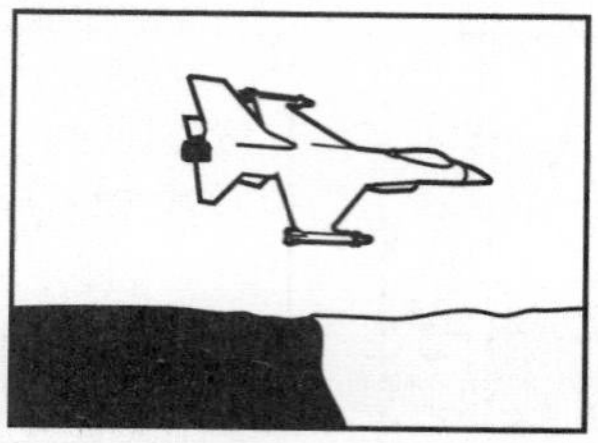

B

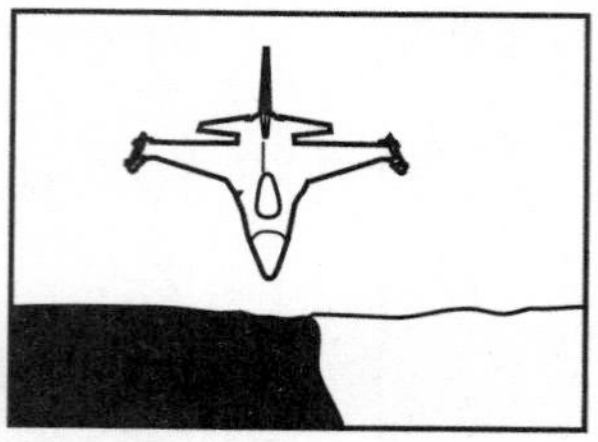

C

D

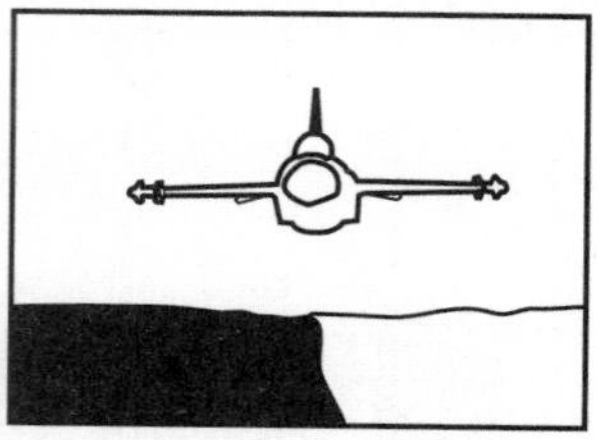

E

17.

A

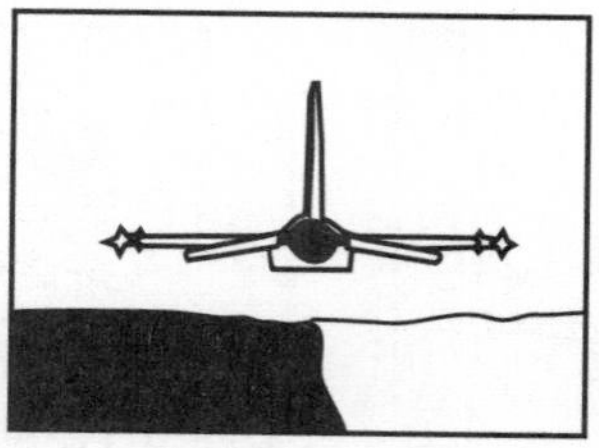

B

C

D

E

18.

A  B  C

D  E

19.

A  B  C

D  E

20.

A B C

D E

21.

A B C

D E

22.

23.

24.

A   B   C

D   E

25.

A   B   C

D   E

Aviation and Nautical Information Test

Directions: This part of the ASTB measures your aviation and nautical knowledge. Each of the questions or incomplete statements is followed by several choices. You must decide which one of the choices best completes the statement or answers the question. Eliminating any obviously incorrect choices first will increase your chances of selecting the right answer. You have fifteen (15) minutes to complete this subtest.

Questions: 30
Time: 15 minutes

1. The front section of a ship is known as the
   a. port side.
   b. starboard side.
   c. bow.
   d. stern.
   e. keel.

2. The rear section of a ship is known as the
   a. port side.
   b. starboard side.
   c. bow.
   d. stern.
   e. keel.

3. The right-hand side of a ship is known as the
   a. port side.
   b. starboard side.
   c. bow.
   d. stern.
   e. keel.

4. The left-hand side of a ship is known as the
   a. port side.
   b. starboard side.
   c. bow.
   d. stern.
   e. keel.

Use the following figure to answer questions 5 through 8.

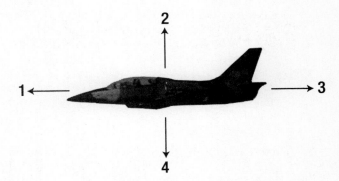

5. The force represented by arrow 1 is
   a. lift.
   b. weight.
   c. drag.
   d. thrust.
   e. none of the above.

6. The force represented by arrow 2 is
   a. lift.
   b. weight.
   c. drag.
   d. thrust.
   e. none of the above.

7. The force represented by arrow 3 is
   a. lift.
   b. weight.
   c. drag.
   d. thrust.
   e. none of the above.

8. The force represented by arrow 4 is
    a. lift.
    b. weight.
    c. drag.
    d. thrust.
    e. none of the above.

Use the following figure to answer questions 9 through 12.

9. Arrow 1 is pointing to the
    a. aileron.
    b. flap.
    c. rudder.
    d. elevator.
    e. fuselage.

10. Arrow 2 is pointing to the
    a. aileron.
    b. flap.
    c. rudder.
    d. elevator.
    e. fuselage.

11. Arrow 3 is pointing to the
    a. aileron.
    b. flap.
    c. rudder.
    d. elevator.
    e. fuselage.

12. Arrow 4 is pointing to the
    a. aileron.
    b. flap.
    c. rudder.
    d. elevator.
    e. fuselage.

13. The _____ is the kitchen compartment of a ship.
    a. hull
    b. keel
    c. bulkhead
    d. galley
    e. forecastle

14. The _____ is the section of the upper deck of a ship located at the bow.
    a. hull
    b. keel
    c. bulkhead
    d. galley
    e. forecastle

15. The _____ is the body of a ship excluding masts, sails, yards, and riggings.
    a. hull
    b. keel
    c. bulkhead
    d. galley
    e. forecastle

16. A _____ is one of the straight upright partitions dividing a ship into compartments.
    a. hull
    b. keel
    c. bulkhead
    d. galley
    e. forecastle

17. The _____ is the principal structural member that forms the centerline of the hull running from bow to stern.
  a. hull
  b. keel
  c. bulkhead
  d. galley
  e. forecastle

18. _____ is the actual velocity of an aircraft traveling through the air.
  a. Indicated airspeed
  b. Calibrated airspeed
  c. Equivalent airspeed
  d. True airspeed
  e. Ground speed

19. _____ is the instrumental indication of the dynamic pressure of the airplane during flight.
  a. Indicated airspeed
  b. Calibrated airspeed
  c. Equivalent airspeed
  d. True airspeed
  e. Ground speed

20. _____ is a measure of the aircraft's actual speed over the ground.
  a. Indicated airspeed
  b. Calibrated airspeed
  c. Equivalent airspeed
  d. True airspeed
  e. Ground speed

21. _____ is the corrected airspeed taking into account instrumental error.
  a. Indicated airspeed
  b. Calibrated airspeed
  c. Equivalent airspeed
  d. True airspeed
  e. Ground speed

22. _____ is found by correcting calibrated airspeed for compressibility error.
  a. Indicated airspeed
  b. Calibrated airspeed
  c. Equivalent airspeed
  d. True airspeed
  e. Ground speed

23. A jet is flying straight and level at 10,000 feet and 400 knots. If the pilot pulls back on the throttle but gives no input to the stick, how will the aircraft react?
  a. The jet will accelerate and climb.
  b. The jet will initially slow down and begin a gradual descent.
  c. The jet will remain level and slow down.
  d. The jet will remain level and accelerate.
  e. The jet will not experience any changes.

24. A jet is flying straight and level at 10,000 feet and 400 knots. If the pilot adds power and pushes the stick forward, how will the aircraft react?
  a. The jet will climb and accelerate.
  b. The jet will descend and slow down.
  c. The jet will descend and accelerate.
  d. The jet will climb and decelerate.
  e. The jet will remain level and decelerate.

25. The average lapse rate of temperature in the atmosphere is the decrease in the air temperature as you climb at a rate of 2° C per 1,000 feet. If the temperature at the airfield is 15° C and you plan to fly a mission with a cruise altitude of 20,000 feet, what temperature can you expect to find during the cruise portion of your flight? The elevation of your airfield is 2,000 feet mean sea level (MSL).
  a. −12° C
  b. −16° C
  c. −21° C
  d. −25° C
  e. −40° C

26. An aircraft's current heading is 180° and your navigator instructs you to turn left 45°. What would be your new heading?
 a. 225
 b. 135
 c. 145
 d. 045
 e. 315

27. An aircraft's current heading is 270°, and your navigator instructs you to turn right 100°. What would be your new heading?
 a. 010
 b. 370
 c. 100
 d. 260
 e. 170

28. Temperature is best described as
 a. the amount of water vapor in the air.
 b. the rate at which sound waves travel through an air mass.
 c. a measure of the average kinetic energy of the air particles.
 d. a measure of the air's resistance to flow and shearing.
 e. the total mass of air particles per unit of volume.

29. Humidity is best described as
 a. the amount of water vapor in the air.
 b. the rate at which sound waves travel through an air mass.
 c. a measure of the average kinetic energy of the air particles.
 d. a measure of the air's resistance to flow and shearing.
 e. the total mass of air particles per unit of volume.

30. Air density is best described as
 a. the amount of water vapor in the air.
 b. the rate at which sound waves travel through an air mass.
 c. a measure of the average kinetic energy of the air particles.
 d. a measure of the air's resistance to flow and shearing.
 e. the total mass of air particles per unit of volume.

Answer Key

Math Skills Test

1. d. 174 is rounded to 200; 364 is rounded to 400. (200)(400) = 80,000.

2. b. Add the corrected value of the sweater ($245) to the value of the two, not three, bracelets ($730), plus the other two items ($78 and $130).

3. c. To solve this problem, convert $5\frac{3}{4}$ to $\frac{23}{4}$ and then divide $\frac{23}{4}$ by $\frac{1}{4}$. The answer is 23.

4. a. Substituting known quantities in the formula yields $20 = \frac{64.8}{x^2}$ Next, you must multiply through by x^2 to get $20x^2 = 64.8$. Now divide through by 20 to get $x^2 = \frac{64.8}{20}$ = 3.24. Now take the square root of both sides to get x equals 1.8.

5. d. Four inches is equal to 16 quarter inches. Each quarter inch is 2 feet, so 16 quarter inches is 32 feet.

6. b. You cannot just take 25% off the original price, because the 15% discount after three years of service is taken off the price that has already been reduced by 10%. Figure the problem in two steps: After the 10% discount, the price is $105.08. Subtracting 5% from that gives you $89.32.

7. d. The simplest way to solve this problem is to divide 1 by 1,500, which is .0006667, and then count off two decimal places to arrive at the percentage, which is .06667 percent. Since the question asks *about* what percentage, the nearest value is .067%.

8. a. You can use logic to arrive at a solution to this problem. After the first hour, the number would be 20, after the second hour 40, after the third hour 80, after the fourth hour 160, and after the fifth hour 320. The other answer choices do not have the same outcome.

9. c. Use the equation .09(1) = .03(x), where x is the total amount of water in the resulting 3% solution. Solving for x, you get 3. Subtracting the 1 liter of water already present in the 9% solution, you will find that 2 liters need to be added.

10. b. In this question, 20% of 15 miles is 3 miles. Adding 3 to 15 gives 18 miles.

11. d. Each 10-foot wall has an area of 10(9), or 90 square feet. There are two such walls, so those two walls combined have an area of 180 square feet. Each 14-foot wall has an area of 14(9), or 126 square feet, and again there are two such walls: 126(2) = 252. Finally, add 180 and 252 to get 432 square feet.

12. c. Substituting 39.6 for C in the equation yields $F = (\frac{9}{5})(39.6) + 32 = 71.28 = 32 =$ 103.3.

13. c. The ratio is $\frac{12cc}{100}$ pounds $= \frac{x}{175}$ pounds, where x is the number of ccs per 175 pounds. Multiply both sides by 175 to get $(175)(\frac{12}{100})$ equals x, so x equals 21.

14. b. On the first day, the hiker walks 40 miles. On the second day, he walks 20 miles. On the third day, he walks 10 miles. On the fourth day, he walks 5 miles. On the fifth day, he walks 2.5 miles. The sum of the miles walked, then, is 77.5 miles. The average over five days is 77.5 divided by 5, or 15.5 miles per day.

15. d. The fugitive will have traveled 5 hours at 50 miles per hour for a distance of 250 miles. To reach her in 4 hours, the police must travel at 250 miles per 4 hours, or 62.5 mph.

16. a. J = 6K, and J + 2 = 2(K + 2), so 6K + 2 = 2K + 4, which means K equals $\frac{1}{2}$. J equals 6K, or 3.

17. d. Add each monthly bill plus $54 for total local service to get $312.90 for three months. Dividing by 3 gives an average of $104.30.

18. d. In this question, 448 miles divided by 16 gallons is 28 miles per gallon.

19. c. In this question, 962,342 bytes free plus 454,783 bytes freed when a file was deleted equals 1,417,125 bytes; 1,417,125 bytes minus 315,926 bytes put into the new file leaves 1,101,199 bytes free.

20. b. Jackie is paid and saves twice a month, while she pays her student loan only once a month. Her monthly salary is $1,644.80. Subtract $300 in savings and $84.71 for the student loan to get $1,260.09.

21. b. The answer to .4 squared is .8.

22. c. First, determine the lowest fraction of parts. Four parts to 12 gallons also equals one part to 3 gallons. Divide 51 gallons of fuel by a factor of 3 to determine 17 parts of fuel additive are required.

23. c. First, determine how long the tanker has been flying: two hours prior to the fighter jet's takeoff, and an additional two hours until rendezvous, which equals four hours. Next, determine how far the tanker has flown in four hours. Four times 300 mph equals 1,200 miles. Finally, divide 1,200 miles by the fighter jet's duration of flight: $\frac{1,200}{2} = 600$ mph.

24. d. First, convert pounds to gallons for the fighter jet burn rate: 4,800 lbs. divided by 6 lbs./gallon equals 800 gallons. Multiply the burn rate of 800 gallons per hour times a three hour flight to get 2,400 gallons. Next, convert the landing fuel requirement: 3,000 lbs. divided by 6 lbs/gallon equals 500 gallons. Add 2,400 gallons plus 500 gallons to get the answer of 2,900 gallons.

25. a. Divide 54 miles by the six-mile orbit circumference to equal 9 orbits.

26. d. The model plane's 10 inches is equal to 20 one-half inches. Each of those is 5 feet. $20 \times 5 = 100$ feet.

27. d. Work backward to find the solution. George has five cousins, which is 11 fewer than Bonnie has; therefore, Bonnie has 16 cousins. Bonnie has twice as many as Robert has, so half of 16 is 8. Robert has eight cousins.

28. c. Set up a proportion with $\frac{milk}{soda}$; $\frac{2}{5} = \frac{10}{x}$. Cross-multiply and solve: $(5)(10) = 2x$. Divide both sides by 2: $\frac{50}{2} = \frac{2x}{2}$; $x = 25$ sodas.

29. b. To earn an average of 93% on four tests, the sum of those four tests must be $(93)(4)$ or 372. The sum of the first three tests is $85 + 92 + 95 = 272$. The difference between the needed sum of four tests, and the sum of the first three tests is 100. He needs a 100 to earn a 93 average.

30. b. Use the order of operations and try each option. The first option results in 14 because $2 \times 5 = 10$, then $10 + 4 = 14$. This does not work. The second option does result in 18. The numbers in parentheses are added first and result in 9, which is then multiplied by 2 to get a final answer of 18. Choice **c** does not work because the operation in parentheses is done first, yielding 6, which is then multiplied by 5 to get a result of 30. Choice **d** does not work because the multiplication is done first, yielding 8, which is added to 5 for a final answer of 13.

Reading Skills Test

1. d. The last sentence in the passage refers to dogs as probably the oldest alarm system. The other choices, even if true, are not in the passage.

2. a. This is the only choice reflected in the passage. Choice **d** may seem attractive at first, but the passage simply says that the local media does not cover local politics—it doesn't give the reason for their neglect.

3. a. The first sentence reflects the idea that the Dvorak keyboard is more efficient than the QWERTY. The other choices are not in the passage.

4. b. The other choices are incorrect because the passage is not concerned with how sanitation workers should deal with sharp objects, but with how everyone should dispose of sharp objects in order to avoid hurting sanitation workers.

5. c. The final sentence indicates that the atmosphere of Mars has been stripped away.

6. d. The passage mentions nothing about main or secondary roads.

7. c. The passage indicates that the city prefers, but does not require, use of the new container provided by the city and that the customers may use more than one container if they purchase an additional one.

8. d. This answer is implied by the statement that redistribution is needed so that people in emerging nations can have proper medical care. Choices **a**, **b**, and **c** are not mentioned in the passage.

9. c. This choice is the best answer because the paragraph indicates that legislators once feared suggesting gas taxes, but now many of them are pushing bills in favor of these taxes. There is no indication that choice **a** is true. Choice **b** is incorrect because the paragraph doesn't say why more gas taxes are being proposed. There is no support for choice **d**.

10. b. Choices **a** and **c** are too narrow to be the main idea. Choice **d** simply supports the main idea that lawyers have received undeserved criticism.

11. b. The support for choice **b** is given in the second sentence of the paragraph. Generation Xers like to work independently, which means they are self-directed. No support is given for choice **a**. Choice **c** is not related to the paragraph. Although the paragraph mentions that Generation Xers liked to be challenged, it does not say they like to challenge their bosses' attitudes; therefore, choice **d** can be ruled out.

12. d. This choice encompasses the main information in the passage. Choices **a**, **b**, and **c** are not mentioned.

13. a. The final sentence states that computer games and virtual reality help children come to terms with the truths of the real world. The other choices are not reflected in the passage.

14. c. The first and second sentences reflect this idea. The passage does not say that Native American art is dreamlike (choice **a**). Choices **b** and **d** are too narrow to be main ideas.

15. b. The passage explains the procedure for bus drivers to follow when their bus gets ahead of schedule. Therefore, *running hot* means running ahead of schedule.

16. c. According to the passage, hazardous waste is defined by the U.S. Environmental Protection Agency.

17. d. The first day of summer in the north is the first day of winter in the south.

18. b. This is the only choice that reflects the idea of interaction among all members of the group spoken of in the first sentence. The other choices are only physical settings.

19. d. The final sentence indicates that the author agrees with the review in *The Sunday Times* that the play was revolutionary (a word which literally means a turning point). Choice **a** underplays and choice **b** overestimates the importance of the work to the author of the passage. Choices **c** and **e** are contradicted by the last sentence.

20. d. The paragraph specifically states that age makes a person less able to respond to long exposure to very hot or very cold temperatures. This would mean that older people are more susceptible to hypothermia. Choices **a, b,** and **c** are not supported by the information given in the paragraph.

21. b. Choice **b** is indicated by the final sentence, which indicates that the RDA approach is useful, but has limitations, implying that a supplemental guide would be a good thing. Choice **a** is contradicted by the final sentence of the passage. Choice **c** is incorrect because the passage says the RDA approach is a useful guide, but does *not* say it is the best guide to good nutrition. Choice **d** is contradicted by the next-to-last sentence of the passage.

22. c. Note that this question asked you to find the answer that is NOT included in the passage. Choice **c** is the best answer because the passage states that after the glacier, the mountain ranges were never to return.

23. e. This detail can be found in the final sentence of the passage.

24. a. The passage states that officers should keep complete notes and use them to refresh their memories about events. None of the other choices is reflected in the passage.

25. c. See the second sentence, which defines *ksa*. The other choices are refuted in the passage.

26. d. See the fourth sentence of the passage.

27. b. The last sentence indicates that there is little or no visible flame with a potential backdraft. The other choices are also listed at the end of the last sentence as warning signs of a potential backdraft.

Mechanical Comprehension Test

1. a. Point A delivers the maximum leverage in the correct direction, because it is as far from the fulcrum as possible.

2. b. The 100 pounds at the right end of the lever creates a moment about the fulcrum of 300 feet-lbs. (100 lbs. × 3 feet). To counter-balance this moment, a 50-pound force must be applied at the opposite end to create the equal 300 feet-lbs. moment (50 pounds × 6 feet).

3. d. Shape D is the best shape to make the dam, because as the flow of the water pushes against it, the arch distributes the force equally and directs it into the banks of the river, instead of the center of the dam, which would cause it to collapse.

4. c. Box A creates a moment about the axle of 450 feet-lbs. (75 lbs. × 6 feet). Since box B is supported by the smaller 2-foot wheel, box B must weigh 225 pounds in order to create an equal moment about the axle (225 lbs. × 2 feet).

5. d. Gears E and F turn counterclockwise and clockwise, respectively.

6. e. If the tire is 3 feet in diameter, then the circumference is 3 feet × pi (3.14) = 9.42 feet. The circumference is also the same distance as one revolution of the tire. So if the tire is turning at 500 revolutions per minute and the circumference is 9.42 feet, then the tire is traveling at 4,710 feet/minute down the road (500 rev/min. × 9.42 ft./rev = 4,710 ft./min.).

7. c. If the block weighs 98 lbs. and the stiffness of the spring is 16 lbs./inch, then the spring will stretch 6.125, or $6\frac{1}{8}$ inches [(98 lbs.)/ (16 lbs./inch)] = 6.125 inches.

8. b. The 50-pound weight at B creates a moment about the fulcrum of 350 feet-lbs. (50 lbs. × 7 feet = 350 feet-lbs.). If the distance from the fulcrum to the lifting point is 10 feet, then only 35 pounds of force must be used to lift the block (350 feet-lbs./10 feet = 35 lbs.).

9. b. Since the pulley shown is fixed, there is no additional mechanical advantage, and it still requires 100 pounds of force to lift the 100-pound weight.

10. e. The top pulley is fixed, but the bottom pulley is raised as shown. This arrangement creates a mechanical advantage of 2. Therefore, the required force to lift the weight is equal to half the weight itself.
In this problem, that equals 150 lbs.

11. c. The first step is determining how much force at point C it takes to stretch the spring itself the required 10 inches. If the stiffness of the spring is 20 lbs./inch, then 200 pounds (20 lbs./inch × 10 inches = 200 lbs.) of force must be applied at point C. To calculate the required force at point A, you must determine the moment about the fulcrum created by the 200-lb. force at C. This is done by multiplying 200 pounds at point C by the distance from C to the fulcrum (4 feet). The result is 200 lbs. × 4 feet = 800 feet-lbs. Now, taking this moment about the fulcrum and applying it to the part of the lever from A to B, you calculate the required force at A as 133.3 pounds (800 feet-lbs./6 feet = 133.3 lbs.).

12. a. Looking at the figure, you will see that the flow of the water pushing against the bottom of the water wheel would cause the water wheel to turn counterclockwise. The flow of the water is 300 feet/minute. This is also the speed that the circumference of the wheel is turning. So if the circumference of the wheel is 28.26 feet (9 feet × 3.14), then the revolutions per minute are (300 feet/ minute)/(28.26 feet/revolution) = 10.6 revolutions/minute, or approximately 10 rpm.

13. b. Gear D will rotate clockwise five rotations.

14. d. Since all the gears shown are connected by the same fan belt, their circumferences are all moving at the same speed. However, since all the gears have different radii and, therefore, different circumferences, the gear with the smallest size (gear D) must turn at the highest rpm to match the speed of the fan belt.

15. e. The first step is determining the moment about the fulcrum created by the weight (150 lbs. × 3 feet = 450 feet-lbs.). Next, apply this same moment to the opposite end of the lever to calculate the force applied to the spring (450 feet-lbs.)/(6 feet) = 75 lbs. If you apply this 75-lb. force to the spring with a stiffness of 25 lbs./inch, the spring will move only 3 inches (75 lbs.)/ (25 lbs./inch) = 3 inches.

16. c. The distance from the pivot point to the point of application of the force (20 feet) is twice the distance from the pivot point to the box (10 feet). Therefore, in order to lift the box, the required force will be one half of the weight of the box (100 pounds), or 50 pounds.

17. a. Because the springs are in a series, their amount of stretch is additive. Spring 1 will stretch 1 inch under 10 pounds, so its total stretch under 20 pounds will be 2 inches. Spring 2 is being subjected to a load of 20 pounds, which is four times the load that will stretch it 2 inches. Therefore, its total stretch will be 8 inches. Adding the amount of stretch for the two springs together gives you 10 inches.

18. a. Gear B will rotate clockwise.

19. a. Since valve D is closed, water will not flow to barrels 3 and 4. Water will flow through valve B but be stopped at valve C. Water will flow through valve A into barrels 1 and 2.

20. d. The box will force the left side of the lever down and the right side of the lever up, which will pull the cable up. The cable will pass across the pulley and apply a pulling force on the spring, so the spring will stretch.

21. c. The two blocks are directly connected by a fixed length of steel cable. Therefore, regardless of the number of pulleys between the two blocks, the distance moved by one block will be the same as that moved by the other block.

22. c. Figure C shows the attachment of the connecting rod to the crankshaft at the bottom of the crankshaft. Another 90° counterclockwise rotation would place the attachment point on the right side of the crankshaft at position C.

23. a. $w_1 \times d_1 = 22 \times d_2$. 27 pounds × 4 feet = 24 pounds × d_2. Solving for d_2 gives 4.5 feet.

24. c. The gauge indicates that any pressure greater than 20 psi is in the danger zone.

25. b. The first step is determining the moment caused by the lift force. Since the lift and weight forces are in opposite directions, they must be subtracted (75,000 − 73,000 = 2,000 lbs.), resulting in a net 2,000-pound force in the up direction. This force is 2.5 feet from the center of gravity of the aircraft, resulting in a moment of (2000 lbs. × 2.5 feet = 5,000 feet-lbs.). The force required at the elevator to balance the moment caused by the lift must be in the down direction. Since the distance from the center of gravity to the elevator is 23 feet, the force at the elevator must be (5,000 feet-lbs./23 feet = 217.4 lbs.).

26. a. Since the weight of the car is evenly distributed on the four wheels, each wheel supports 1,200 pounds (4,800 lbs./4 wheels = 1,200 lbs./wheel).

27. b. In calculating the amount each spring will stretch, each weight must be divided by the corresponding spring resistance. In doing so, it is found that weight B has the greatest displacement with 3 inches [(15 lbs.)/ (5 lbs./in) = 3 inches].

28. c. Wheel B is the only wheel in the diagram that turns counterclockwise. All the other wheels turn clockwise.

29. d. To calculate the required weight to compress the spring 10 inches, you must multiply the spring resistance by the amount of desired compression: (20 lbs./inch) × (10 inches) = 200 lbs. Since the weight is placed directly over the spring, the distance from the hinge does not matter.

30. e. The 300-lb. force creates a 900 feet-lbs. moment at point A. This results in a 90-pound force being applied to the spring at point B [(900 feet-lbs.)/(10 feet) = 90 lbs.]. A 90-pound force applied to the spring will compress it 6 inches [(90 lbs.)/(15 lbs./inch) = 6 inches].

Spatial Apperception Test

QUESTION	ANSWER	PITCH	ROLL	DIRECTION
1.	A	diving	no bank angle	flying out to sea
2.	C	diving	banking right	flying out to sea
3.	B	diving	banking right	flying out to sea
4.	E	level	no bank angle	coastline on left
5.	E	level	banking right	coastline on left
6.	B	level	banking left	coastline on left
7.	B	climbing	banking left	flying out to sea
8.	B	level	no bank angle	coastline on right
9.	D	climbing	banking left	flying out to sea
10.	B	level	banking left	coastline on right
11.	A	level	banking right	coastline on right
12.	B	level	banking right	coastline on left
13.	D	diving	no bank angle	flying out to sea
14.	C	level	no bank angle	coastline on right
15.	A	level	no bank angle	coastline on right
16.	C	diving	no bank angle	coastline on right
17.	A	climbing	banking right	flying out to sea
18.	E	climbing	banking right	flying out to sea
19.	E	diving	banking left	flying out to sea
20.	B	level	banking left	flying out to sea
21.	A	diving	banking left	flying out to sea
22.	D	level	no bank angle	coastline on left
23.	B	level	banking right	coastline on right
24.	E	level	no bank angle	flying out to sea
25.	A	level	no bank angle	flying out to sea

Aviation and Nautical Information Test

1. c. The front section of a ship is known as the bow.

2. d. The rear section of a ship is known as the stern.

3. b. The right-hand side of a ship is known as the starboard side.

4. a. The left-hand side of a ship is known as the port side.

5. d. Thrust acts in the direction of flight.

6. a. Lift acts perpendicular to the wings.

7. c. Drag acts in the opposite direction of flight.

8. b. Weight acts in the direction that always points to the center of the earth.

9. a. Arrow 1 points to the aileron.

10. b. Arrow 2 points to the flap.

11. d. Arrow 3 points to the elevator.

12. c. Arrow 4 points to the rudder.

13. d. The galley is the kitchen compartment of a ship.

14. e. The forecastle is the section of the upper deck of a ship located at the bow.

15. a. The hull is the body of a ship excluding masts, sails, yards, and riggings.

16. c. A bulkhead is one of the straight upright partitions dividing a ship into compartments.

17. b. The keel is the principal structural member that forms the centerline of the hull running from bow to stern.

18. d. True airspeed is the actual velocity of an aircraft traveling through the air.

19. a. Indicated airspeed is the instrumental indication of the dynamic pressure of the airplane during flight.

20. e. Ground speed is a measure of the aircraft's actual speed over the ground.

21. b. Calibrated airspeed is the corrected airspeed taking into account instrumental error.

22. c. Equivalent airspeed is found by correcting calibrated airspeed for compressibility error.

23. b. The jet will initially slow down due to the power reduction and will begin a gradual descent.

24. c. The jet will descend with the push forward on the stick and will accelerate with the addition of power.

25. c. If the airfield is located at an elevation of 2,000 feet MSL and your planned cruise altitude is 20,000 feet, this is a difference of 18,000 feet. Using the standard lapse rate of 2° C per 1,000 feet in altitude change, this results in a total change in temperature of 36° C. If the starting temperature at the airfield is 15° C, then the temperature at the cruise altitude is –21°C (15° C – 36°C = –21°C).

26. b. 180 minus a left turn of 45° equals a new heading of 135.

27. a. A heading of 270° added to a right turn of 100 degrees equals 370°. In a compass there are only 360° as you pass through north. 370 minus 360 equals 10°.

28. c. Temperature is best described as a measure of the average kinetic energy of the air particles.

29. a. Humidity is best described as the amount of water vapor in the air.

30. e. Air density is best described as the total mass of air particles per unit volume.

For information about how the official ASTB is scored, see Chapter 3.

11 ▶ PRACTICE TEST FOR THE ARMED SERVICES VOCATIONAL APTITUDE BATTERY

CHAPTER SUMMARY

Here is another practice test for the Armed Services Vocational Aptitude Battery (ASVSB).

For this test, simulate the actual test-taking experience as closely as you can. Find a quiet place to work where you will not be disturbed. If you own this book, tear out the answer sheet on the following pages and find some #2 pencils to fill in the circles. Use a timer or a stopwatch to time each subtest. The time allotted is marked at the beginning of each subtest. When you have finished the whole test, use the detailed answer explanations in the Answer Key at the end of this chapter to review any questions you missed.

Subtest 1: General Science (GS)

1.	(a)	(b)	(c)	(d)	10.	(a)	(b)	(c)	(d)	18.	(a)	(b)	(c)	(d)
2.	(a)	(b)	(c)	(d)	11.	(a)	(b)	(c)	(d)	19.	(a)	(b)	(c)	(d)
3.	(a)	(b)	(c)	(d)	12.	(a)	(b)	(c)	(d)	20.	(a)	(b)	(c)	(d)
4.	(a)	(b)	(c)	(d)	13.	(a)	(b)	(c)	(d)	21.	(a)	(b)	(c)	(d)
5.	(a)	(b)	(c)	(d)	14.	(a)	(b)	(c)	(d)	22.	(a)	(b)	(c)	(d)
6.	(a)	(b)	(c)	(d)	15.	(a)	(b)	(c)	(d)	23.	(a)	(b)	(c)	(d)
7.	(a)	(b)	(c)	(d)	16.	(a)	(b)	(c)	(d)	24.	(a)	(b)	(c)	(d)
8.	(a)	(b)	(c)	(d)	17.	(a)	(b)	(c)	(d)	25.	(a)	(b)	(c)	(d)
9.	(a)	(b)	(c)	(d)										

Subtest 2: Arithmetic Reasoning (AR)

1.	(a)	(b)	(c)	(d)	11.	(a)	(b)	(c)	(d)	21.	(a)	(b)	(c)	(d)
2.	(a)	(b)	(c)	(d)	12.	(a)	(b)	(c)	(d)	22.	(a)	(b)	(c)	(d)
3.	(a)	(b)	(c)	(d)	13.	(a)	(b)	(c)	(d)	23.	(a)	(b)	(c)	(d)
4.	(a)	(b)	(c)	(d)	14.	(a)	(b)	(c)	(d)	24.	(a)	(b)	(c)	(d)
5.	(a)	(b)	(c)	(d)	15.	(a)	(b)	(c)	(d)	25.	(a)	(b)	(c)	(d)
6.	(a)	(b)	(c)	(d)	16.	(a)	(b)	(c)	(d)	26.	(a)	(b)	(c)	(d)
7.	(a)	(b)	(c)	(d)	17.	(a)	(b)	(c)	(d)	27.	(a)	(b)	(c)	(d)
8.	(a)	(b)	(c)	(d)	18.	(a)	(b)	(c)	(d)	28.	(a)	(b)	(c)	(d)
9.	(a)	(b)	(c)	(d)	19.	(a)	(b)	(c)	(d)	29.	(a)	(b)	(c)	(d)
10.	(a)	(b)	(c)	(d)	20.	(a)	(b)	(c)	(d)	30.	(a)	(b)	(c)	(d)

Subtest 3: Word Knowledge (WK)

1.	(a)	(b)	(c)	(d)	13.	(a)	(b)	(c)	(d)	25.	(a)	(b)	(c)	(d)
2.	(a)	(b)	(c)	(d)	14.	(a)	(b)	(c)	(d)	26.	(a)	(b)	(c)	(d)
3.	(a)	(b)	(c)	(d)	15.	(a)	(b)	(c)	(d)	27.	(a)	(b)	(c)	(d)
4.	(a)	(b)	(c)	(d)	16.	(a)	(b)	(c)	(d)	28.	(a)	(b)	(c)	(d)
5.	(a)	(b)	(c)	(d)	17.	(a)	(b)	(c)	(d)	29.	(a)	(b)	(c)	(d)
6.	(a)	(b)	(c)	(d)	18.	(a)	(b)	(c)	(d)	30.	(a)	(b)	(c)	(d)
7.	(a)	(b)	(c)	(d)	19.	(a)	(b)	(c)	(d)	31.	(a)	(b)	(c)	(d)
8.	(a)	(b)	(c)	(d)	20.	(a)	(b)	(c)	(d)	32.	(a)	(b)	(c)	(d)
9.	(a)	(b)	(c)	(d)	21.	(a)	(b)	(c)	(d)	33.	(a)	(b)	(c)	(d)
10.	(a)	(b)	(c)	(d)	22.	(a)	(b)	(c)	(d)	34.	(a)	(b)	(c)	(d)
11.	(a)	(b)	(c)	(d)	23.	(a)	(b)	(c)	(d)	35.	(a)	(b)	(c)	(d)
12.	(a)	(b)	(c)	(d)	24.	(a)	(b)	(c)	(d)					

Subtest 4: Paragraph Comprehension (PC)

1.	ⓐ	ⓑ	ⓒ	ⓓ	6.	ⓐ	ⓑ	ⓒ	ⓓ	11.	ⓐ	ⓑ	ⓒ	ⓓ
2.	ⓐ	ⓑ	ⓒ	ⓓ	7.	ⓐ	ⓑ	ⓒ	ⓓ	12.	ⓐ	ⓑ	ⓒ	ⓓ
3.	ⓐ	ⓑ	ⓒ	ⓓ	8.	ⓐ	ⓑ	ⓒ	ⓓ	13.	ⓐ	ⓑ	ⓒ	ⓓ
4.	ⓐ	ⓑ	ⓒ	ⓓ	9.	ⓐ	ⓑ	ⓒ	ⓓ	14.	ⓐ	ⓑ	ⓒ	ⓓ
5.	ⓐ	ⓑ	ⓒ	ⓓ	10.	ⓐ	ⓑ	ⓒ	ⓓ	15.	ⓐ	ⓑ	ⓒ	ⓓ

Subtest 5: Mathematics Knowledge (MK)

1.	ⓐ	ⓑ	ⓒ	ⓓ	10.	ⓐ	ⓑ	ⓒ	ⓓ	18.	ⓐ	ⓑ	ⓒ	ⓓ
2.	ⓐ	ⓑ	ⓒ	ⓓ	11.	ⓐ	ⓑ	ⓒ	ⓓ	19.	ⓐ	ⓑ	ⓒ	ⓓ
3.	ⓐ	ⓑ	ⓒ	ⓓ	12.	ⓐ	ⓑ	ⓒ	ⓓ	20.	ⓐ	ⓑ	ⓒ	ⓓ
4.	ⓐ	ⓑ	ⓒ	ⓓ	13.	ⓐ	ⓑ	ⓒ	ⓓ	21.	ⓐ	ⓑ	ⓒ	ⓓ
5.	ⓐ	ⓑ	ⓒ	ⓓ	14.	ⓐ	ⓑ	ⓒ	ⓓ	22.	ⓐ	ⓑ	ⓒ	ⓓ
6.	ⓐ	ⓑ	ⓒ	ⓓ	15.	ⓐ	ⓑ	ⓒ	ⓓ	23.	ⓐ	ⓑ	ⓒ	ⓓ
7.	ⓐ	ⓑ	ⓒ	ⓓ	16.	ⓐ	ⓑ	ⓒ	ⓓ	24.	ⓐ	ⓑ	ⓒ	ⓓ
8.	ⓐ	ⓑ	ⓒ	ⓓ	17.	ⓐ	ⓑ	ⓒ	ⓓ	25.	ⓐ	ⓑ	ⓒ	ⓓ
9.	ⓐ	ⓑ	ⓒ	ⓓ										

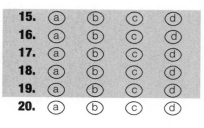

Subtest 6: Electronics Information (EI)

1.	ⓐ	ⓑ	ⓒ	ⓓ	8.	ⓐ	ⓑ	ⓒ	ⓓ	15.	ⓐ	ⓑ	ⓒ	ⓓ
2.	ⓐ	ⓑ	ⓒ	ⓓ	9.	ⓐ	ⓑ	ⓒ	ⓓ	16.	ⓐ	ⓑ	ⓒ	ⓓ
3.	ⓐ	ⓑ	ⓒ	ⓓ	10.	ⓐ	ⓑ	ⓒ	ⓓ	17.	ⓐ	ⓑ	ⓒ	ⓓ
4.	ⓐ	ⓑ	ⓒ	ⓓ	11.	ⓐ	ⓑ	ⓒ	ⓓ	18.	ⓐ	ⓑ	ⓒ	ⓓ
5.	ⓐ	ⓑ	ⓒ	ⓓ	12.	ⓐ	ⓑ	ⓒ	ⓓ	19.	ⓐ	ⓑ	ⓒ	ⓓ
6.	ⓐ	ⓑ	ⓒ	ⓓ	13.	ⓐ	ⓑ	ⓒ	ⓓ	20.	ⓐ	ⓑ	ⓒ	ⓓ
7.	ⓐ	ⓑ	ⓒ	ⓓ	14.	ⓐ	ⓑ	ⓒ	ⓓ					

Subtest 7: Auto and Shop Information (AS)

1.	ⓐ	ⓑ	ⓒ	ⓓ	10.	ⓐ	ⓑ	ⓒ	ⓓ	18.	ⓐ	ⓑ	ⓒ	ⓓ
2.	ⓐ	ⓑ	ⓒ	ⓓ	11.	ⓐ	ⓑ	ⓒ	ⓓ	19.	ⓐ	ⓑ	ⓒ	ⓓ
3.	ⓐ	ⓑ	ⓒ	ⓓ	12.	ⓐ	ⓑ	ⓒ	ⓓ	20.	ⓐ	ⓑ	ⓒ	ⓓ
4.	ⓐ	ⓑ	ⓒ	ⓓ	13.	ⓐ	ⓑ	ⓒ	ⓓ	21.	ⓐ	ⓑ	ⓒ	ⓓ
5.	ⓐ	ⓑ	ⓒ	ⓓ	14.	ⓐ	ⓑ	ⓒ	ⓓ	22.	ⓐ	ⓑ	ⓒ	ⓓ
6.	ⓐ	ⓑ	ⓒ	ⓓ	15.	ⓐ	ⓑ	ⓒ	ⓓ	23.	ⓐ	ⓑ	ⓒ	ⓓ
7.	ⓐ	ⓑ	ⓒ	ⓓ	16.	ⓐ	ⓑ	ⓒ	ⓓ	24.	ⓐ	ⓑ	ⓒ	ⓓ
8.	ⓐ	ⓑ	ⓒ	ⓓ	17.	ⓐ	ⓑ	ⓒ	ⓓ	25.	ⓐ	ⓑ	ⓒ	ⓓ
9.	ⓐ	ⓑ	ⓒ	ⓓ										

Subtest 8: Mechanical Comprehension (MC)

1.	ⓐ ⓑ ⓒ ⓓ	10.	ⓐ ⓑ ⓒ ⓓ	18.	ⓐ ⓑ ⓒ ⓓ
2.	ⓐ ⓑ ⓒ ⓓ	11.	ⓐ ⓑ ⓒ ⓓ	19.	ⓐ ⓑ ⓒ ⓓ
3.	ⓐ ⓑ ⓒ ⓓ	12.	ⓐ ⓑ ⓒ ⓓ	20.	ⓐ ⓑ ⓒ ⓓ
4.	ⓐ ⓑ ⓒ ⓓ	13.	ⓐ ⓑ ⓒ ⓓ	21.	ⓐ ⓑ ⓒ ⓓ
5.	ⓐ ⓑ ⓒ ⓓ	14.	ⓐ ⓑ ⓒ ⓓ	22.	ⓐ ⓑ ⓒ ⓓ
6.	ⓐ ⓑ ⓒ ⓓ	15.	ⓐ ⓑ ⓒ ⓓ	23.	ⓐ ⓑ ⓒ ⓓ
7.	ⓐ ⓑ ⓒ ⓓ	16.	ⓐ ⓑ ⓒ ⓓ	24.	ⓐ ⓑ ⓒ ⓓ
8.	ⓐ ⓑ ⓒ ⓓ	17.	ⓐ ⓑ ⓒ ⓓ	25.	ⓐ ⓑ ⓒ ⓓ
9.	ⓐ ⓑ ⓒ ⓓ				

Subtest 9: Assembling Objects (AO)

1.	ⓐ ⓑ ⓒ ⓓ	10.	ⓐ ⓑ ⓒ ⓓ	18.	ⓐ ⓑ ⓒ ⓓ
2.	ⓐ ⓑ ⓒ ⓓ	11.	ⓐ ⓑ ⓒ ⓓ	19.	ⓐ ⓑ ⓒ ⓓ
3.	ⓐ ⓑ ⓒ ⓓ	12.	ⓐ ⓑ ⓒ ⓓ	20.	ⓐ ⓑ ⓒ ⓓ
4.	ⓐ ⓑ ⓒ ⓓ	13.	ⓐ ⓑ ⓒ ⓓ	21.	ⓐ ⓑ ⓒ ⓓ
5.	ⓐ ⓑ ⓒ ⓓ	14.	ⓐ ⓑ ⓒ ⓓ	22.	ⓐ ⓑ ⓒ ⓓ
6.	ⓐ ⓑ ⓒ ⓓ	15.	ⓐ ⓑ ⓒ ⓓ	23.	ⓐ ⓑ ⓒ ⓓ
7.	ⓐ ⓑ ⓒ ⓓ	16.	ⓐ ⓑ ⓒ ⓓ	24.	ⓐ ⓑ ⓒ ⓓ
8.	ⓐ ⓑ ⓒ ⓓ	17.	ⓐ ⓑ ⓒ ⓓ	25.	ⓐ ⓑ ⓒ ⓓ
9.	ⓐ ⓑ ⓒ ⓓ				

Subtest 1: General Science

Questions: 25
Time: 11 minutes

1. Elements on the right side of the periodic table have the following characteristics *except*
   a. being gaseous at room temperature.
   b. accepting electrons.
   c. having smaller electronegativity.
   d. being poor conductors.

2. Which of the following plant groups produces seeds in cones?
   a. angiosperms
   b. bryophytes
   c. all vascular plants
   d. gymnosperms

3. When two atoms form a molecule and there is an unequal sharing of electrons within their bond, this is called
   a. a covalent bond.
   b. an ionic bond.
   c. hydrogen bonding.
   d. Van der Waals forces.

4. A predator-prey relationship is balanced in a specific area. If another predator is introduced to this area, what is expected to happen?
   a. The balance would not change.
   b. Only the population of the prey would decrease.
   c. Only the population of the predators would decrease.
   d. The populations of both the prey and the predators would decrease.

5. If during an experiment you wanted to measure the kinetic energy of a system, what would be the best instrument to use?
   a. a thermometer
   b. a voltmeter
   c. a pH monitor
   d. a stopwatch

6. Compared to magma, lava is
   a. deeper and cooler.
   b. shallower and cooler.
   c. deeper and hotter.
   d. shallower and hotter.

7. Mutations are favored when they lead to adaptations. Which of the following does NOT cause a beneficial mutation?
   a. RNA
   b. a carcinogen
   c. gene linkage
   d. codons

8. The pH of an alkaline solution is
   a. less than 0.
   b. less than 7.
   c. more than 14.
   d. more than 7.

9. What coefficients are needed to balance the reaction?

   $$?Fe_2O_3 + 3C \rightarrow ?Fe + 3CO_2$$

   a. $2Fe_2O_3$ and 2Fe
   b. $2Fe_2O_3$ and 4Fe
   c. $3Fe_2O_3$ and 2Fe
   d. $3Fe_2O_3$ and 3Fe

10. A watershed is
   a. a zone of water whose salt content is between that of fresh water and that of the ocean.
   b. an underground layer of porous rock that conducts water.
   c. a place where groundwater seeps out to the surface.
   d. the area of land that collects water that is eventually drained into a river.

11. Two parents do not show a genetic trait that shows up in their offspring. Which of the following explains this phenomenon?
   a. The environment of the offspring brought out the trait.
   b. Both parents were carriers of a recessive trait.
   c. The offspring was actually adopted.
   d. One parent was a carrier of a recessive trait.

12. In order to be considered organic, a compound must contain which of the following elements?
   a. hydrogen
   b. sodium
   c. nitrogen
   d. carbon

13. The mass number of an atom consists of
   a. protons and electrons.
   b. neutrons and electrons.
   c. protons, neutrons, and electrons.
   d. protons and neutrons.

14. What should a population of humans do to maintain an increasing population?
   a. improve their farming
   b. increase their grazing animals
   c. expand their population's boundaries
   d. defend against predators

15. Deserts are usually defined by the criterion that the rainfall is less than
   a. 2 inches per year.
   b. 5 inches per year.
   c. 10 inches per year.
   d. 20 inches per year.

16. What factor would be most helpful to increasing the reaction rate of an endothermic reaction?
   a. increasing its activation energy
   b. increasing the reactor size
   c. using a catalyst
   d. increasing concentration of products

17. The principal function of blood platelets is to
   a. help clot blood.
   b. carry oxygen.
   c. produce antibodies.
   d. consume bacteria.

18. The surface tension of water is relatively strong due to the intermolecular force of
   a. hydrogen bonds.
   b. ionic bonds.
   c. polar covalent bonds.
   d. covalent bonds.

19. A father presents an X-linked trait and a mother does not. What is the probability that the mother is a carrier of this trait if they produce a son who also presents the X-linked trait?
   a. 0%
   b. 25%
   c. 50%
   d. 100%

20. The third-largest reservoir of water on Earth is
   a. the ocean.
   b. glaciers and ice caps.
   c. groundwater.
   d. lakes.

21. What needs to be added to the following equation to get the fission reaction started?

$$^{235}_{92}U + ? \rightarrow {}^{142}_{142}Ba + {}^{91}_{36}Kr + 3{}^{1}_{0}n$$

   a. an electron
   b. a neutron
   c. a proton
   d. nothing, U-235 is unstable enough

22. Complete the two missing parts of the following food chain: $X \rightarrow$ plant $\rightarrow X \rightarrow$ snake
   a. water, owl
   b. water, mouse
   c. sunlight, deer
   d. sunlight, mouse

23. What adaptation would you NOT expect an animal native to tundra to have?
   a. migratory patterns
   b. long times between feedings
   c. insulation
   d. hairless skin

24. What is true about the elements when moving from top to bottom in a family on the periodic table?
   a. They are more reactive.
   b. Their atomic numbers decrease.
   c. They are more stable.
   d. They have smaller mass numbers.

25. What type of bond is formed when electrons are shared between two atoms?
   a. a shared bond
   b. an ionic bond
   c. a covalent bond
   d. a multiple bond

Subtest 2: Arithmetic Reasoning

Questions: 30
Time: 36 minutes

1. A survey has shown that a family of four can save about $40 a week by purchasing generic items rather than brand-name ones. How much can a particular family save over six months? (one month = 4.3 weeks)
   a. $1,032
   b. $1,320
   c. $1,310
   d. $1,300

2. Bart's eight-ounce glass is $\frac{4}{5}$ full of water. How many ounces of water does he have?
   a. $4\frac{5}{8}$ ounces
   b. 5 ounces
   c. 6 ounces
   d. $6\frac{2}{5}$ ounces

Use the following pie chart to answer questions 3 and 4.

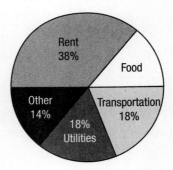

Harold's Monthly Budget

3. What should be the percent budgeted for food?
   a. 12%
   b. 18%
   c. 28%
   d. 38%

4. If Harold's monthly income is $2,450, how much does he spend on rent each month?
  a. $686
  b. $735
  c. $882
  d. $931

Recycler	Aluminum	Cardboard	Glass	Plastic
X	.06/pound	.03/pound	.08/pound	.02/pound
Y	.07/pound	.04/pound	.07/pound	.03/pound

5. If you take recyclables to whichever recycler will pay the most, what is the greatest amount of money you could get for 2,200 pounds of aluminum, 1,400 pounds of cardboard, 3,100 pounds of glass, and 900 pounds of plastic?
  a. $409
  b. $440
  c. $447
  d. $485

6. Five oranges, when removed from a basket containing three more than seven times as many oranges, leaves how many in the basket?
  a. 21
  b. 28
  c. 33
  d. 38

7. Ribbon in a craft store costs $0.75 per yard. Vernon needs to buy $7\frac{1}{3}$ yards. How much will it cost?
  a. $7.33
  b. $6.95
  c. $5.50
  d. $4.25

8. R.J. found a lamp on sale for 0.25 off its original price. What fraction of its original price will R.J. have to pay for the lamp?
  a. $\frac{1}{4}$
  b. $\frac{3}{4}$
  c. $\frac{1}{2}$
  d. $\frac{2}{3}$

9. How many $\frac{1}{4}$-pound hamburgers can be made from six pounds of ground beef?
  a. 18 hamburgers
  b. $20\frac{1}{2}$ hamburgers
  c. 24 hamburgers
  d. $26\frac{1}{4}$ hamburgers

10. The markup on a pair of sneakers is 150%. If the sneakers originally cost $45, what is the price after the markup?
  a. $22.50
  b. $57.50
  c. $67.50
  d. $112.50

11. Matthew had 200 baseball cards. He sold 5% of the cards on Saturday and 10% of the remaining cards on Sunday. How many cards are left?
  a. 170
  b. 171
  c. 175
  d. 185

12. A teacher purchased a number of supplies to start the new school year. The costs are listed as follows: $12.98, $5.68, $20.64, and $6.76. What is the total cost?
  a. $45.96
  b. $46.06
  c. $46.16
  d. $47.16

13. How many hours are in five days?
   a. 60 hours
   b. 100 hours
   c. 120 hours
   d. 240 hours

14. A truck is carrying 1,000 television sets; each set weighs 21.48 pounds. What is the total weight, in pounds, of the entire load?
   a. 214.8 pounds
   b. 2,148 pounds
   c. 21,480 pounds
   d. 214,800 pounds

15. Hilga and Jerome leave from different points walking directly toward each other. Hilga walks $2\frac{1}{2}$ miles per hour, and Jerome walks 4 miles per hour. If they meet in $2\frac{1}{2}$ hours, how far apart were they?
   a. 9 miles
   b. 13 miles
   c. $16\frac{1}{4}$ miles
   d. $18\frac{1}{2}$ miles

16. Des Moines recently received a snowstorm that left a total of 8 inches of snow. If it snowed at a consistent rate of 3 inches every two hours, how much snow had fallen in the first five hours of the storm?
   a. 3 inches
   b. 3.3 inches
   c. 5 inches
   d. 7.5 inches

Use the following graph to answer question 17.

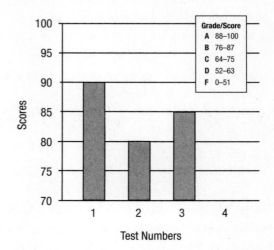

17. Avi's final math grade is based on his scores on four tests. To get an A, Avi needs an average test score of 88 or higher. The graph shown here represents Avi's first three test scores. What is the lowest score Avi can get on the fourth test and still earn an A?
   a. 99
   b. 97
   c. 95
   d. 93

18. Joan will be twice Tom's age in three years when Tom will be 40. How old is Joan now?
   a. 20
   b. 80
   c. 77
   d. 37

19. Kari is running for student council. The rules restrict the candidates to four two-foot-by-three-foot posters. Kari has dozens of four-inch-by-six-inch pictures that she would like to cover the posters with. What is the maximum number of pictures she will be able to use on the four posters?
   a. 144
   b. 130
   c. 125
   d. 111

20. It takes five-year-old Carlos 1.6 minutes to tie the lace on his right shoe and 1.5 minutes to tie the lace on his left shoe. How many minutes does it take Carlos to tie both shoes?
   a. 2.1 minutes
   b. 3.0 minutes
   c. 3.1 minutes
   d. 4.1 minutes

21. Tamika is restoring an antique storage chest that is in the shape of a rectangular box. She is painting only the outside of the chest. The chest is 4 feet long, 18 inches wide, and 2 feet tall. There is a 1-square-foot brass ornament on the outside of the trunk that will not get painted. How much paint does she need, in square feet, to cover the outside of the trunk?
   a. 33 square feet
   b. 34 square feet
   c. 143 square feet
   d. 231 square feet

22. 2,520 seconds is equivalent to how many minutes?
   a. 84 minutes
   b. 42 minutes
   c. 151,200 minutes
   d. 126 minutes

23. Belinda is building a garden shed. When she helped her neighbor build an identical shed, it took them 22 hours to complete the job together. If it would have taken her neighbor, working alone, 38 hours to build the shed, how long will it take Belinda, working alone, to build her shed?
   a. 33.75 hours
   b. 41.00 hours
   c. 41.25 hours
   d. 52.25 hours

24. An empty crate weighs 8.16 kg and an orange weighs 220 g. If Jon can lift 11,000 g, how many oranges can he pack in the crate before lifting it onto his truck?
   a. 12
   b. 13
   c. 37
   d. 46

25. Jeff was 10 minutes early for class. Dee came in four minutes after Mae, who was half as early as Jeff. How many minutes early was Dee?
   a. 1 minute
   b. 2 minutes
   c. 2.5 minutes
   d. 6 minutes

26. A certain radio station plays classical music during 20% of its airtime. If the station is on the air 24 hours a day, how many hours each day is the station NOT playing classical music?
   a. 8.0 hours
   b. 15.6 hours
   c. 18.2 hours
   d. 19.2 hours

27. Change $\frac{55}{6}$ to a mixed number.
   a. $8\frac{1}{6}$
   b. $9\frac{1}{6}$
   c. $9\frac{1}{55}$
   d. $9\frac{6}{55}$

28. The animal shelter is developing a new outdoor grass area for dogs. A fence needs to be purchased that will surround the entire grassy section. The dimensions of the area are 120 feet by 250 feet. How much fencing needs to be purchased?
a. 740 feet
b. 30,000 square feet
c. 740 square feet
d. 30,000 feet

29. If it takes Danielle 22.4 minutes to walk 1.25 miles, how many minutes will it take her to walk one mile?
a. 17.92 minutes
b. 18 minutes
c. 19.9 minutes
d. 21.15 minutes

30. Luis is mailing two packages. One weighs 12.9 pounds, and the other weighs half as much. What is the total weight, in pounds, of the two packages?
a. 6.45 pounds
b. 12.8 pounds
c. 18.5 pounds
d. 19.35 pounds

Subtest 3: Word Knowledge
Questions: 35
Time: 11 minutes

1. *Noisome* most nearly means
a. loud.
b. harmful.
c. full.
d. clean.

2. *Capsize* most nearly means
a. enlarge.
b. profit.
c. overturn.
d. shrink.

3. *Arsenal* most nearly means
a. stockpile.
b. fire.
c. crime.
d. warfare.

4. *Inert* most nearly means
a. reversed.
b. introduce.
c. motionless.
d. buried.

5. *Affix* most nearly means
a. repair.
b. suffer.
c. fasten.
d. send.

6. *Aptitude* most nearly means
a. capability.
b. mood.
c. height.
d. attention.

7. *Fractious* most nearly means
a. make-believe.
b. true.
c. friendly.
d. quarrelsome.

8. *Serene* most nearly means
a. loud.
b. calm.
c. melodious.
d. stern.

9. *Improbable* most nearly means
   a. unlikeable.
   b. unlikely.
   c. unsuitable.
   d. unmistakable.

10. *Practical* most nearly means
   a. expert.
   b. healthy.
   c. useless.
   d. convenient.

11. *Elementary* most nearly means
   a. basic.
   b. school.
   c. fancy.
   d. specific.

12. *Impart* most nearly means
   a. separate.
   b. incomplete.
   c. give.
   d. finish.

13. *Cower* most nearly means
   a. farm.
   b. creep.
   c. recoil.
   d. frighten.

14. *Spartan* most nearly means
   a. strong.
   b. simple.
   c. complicated.
   d. experienced.

15. *Adept* most nearly means
   a. skilled.
   b. unrelated.
   c. included.
   d. accepted.

16. *Agility* most nearly means
   a. weakness.
   b. harmony.
   c. irritability.
   d. dexterity.

17. *Harry* most nearly means
   a. bother.
   b. accelerate.
   c. furry.
   d. congratulate.

18. *Remorse* most nearly means
   a. solitude.
   b. punishment.
   c. regret.
   d. frailty.

19. *Haggard* most nearly means
   a. tiny.
   b. rough.
   c. exhausted.
   d. strong.

20. *Prominent* most nearly means
   a. appropriate.
   b. important.
   c. supportive.
   d. unnoticeable.

21. Never one to ignore a suggestion, Max was
   _____ to his student's ideas.
   a. dismissive
   b. apathetic
   c. attentive
   d. reciprocal

22. Unsure of what lay ahead, the careful explorer
   went forward _____.
   a. brazenly
   b. cautiously
   c. hurriedly
   d. progressively

23. Suspecting the salesperson of being less than truthful, Lindsay did not buy the chair, because of its _____ quality.
   a. comfortable
   b. excellent
   c. expensive
   d. dubious

24. _____ by the reputation of her more experienced opponent, Nancy took the field with confidence.
   a. Daunted
   b. Unfazed
   c. Informed
   d. Terrified

25. The two generals differed markedly in their strategies; Percy was calculating and cautious while Norton was hasty and _____.
   a. guarded
   b. brave
   c. reckless
   d. prudent

26. Because so much of academia is _____ to many people, its theories are often dismissed as highbrow and farfetched.
   a. inaccessible
   b. important
   c. understandable
   d. controversial

27. _____ the upscale dress code, Wes came to work in jeans and a T-shirt every day.
   a. Obeying
   b. Flouting
   c. Wearing
   d. Knowing

28. The _____ of the mansion stood in stark contrast to the nondescript, ramshackle buildings surrounding the square.
   a. drabness
   b. grandeur
   c. importance
   d. location

29. Jodi's parents were surprised when she went to bed when they asked; she was usually very _____.
   a. agreeable
   b. tired
   c. hopeful
   d. stubborn

30. As he aged, he became increasingly _____, repeating himself and forgetting where he put things.
   a. weak
   b. tired
   c. senile
   d. thoughtless

31. It seems strange that a poem about such a _____ subject as waiting for the bus could be so fascinating and beautiful.
   a. random
   b. mundane
   c. remarkable
   d. controversial

32. Under fire from the press for taking so long to find the culprit, the police _____ their search.
   a. intensified
   b. canceled
   c. doubted
   d. undertook

33. The final scene of the film is so touching that even the most _____ crowd would be moved to tears.
  a. sullen
  b. impassive
  c. emotional
  d. peaceable

34. Upon their return home, the soldiers were lauded as _____.
  a. victims
  b. heroes
  c. veterans
  d. reinforcements

35. The short-tempered clerk was so _____ to customers that soon the store had no more business.
  a. helpful
  b. serious
  c. rude
  d. outgoing

Subtest 4:
Paragraph Comprehension
Questions: 15
Time: 13 minutes

Every 10 years in America, the federal government conducts a national census to *enumerate* the national population. The U.S. Constitution actually requires that all American citizens, non-citizen long-term visitors, and both legal and illegal immigrants be counted on a *decennial* basis, with specific information gathered regarding population density in all voting districts. This information is what determines how many seats each state is permitted within the House of Representatives. The census has been conducted every 10 years since 1790. Specific questions have varied from one census to another, but the basic information gathered has been the same since the beginning: how many people live in a particular voting district. This information is vitally important, since it determines the extent of political representation the voters have in Washington, DC.

1. According to the passage, the basic purpose of the census is to
  a. learn information about American voters.
  b. see how population densities influence political trends.
  c. determine a voting district's political representation.
  d. keep the Postal Service in business.

2. As used in the passage, *enumerate* most nearly means to
  a. expound on.
  b. count.
  c. make amends.
  d. steal from the treasury.

3. The census is conducted every 10 years because
  a. population trends can best be tracked in 10-year intervals.
  b. seats in the House of Representatives expire every 10 years.
  c. the American people get angry if it is more frequent.
  d. the Constitution requires it.

4. As used in the passage, *decennial* most nearly means
  a. Constitutional.
  b. every 10 years.
  c. decaying.
  d. irritating.

The stories about King Arthur are an *enduring* legend in Western literature. Most people are familiar with the Round Table and famous characters such as Merlin, Sir Lancelot, Guinevere, and King Arthur himself. The stories date back to the Middle Ages, with such classic works as Sir Thomas Malory's famous *Le Morte d'Arthur* (*The Death of Arthur*), Alfred Lord Tennyson's *Idylls of the King*, and T. H. White's *The Once and Future King*. The legend is so enjoyable that writers even today use it to create new works of fiction. But many people are not aware that there was a real King Arthur, a real Merlin, and even a real castle of Camelot!

The actual details of these historical facts and personalities are very sketchy, but historical documents record a warrior named Arthur who led an army against Anglo-Saxon invasions during the sixth century. A man named *Merlinus Ambrosius* was instrumental in establishing a lasting British independence, and he was probably the *prototype* of Merlin. Perhaps someday historians will unveil more about this legendary topic.

5. The author of this passage would most likely agree with which statement?
   a. King Arthur is an old-fashioned story.
   b. Alfred Lord Tennyson wrote many poems.
   c. The legend of King Arthur is based loosely on historical facts.
   d. The future of the Arthurian legend is in question.

6. As used in the passage, *enduring* most nearly means
   a. lasting a long time.
   b. ending quickly.
   c. interesting and lively.
   d. historically accurate.

7. According to the passage, Merlin should be best remembered for
   a. being a powerful magician.
   b. inventing the Round Table.
   c. helping to establish British independence.
   d. wearing funny hats.

8. As used in the passage, *prototype* most nearly means
   a. clearly written.
   b. historical basis.
   c. fictional character.
   d. well fed.

In 1440, a German named Johannes Gutenberg created a new invention which revolutionized Western society—the printing press. In modern times, most of us take printing for granted, being able to create printed documents with the push of a button and the click of a mouse, but 600 years ago no such technology existed. Books were produced by hand, by people working long hours to write out each page using pens made from feathers! The closest thing to a printing press was the art of *xylography*, which involved engraving an entire page of text onto a wooden block, which was then covered with ink and pressed against paper.

Gutenberg invented something called "moveable type," which consisted of individual letters made of lead that could be placed together to form words and sentences. His press allowed a printer to set those lead letters together to produce an entire page of text, which was then inked and printed onto paper. Books could be reproduced on a large scale very quickly, which allowed printers to *disseminate* ideas around the world without much effort and expense.

9. The printing press revolutionized Western society because
  a. it allowed people to make money.
  b. it was fast.
  c. it enabled people to share ideas worldwide.
  d. there had never been anything like it.

10. As used in the passage, *disseminate* most nearly means to
  a. spread around.
  b. heat up quickly.
  c. cool down quickly.
  d. cause pain.

11. Moveable type is made of
  a. ink.
  b. paper.
  c. lead.
  d. feathers.

12. The art of *xylography* involves
  a. playing music.
  b. engraving lead.
  c. making paper.
  d. engraving on wood.

Reality TV shows will have an adverse effect on traditional dramas and comedies. As reality TV increases in popularity, network executives will begin canceling more traditional programs and replacing them with the latest in reality TV.

13. This passage best supports the statement that
  a. Reality TV is low quality.
  b. Reality TV shows get the highest ratings.
  c. More and more people love to watch and participate in reality TV.
  d. As reality TV gets more popular, more traditional television shows may be threatened.

In cities throughout the country, there is a new direction in local campaign coverage. Frequently in local elections, journalists are not giving voters enough information to understand the issues and evaluate the candidates. The local news media devote too much time to scandal and not enough time to policy.

14. This paragraph best supports the statement that the local news media
  a. are not doing an adequate job when it comes to covering local campaigns.
  b. do not understand either campaign issues or politics.
  c. should learn how to cover politics by watching the national news media.
  d. have no interest in covering stories about local political events.

The entire low-carbohydrate versus low-fat diet argument is so prevalent that one would think that these are the only two options available for losing weight and staying healthy. Some experts even feel that the low-carb and low-fat debate distracts us from an even more important issue—our culture's reliance on processed and manufactured foods.

15. The paragraph best supports the statement that
  a. experts state that not all fats are equal, so we need not reduce our intake of all fats—just those that contain partially hydrogenated oils.
  b. important health concerns get overlooked when we focus exclusively on the low-fat versus low-carb question.
  c. low-carbohydrate diets lead to significant and sustained weight loss.
  d. processed foods can lead to many adverse health problems including heart disease, cancer, diabetes, and obesity.

Subtest 5: Mathematics Knowledge

Questions: 25
Time: 24 minutes

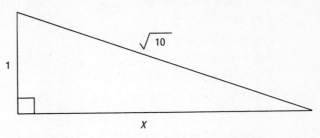

1. Which of the following is equivalent to
   $(x-3)(x+7)$?
   a. $x^2 - 3x - 21$
   b. $x^2 - 4x - 21$
   c. $x^2 + 4x - 21$
   d. $x^2 - 21$

2. Which of the following represents a composite number?
   a. 11
   b. 29
   c. 41
   d. 91

3. Choose the answer to the following problem:
   $\frac{5}{12} \times \frac{1}{6} \times \frac{2}{3} =$
   a. $\frac{10}{12}$
   b. $\frac{5}{6}$
   c. $\frac{5}{108}$
   d. $\frac{5}{216}$

4. Find the median of the following group of numbers: 14 12 20 22 14 16
   a. 12
   b. 14
   c. 15
   d. 16

5. What is the value of x in this figure?
   a. 3
   b. 4
   c. 5
   d. 9

6. In which of the following are the diagonals of the figure always congruent and perpendicular?
   a. isosceles trapezoid
   b. square
   c. isosceles triangle
   d. rhombus

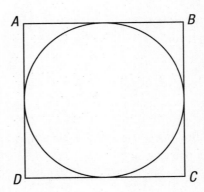

7. In this diagram, a circle of area 100π square inches is inscribed in a square. What is the length of side AB?
   a. 10 inches
   b. 20 inches
   c. 100 inches
   d. 400 inches

8. Which of the following expressions is equal to 40,503?
- **a.** 400 + 50 + 3
- **b.** 4,000 + 500 + 3
- **c.** 40,000 + 50 + 3
- **d.** 40,000 + 500 + 3

9. If the perimeter of a rectangle is 40 centimeters and the shorter sides are 4 centimeters, what is the length of the longer sides?
- **a.** 12 centimeters
- **b.** 10 centimeters
- **c.** 18 centimeters
- **d.** 16 centimeters

10. A straight angle is
- **a.** exactly 180°.
- **b.** between 90° and 180°.
- **c.** 90°.
- **d.** less than 90°.

11. If $\frac{1}{19} = \frac{x}{76}$, what is x?
- **a.** 3
- **b.** 3.5
- **c.** 4
- **d.** 5

12. Which value of x will make the following inequality true: $12x - 1 < 35$
- **a.** 2
- **b.** 3
- **c.** 4
- **d.** 5

13. Which of the following could describe a quadrilateral with two pairs of parallel sides and two interior angles that measure 65°?
- **a.** square
- **b.** triangle
- **c.** rectangle
- **d.** rhombus

14. Simplify the radical completely: $\sqrt{64x^5y^8}$.
- **a.** $8x^2y^4 \sqrt{x}$
- **b.** $8x^4y^8 \sqrt{x}$
- **c.** $64x^2y^4$
- **d.** $8x^5y^8$

15. Write ten thousand, four hundred forty-seven in numerals.
- **a.** 10,499,047
- **b.** 104,447
- **c.** 10,447
- **d.** 1,047

16. Which of the following numbers is represented by the prime factors $2 \times 3 \times 7$?
- **a.** 21
- **b.** 42
- **c.** 84
- **d.** 237

17. Solve the equation for a: $\sqrt{2a+6} - 4 = 6$.
- **a.** 2
- **b.** 17
- **c.** 23
- **d.** 47

18. Find the sum of $4x - 7y$ and $7x + 7y$.
- **a.** $11x$
- **b.** $14y$
- **c.** $11x + 14y$
- **d.** $11x - 14y$

19. 3 hours 20 minutes − 1 hour 48 minutes =
- **a.** 5 hours 8 minutes
- **b.** 4 hours 8 minutes
- **c.** 2 hours 28 minutes
- **d.** 1 hour 32 minutes

[shaded bar figure]

20. Name the fraction that indicates the shaded part of this figure.

a. $\frac{2}{5}$

b. $\frac{3}{5}$

c. $\frac{5}{3}$

d. $\frac{5}{2}$

21. Which expression best describes the sum of three numbers multiplied by the sum of their reciprocals?

a. $(a + b + c)(\frac{1}{a} + \frac{1}{b} + \frac{1}{c})$

b. $(a)(\frac{1}{a}) + (b)(\frac{1}{b}) + (c)(\frac{1}{c})$

c. $(a + b + c) \div (\frac{1}{a})(\frac{1}{b})(\frac{1}{c})$

d. $(a)(b)(c) + (\frac{1}{a})(\frac{1}{b})(\frac{1}{c})$

22. Find three consecutive odd integers whose sum is 117.

a. 39, 39, 39

b. 38, 39, 40

c. 37, 39, 41

d. 39, 41, 43

23. Which of the following points is the solution to the following system of equations?

$y = -x + 10$

$y = x - 2$

a. (2,10)

b. (2,0)

c. (3,6)

d. (6,4)

24. Find the sum: $\frac{2w}{z} + \frac{5w}{z}$.

a. $\frac{7w}{2z}$

b. $\frac{7w}{z^2}$

c. $\frac{7w}{z}$

d. $7w$

25. Divide: $\frac{6a2b}{2c} \div \frac{ab^2}{4c^4}$

a. $\frac{24ac}{b}$

b. $\frac{12ac^3}{b}$

c. $\frac{24ac^3}{b}$

d. $12abc^3$

Subtest 6: Electronics Information

Questions: 20

Time: 9 minutes

1. For safety purposes, electrical devices need to be

a. inspected daily.

b. limited in volt and amperage.

c. grounded to prevent electrical shock.

d. designed under international guidelines.

2. What is the frequency of the alternating voltage and current typically used in the United States?

a. 20 Hz

b. 40 Hz

c. 60 Hz

d. 110 Hz

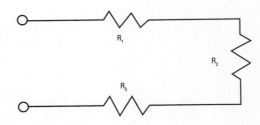

3. If resistors R_1, R_2, and R_3 are all rated at 500 ohms, what is the total resistance?

a. 500 watts

b. 500 ohms

c. 1,500 ohms

d. 1,500 watts

4. Cooking with metal in a microwave should be avoided because
   a. it can melt.
   b. parts of the microwave can be damaged by reflected energy.
   c. it could cause a reverse polarity of the structural wiring system.
   d. none of the above.

5. What is the total current in a parallel resistance circuit with three parallel paths that each have four amperes flowing through them?
   a. 2A
   b. 12A
   c. 4A
   d. 8A

6. The abbreviation FM stands for
   a. frequency modulation.
   b. frequency multiplier.
   c. feedback multiplex.
   d. farad magnet.

7. What does this electronic circuit symbol depict?
   a. a conversion from AC to DC power
   b. an electrical surge
   c. a wire that does not join another
   d. a wire that intersects another

8. A volt is a unit of electric(al)
   a. potential.
   b. energy.
   c. pressure.
   d. current.

9. Coulomb's law describes
   a. electromagnetic fields and their association with the electric grid.
   b. the relationship between direct current (DC) and alternating current (AC).
   c. the electrostatic force between electric charges.
   d. the electrical differential between resistors.

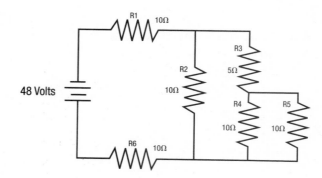

10. Total resistance in this schematic is 25Ω. What is the voltage drop across R1?
   a. 6.2 V
   b. 12.4 V
   c. 19.2 V
   d. 48 V

11. If a vacuum cleaner is rated at 1,200 watts and operates at 120 volts, how many ampereres (amps) of current will it draw?
   a. 10
   b. 100
   c. 120
   d. 144,000

12. The term given to a unit of electromotive force is a(n)
   a. ohm.
   b. amp.
   c. megawatt.
   d. volt.

13. The best antenna to use when working with frequencies below 300kHz would be a
   a. parabolic antenna.
   b. loopstick antenna.
   c. dish antenna.
   d. wire hanger antenna.

14. Which of the following is an advantage of a corner reflector antenna?
   a. broad spectrum capability
   b. its wireless design
   c. low power out
   d. increased directivity

15. In a directional antenna, what is the correlation between the diameter of a reflector in wave lengths and the gain?
   a. The smaller the diameter, the narrower the lobe.
   b. The smaller the diameter, the greater the gain.
   c. The larger the diameter, the greater the gain.
   d. None of the above.

16. In series circuit A, a 10Ω load dissipates 1 watt. In series circuit B, a 10Ω load dissipates 2 watts. What can be said about the current through the load in circuit A if the voltages in both circuits are equal?
   a. The current through load A is equal to the current through load B.
   b. The current through load A is twice the current through load B.
   c. The current through load A is half the current through load B.
   d. The current through load A is zero.

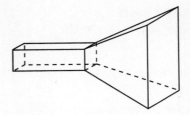

17. What type of antenna is this?
   a. a corner reflector
   b. a horn
   c. a dish
   d. a helical

18. FM radio broadcasting, amateur radio, broadcast television, and commercial aircraft transmit on what radio frequency?
   a. low frequency (LF)
   b. medium frequency (MF)
   c. very high frequency (VHF)
   d. ultra high frequency (UHF)

19. What is the purpose of a tuning capacitor?
   a. It allows an antenna to transmit.
   b. It is used to vary the time period.
   c. It adjusts the resonant frequency.
   d. None of the above.

20. A transformer changes which of the following?
   a. power and pressure
   b. voltage and amperage
   c. voltage and current
   d. chemical energy

Subtest 7: Auto and Shop Information

Questions: 25
Time: 11 minutes

1. One way to ensure optimum gas mileage is to
   a. keep the engine coolant system replenished every 3,000 to 5,000 miles.
   b. keep the fuel tank topped off.
   c. keep the tires properly inflated.
   d. minimize the use of cruise control.

2. A flow meter measures the
   a. projected rate at which fuel is being burned.
   b. remaining volume of liquid in a container.
   c. specific gravity of a given fluid.
   d. rate at which a fluid is flowing through a piping system.

3. Which of the following is an example of a flow meter?
   a. speedometer
   b. oil pressure gauge
   c. gas pump gauge
   d. none of the above

4. The abbreviation PCV, when associated with an automobile, stands for
   a. positive crankcase ventilation.
   b. pollution control valve.
   c. primary catalytic volume.
   d. post critical valance.

5. After an oil change, the used oil should be
   a. disposed of in the most convenient manner.
   b. reused immediately to take advantage of its viscosity.
   c. recycled for reuse.
   d. tested for metal parts from excessive engine wear.

6. An automobile's fuel gauge typically measures its contents in
   a. gallons or liters.
   b. pounds per square inch.
   c. degrees Fahrenheit or Celsius.
   d. miles per hour.

7. An automobile alternator performs which of the following functions?
   a. It provides the spark to ignite the air-fuel mixture.
   b. It recycles the coolant.
   c. It recharges the battery.
   d. It powers the brake system.

8. An acoustical chamber in the exhaust system that reduces engine noise is
   a. the radiator.
   b. the muffler.
   c. the catalytic converter.
   d. none of the above.

9. Which of the following types of springs are found in a suspension system?
   a. leaf springs
   b. universal springs
   c. coil compression springs
   d. both a and c

10. To determine the strength of a solution of antifreeze, you would use a
    a. voltmeter.
    b. hydrometer.
    c. thermometer.
    d. dosimeter.

11. The burning of gasoline during the operation of an internal combustion engine generates what three major pollutants?
   a. oxygen, nitrogen, and carbon dioxide
   b. oxygen, nitrogen, and carbon monoxide
   c. carbon monoxide, nitrogen oxides, and helium
   d. hydrocarbons, carbon monoxide, and nitrogen oxides

12. The oil pump ensures that
   a. oil is pumped throughout all the engine oil passages.
   b. the correct oil-fuel mixture is maintained.
   c. oil is supplied to the cooling system.
   d. used oil is cleaned and recycled within the oil system.

13. Front-wheel drive vehicles have their transmission and differential combined in a
   a. crossaxle.
   b. through-put drive.
   c. transaxle.
   d. universal joint.

14. A *hinge mortise* would typically be found
   a. on soffit facing
   b. on a floor joist
   c. on a door or door jamb
   d. on a stair stringer

15. All the cuts listed are one of the six basic woodworking cuts *except*
   a. a crosscut.
   b. a rip.
   c. a miter.
   d. a lateral.

16. Which of the following will provide the strongest joint?
   a. a nail
   b. a screw
   c. a solder
   d. a weld

17. The chemical process that results in the hardening of concrete is called
   a. evaporation.
   b. condensation.
   c. hydration.
   d. dissipation.

18. The tool used to smooth out the surface of poured concrete is called
   a. a float.
   b. a screed.
   c. a tamp.
   d. a form.

19. What sort of washer would you use to ensure that a bolt does not come loose?
   a. flat
   b. fender
   c. ogee
   d. split lock

20. Concrete is typically used in conjunction with which of the following building materials in order to provide a stronger product?
   a. bronze reinforcement
   b. aluminum reinforcement
   c. steel reinforcement
   d. plastic reinforcement

21. Concrete is made up of which of the following components?
   a. cement, water, and steel
   b. gravel and sand
   c. gravel, water, and glass
   d. cement, sand, gravel, and water

22. Which material may be used as the outer material on a roof in order to keep out rain?
 a. tile
 b. wood
 c. asphalt
 d. all of the above

23. This hand tool is known as a
 a. screwdriver.
 b. hammer.
 c. crescent wrench.
 d. pair of pliers.

24. Which of the following is NOT a type of hammer?
 a. ball-peen
 b. sledge
 c. claw
 d. box

25. If a line is *plumb*, what would be its defining characteristic?
 a. It would be as tightly drawn as possible.
 b. It would form a perfect square.
 c. It would be perfectly vertical.
 d. It would form a precise 45° angle.

Subtest 8:
Mechanical Comprehension
Questions: 25
Time: 19 minutes

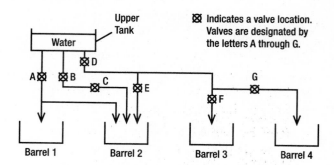

1. In this figure, all valves are initially closed. Gravity will cause the water to drain down into the barrels when the valves are opened. Which barrels will be filled if valves A, B, E, F, and G are opened and valves C and D are left closed?
 a. barrels 1 and 2
 b. barrels 3 and 4
 c. barrels 1, 2, 3, and 4
 d. barrels 1, 2, and 3
 e. barrels 1 and 4

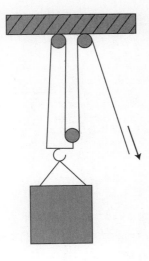

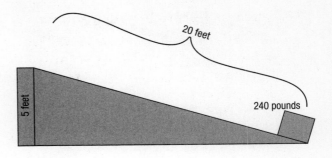

4. A 240-pound block is being pulled up an incline by a pulley. The incline is 20 feet long and rises 5 feet. Neglecting friction, how much force is necessary to move the block up the incline?
- **a.** 60 pounds
- **b.** 100 pounds
- **c.** 260 pounds
- **d.** 240 pounds

2. If the rope on the end of this pulley system is pulled with 160 pounds of force, what is the maximum weight that can be lifted?
- **a.** 640 pounds
- **b.** 480 pounds
- **c.** 320 pounds
- **d.** 80 pounds

5. A jack is able to lift a 3,000-pound car using only 50 pounds of force. What is the mechanical advantage of the jack?
- **a.** 4
- **b.** 60
- **c.** 600
- **d.** 2,950

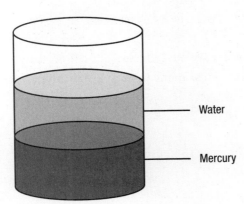

6. The tires of a car are filled in a garage to a pressure of 35 psi (pounds per square inch). Driving the car to a hot desert will have what effect on the tires?
- **a.** Their pressure will increase.
- **b.** Their pressure will decrease.
- **c.** Their weight will increase.
- **d.** Their weight will decrease.

3. A beaker is filled with mercury and water. Mercury is a liquid with a density of 8 g/cm^3 and water has a density of 1 g/cm^3. If a penny with a density of 5 g/cm^3 is dropped into the beaker, where will it settle?
- **a.** at the bottom of the beaker
- **b.** in the middle of the mercury layer
- **c.** in between the mercury and water layers
- **d.** on top of the water layer

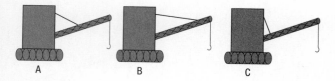

7. A crane raises its arm using a powerful cable attached to the main body. Which cable position offers the greatest mechanical advantage?

a. A
b. B
c. C
d. They all offer the same advantage.

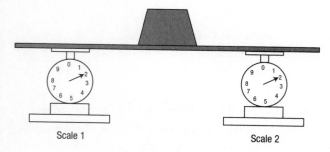

Scale 1   Scale 2

8. Two scales are connected by a plank weighing 2 pounds. A 12-pound block is placed directly in between the two scales. How many pounds will Scale 1 read?

a. 7 pounds
b. 10 pounds
c. 12 pounds
d. 14 pounds

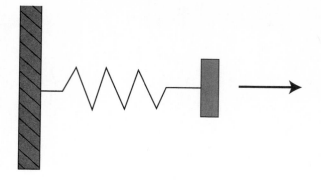

9. A force of 9 pounds stretches a spring 3 inches. How far will the spring move under 12 pounds of force?

a. 3 inches
b. 4 inches
c. 6 inches
d. 36 inches

10. A solid object will float on water when

a. it is less dense than water.
b. it is more dense than water.
c. it has a large surface area.
d. it has a small surface area.

11. A nut travels 1.25 inches after 15 turns of the screw. How many threads per inch does the screw have?

a. 10
b. 12
c. 15
d. 20

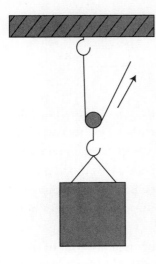

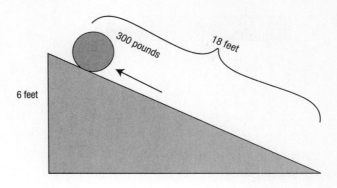

12. Using the pulley system shown above, how much force is required to lift a 200-pound load?

    a. 50 pounds

    b. 100 pounds

    c. 200 pounds

    d. 400 pounds

13. Which material expands most when heated?

    a. wood

    b. steel

    c. glass

    d. rubber

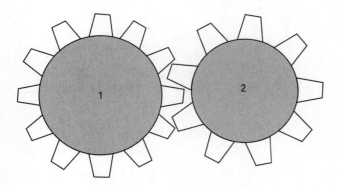

14. Gear 1 has 12 teeth and gear 2 has 9. If gear 1 turns at 30 revolutions per minute (rpm), how fast will gear 2 turn?

    a. 20 rpm

    b. 30 rpm

    c. 40 rpm

    d. 60 rpm

15. A 300-pound barrel is being supported on an incline. The incline is 18 feet long and rises 6 feet. How much force is necessary to prevent the barrel from rolling down?

    a. 50 pounds

    b. 100 pounds

    c. 150 pounds

    d. 300 pounds

16. A single-speed bicycle has a front chain ring with 55 teeth. The back gear has 11 teeth. If the bicycle is pedaled for 80 rpm, how many complete revolutions will the rear wheel make in 30 seconds?

    a. 40 revolutions

    b. 80 revolutions

    c. 200 revolutions

    d. 400 revolutions

17. Why do helium-filled balloons float?

    a. Helium is less dense than air.

    b. Helium is a noble gas.

    c. Helium is hotter than air.

    d. Helium is colder than air.

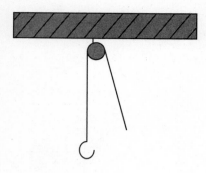

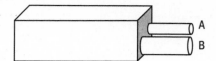

18. The pulley system shown in the figure offers what advantage?
a. a two-fold mechanical advantage
b. a three-fold mechanical advantage
c. a change in the direction of force
d. no advantage

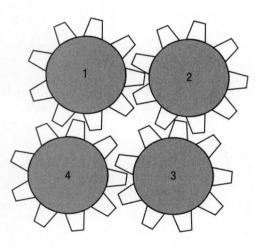

19. If gear 4 turns clockwise, which other gear(s) will turn counterclockwise?
a. 1 only
b. 2 only
c. 3 only
d. 1 and 3

20. Two cylindrical pipes are used to drain a tank. Pipe A has a diameter of 2 inches and pipe B has a diameter of 6 inches. If there is equal water pressure inside the tank, how much more water will flow out of pipe B than out of pipe A?
a. The same amount will flow out of both pipes.
b. Three times more will flow out of pipe B.
c. Six times more will flow out of pipe B.
d. Nine times more will flow out of pipe B.

21. Steve goes on a run at 8 mph and travels 14 miles. How long did Steve run?
a. 1 hour 15 minutes
b. 1 hour 30 minutes
c. 1 hour 45 minutes
d. 2 hours

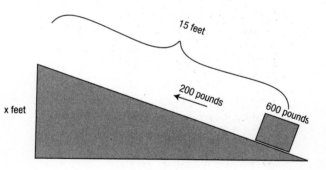

22. A 600-pound block is being pulled up a 15-foot incline. Neglecting friction, if 200 pounds of force is necessary to move the block up the incline, how tall is the ramp?
a. 4 feet
b. 10 feet
c. 5 feet
d. 15 feet

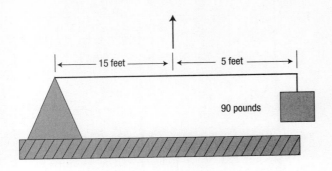

23. In the diagram, Paul wants to lift a 90-pound block using a lever. If the block is 20 feet from the pivot point and Paul is 15 feet from the pivot point, how much force must he apply to lift the block?

    a. 120 pounds

    b. 450 pounds

    c. 20 pounds

    d. 90 pounds

24. A helium balloon is released from the ground and quickly rises 2,000 feet. What will happen to the balloon?

    a. The balloon will become heavier.

    b. The balloon will become lighter.

    c. The size of the balloon will increase.

    d. The size of the balloon will decrease.

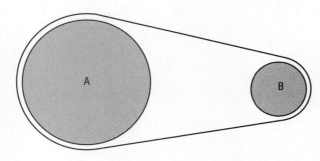

25. Pulley A has 1.5 times the circumference of pulley B. If pulley A rotates counterclockwise at 30 revolutions per minute (rpm), how fast and in what direction will pulley B rotate?

    a. 30 rpm clockwise

    b. 30 rpm counterclockwise

    c. 45 rpm clockwise

    d. 45 rpm counterclockwise

Subtest 9: Assembling Objects

Each question is composed of five separate drawings. The problem is presented in the first drawing, and the remaining four drawings are possible solutions. Determine which of the four choices contains all of the pieces assembled properly that are shown in the first picture. Note: images are not drawn to scale. You have 15 minutes to complete this subtest.

Questions: 25
Time: 15 minutes

1.
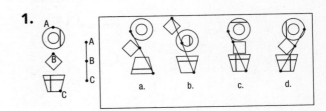

2.
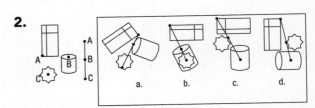

3.
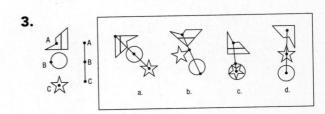

4.
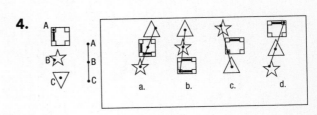

5.
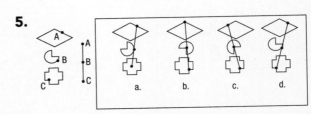

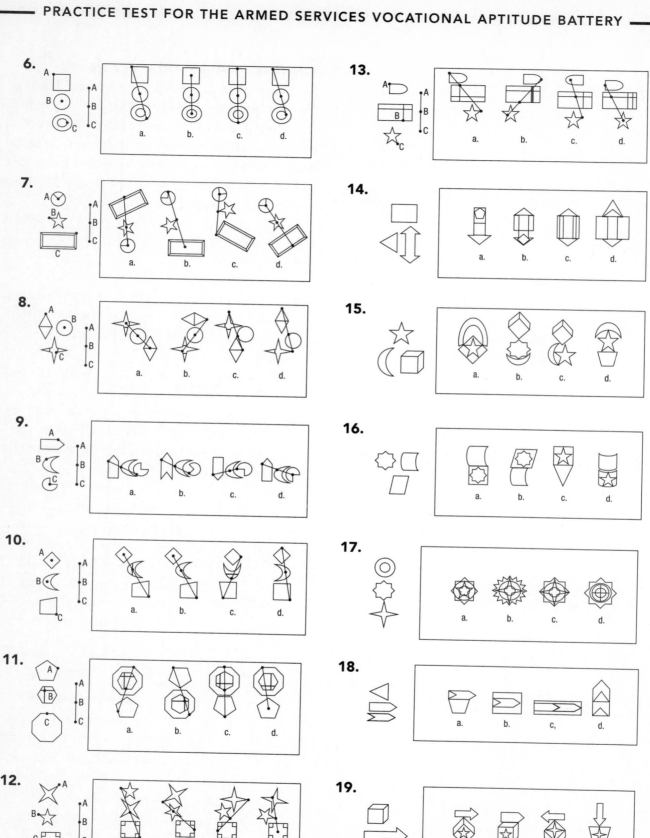

20.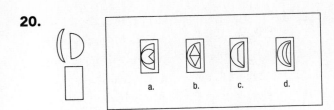

21.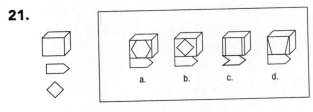

22.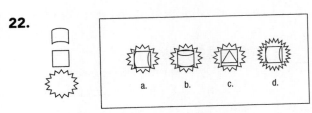

23.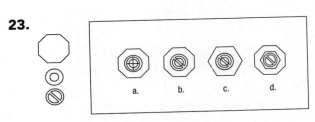

24.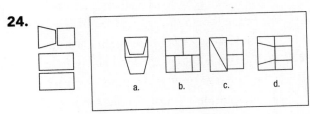

25.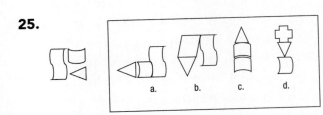

Answer Key

Part 1: General Science

1. **c.** Elements on the right of the periodic table tend to be nonmetal gases. Moving to the right in the periodic table, elements increase their electronegativity (tendency to accept electrons).

2. **d.** Gymnosperms are conifer plants that store their seeds in cones instead of in fruit like angiosperms.

3. **b.** When there is an unequal sharing of electrons between atoms, one atom becomes negatively charged and the other positively charged. These ions are held together through an ionic bond.

4. **d.** The addition of another predator introduces competition for a limited resource, the prey. As a result, the prey population will decrease and the predator populations will have less food and their populations will decrease as well.

5. **a.** Temperature is the measure of the average kinetic energy of molecules, which is measured by a thermometer.

6. **b.** Magma is deep in the earth and extremely hot. When magma reaches the surface of the earth it cools and is considered lava.

7. **b.** Carcinogens cause mutations that lead to cancerous growth, which in most cases is unhealthy.

8. **d.** Alkaline solutions are basic so they have a pH between 8 and 14.

9. **b.** Start by balancing the reactants first. From the products it is determined that there are six oxygen atoms, so six are needed in the reactants. This would lead to $2Fe_2O_3$. Now, determine the total iron (Fe) on the product side by looking at what is present as reactants. There are four iron atoms, therefore 4Fe is needed in the products.

10. d. A watershed collects water and drains it into a river.

11. b. Most likely the parents expressed the dominant trait and carried the recessive allele, which was not expressed, as well. There is a 25% chance that each parent gives the offspring the recessive allele and the offspring expresses the recessive trait not expressed in its parents.

12. d. All organic compounds and organisms contain carbon in addition to other elements.

13. d. Electrons have negligible mass and are not included in the mass number.

14. a. Energy only enters the food chain through primary consumers. Improved farms would provide more energy from primary producers. Choice **b** would benefit the population, but not without choice **a**. Choice **d** is helpful, but humans are secondary consumers and have fewer predators than primary consumers.

15. c. Although some deserts get less than 2 inches per year, any place that gets less than 10 inches of rain per year is considered a desert.

16. c. An endothermic reaction most likely has a high activation energy. Catalysts reduce the activation energy of a reaction, which increases the rate of reaction. Choice **d** would cause the reaction to run in the reverse direction. Choice **b** would likely lead to more space between reactants and less collisions, decreasing the reaction rate.

17. a. Platelets are responsible for clotting blood.

18. a. Intermolecular forces refer to forces between molecules. Water is formed by covalent bonds between hydrogen and oxygen. There is an unequal sharing of electrons in the bonds, which creates a dipole in the molecule—one end has a positive charge and the other a negative. The dipoles of water molecules attract other water molecules and hold the solution strongly together (surface tension).

19. d. The father gives only his Y chromosome to the son, so the mother must have given the son the X-linked trait. Because the mother does not show the X-linked trait, she is considered a carrier of the trait.

20. c. The first and second largest reservoirs are the ocean and the glaciers and ice caps.

21. b. Fission reactions occur when a heavy nucleus, like uranium U-235, is bombarded by a neutron, and splits into two lighter nuclei, in this case barium and krypton, releasing enormous amounts of energy.

22. d. The food chain is the exchange of energy and starts with producers (plants) making energy from sunlight, then primary consumers eating the producers, and finally secondary consumers eating the primary consumers.

23. d. Tundra is cold and windy permafrost areas in polar regions and alpine locations. Adaptations favored in this biome would resist cold and adjust to scarce food supply. Choice **a** benefits animals by moving to warmer locations and searching for food.

24. a. A family represents a column on the periodic table. The atomic radius of elements increases toward the bottom of a family, leaving electrons farther away from the nucleus. Elements toward the bottom are less stable and more reactive.

25. c. When elements share their electrons they form a covalent bond.

Subtest 2: Arithmetic Reasoning

1. a. This is a two-step multiplication problem. First, multiply to find out how many weeks there are in six months: $6 \times 4.3 = 25.8$. Then, multiply to find out how much is saved: $\$40 \times 25.8 = \$1,032$.

2. d. In this problem, you must multiply a fraction by a whole number. First, rewrite the whole number as a fraction: $8 = \frac{8}{1}$. Next, multiply: $\frac{8}{1} \times \frac{4}{5} = \frac{32}{5}$. Finally, convert to a mixed number: $\frac{32}{5} = 6\frac{2}{5}$.

3. a. Add each of the known sectors, and subtract the sum from 100% to get 12%.

4. d. Since the rent sector is labeled 38%, find 38% of $2,450: $0.38 \times 2,450 = \$931$.

5. d. First, determine which recycler pays the most for each material. Recycler X pays the most for aluminum, cardboard, and plastic; recycler Y pays the most for glass. Next, multiply the amount in pounds of each material by the price per pound you determined in the first step. Then add these totals together to get your answer: $2,200 \times .07 + 1,400 \times .04 + 3,100 \times .08 + 900 \times .03 = 485$.

6. c. Let x equal the number of oranges left in the basket. Three more than seven times as many oranges as five is $7(5) + 3 = 38$. Removing five leaves $x = 38 - 5 = 33$ oranges.

7. c. Convert both the cost and the length to fractions: $\frac{3}{4} \times \frac{22}{3} = \frac{66}{12}$ or $5\frac{1}{2}$, which is $5.50.

8. b. If the lamp is 0.25 off of its original price, then the sale price will be 0.75 $(1.0 - 0.25 = 0.75)$. Convert 0.75 into a fraction and reduce; $\frac{75}{100} = \frac{3}{4}$.

9. c. This is a division of fractions problem. First, change the whole number to a fraction: $6 = \frac{6}{1}$. Then, invert the second fraction and multiply: $\frac{6}{1} \times \frac{4}{1} = 24$.

10. d. To find 150% of $45, change the percent to a decimal and multiply: $1.50 \times 45 = 67.50$. Since this is the markup of the price, add $67.50 to $45 to find the new price of $112.50.

11. b. This is a three-step problem involving multiplication and addition and subtraction. First, determine how many cards were sold on Saturday: $0.05 \times 200 = 10$. That leaves 190 cards. Then, find out how many cards were sold on Sunday: $0.10 \times 190 = 19$. Next, add the cards that were sold: $10 + 19 = 29$. Finally, subtract from the original number: $200 - 29 = 171$.

12. b. This is a simple addition problem. Be sure to align the decimal points: $12.98 + 5.68 + 20.64 + 6.76 = 46.06$.

13. c. Multiply the number of hours in a day by the given number of days. There are 24 hours in each day. There are 120 hours in 5 days; 5 days $\times$ 24 hours = 120 hours.

14. c. This is a multiplication problem. To multiply a number by 1,000 quickly, move the decimal point three digits to the right—one digit for each zero. In this situation, because there are only two decimal places, add a zero.

15. c. Hilga and Jerome's initial distance apart equals the sum of the distance each travels in 2.5 hours. Hilga travels a distance of $(2.5)(2.5) = 6.25$ miles, while Jerome travels $(4)(2.5) = 10$ miles. This means that they were $6.25 + 10 = 16.25$ miles apart.

16. d. Three inches every 2 hours = 1.5 inches per hour $\times$ 5 hours = 7.5 inches.

17. b. For the lowest score Avi needs to get an A, assume his final average is 88. Average = $(90 + 80 + 85 + a) \div 4 = 88$. To find a, multiply 88 by 4. Then subtract Avi's first three scores: $88 \times 4 = 352$; $352 - (90 + 80 + 85) = 352 - 255 = 97$.

18. c. The problem is to find J, Joan's present age, in years. Begin by breaking the problem up into smaller parts: Joan will be twice Tom's age in three years becomes J + 3 = 2T; Tom will be 40 becomes T = 40. Substitute: J + 3 = 2(40). Simplify: J = 80 – 3, or J = 77 years old.

19. a. The area of each poster is 864 square inches (24 inches × 36 inches). Kari may use four posters, for a total of 3,456 square inches (864 × 4). Each picture has an area of 24 square inches (4 × 6); the total area of the posters should be divided by the area of each picture, or 3,456 ÷ 24 = 144.

20. c. This is a simple addition problem. Add 1.6 and 1.5, keeping the decimal points aligned: 1.6 + 1.5 = 3.1.

21. a. The surface area of the chest can be found by finding the sum of the areas of each of the six faces of the chest. Since the answer is in square feet, change 18 inches to 1.5 feet: 2(4 × 2) + 2(4 × 1.5) + 2(2 × 1.5) = 2(8) + 2(6) + 2(3) = 16 + 12 + 6 = 34. Subtract the area of the brass ornament: 34 – 1 = 33 square feet.

22. b. Divide the total number of seconds by the number of seconds in a minute. There are 60 seconds in a minute; 2,520 seconds ÷ 60 seconds = 42 minutes.

23. d. Let x equal the number of hours it takes Belinda to complete the job. In one hour, the neighbor can do $\frac{1}{38}$ of the job, while Belinda can do $\frac{1}{x}$. Working together, they take 22 hours to complete 100% of the job or: $\frac{1}{38}(22) + \frac{1}{x}(22) = 1$ (where 1 represents 100% of the job). Simplify: $\frac{22}{38} + \frac{22}{x} = 1$ or $\frac{22}{x} = 1 - \frac{22}{38}$, which reduces to $\frac{22}{x} = \frac{16}{38}$. Cross-multiply: $16x = (22)(38)$, or $x = 52.25$ hours.

24. a. The empty crate weighs 8.16 kg, or 8,160 g. If Jon can lift 11,000 g and one orange weighs 220 g, then the number of oranges that he can pack into the crate is equal to $\frac{(11,000 - 8,160)}{220} = \frac{2,840}{220} \approx 12.9$. Jon cannot pack a fraction of an orange. He can pack 12 whole oranges into the crate.

25. a. Let D equal the time Dee arrived before class. Choosing to represent time before class as a negative number, you have: Jeff arrived 10 minutes early means J = –10, Dee came in four minutes after Mae means D = M + 4, Mae, who was half as early as Jeff means M = $(\frac{1}{2})$J. Substitute: M = –5, so D = –5 + 4 = –1. Thus, D = 1 minute before class.

26. d. First, determine the percent of time that the station is NOT playing classical music. Subtract from 100%: 100 – 20 = 80. Eighty percent of the time the station does NOT play classical music. Then change the percent to a decimal and multiply: 0.8 × 24 = 19.2.

27. b. Divide the numerator by the denominator to find the whole number of the mixed number. The remainder, if any, becomes the numerator of the fraction: 55 ÷ 6 = 9, remainder 1. The denominator stays the same. Therefore, the mixed number is $9\frac{1}{6}$.

28. a. In order to find the amount of fencing, the perimeter needs to be determined: 120 + 120 + 250 + 250 = 740 feet.

29. a. This is a division problem. Because there are two decimal points in 1.25, move the decimal point two places in both numbers: $\frac{2,240}{125} = 17.92$.

30. d. This is a two-step problem involving division and addition. Divide 12.9 by 2 to get 6.45, and then add both numbers: 12.90 + 6.45 = 19.35.

Subtest 3: Word Knowledge

1. b. *Noisome* means offensive, noxious, or *harmful*. Choice **a** might seem like a good choice, but noisome does not mean noisy.

2. c. To *capsize* means to flip or *overturn*. If you chose choice **a** or **b**, you may have been thinking of *capitalize* .

3. a. An *arsenal* is a collection of weapons and munitions; a *stockpile* is a supply of items. Do not confuse *arsenal* with *arson*, which is a crime related to setting fires.

4. c. *Inert* means inactive, powerless, or *motionless*. If you chose choice **a**, **b**, or **d** you may have been thinking of *inverted*, *insert*, or *interred*, respectively.

5. c. *Affix* and *fasten* both mean to join, attach, or secure.

6. a. *Aptitude* means ability, fitness in a task, or *capability*. If you chose choice **b**, you may have been thinking of *attitude*.

7. d. *Fractious* means mutinous, contentious, or *quarrelsome*. If you chose choice **a**, you might have been thinking of *fictional*. *Fractious* is related to *fraction*, which means a piece broken off.

8. b. *Serene* means peaceful or *calm*. You might have been thinking of siren if you chose choice **a**.

9. b. *Improbable* means doubtful or *unlikely*. You might have chosen choice **a**, unlikeable, but that means not liked, or displeasing.

10. d. *Practical* can be used to describe something that is worth doing, useful, or *convenient*.

11. a. Something that is *elementary* is simple, rudimentary, or *basic*. Elementary school is where children learn basic concepts, but by themselves the terms elementary and school are not synonyms.

12. c. To *impart* means to tell, reveal, or *give*. Even though its root word is *part*, the word *impart* does not relate to separation or lack.

13. c. To *cower* means to cringe or crouch in fear, to *recoil*. Be careful not to confuse frighten, a verb meaning to scare, with frightened, an adjective meaning to be scared.

14. b. *Spartan* means disciplined, frugal or *simple*.

15. a. Someone who is *adept* is highly proficient or *skilled*; an expert. Do not confuse *adept* with adopt, a verb that means to incorporate or include.

16. d. Both *agility* and *dexterity* refer to being quick or nimble, or clever.

17. a. *Harry* means to assault, pester, or *bother*. Be careful not to confuse harry with hurry, hairy, or hurray.

18. c. *Remorse* is a feeling of compunction or *regret*.

19. c. *Haggard* means worn out, weak, or *exhausted*.

20. b. *Prominent* means well known, celebrated, or *important*.

21. c. The key phrase is *Never one to ignore a suggestion*. This tells you that Max considers suggestions, or pays attention to them, which eliminates choices **a** and **b**. Choice **c**, *attentive*, means considerate or receptive.

22. b. If a careful explorer is unsure, he or she would probably act with caution, or *cautiously*. Choices **a**, **c**, and **d** do not reflect a careful approach.

23. d. The sentence tells us that Lindsay is suspicious of the salesperson, that she believes there is something wrong with the chair. While choice **c** is a likely reason why someone might decide not to buy a chair, only choice **d** agrees with Lindsay's suspicion.

24. b. The clues in this sentence are the words *experienced* and *confidence*; they tell you that Nancy is facing a challenging opponent, but she is not worried. Therefore, you should eliminate choices **a** and **d**. Choice **c**, though it might make sense, is not as strong a choice as **b**.

25. c. Choices **a** and **d** better describe Percy. Choice **b**, *brave*, is not necessarily the opposite of cautious, but *reckless* certainly is.

26. a. The key phrase in this sentence is *dismissed as highbrow and farfetched*; it tells you that the missing word should be negatively connoted, which rules out choices **b** and **c**. Choice **d** does not provide an adequate reason why the theories would be dismissed, but *inaccessible* means *unfamiliar* or *obscure*, which explains people's rejection.

27. b. Jeans and a T-shirt probably do not comply with an upscale dress code, so choice **a** is incorrect. Choice **c** does not make any sense. Choice **b** better connects and explains the second half of the sentence than choice **d**, even though both might be true.

28. b. The sentence asks for the opposite of *nondescript* and *ramshackle*. Choice **b** is the only logical answer.

29. d. The sentence implies that Jodi usually does not go to bed when asked; choice **d** is the only choice that reflects this idea.

30. c. Someone who is *senile* has difficulty remembering things. *Thoughtless* does not mean forgetful, but rather, inconsiderate or rude.

31. b. The missing word should mean the opposite of fascinating and beautiful; *mundane* means ordinary.

32. a. If the police are being criticized for taking too much time, then a logical response would be something to speed up the process and increase the chance of catching the culprit, to intensify efforts.

33. b. From the sentence you know that the missing word should describe a crowd that is insensitive. *Impassive*, meaning without emotion or apathetic, is the only word that fits.

34. b. The verb *laud* means to praise or honor; the only word that fits logically with that behavior is *heroes*.

35. c. A short-tempered person is likely to be *rude*, and such behavior would certainly have a negative impact on the customers. The other answer choices do not convey this meaning.

Subtest 4: Paragraph Comprehension

1. c. The passage states that the census is used to determine how many representatives each voting district can have in Washington, DC. None of the other choices is addressed.

2. b. The word *enumerate* means to count. The census counts the number of people who live in any voting district; thus, the people who work for the census are called enumerators or counters.

3. d. The passage states in the first paragraph that the 10-year census is required by the U.S. Constitution. None of the other choices is addressed.

4. b. The word *decennial* means occurring every 10 years. The prefix dec- means 10, and the root -ennial is the same as our word annual.

5. c. The passage states that many details of the Arthurian legend are based on historical facts. The author does touch on Tennyson's works, and mentions the legend's existence from the past into the future, but only choice **c** can be fully supported from the passage.

6. a. Something that *endures* lasts a long time despite difficulties and opposition. The legend of King Arthur is enduring because it has been written and read about for hundreds of years.

7. c. The passage states that the real-life Merlin was influential in helping to establish British independence. None of the other choices is mentioned in the text.

8. b. The prefix *proto-* means first in time or earliest, so a *prototype* would be the first historical appearance of a person or thing.

9. c. The printing press revolutionized Western society because it allowed people to share ideas easily, as stated in the last sentence. The other choices might or might not be true, but they are not addressed in the passage.

10. a. To *disseminate* means to spread or to scatter in different directions. Farmers and gardeners disseminate seeds when they scatter them.

11. c. The passage states that moveable type consisted of letters molded in lead.

12. d. The passage defines *xylography* as the art of engraving a page of text onto a wooden block.

13. d. Both sentences in the passage support this choice. Choice **a** is an opinion and is not in the paragraph. Choices **b** and **c** may be true, but they are also not supported by the paragraph.

14. a. Choice **d** may seem attractive at first, but the passage simply says that the local media do not adequately cover local politics.

15. b. Both sentences in this passage support the idea that the emphasis on the low-carb and low-fat debate is misleading and might distract us from other important ideas. The other choices are not supported by or developed in this passage.

Subtest 5: Mathematics Knowledge

1. c. Multiply the two binomials using the distributive property so that each term from the first set of parentheses gets multiplied by each term of the second set of parentheses: $(x - 3)(x + 7) = x(x + 7) + -3(x + 7)$. Simplify the multiplication next: $x^2 + 7x - 3x - 21$. Combine like terms: $x^2 + 4x - 21$.

2. d. A composite number is a whole number greater than one that has other factors besides one and itself; in other words, it is not prime. Each of the answer choices is a prime number except 91, which has factors of 1, 7, 13, and 91.

3. c. Multiply across: $\frac{10}{216}$. Then reduce to lowest terms to get the answer: $\frac{5}{108}$.

4. c. The median of a group of numbers is found by arranging the numbers in ascending or descending order, and then finding the number in the middle of the set. First, arrange the numbers in order: 12, 14, 14, 16, 20, 22. Since there is an even number of numbers in the list, find the average of the two numbers that share the middle. In this case, the numbers in the middle are 14 and 16, and the average between them is 15.

5. a. The Pythagorean theorem states that the square of the length of the hypotenuse of a right triangle is equal to the sum of the squares of the other two sides, so you know that the following equation applies: $1^2 + x^2 = 10$, so $x^2 = 10 - 1 = 9$, so $x = 3$.

6. b. Both the isosceles trapezoid and the square have congruent diagonals, but only the square has diagonals that are both congruent and perpendicular.

7. b. If the circle is 100π square inches, its radius must be 10 inches, using the formula $A = \pi r^2$. Side AB is twice the radius, so it is 20 inches.

8. d. Use the place value of each of the nonzero numbers. The four is in the ten thousands place, so it is equal to 40,000, the five is in the hundreds place, so it is equal to 500, and the three is in the ones place, so it is equal to 3; $40,000 + 500 + 3 = 40,503$.

9. d. If the shorter sides are each 4 centimeters, then the longer sides must each equal $40 - 8 \div 2$; therefore, the length of each of the longer sides is 16 centimeters.

10. a. A straight angle is exactly $180°$.

11. c. In order to find an equivalent fraction, you need to perform the same action on both the numerator and the denominator. One way to solve for x is to ask the question, "What is multiplied by 19 (the denominator) to get a product of 76?" Divide: $76 \div 19 = 4$. Then, multiply the numerator by 4 in order to find the value of x: $4 \times 1 = 4$.

12. a. To solve the inequality $12x - 1 < 35$, first solve the equation $12x - 1 = 35$. In this case, the solution is $x = 3$. Replace the equal sign with the *less than* symbol (<): $x < 3$. Since values of x *less than* 3 satisfy this inequality, 2 is the only answer choice that would make the inequality true.

13. d. Squares, rectangles, and rhombuses are quadrilateral (have four sides), and each has two pairs of parallel sides. However, all angles in both squares and rectangles are $90°$. Therefore, only a rhombus could contain two angles that measure $65°$.

14. a. To simplify the radical, first find the square root of 64, which is 8. Then divide each exponent on the variables by 2 to find the square root of the variables. If the exponent is odd, the remainder stays inside the radical: $\sqrt{x^5} = x^2\sqrt{x}$ and $\sqrt{y^8} = y^4$. Thus, the result is $8x^2y^4\sqrt{x}$.

15. c. The correct answer is 10,447. It helps, if you are in a place where you can do so, to read the answer aloud; that way, you will likely catch any mistake. When writing numbers with four or more digits, begin at the right and separate the digits into groups of three with commas.

16. b. A prime number is a whole number whose only factors are one and itself. Two, three, and seven are all prime numbers. The prime factors of a number are the prime numbers that multiply to equal that number: $2 \times 3 \times 7 = 42$.

17. d. First, add 4 to both sides of the equation: $\sqrt{2a+6} - 4 + 4 = 6 + 4$. The equation simplifies to $\sqrt{2a+6} = 10$. Square each side to eliminate the radical sign: $(\sqrt{2a+6})^2 = 10^2$. The equation becomes $2a + 6 = 100$. Subtract 6 from each side of the equal sign and simplify: $2a + 6 - 6 = 100 - 6$; $2a = 94$. Divide each side by 2: $\frac{2a}{2} = \frac{94}{2}$. Therefore, $a = 47$.

18. a. Only like terms can be added: $4x - 7y + 7x + 7y$; $4x + 7x$ and $-7y + 7y$. The y terms cancel each other out, leaving $11x$ as the correct answer.

19. d. You must borrow 60 minutes from the three hours in order to be able to subtract: 2 hours 80 minutes – 1 hour 48 minutes = 1 hour 32 minutes.

20. b. Since there are three sections shaded out of a total of five sections, the part shaded is $\frac{3}{5}$.

21. a. The sum of three numbers means $(a + b + c)$, the sum of their reciprocals means $(\frac{1}{a} + \frac{1}{b} + \frac{1}{c})$. Combine terms: $(a + b + c)(\frac{1}{a} + \frac{1}{b} + \frac{1}{c})$. Thus, choice **a** is the correct answer.

22. c. Consecutive odd integers are positive or negative whole numbers in a row that are two apart, such as 1, 3, 5 or –23, –21, –19. To find three consecutive odd integers whose sum is 117, divide 117 by 3 to get 39; $39 - 2 = 37$ and $39 + 2 = 41$. To check, add the three integers: $37 + 39 + 41 = 117$.

23. d. By adding the two equations vertically, you end up with $2y = 8$, so y must equal 4. Substitute 4 for y in either original equation to get $x = 6$. Therefore, the point of intersection where the two lines are equal is (6,4).

24. c. Since there is a common denominator, add the numerators and keep the denominator: $\frac{7w}{z}$.

25. b. Take the reciprocal of the fraction being divided by, change the operation to multiplication, and cancel common factors between the numerators and the denominators: $\frac{6a^2b}{2c} \div \frac{ab^2}{4c^4}$ becomes $\frac{6a^2b}{2c} \times \frac{4c^4}{ab^2} = \frac{12ac^3}{b}$.

Subtest 6: Electronics Information

1. c. Not grounding an electrical device runs the risk of electrocution.

2. c. 60 Hz is the frequency of the alternating voltage, which is the type of voltage used in the United States.

3. c. To determine the total resistance in a series circuit similar to the one presented, total resistance is equal to the sum of the individual resistors. Hence, the total resistance in this schematic would be $R_1 + R_2 + R_3 = 1,500$ ohms.

4. b. Metal in a microwave oven reflecting the microwave energy generated by the microwave's magnetron can be reflected back. The metal can also cause arcing and sparks from interaction with the microwaves.

5. b. The total current is equal to the sum of the currents through each resistor. Therefore, $4A + 4A + 4A = 12A$.

6. a. FM stands for frequency modulation.

7. c. This symbol in a schematic depicts a wire that does not join another.

8. c. Electrical pressure results from a difference of electrical force between two points. Hence, voltage is what pushes electricity through a circuit.

9. c. Coulomb's law describes the electrostatic force between electric charges.

10. c. The total resistance (25Ω) is already known. Using Ohm's law to determine the voltage drop, we first solve for I, which gives the total current flowing through the circuit. Since the resistors are in series, the same amount of current flows through each resistor. Once I is known, Ohm's law again lets us solve for E across R1:
$I = E/R = 48/25 = 1.92$ A
$E = IR = 1.92 \times 10 = 19.2$ V

11. a. If a vacuum cleaner is rated at 1,200 watts and operates at 120 volts, it will draw 10 amps of current. The Power Law can be applied:
$P = I \times E$; $I = P \div E$; $I = 1,200$ watts $\div 120$ volts; $I = 10$ amperes.

12. d. The electronic term given to a unit of electromotive force is a *volt*.

13. b. A loopstick antenna is optimized for frequencies below 300kHz. Parabolic-shaped or dish antennas typically operate in the gigahertz range.

14. d. The design of a corner reflector antenna includes a conductive sheet behind it to direct radiation in the forward direction, enhancing reception by increasing the directivity of the radiofrequency (RF) signals.

15. c. In antenna design, the larger the diameter of the reflector, the greater the reception effectiveness of a directional antenna, also known as gain.

16. c. The power in circuit A is one-half the power in B, so the current through A must be one-half the current through B. If either circuit had no current flowing, there would be zero power dissipated.

17. b. The image shown is a horn antenna.

18. c. FM radio broadcasting, amateur radio, broadcast television, and commercial aircraft transmit on very high frequency (VHF). VHF bands use the 30–300 MHz frequency band.

19. c. A tuning capacitor is used in a radio device to adjust the resonant frequency or tune a radio frequency.

20. b. A transformer changes voltage and amperage.

Subtest 7: Auto and Shop Information

1. c. Properly inflated tires, along with a tuned-up engine, will help to ensure you are getting the best gas mileage possible out of your vehicle.

2. d. A flow meter will measure the rate at which a fluid is flowing through the piping system.

3. c. An example of a flow meter would be a gas pump gauge. The pump gauge measures how much fuel is passing from the pump, through the nozzle, and into your tank.

4. a. The positive crankcase ventilation (PCV) system recirculates harmful emissions from the engine that would otherwise be vented out into the atmosphere.

5. c. Recycled oil can have any number of uses from refinement into lubricating oil, recycling into oil to be burned for energy consumption, or for use in smaller oil-burning heaters. Discarding the used oil into the ecosystem via a wastewater drain is not only wasteful but will result in oil pollution of our waterways and our groundwater systems.

6. a. Fuel gauges will typically read in gallons or liters.

7. c. The automobile battery stores electricity and supplies power for a number of vehicle functions, including starting and ignition requirements. When the battery is drained of power, the alternator recharges the battery while the engine is running, in essence making electricity through rotary motion from a belt assembly powered by the engine.

8. b. The muffler is a component mounted midway between the engine and the exhaust where baffles and other sound-deadening materials are positioned to quiet and block the noise of the engine cylinder explosions and power cycles.

9. d. Leaf springs and coil compression springs are both suspension devices used to provide a smoother ride.

10. b. A hydrometer is an instrument used to measure the specific gravity (or relative density) of liquids. It examines the ratio of the density of the solution of antifreeze to the density of water.

11. d. Carbon monoxide (CO) results from the incomplete combustion of vehicle fuels. Gasoline engines emit a higher proportion of CO than diesel engines, due to the lower combustion temperature. Nitrogen oxides (NOx) are precursors for the formation of smog components such as ground-level ozone. Hydrocarbons contribute to the formation of tropospheric ozone and greenhouse gases.

12. a. Engines need a thin film of lubricant to ensure that the various metal-on-metal contact points do not overheat or suffer excessive wear. The oil pump pushes oil through engine oil passages.

13. c. The transaxle combines a transmission, the differential, and associated components into one integrated assembly. Automobile configurations that have the engine at the same end of the car as the driven wheels (e.g., front-wheel drive/front-engine mounted or rear-wheel drive/rear-engine mounted) use a transaxle since space and mechanical restrictions make it difficult to mount a conventional drivetrain.

14. c. A hinge mortise is a recessed notch cut into a piece of wood so that a door hinge will fit flush within the mortise.

15. d. A lateral cut is not one of the six basic woodworking cuts. In addition to crosscut, rip, and miter, the remaining three are bevel crosscut, bevel rip, and bevel miter cuts.

16. d. A weld melts the two materials needing to be joined so that when they cool they become one piece through the process of coalescence. A nail or a screw merely joins two pieces of wood together. A solder uses a fusible metal alloy that joins two pieces together but lacks the strength of a weld.

17. c. Hydration is the process by which the water reacts with the cement and bonds the other components together, eventually creating a stonelike material.

18. a. A float, sometimes called a bull float, is used to put a smooth final finish to concrete floors. A screed (choice **b**) is used to level the just-poured concrete. Tamping (choice **c**) is a process whereby the materials in concrete are consolidated and it forces coarse aggregates below the surface. Forms (choice **d**) are the temporary structure or mold for the support of concrete while it is setting and curing.

19. d. A split lock washer is designed to prevent nuts and bolts from backing out. A flat washer (choice **a**) is used to distribute loads evenly through the connection. A fender washer (choice **b**) is an oversize flat washer used to further distribute load, especially on soft materials. An ogee washer (choice **c**) is typically used in dock and wood construction.

20. c. Steel is most often used to provide additional strength in concrete slabs and walls because of its high strength and relatively low cost.

21. d. Cement, sand, gravel, and water are the four primary ingredients in concrete.

22. d. Tile shingles are expensive but have a long life. Wooden shake shingles are also used as roofing material. The most common outer roofing material is asphalt shingles, since they are low in cost and provide good protection.

23. c. The hand tool depicted is a crescent wrench.

24. d. There is no tool known as a box hammer.

25. c. If a line is plumb, it is perfectly vertical.

Subtest 8: Mechanical Comprehension

1. a. Since valve D is closed, water will not flow to barrels 3 and 4. Water will flow through valve B but be stopped at valve C. Water will flow through valve A into barrels 1 and 2.

2. b. A pulley system of this type has a mechanical advantage of 3. If 160 pounds of force is applied, a maximum weight of 160 pounds × 3 = 480 pounds can be lifted.

3. c. An object will float on top of a liquid if its density is less than the liquid it is in and sink if its density is greater. In this case, the penny is less dense than mercury and denser than water, so it will float on top of the mercury and sink in water, meaning it will settle directly in between the two layers.

4. a. The mechanical advantage (MA) of a ramp is determined by the length of the ramp, l, divided by the height gained, h. In this case, MA = $\frac{l}{h}$ = 20 feet ÷ 5 feet = 4. The force required to pull a 240-pound block up a ramp is 240 pounds ÷ 4 = 60 pounds.

5. b. Mechanical advantage = output force ÷ input force. Here, 50 pounds of force is input into a jack to lift a 3,000-pound car. The mechanical advantage is 3,000 ÷ 50 = 60.

6. a. Heating leads to an increase in pressure of a contained gas. Since no air is added or removed from the tires, their overall weight remains constant.

7. b. The arm acts as a lever with the pivot point being where it intersects the crane body. By attaching the cable as far along the arm as possible, the greatest mechanical advantage is achieved.

8. a. The total weight of the block and the plank is 14 pounds. The weight is distributed evenly between the two scales, meaning that Scale 1 will read 7 pounds.

9. b. The force constant of the spring is 9 pounds ÷ 3 inches = 3 pounds per inch. Using the equation, $F = kx$, we have 12 pounds = 3 pounds per inch × x. Solving for x gives 4 inches.

10. a. An object's density determines whether it will float or sink. To float, it must have a lower density than water. Surface area will not affect whether an object ultimately floats or sinks.

11. b. If 15 turns move the nut 1.25 inches, there are 15 turns ÷ 1.25 inches = 12 threads per inch.

12. b. The mechanical advantage of this pulley system is 2. The force required to lift the 200-pound load is 200 pounds ÷ 2 = 100 pounds.

13. b. Metals such as steel tend to expand considerably when heated. The other materials may expand somewhat when heated, but to a lesser extent.

14. c. Each revolution of gear 1 will turn gear 2 12 teeth ÷ 9 teeth = $1\frac{1}{3}$ times. At 30 revolutions per minute, gear 2 will turn at 30 rpm × $1\frac{1}{3}$ = 40 rpm.

15. b. The mechanical advantage (MA) of a ramp is determined by the length of the ramp, l, divided by the height gained, h. In this case, MA = $\frac{l}{h}$ = 18 feet ÷ 6 feet = 3. Since the barrel weighs 300 pounds, a force of 300 ÷ 3 = 100 pounds is required to keep the barrel in place.

16. c. Each turn of the pedals will move the rear wheel 55 ÷ 11 = 5 revolutions. If the bike is pedaled at 80 rpm, the rear wheel will rotate at 80 rpm × 5 revolutions = 400 rpm. Since 30 seconds is half of one minute, the rear wheel will complete 400 rpm ÷ 2 = 200 revolutions

17. a. Helium is less dense than air. Objects will float when they are less dense than air. Helium will float regardless of its temperature.

18. c. While no mechanical advantage is gained, a pulley system such as this one allows one to raise an object while pulling downward, rather than having to climb above the object to pull it.

19. d. If gear 4 turns clockwise, the neighboring gears 1 and 3 will turn counterclockwise.

20. d. The amount of water that flows out through the pipes is proportional to the size of the pipe opening. Since the area of the opening is proportional to the square of the diameter, the ratio of the amount of water that flows out of A and B is $6^2 ÷ 2^2 = 9$.

21. c. 14 miles ÷ 8 mph = 1.75 hours = 1 hour 45 minutes.

22. c. If the 600-pound block can be lifted with 200 pounds of force, the ramp has a mechanical advantage (MA) of 3. The MA of a ramp is determined by the length of the ramp, l, divided by the height gained, h. In this case, MA $= 3 = \frac{l}{h} = \frac{15 \text{ feet}}{h}$. Solving for h tells us the ramp is 5 feet high.

23. a. $w_1 \times d_1 = w_2 \times d_2$. Paul is 15 feet away from the pivot point and the block is 20 feet away. 90×20 feet $= 15$ feet $\times w_2$. Solving for w_2 gives 120 pounds.

24. c. As the balloon rises, the air pressure surrounding it will decrease and the internal pressure from the helium will press outward on the walls of the balloon, increasing it in size. Since the balloon is a closed system, its weight will be unaffected.

25. d. Since pulley A is 1.5 times greater in circumference than pulley B, each revolution of A will lead to 1.5 revolutions of B. The belt of the pulley will cause pulley B to move in the same direction (counter-clockwise) as pulley A.

Subtest 9: Assembling Objects

1. c.
2. b.
3. c.
4. d.
5. d.
6. d.
7. c.
8. b.
9. d.
10. b.

11. b.
12. c.
13. a.
14. d.
15. c.
16. b.
17. c.
18. d.
19. a.
20. d.
21. b.
22. a.
23. b.
24. d.
25. a.

For information on how the official ASVAB is scored see Chapter 3.